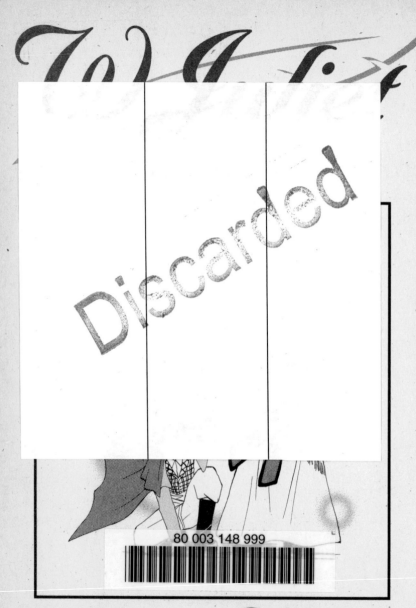

Story & Art by **Emura**

W Juliet
Volume 3

Story and Art by Emura

Translation & English Adaptation/William Flanagan
Touch-up Art & Lettering/Mark McMurray
Graphic Design/Hidemi Sahara
Editor/Megan Bates

Managing Editor/Annette Roman
Director of Production/Noboru Watanabe
Editorial Director/Alvin Lu
Sr. Director of Acquisitions/Rika Inouye
Vice President of Sales & Marketing/Liza Coppola
Executive Vice President/Hyoe Narita
Publisher/Seiji Horibuchi

© Emura 1999. All rights reserved. First published in Japan in 1999 by HAKUSENSHA, Inc., Tokyo. English language translation rights in America and Canada arranged with HAKUSEN-SHA, Inc., Tokyo. The W JULIET logo is a trademark of VIZ, LLC. All rights reserved. The stories, characters and incidents mentioned in this publication are entirely fictional.

Printed in the U.S.A..

Published by VIZ, LLC
P.O. Box 77010
San Francisco, CA 94107

10 9 8 7 6 5 4 3 2 1
First printing, February 2005

www.viz.com

store.viz.com

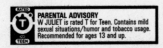

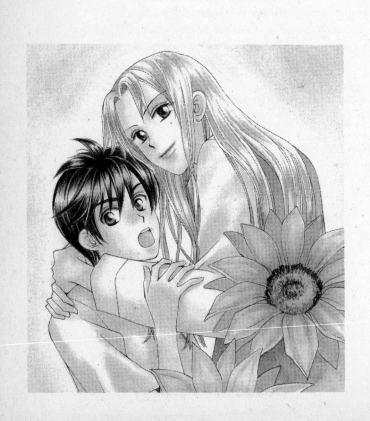

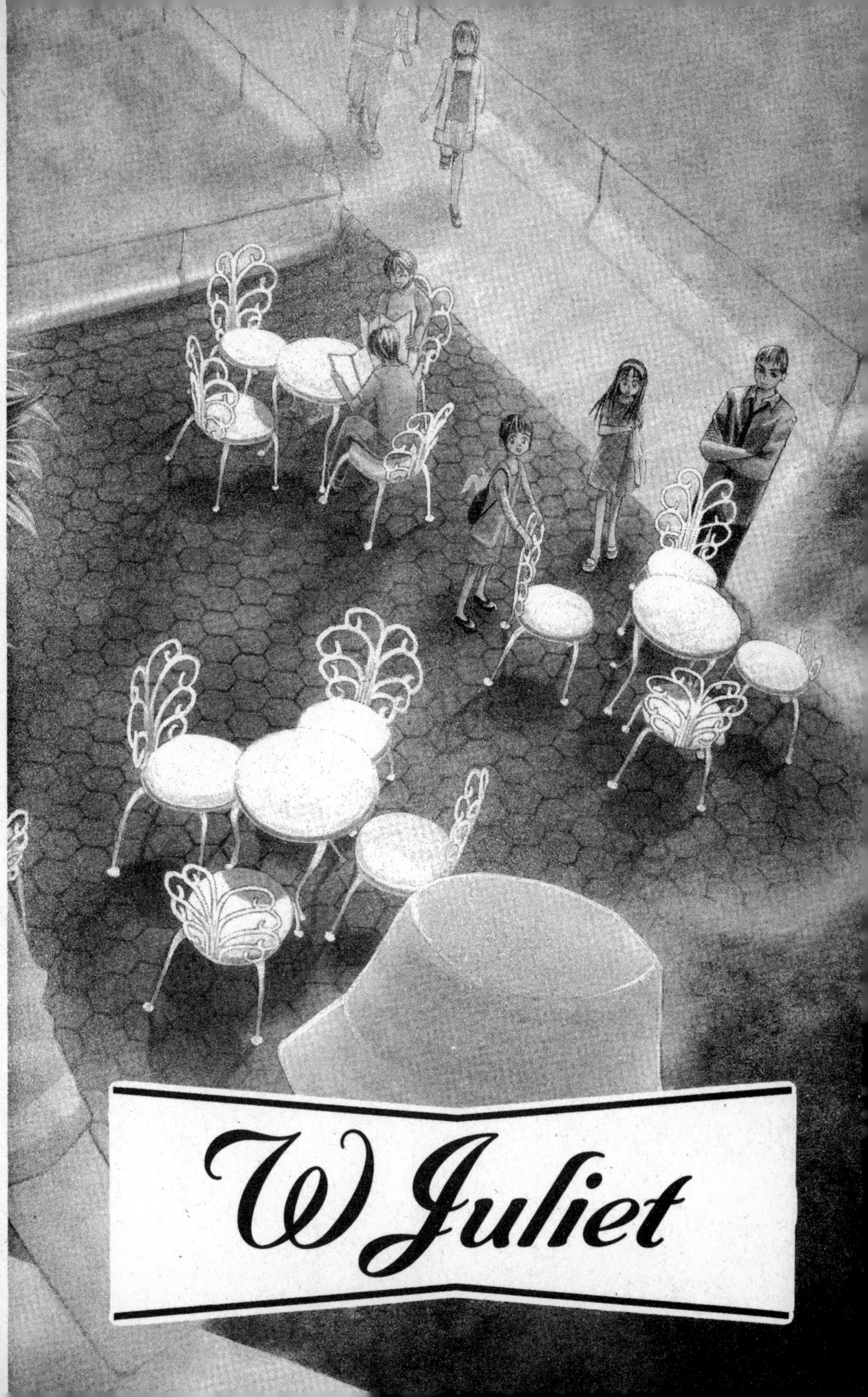
W Juliet

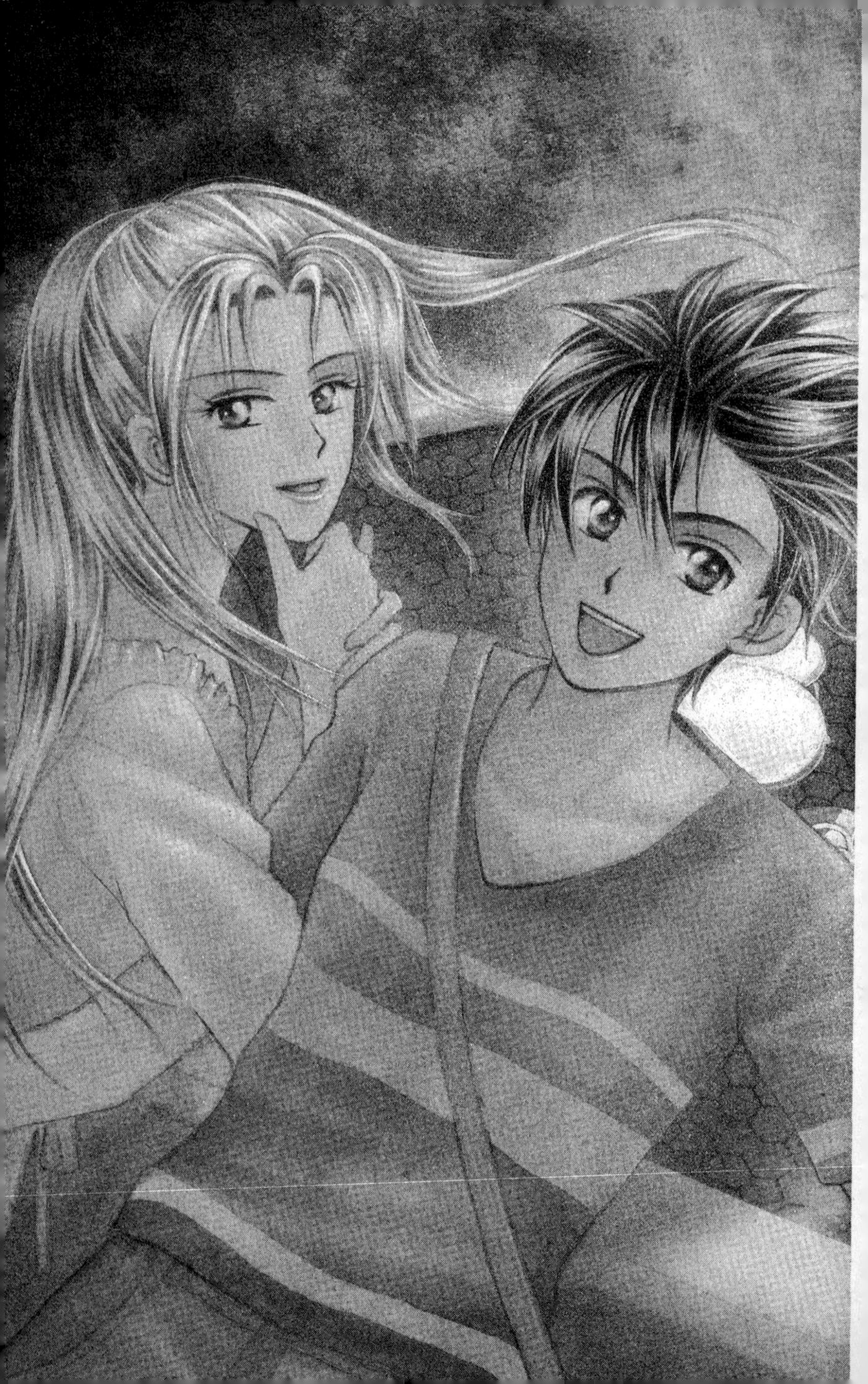

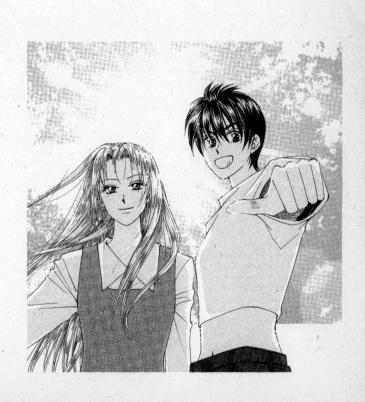

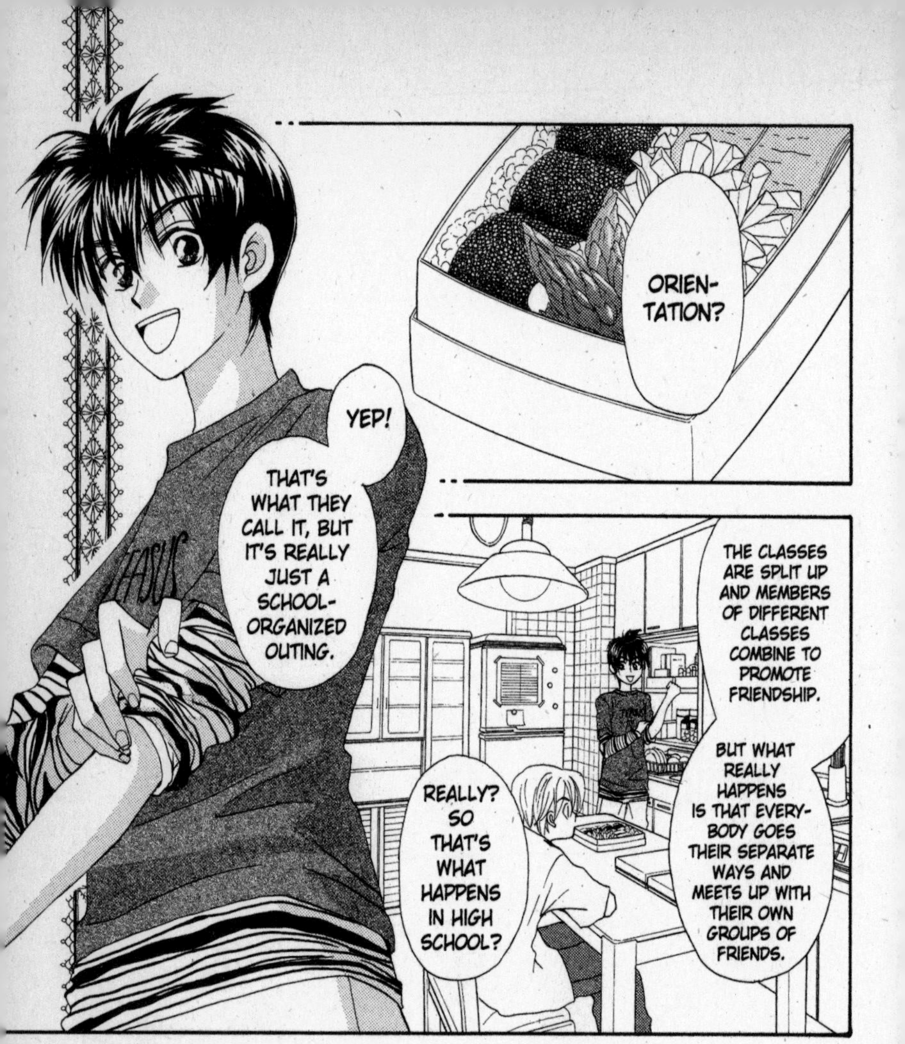
ORIEN-TATION?
YEP!
THAT'S WHAT THEY CALL IT, BUT IT'S REALLY JUST A SCHOOL-ORGANIZED OUTING.
THE CLASSES ARE SPLIT UP AND MEMBERS OF DIFFERENT CLASSES COMBINE TO PROMOTE FRIENDSHIP.
BUT WHAT REALLY HAPPENS IS THAT EVERY-BODY GOES THEIR SEPARATE WAYS AND MEETS UP WITH THEIR OWN GROUPS OF FRIENDS.
REALLY? SO THAT'S WHAT HAPPENS IN HIGH SCHOOL?

-Behind the Scenes Story- ①

This was the first time I was able to do the color pages at the beginning of the manga anthology, and I was able to use a huge page count—50 pages!! (Up until now, the closest I got was 46 pages for the Summer Retreat episode... which we haven't mentioned yet.)

The thumbnails and outline were difficult but I remember that in drawing it, I didn't feel the story was rushed. I guess I'm just a girl who tells a lot of story, so the extra pages really helped out! But drawing the pages was hell! I'd draw and draw, and I'd never get to the end! To think that others draw 10 to 100 pages in the same amount of time...! And when I think of that, with only 50 pages, I've still got a long way to go. But still, that time was really hard! Hard, but fun!

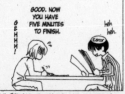

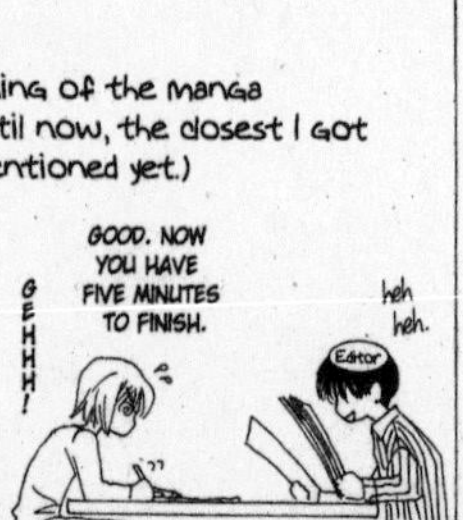
GOOD. NOW YOU HAVE FIVE MINUTES TO FINISH.
GEHHH!
heh heh.
Editor

In the end, the Editorial department helped put down screen tone.

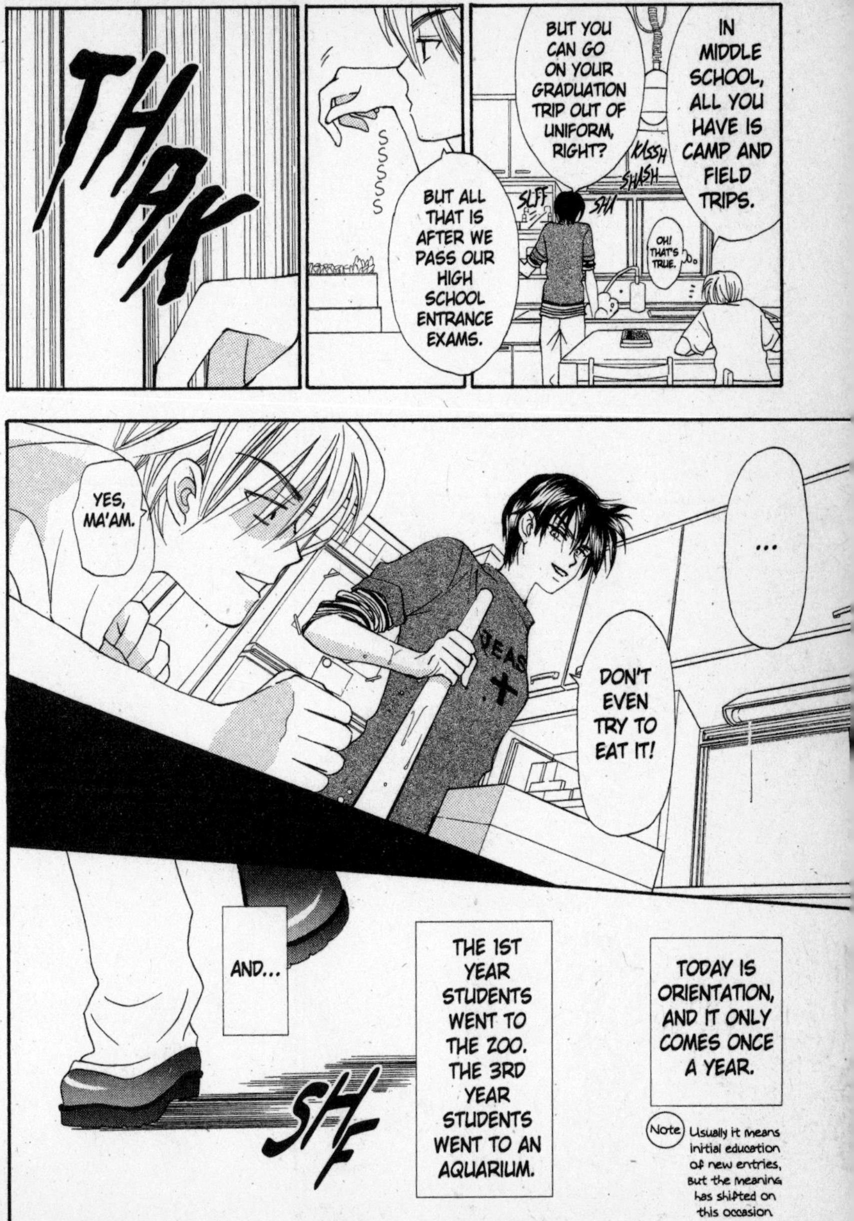
IN MIDDLE SCHOOL, ALL YOU HAVE IS CAMP AND FIELD TRIPS.
BUT YOU CAN GO ON YOUR GRADUATION TRIP OUT OF UNIFORM, RIGHT?
KASSH
SHASH
SHA
SLFF
OH! THAT'S TRUE.
SSSSS
BUT ALL THAT IS AFTER WE PASS OUR HIGH SCHOOL ENTRANCE EXAMS.
THAK
...
DON'T EVEN TRY TO EAT IT!
YES, MA'AM.
TODAY IS ORIENTATION, AND IT ONLY COMES ONCE A YEAR.
Note Usually it means initial education of new entries, but the meaning has shifted on this occasion.
THE 1ST YEAR STUDENTS WENT TO THE ZOO. THE 3RD YEAR STUDENTS WENT TO AN AQUARIUM.
AND...
SHF

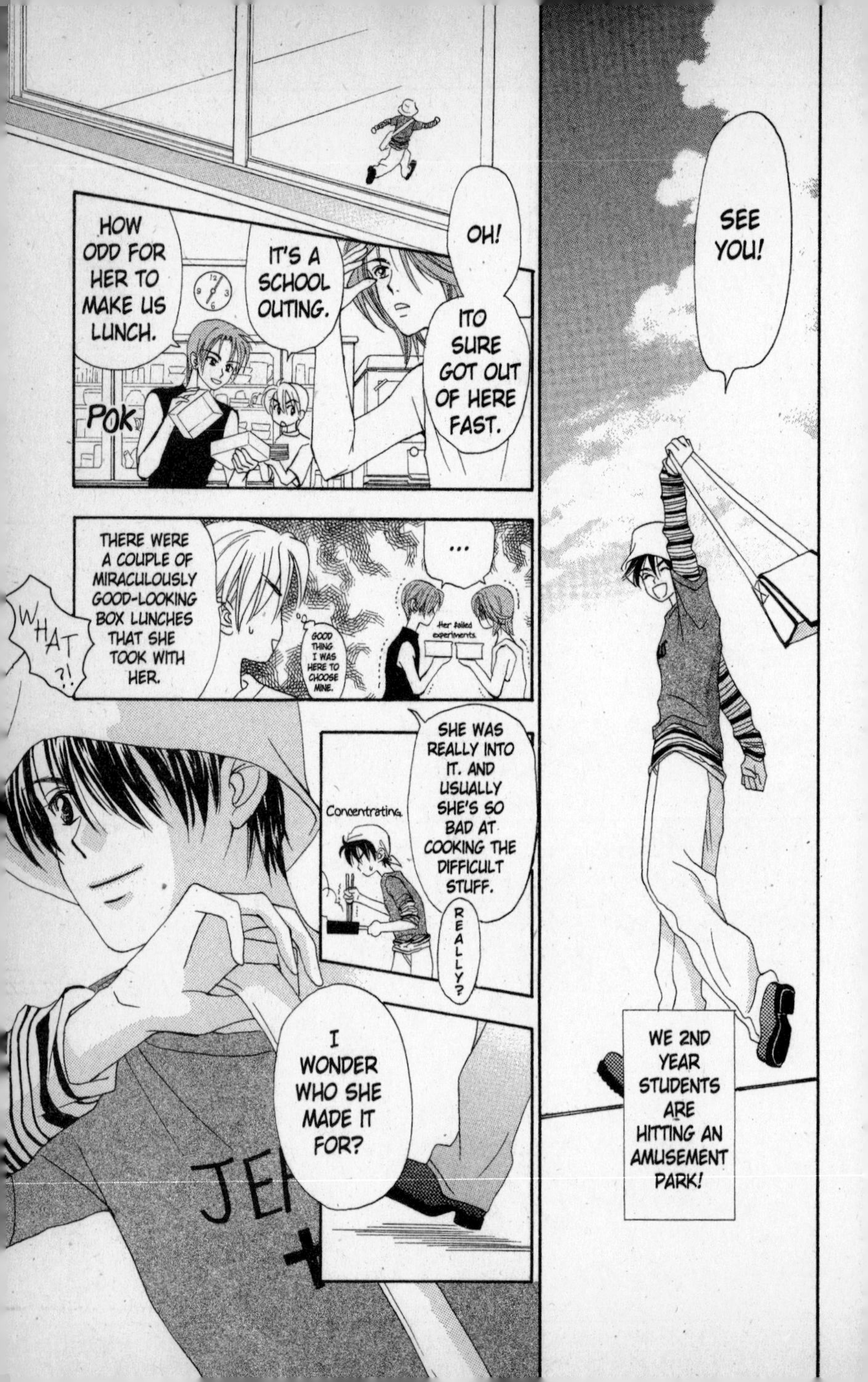
SEE YOU!
WE 2ND YEAR STUDENTS ARE HITTING AN AMUSEMENT PARK!
OH!
ITO SURE GOT OUT OF HERE FAST.
IT'S A SCHOOL OUTING.
HOW ODD FOR HER TO MAKE US LUNCH.
POK
...
Her failed experiments.
GOOD THING I WAS HERE TO CHOOSE MINE.
THERE WERE A COUPLE OF MIRACULOUSLY GOOD-LOOKING BOX LUNCHES THAT SHE TOOK WITH HER.
WHAT?!
SHE WAS REALLY INTO IT. AND USUALLY SHE'S SO BAD AT COOKING THE DIFFICULT STUFF.
REALLY?
Concentrating.
I WONDER WHO SHE MADE IT FOR?

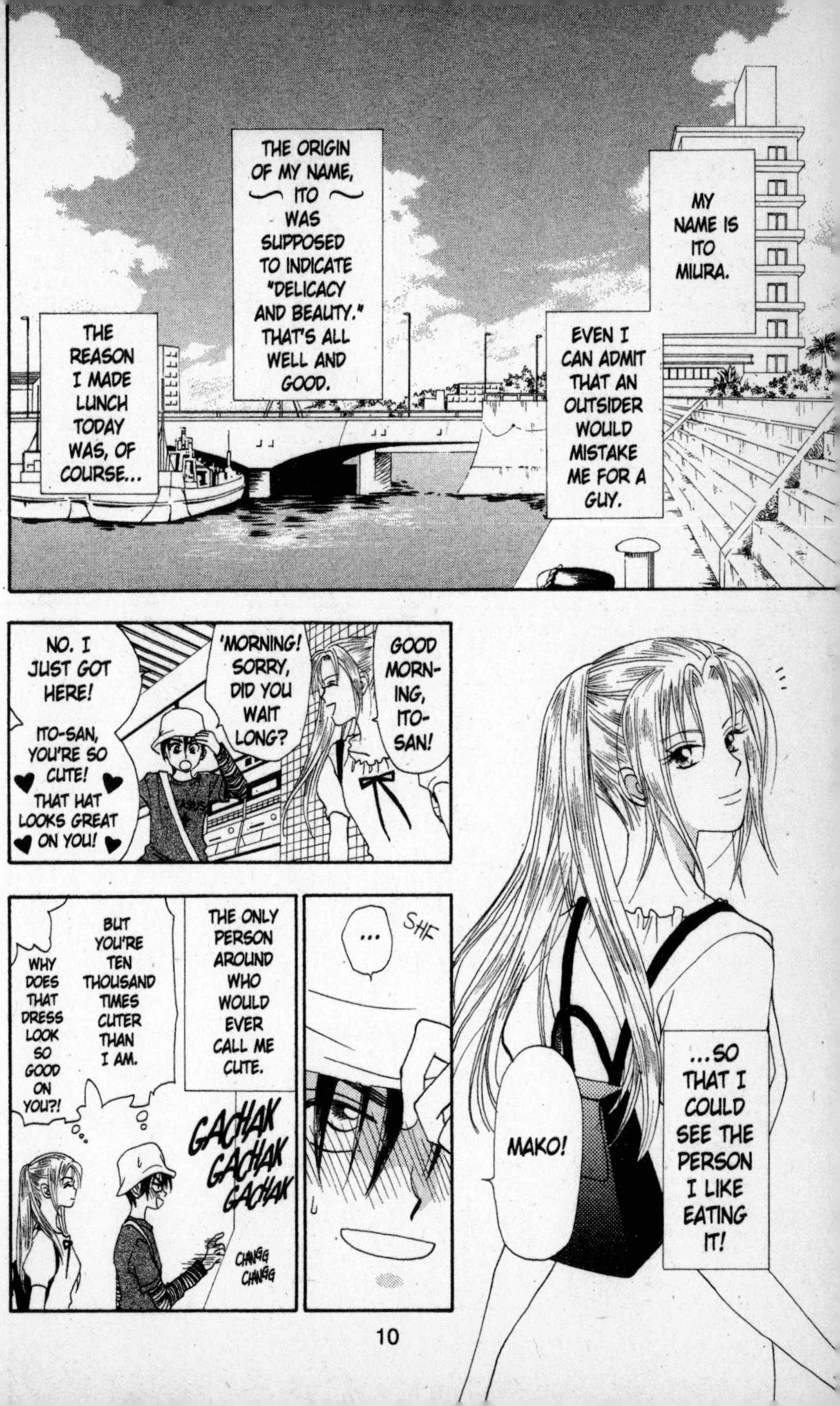
MY NAME IS ITO MIURA.
EVEN I CAN ADMIT THAT AN OUTSIDER WOULD MISTAKE ME FOR A GUY.
THE ORIGIN OF MY NAME, ~ ITO ~ WAS SUPPOSED TO INDICATE "DELICACY AND BEAUTY." THAT'S ALL WELL AND GOOD.
THE REASON I MADE LUNCH TODAY WAS, OF COURSE...
...SO THAT I COULD SEE THE PERSON I LIKE EATING IT!
MAKO!
GOOD MORNING, ITO-SAN!
'MORNING! SORRY, DID YOU WAIT LONG?
NO. I JUST GOT HERE!
ITO-SAN, YOU'RE SO CUTE! ♥ THAT HAT LOOKS GREAT ON YOU! ♥
SHF
...
THE ONLY PERSON AROUND WHO WOULD EVER CALL ME CUTE.
BUT YOU'RE TEN THOUSAND TIMES CUTER THAN I AM.
WHY DOES THAT DRESS LOOK SO GOOD ON YOU?!
GACHAK GACHAK GACHAK
CHANGG CHANGG

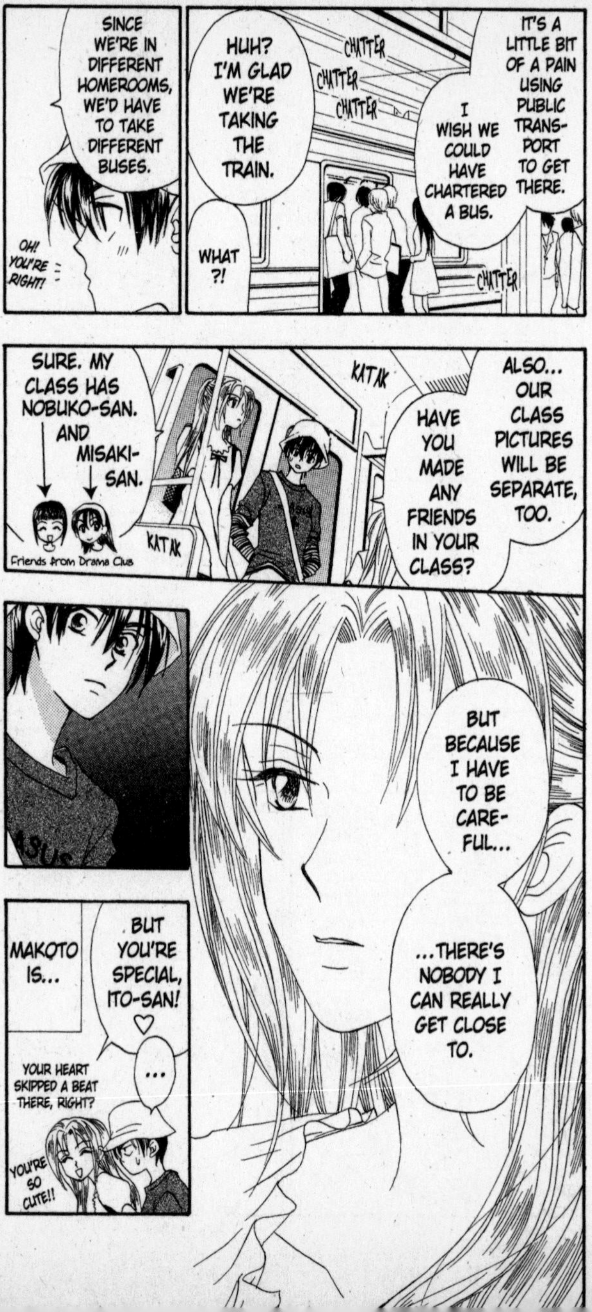
IT'S A LITTLE BIT OF A PAIN USING PUBLIC TRANSPORT TO GET THERE.
I WISH WE COULD HAVE CHARTERED A BUS.
CHATTER
CHATTER
CHATTER
CHATTER
HUH? I'M GLAD WE'RE TAKING THE TRAIN.
WHAT ?!
SINCE WE'RE IN DIFFERENT HOMEROOMS, WE'D HAVE TO TAKE DIFFERENT BUSES.
OH! YOU'RE RIGHT!
ALSO... OUR CLASS PICTURES WILL BE SEPARATE, TOO.
HAVE YOU MADE ANY FRIENDS IN YOUR CLASS?
KATAK
KATAK
SURE. MY CLASS HAS NOBUKO-SAN. AND MISAKI-SAN.
Friends from Drama Club
BUT BECAUSE I HAVE TO BE CAREFUL...
...THERE'S NOBODY I CAN REALLY GET CLOSE TO.
BUT YOU'RE SPECIAL, ITO-SAN! ♡
MAKOTO IS...
...
YOUR HEART SKIPPED A BEAT THERE, RIGHT?
YOU'RE SO CUTE!!

GREETINGS

Or in other words... Hello! I'm Emura! W·J has quickly gone to its third volume! Since the first volume came out in May (1999 in Japan), I never thought that I would have three volumes out in the first year! Thank you so much, everybody!! I thought that Volume Three would come out in January of next year, but it was announced as a December book! I'm happy, but on the other hand, I have to write these 1/4 page chat spaces and draw original work for the book at the same time that I'm right in the middle of drawing the continuing story! ᕲᕲ And some very detailed requests have been coming in, too! (prize advertisements, prizes, telephone cards, etc... All of them for color images!) It's like I'm finally succumbing to death by overwork.

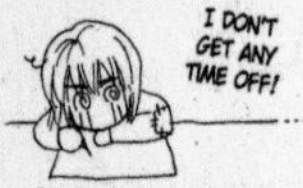
I DON'T GET ANY TIME OFF!

Right now, it's slightly past the deadline for the 24th issue of 1999's Hana to Yume anthology, and all the 1/4 page sections, both the ones on the bottom and these thin side columns are due today. So I'm going to do my best on all 10 sections!! What an awful greeting this was!

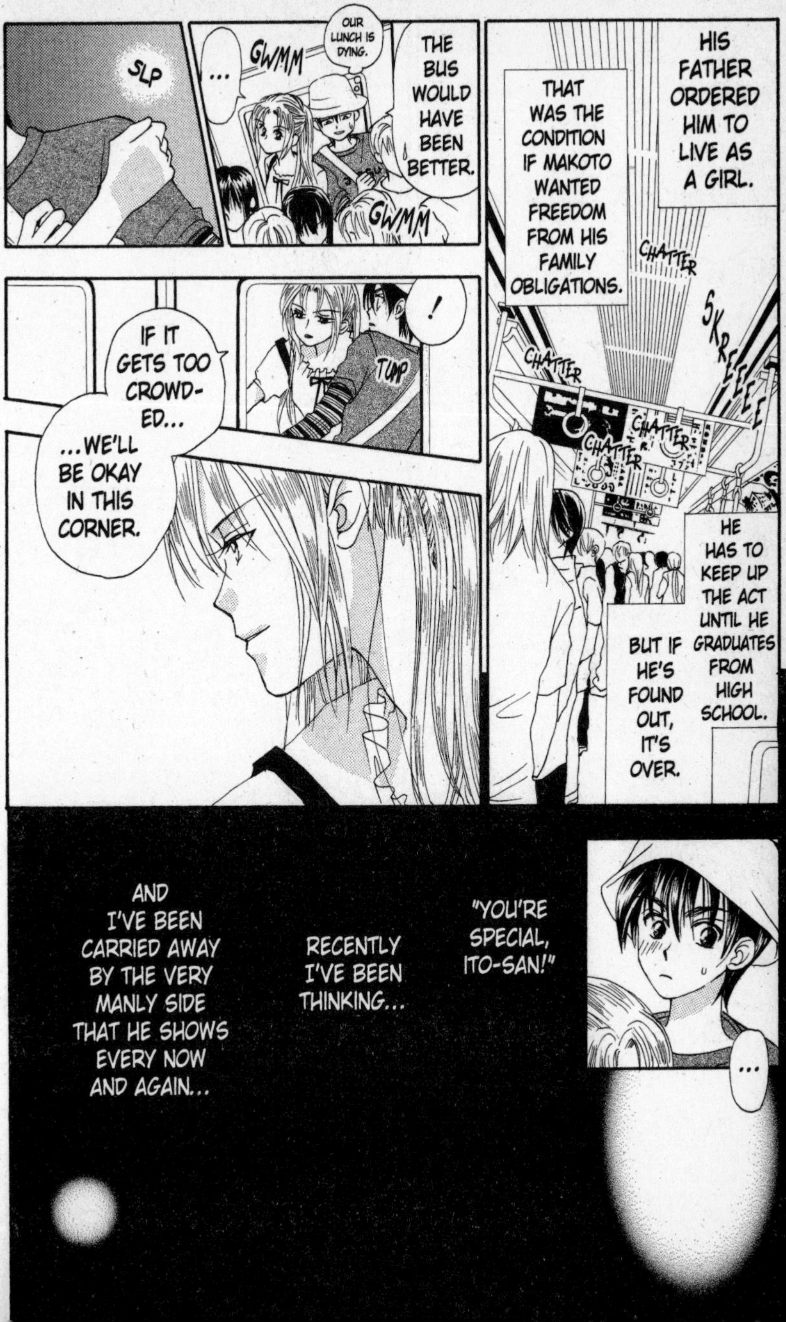
HIS FATHER ORDERED HIM TO LIVE AS A GIRL.
THAT WAS THE CONDITION IF MAKOTO WANTED FREEDOM FROM HIS FAMILY OBLIGATIONS.
CHATTER
SKREEEEE
CHATTER
CHATTER
CHATTER
HE HAS TO KEEP UP THE ACT UNTIL HE GRADUATES FROM HIGH SCHOOL.
BUT IF HE'S FOUND OUT, IT'S OVER.
THE BUS WOULD HAVE BEEN BETTER.
OUR LUNCH IS DYING.
GWMM
...
GWMM
SLP
!
TUMP
IF IT GETS TOO CROWD-ED...
...WE'LL BE OKAY IN THIS CORNER.
...
"YOU'RE SPECIAL, ITO-SAN!"
RECENTLY I'VE BEEN THINKING...
AND I'VE BEEN CARRIED AWAY BY THE VERY MANLY SIDE THAT HE SHOWS EVERY NOW AND AGAIN...

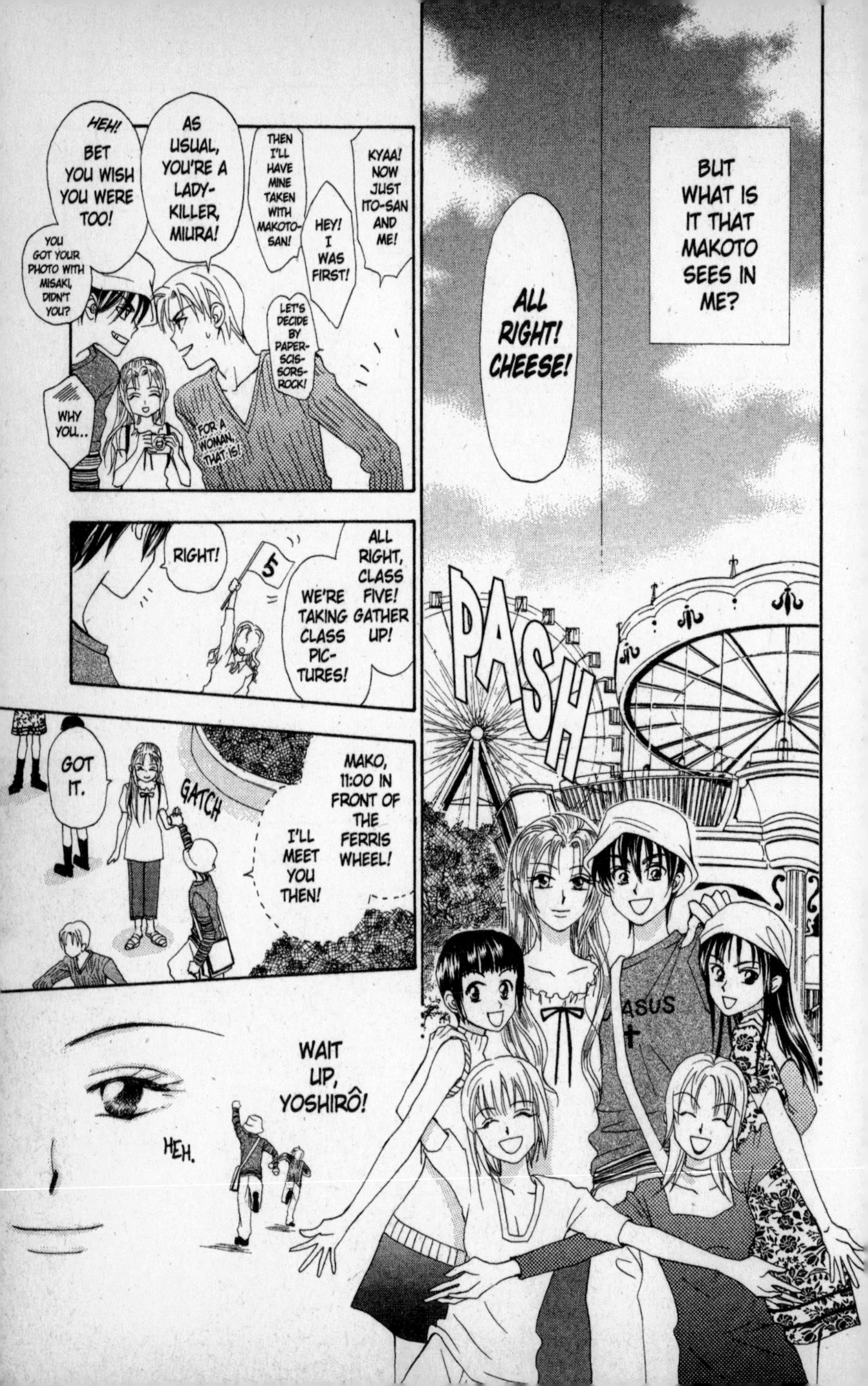
BUT WHAT IS IT THAT MAKOTO SEES IN ME?
ALL RIGHT! CHEESE!
PASH
KYAA! NOW JUST ITO-SAN AND ME!
HEY! I WAS FIRST!
THEN I'LL HAVE MINE TAKEN WITH MAKOTO-SAN!
LET'S DECIDE BY PAPER-SCISSORS-ROCK!
AS USUAL, YOU'RE A LADY-KILLER, MIURA!
FOR A WOMAN, THAT IS!
HEH! BET YOU WISH YOU WERE TOO!
YOU GOT YOUR PHOTO WITH MISAKI, DIDN'T YOU?
WHY YOU...
ALL RIGHT, CLASS FIVE! GATHER UP!
WE'RE TAKING CLASS PICTURES!
5
RIGHT!
MAKO, 11:00 IN FRONT OF THE FERRIS WHEEL!
I'LL MEET YOU THEN!
GATCH
GOT IT.
WAIT UP, YOSHIRÔ!
HEH.
ASUS

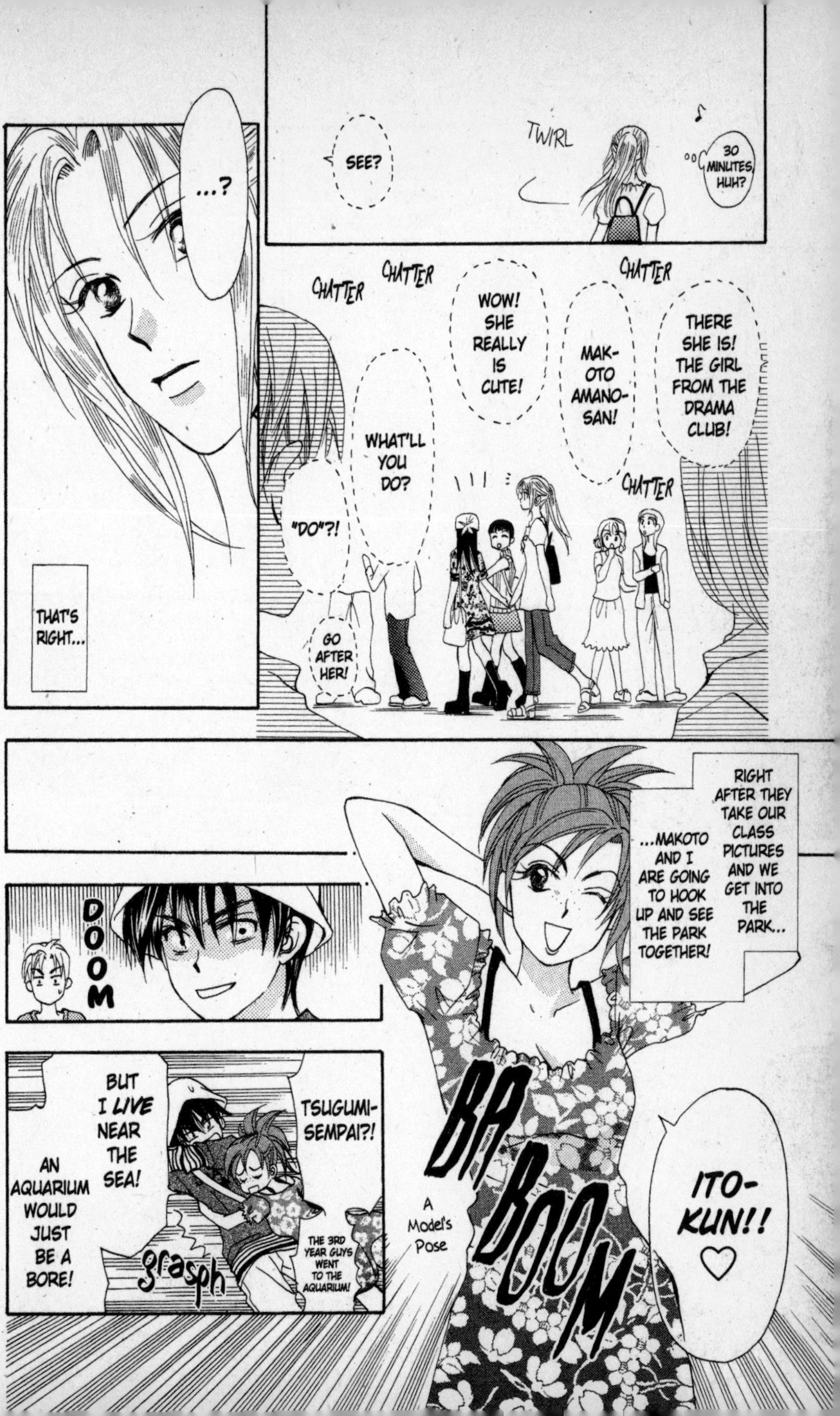

30 MINUTES, HUH?
TWIRL
SEE?
CHATTER
THERE SHE IS! THE GIRL FROM THE DRAMA CLUB!
MAKOTO AMANO-SAN!
CHATTER
WOW! SHE REALLY IS CUTE!
CHATTER
CHATTER
WHAT'LL YOU DO?
"DO"?!
GO AFTER HER!
CHATTER
...?
THAT'S RIGHT...
RIGHT AFTER THEY TAKE OUR CLASS PICTURES AND WE GET INTO THE PARK...
...MAKOTO AND I ARE GOING TO HOOK UP AND SEE THE PARK TOGETHER!
ITO-KUN!! ♡
BA BOOM
A Model's Pose
DOOM
TSUGUMI-SEMPAI?!
BUT I *LIVE* NEAR THE SEA!
AN AQUARIUM WOULD JUST BE A BORE!
grasph
THE 3RD YEAR GUYS WENT TO THE AQUARIUM!

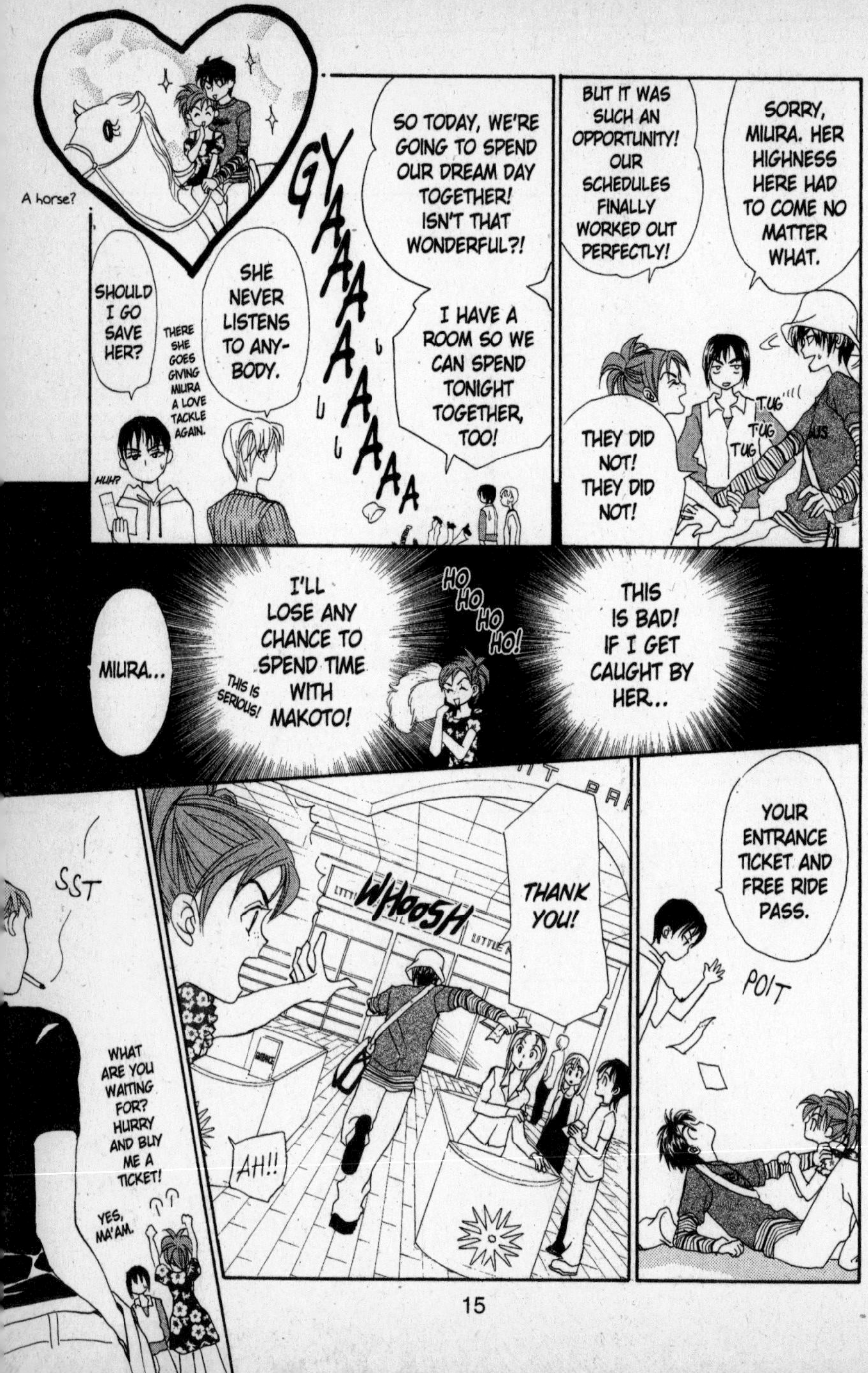
SORRY, MIURA. HER HIGHNESS HERE HAD TO COME NO MATTER WHAT.
BUT IT WAS SUCH AN OPPORTUNITY! OUR SCHEDULES FINALLY WORKED OUT PERFECTLY!
TUG
TUG
TUG
THEY DID NOT! THEY DID NOT!
SO TODAY, WE'RE GOING TO SPEND OUR DREAM DAY TOGETHER! ISN'T THAT WONDERFUL?!
I HAVE A ROOM SO WE CAN SPEND TONIGHT TOGETHER, TOO!
GYAAAAAAAAA
A horse?
SHE NEVER LISTENS TO ANYBODY.
THERE SHE GOES GIVING MIURA A LOVE TACKLE AGAIN.
SHOULD I GO SAVE HER?
HUH?
THIS IS BAD! IF I GET CAUGHT BY HER...
HO HO HO HO!
I'LL LOSE ANY CHANCE TO SPEND TIME WITH MAKOTO!
THIS IS SERIOUS!
MIURA...
YOUR ENTRANCE TICKET AND FREE RIDE PASS.
POIT
THANK YOU!
WHOOSH
AH!!
SST
WHAT ARE YOU WAITING FOR? HURRY AND BUY ME A TICKET!
YES, MA'AM.

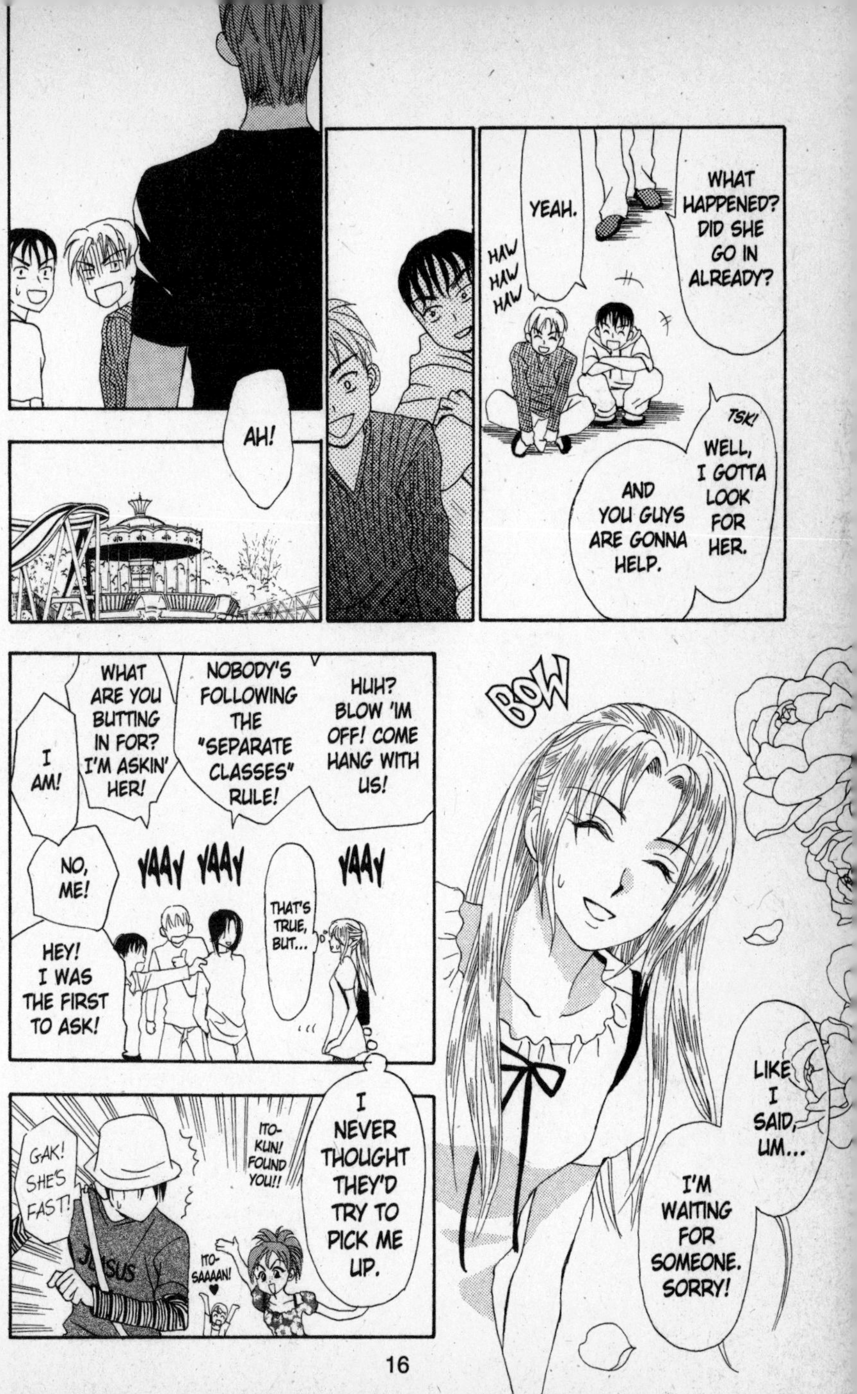
WHAT HAPPENED? DID SHE GO IN ALREADY?
YEAH.
HAW HAW HAW
TSK!
WELL, I GOTTA LOOK FOR HER.
AND YOU GUYS ARE GONNA HELP.
AH!
BOW
LIKE I SAID, UM...
I'M WAITING FOR SOMEONE. SORRY!
HUH? BLOW 'IM OFF! COME HANG WITH US!
NOBODY'S FOLLOWING THE "SEPARATE CLASSES" RULE!
WHAT ARE YOU BUTTING IN FOR? I'M ASKIN' HER!
I AM!
YAAY
YAAY YAAY
NO, ME!
THAT'S TRUE, BUT...
HEY! I WAS THE FIRST TO ASK!
I NEVER THOUGHT THEY'D TRY TO PICK ME UP.
ITO-KUN! FOUND YOU!!
ITO-SAAAAN! ♥
GAK! SHE'S FAST!

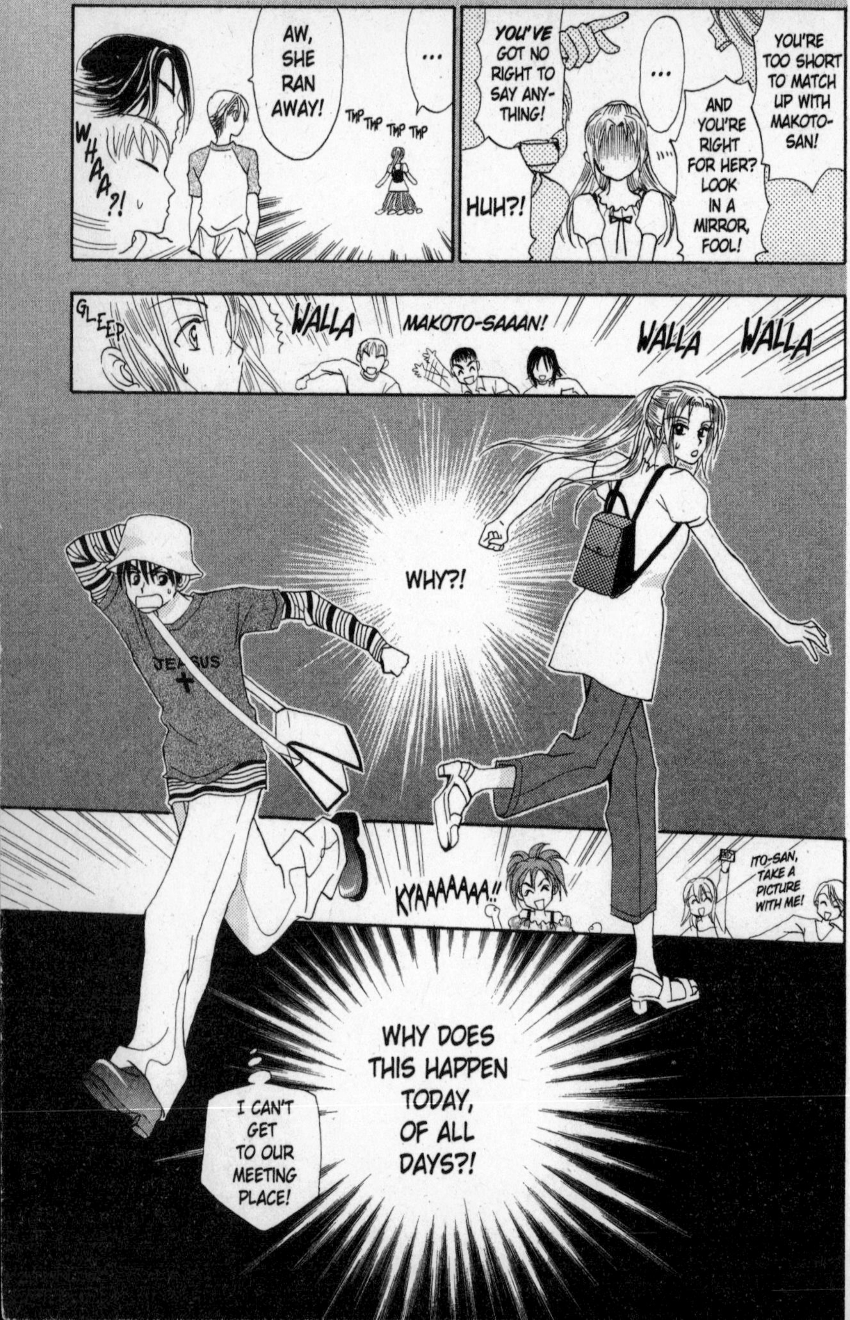
YOU'RE TOO SHORT TO MATCH UP WITH MAKOTO-SAN!
...
AND YOU'RE RIGHT FOR HER? LOOK IN A MIRROR, FOOL!
YOU'VE GOT NO RIGHT TO SAY ANYTHING!
HUH?!
...
AW, SHE RAN AWAY!
TMP TMP TMP TMP
WHAA?!
WALLA WALLA
MAKOTO-SAAAN!
WALLA
GLEEP
WHY?!
ITO-SAN, TAKE A PICTURE WITH ME!
KYAAAAAAA!!
WHY DOES THIS HAPPEN TODAY, OF ALL DAYS?!
I CAN'T GET TO OUR MEETING PLACE!

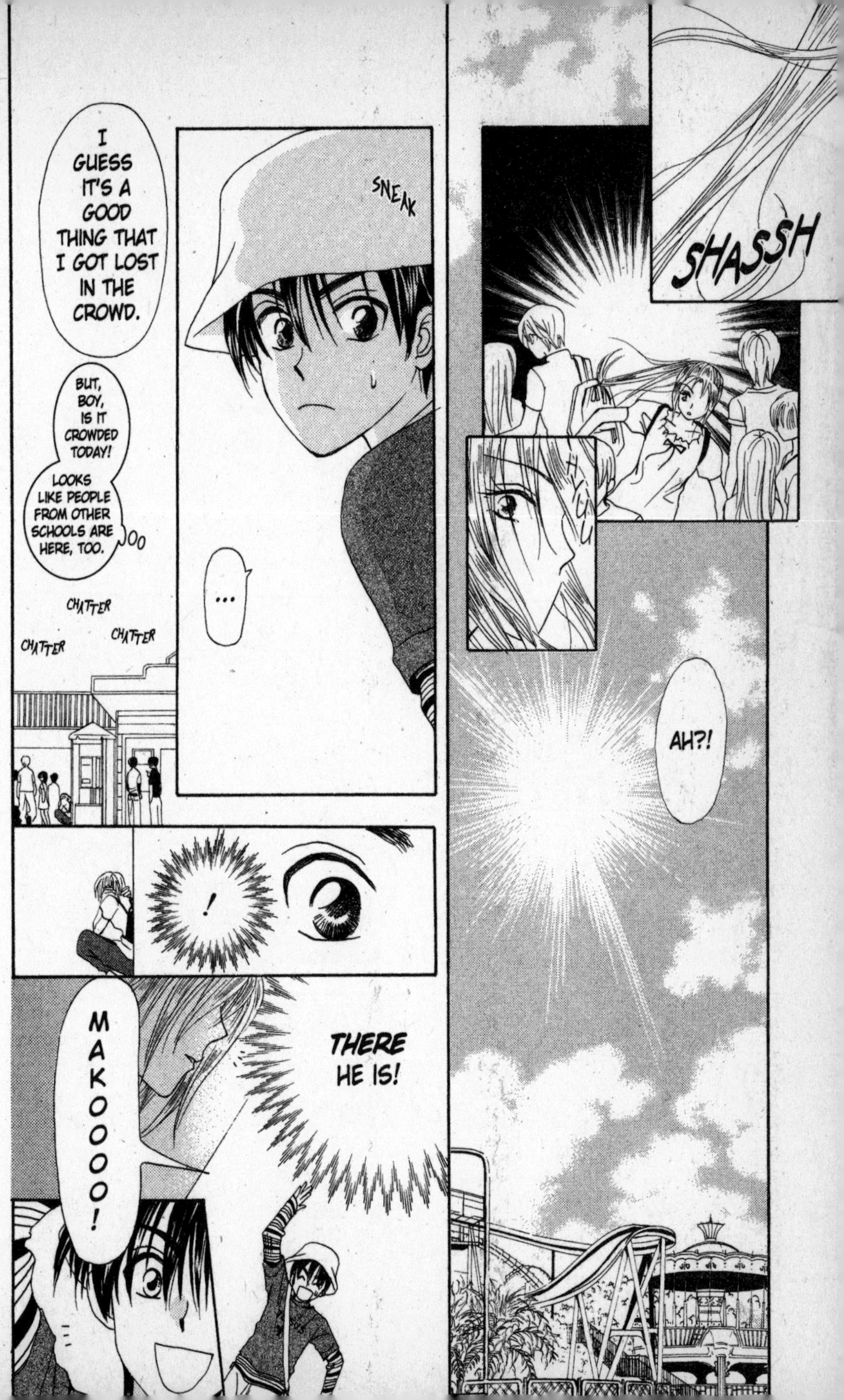
SHASSH
AH?!
SNEAK
I GUESS IT'S A GOOD THING THAT I GOT LOST IN THE CROWD.
BUT, BOY, IS IT CROWDED TODAY!
LOOKS LIKE PEOPLE FROM OTHER SCHOOLS ARE HERE, TOO.
CHATTER
CHATTER
CHATTER
...
!
THERE HE IS!
MAKOOOOO!

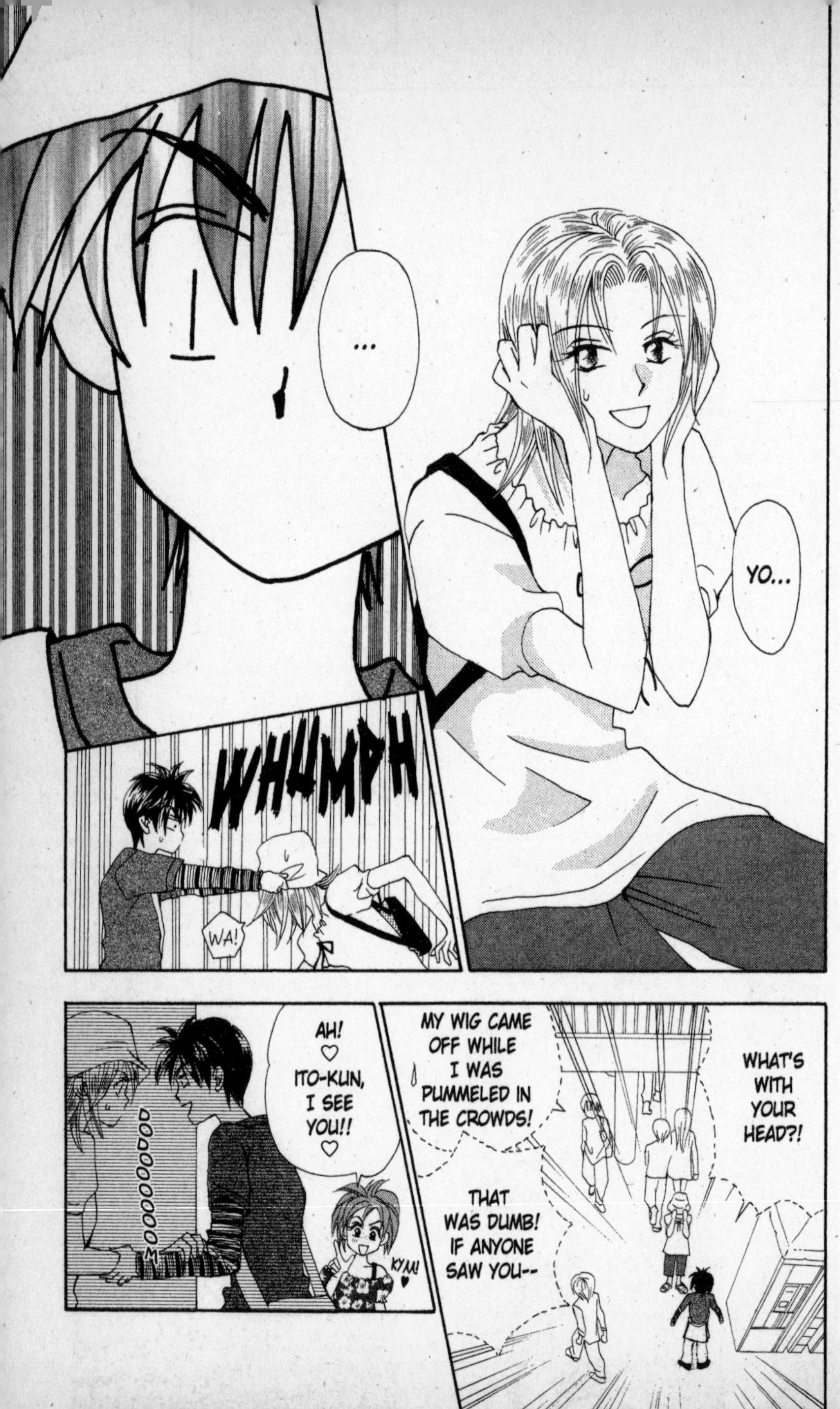

YO...
...
WHUMPH
WA!
WHAT'S WITH YOUR HEAD?!
MY WIG CAME OFF WHILE I WAS PUMMELED IN THE CROWDS!
THAT WAS DUMB! IF ANYONE SAW YOU--
AH! ♡ ITO-KUN, I SEE YOU!! ♡
KYA! ♡
DODOOOOOOOOM

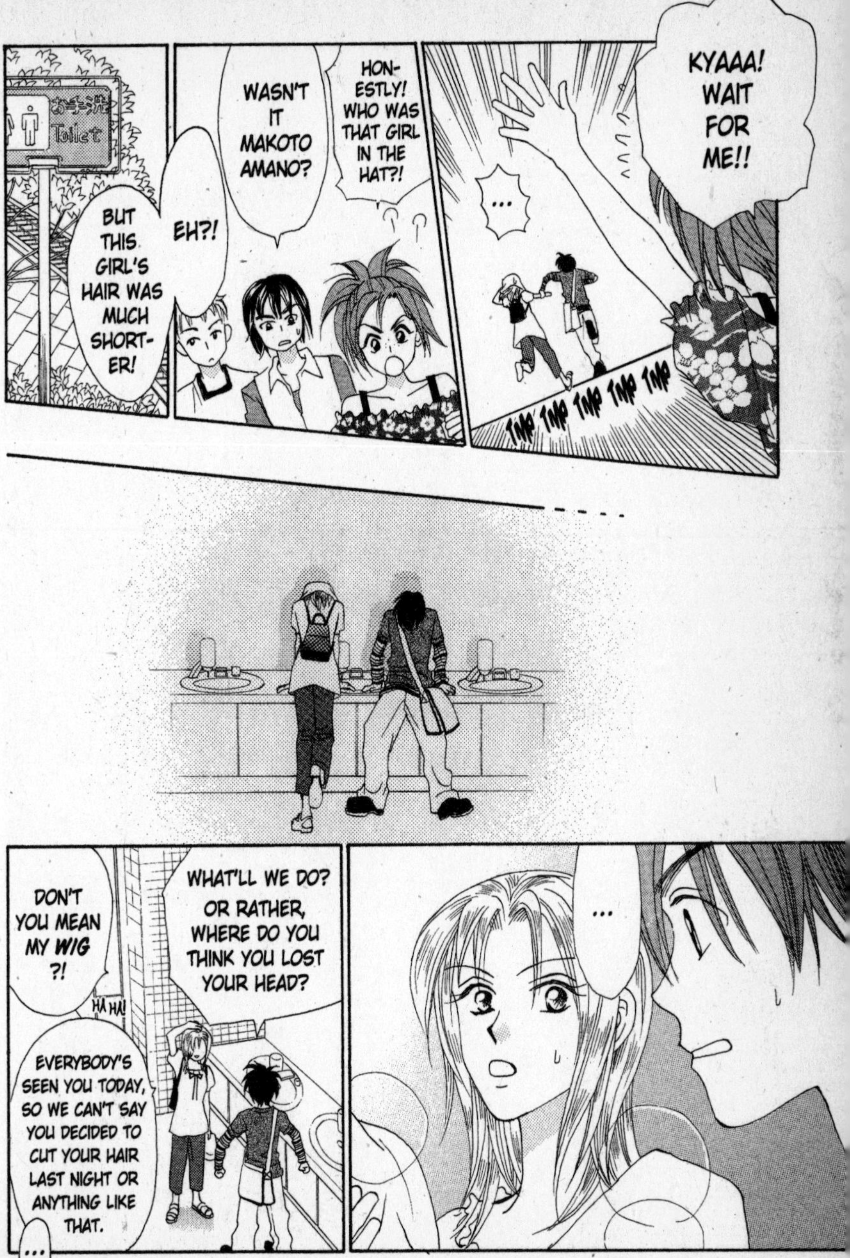
KYAAA! WAIT FOR ME!!
...
TMP TMP TMP TMP TMP TMP
HON-ESTLY! WHO WAS THAT GIRL IN THE HAT?!
WASN'T IT MAKOTO AMANO?
EH?!
BUT THIS GIRL'S HAIR WAS MUCH SHORT-ER!
Toilet
...
WHAT'LL WE DO? OR RATHER, WHERE DO YOU THINK YOU LOST YOUR HEAD?
DON'T YOU MEAN MY *WIG* ?!
HA HA!
EVERYBODY'S SEEN YOU TODAY, SO WE CAN'T SAY YOU DECIDED TO CUT YOUR HAIR LAST NIGHT OR ANYTHING LIKE THAT.
...

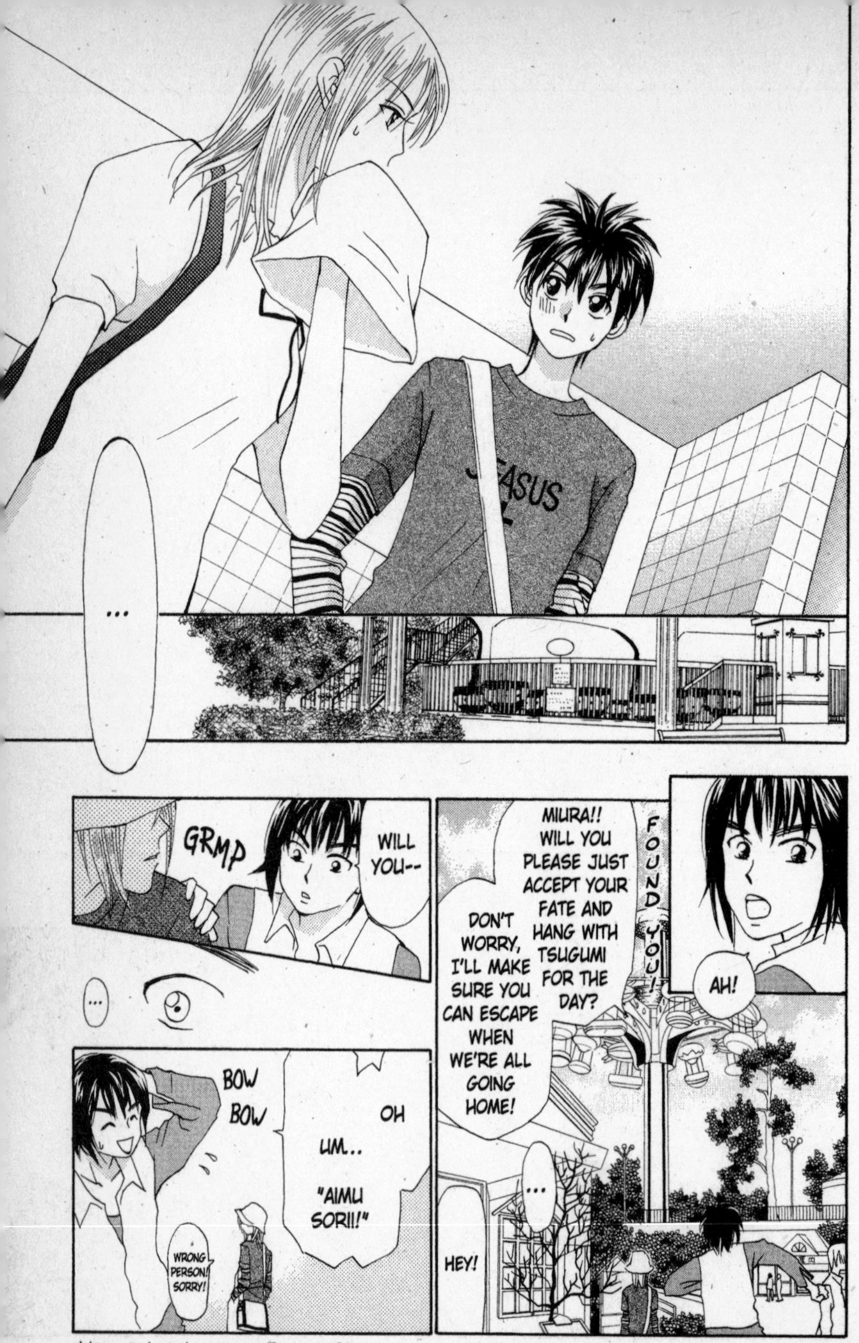
...
AH!
FOUND YOU!
MIURA!! WILL YOU PLEASE JUST ACCEPT YOUR FATE AND HANG WITH TSUGUMI FOR THE DAY?
DON'T WORRY, I'LL MAKE SURE YOU CAN ESCAPE WHEN WE'RE ALL GOING HOME!
...
HEY!
WILL YOU--
GRMP
...
OH
UM...
"AIMU SORII!"
BOW BOW
WRONG PERSON! SORRY!

*Kubota is trying to say, "I'm sorry," in English to the foreigner.

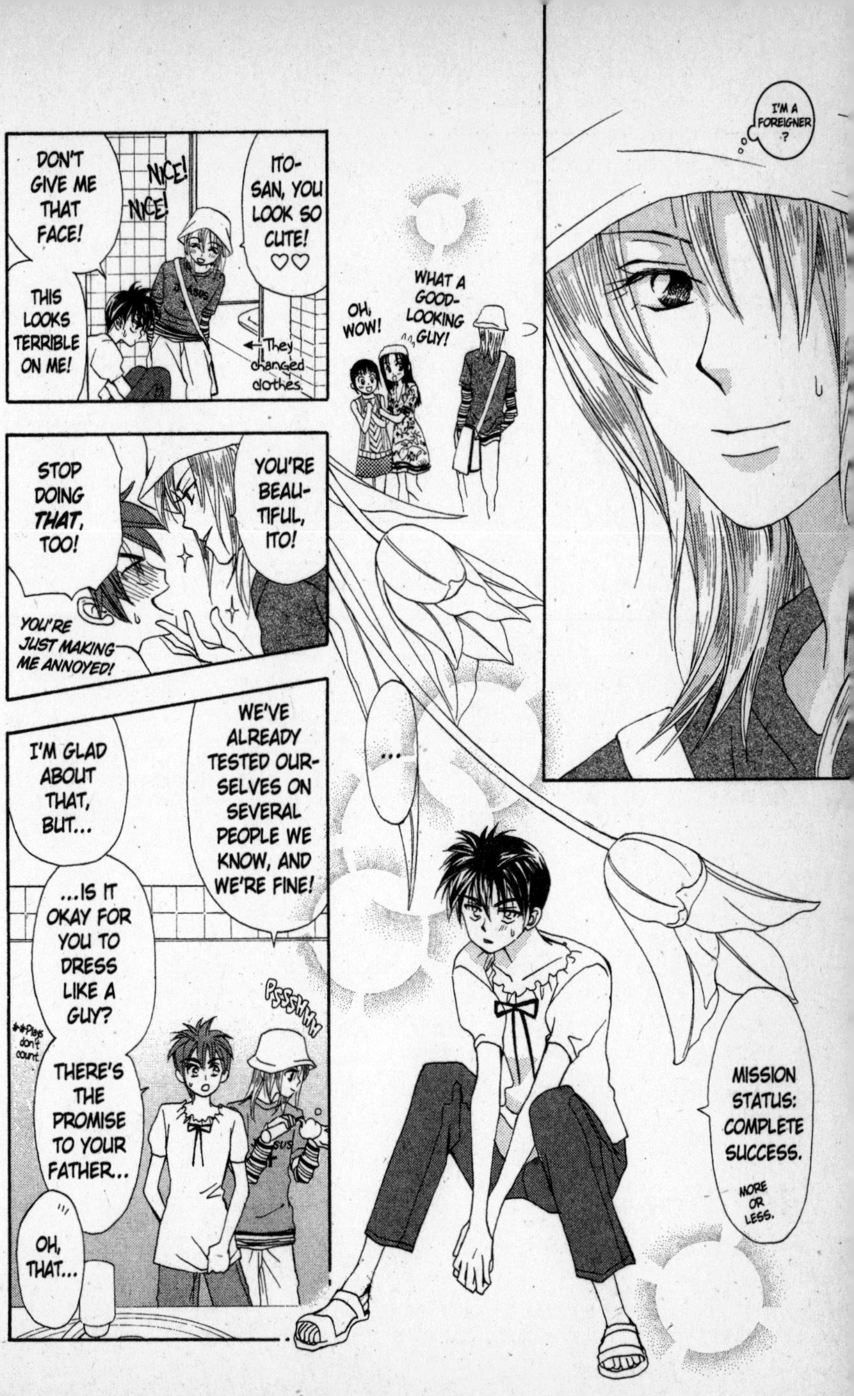
I'M A FOREIGNER?
WHAT A GOOD-LOOKING GUY!
OH, WOW!
MISSION STATUS: COMPLETE SUCCESS.
MORE OR LESS.
...
ITO-SAN, YOU LOOK SO CUTE! ♡♡
NICE!
NICE!
DON'T GIVE ME THAT FACE!
THIS LOOKS TERRIBLE ON ME!
← They changed clothes.
YOU'RE BEAUTIFUL, ITO!
STOP DOING THAT, TOO!
YOU'RE JUST MAKING ME ANNOYED!
WE'VE ALREADY TESTED OURSELVES ON SEVERAL PEOPLE WE KNOW, AND WE'RE FINE!
I'M GLAD ABOUT THAT, BUT...
...IS IT OKAY FOR YOU TO DRESS LIKE A GUY?
PSSSHHH
**Plays don't count.
THERE'S THE PROMISE TO YOUR FATHER...
OH, THAT...

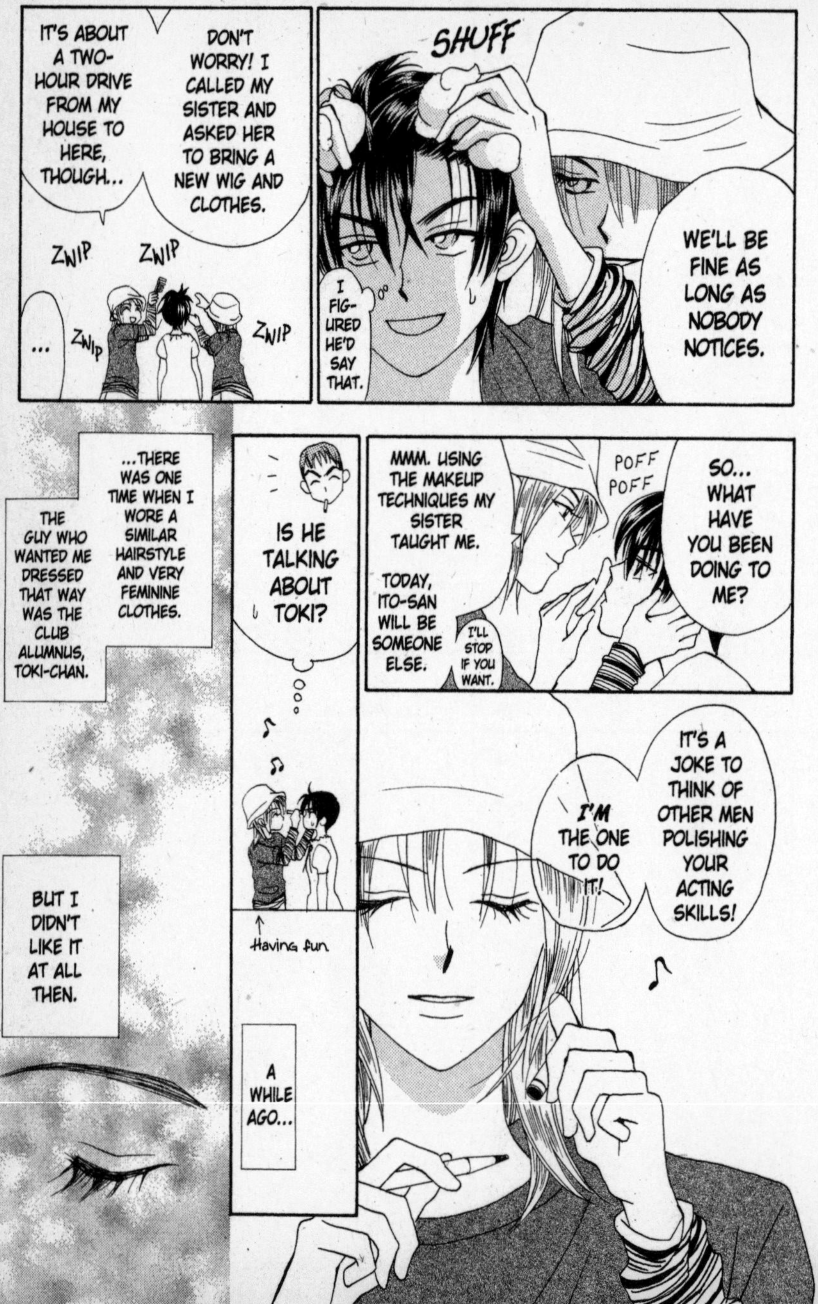
SHUFF
WE'LL BE FINE AS LONG AS NOBODY NOTICES.
I FIGURED HE'D SAY THAT.
DON'T WORRY! I CALLED MY SISTER AND ASKED HER TO BRING A NEW WIG AND CLOTHES.
IT'S ABOUT A TWO-HOUR DRIVE FROM MY HOUSE TO HERE, THOUGH...
ZWIP
ZWIP
ZWIP
ZWIP
...
SO... WHAT HAVE YOU BEEN DOING TO ME?
POFF POFF
MMM. USING THE MAKEUP TECHNIQUES MY SISTER TAUGHT ME.
TODAY, ITO-SAN WILL BE SOMEONE ELSE.
I'LL STOP IF YOU WANT.
IT'S A JOKE TO THINK OF OTHER MEN POLISHING YOUR ACTING SKILLS!
I'M THE ONE TO DO IT!
IS HE TALKING ABOUT TOKI?
Having fun
A WHILE AGO...
...THERE WAS ONE TIME WHEN I WORE A SIMILAR HAIRSTYLE AND VERY FEMININE CLOTHES.
THE GUY WHO WANTED ME DRESSED THAT WAY WAS THE CLUB ALUMNUS, TOKI-CHAN.
BUT I DIDN'T LIKE IT AT ALL THEN.

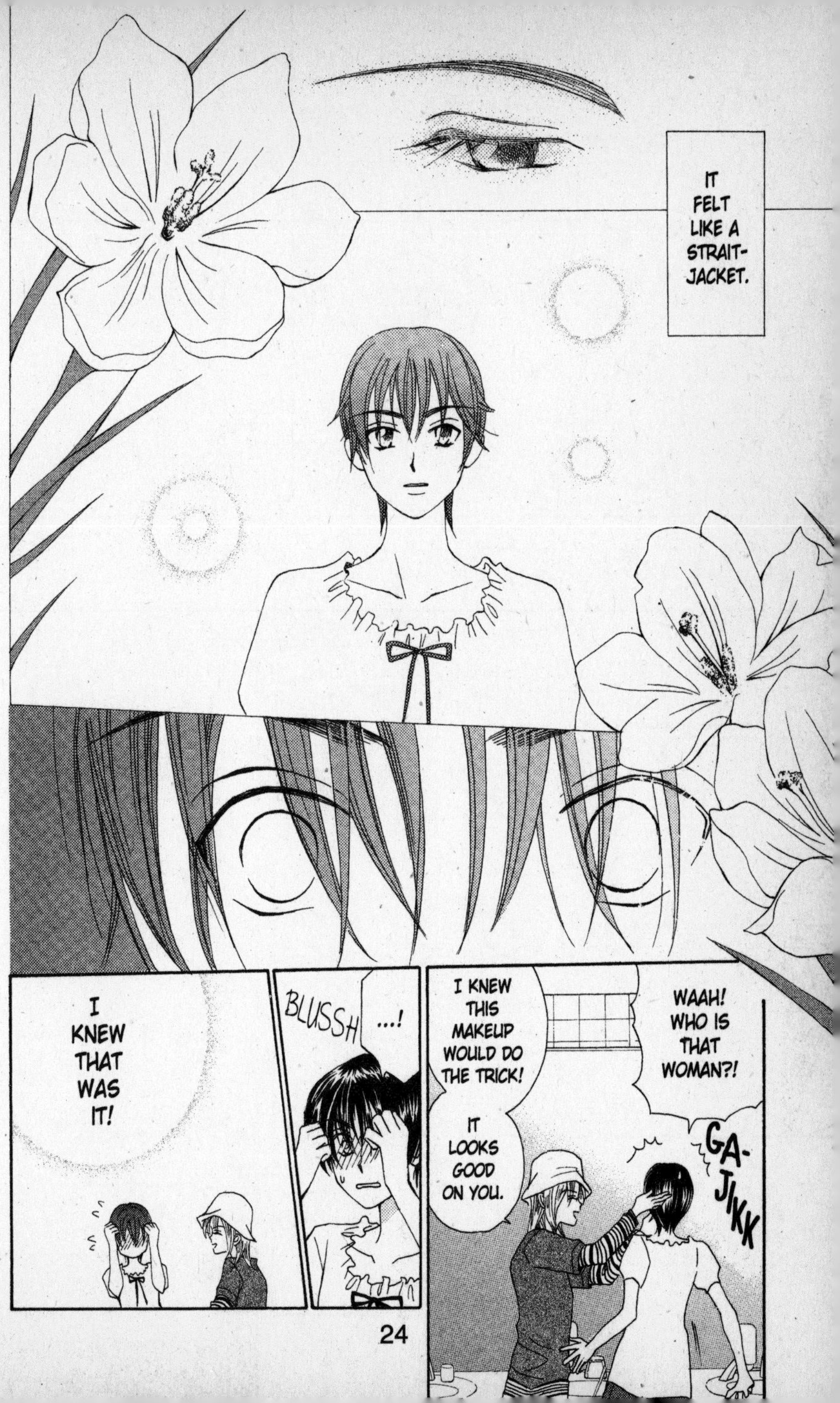
IT FELT LIKE A STRAIT-JACKET.
WAAH! WHO IS THAT WOMAN?!
GA-JIKK
I KNEW THIS MAKEUP WOULD DO THE TRICK!
IT LOOKS GOOD ON YOU.
BLUSSH
...!
I KNEW THAT WAS IT!

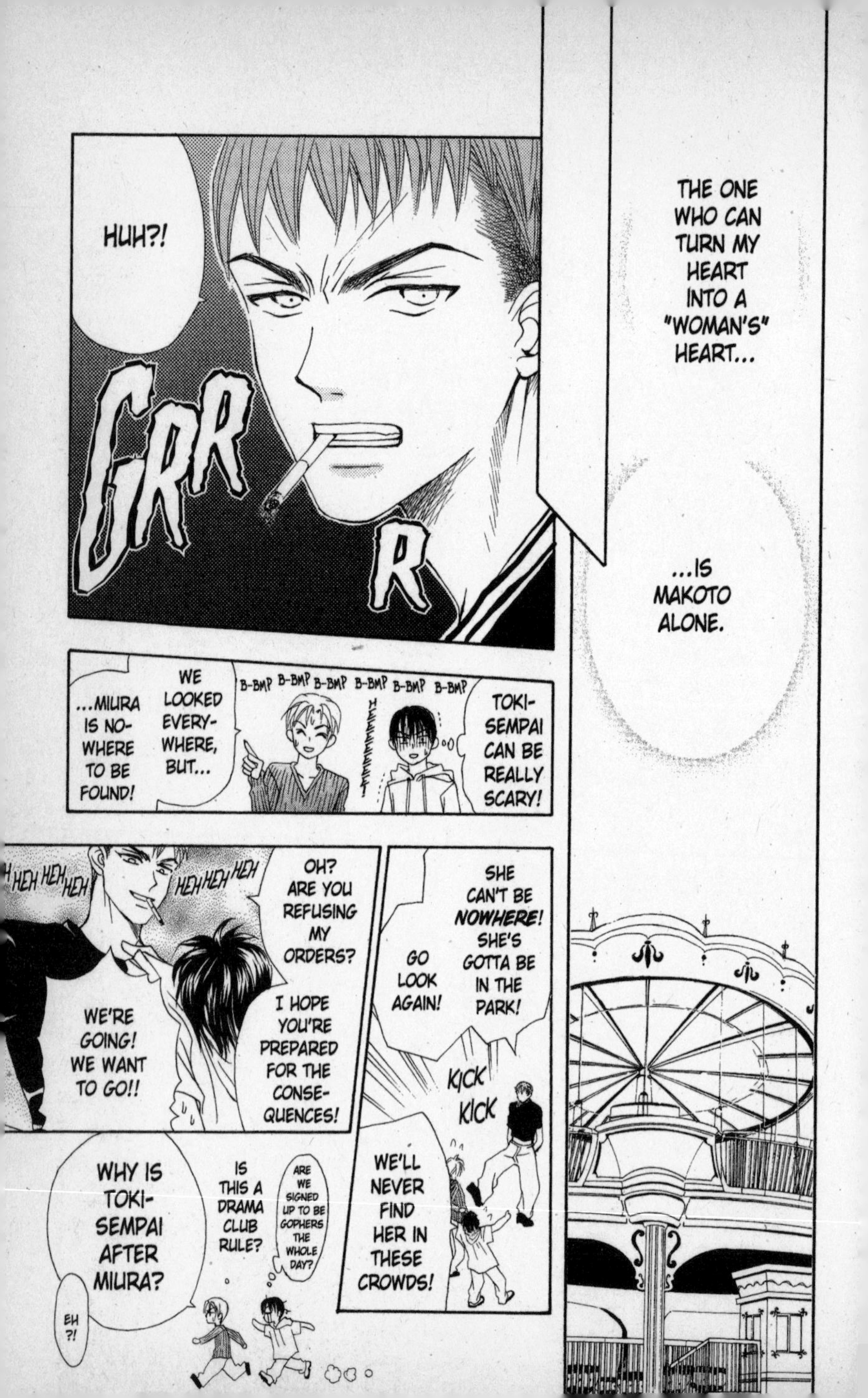
THE ONE WHO CAN TURN MY HEART INTO A "WOMAN'S" HEART...
...IS MAKOTO ALONE.
HUH?!
GRR
R
TOKI-SEMPAI CAN BE REALLY SCARY!
B-BMP B-BMP B-BMP B-BMP B-BMP B-BMP
HEEEEEEE!
WE LOOKED EVERY-WHERE, BUT...
...MIURA IS NO-WHERE TO BE FOUND!
SHE CAN'T BE *NOWHERE*! SHE'S GOTTA BE IN THE PARK!
GO LOOK AGAIN!
KICK KICK
WE'LL NEVER FIND HER IN THESE CROWDS!
HEH HEH HEH HEH HEH HEH HEH
OH? ARE YOU REFUSING MY ORDERS?
I HOPE YOU'RE PREPARED FOR THE CONSE-QUENCES!
WE'RE GOING! WE WANT TO GO!!
ARE WE SIGNED UP TO BE GOPHERS THE WHOLE DAY?
IS THIS A DRAMA CLUB RULE?
WHY IS TOKI-SEMPAI AFTER MIURA?
EH ?!

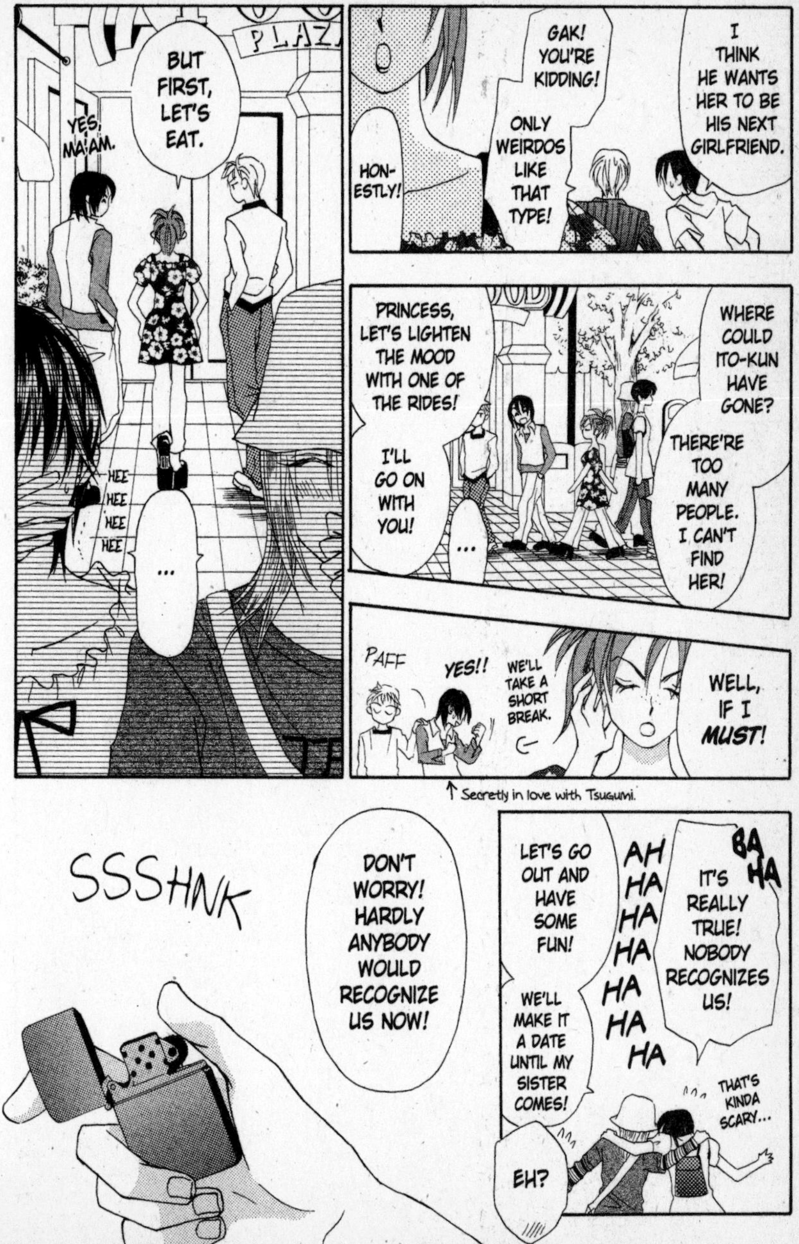
I THINK HE WANTS HER TO BE HIS NEXT GIRLFRIEND.
GAK! YOU'RE KIDDING!
ONLY WEIRDOS LIKE THAT TYPE!
HON-ESTLY!
WHERE COULD ITO-KUN HAVE GONE?
THERE'RE TOO MANY PEOPLE. I CAN'T FIND HER!
PRINCESS, LET'S LIGHTEN THE MOOD WITH ONE OF THE RIDES!
I'LL GO ON WITH YOU!
...
WELL, IF I *MUST*!
WE'LL TAKE A SHORT BREAK.
YES!!
PAFF
BUT FIRST, LET'S EAT.
YES, MA'AM.
HEE HEE HEE HEE
...
↑ Secretly in love with Tsugumi.
BA HA
IT'S REALLY TRUE! NOBODY RECOGNIZES US!
AH HA HA HA HA HA HA
LET'S GO OUT AND HAVE SOME FUN!
WE'LL MAKE IT A DATE UNTIL MY SISTER COMES!
THAT'S KINDA SCARY...
EH?
DON'T WORRY! HARDLY ANYBODY WOULD RECOGNIZE US NOW!
SSSHNK

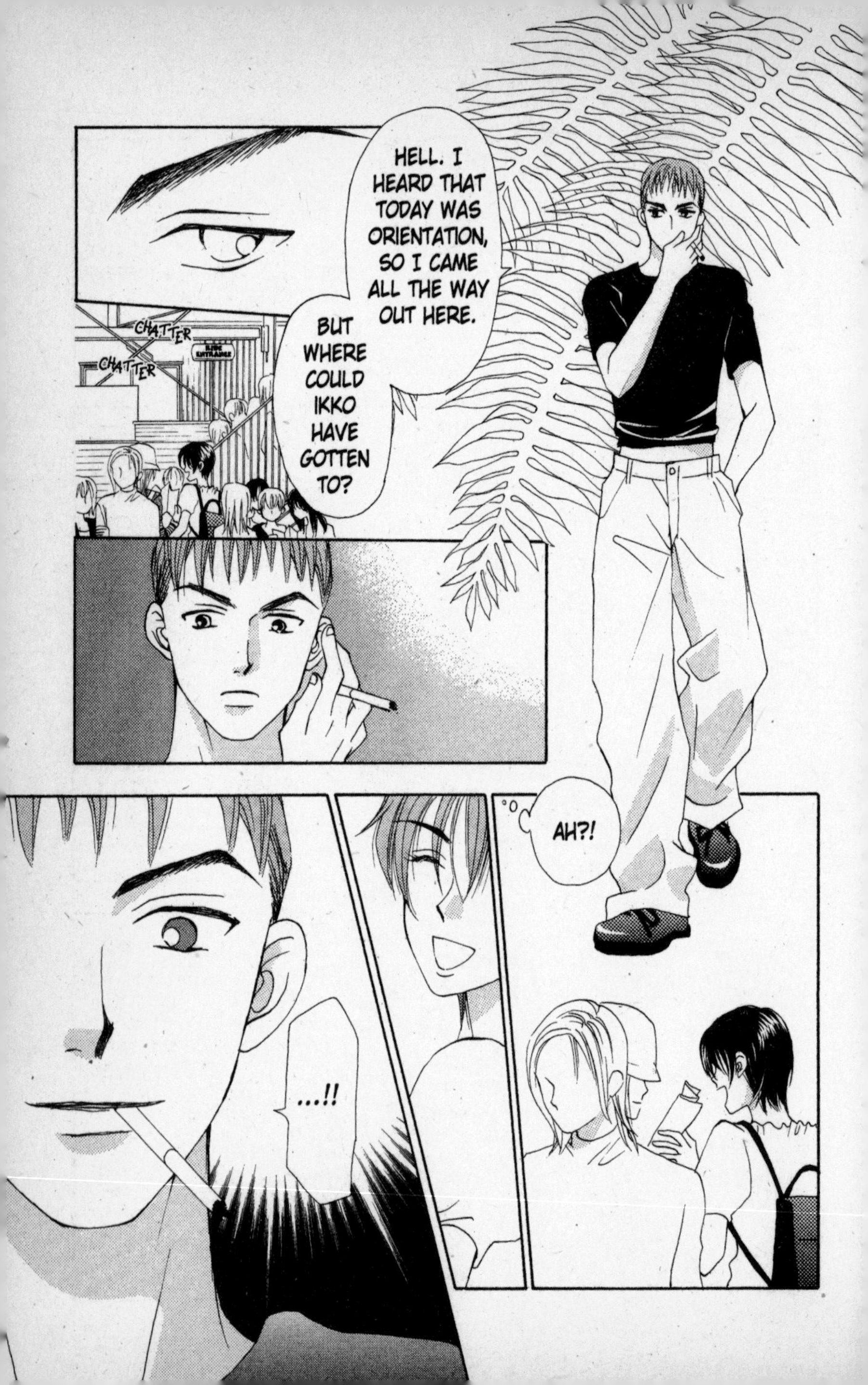
HELL. I HEARD THAT TODAY WAS ORIENTATION, SO I CAME ALL THE WAY OUT HERE.
CHATTER
CHATTER
BUT WHERE COULD IKKO HAVE GOTTEN TO?
AH?!
...!!

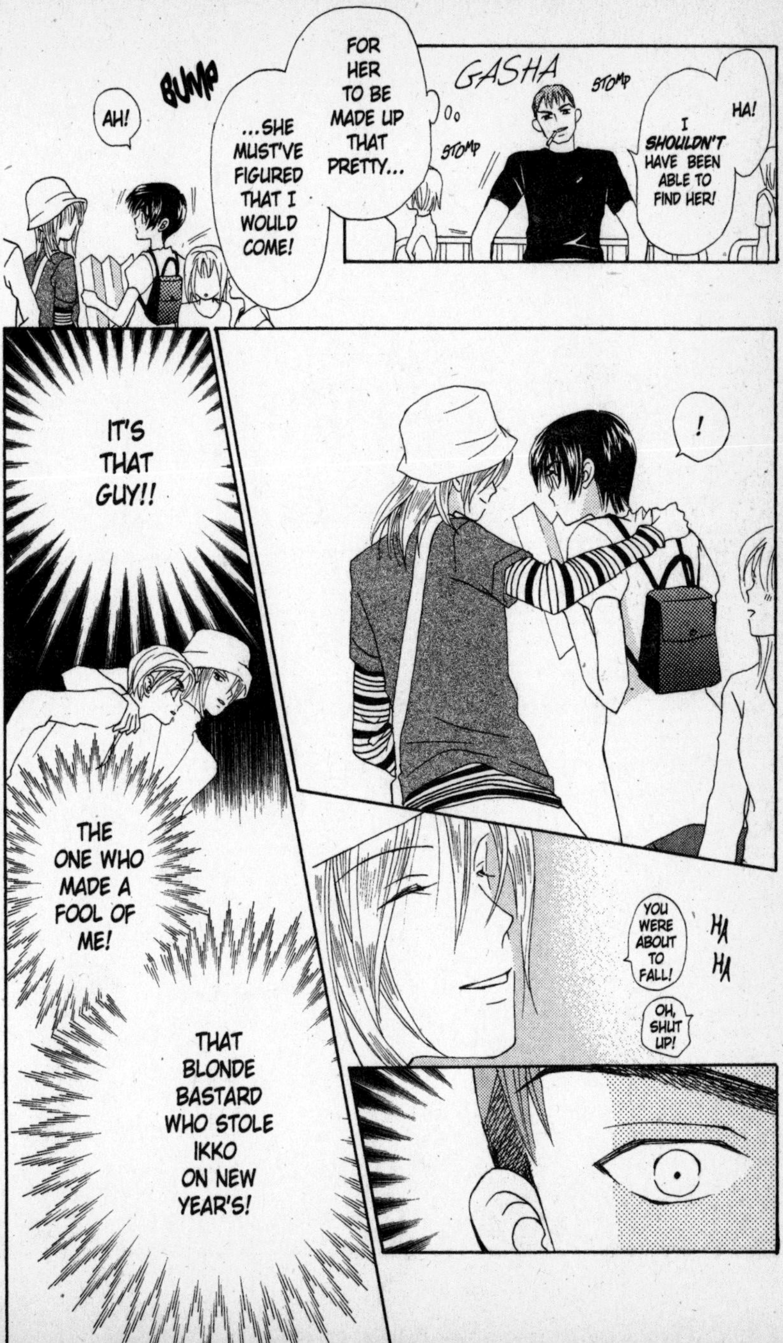
GASHA
STOMP
STOMP
HA!
I SHOULDN'T HAVE BEEN ABLE TO FIND HER!
FOR HER TO BE MADE UP THAT PRETTY...
...SHE MUST'VE FIGURED THAT I WOULD COME!
BUMP
AH!
!
YOU WERE ABOUT TO FALL!
HA HA
OH, SHUT UP!
IT'S THAT GUY!!
THE ONE WHO MADE A FOOL OF ME!
THAT BLONDE BASTARD WHO STOLE IKKO ON NEW YEAR'S!

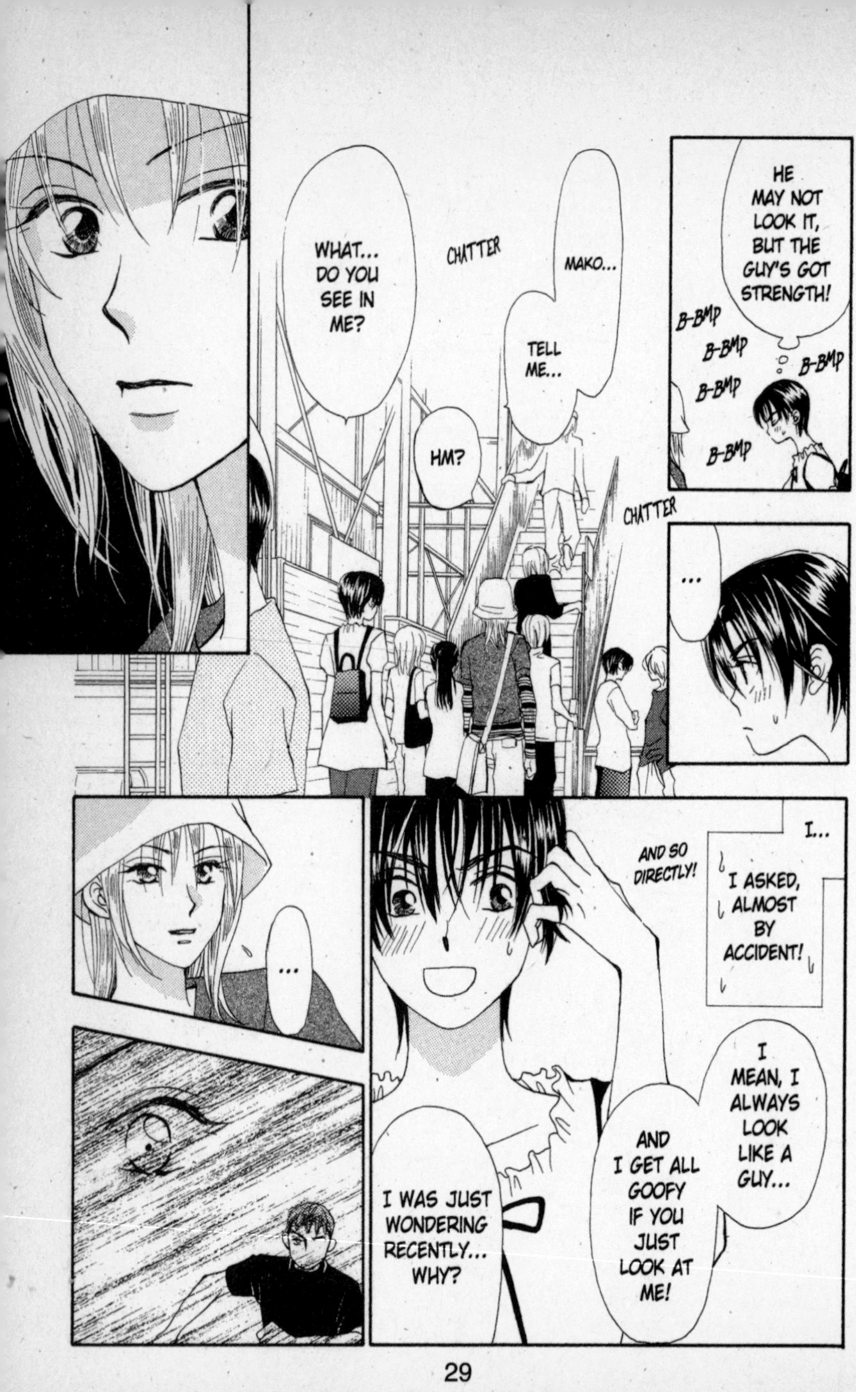
HE MAY NOT LOOK IT, BUT THE GUY'S GOT STRENGTH!
B-BMP
B-BMP
B-BMP
B-BMP
B-BMP
...
CHATTER
MAKO...
TELL ME...
WHAT... DO YOU SEE IN ME?
HM?
CHATTER
I...
I ASKED, ALMOST BY ACCIDENT!
AND SO DIRECTLY!
I MEAN, I ALWAYS LOOK LIKE A GUY...
AND I GET ALL GOOFY IF YOU JUST LOOK AT ME!
I WAS JUST WONDERING RECENTLY... WHY?
...

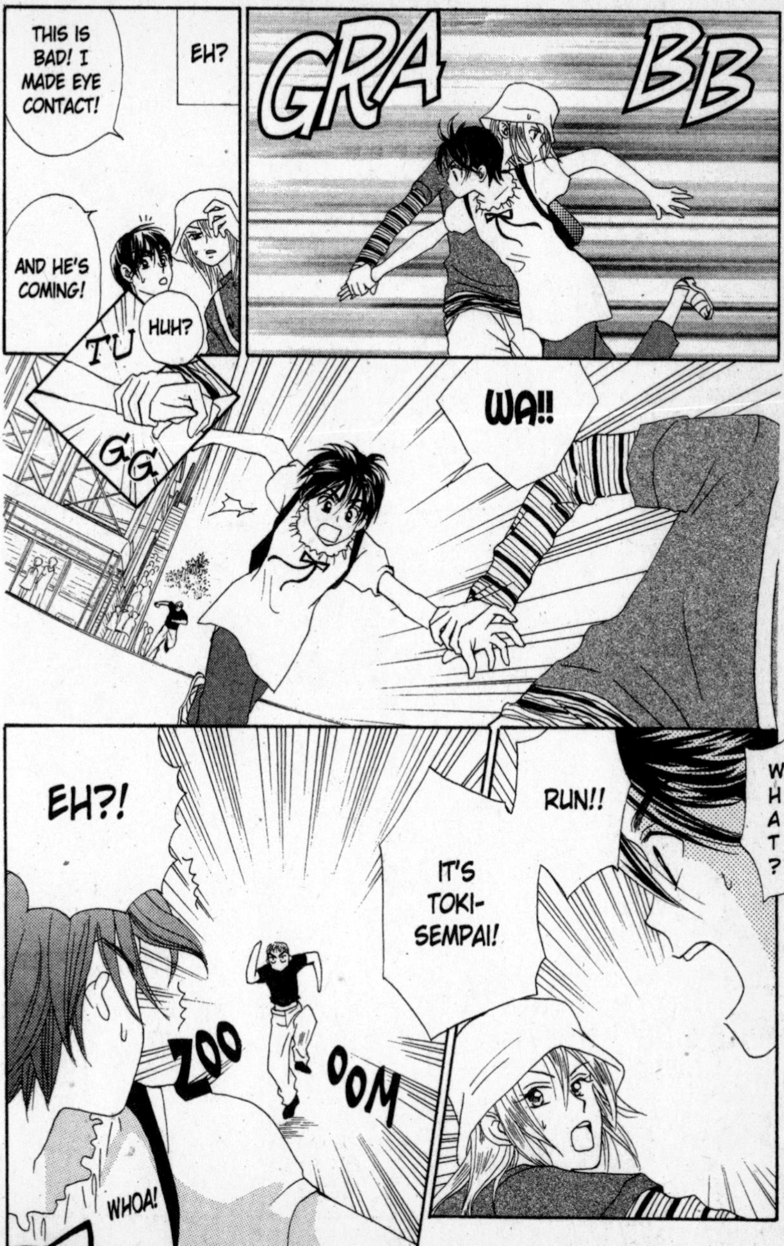
GRABB
EH?
THIS IS BAD! I MADE EYE CONTACT!
AND HE'S COMING!
HUH?
TUGG
WA!!
WHAT?
RUN!!
IT'S TOKI-SEMPAI!
EH?!
ZOOOOM
WHOA!

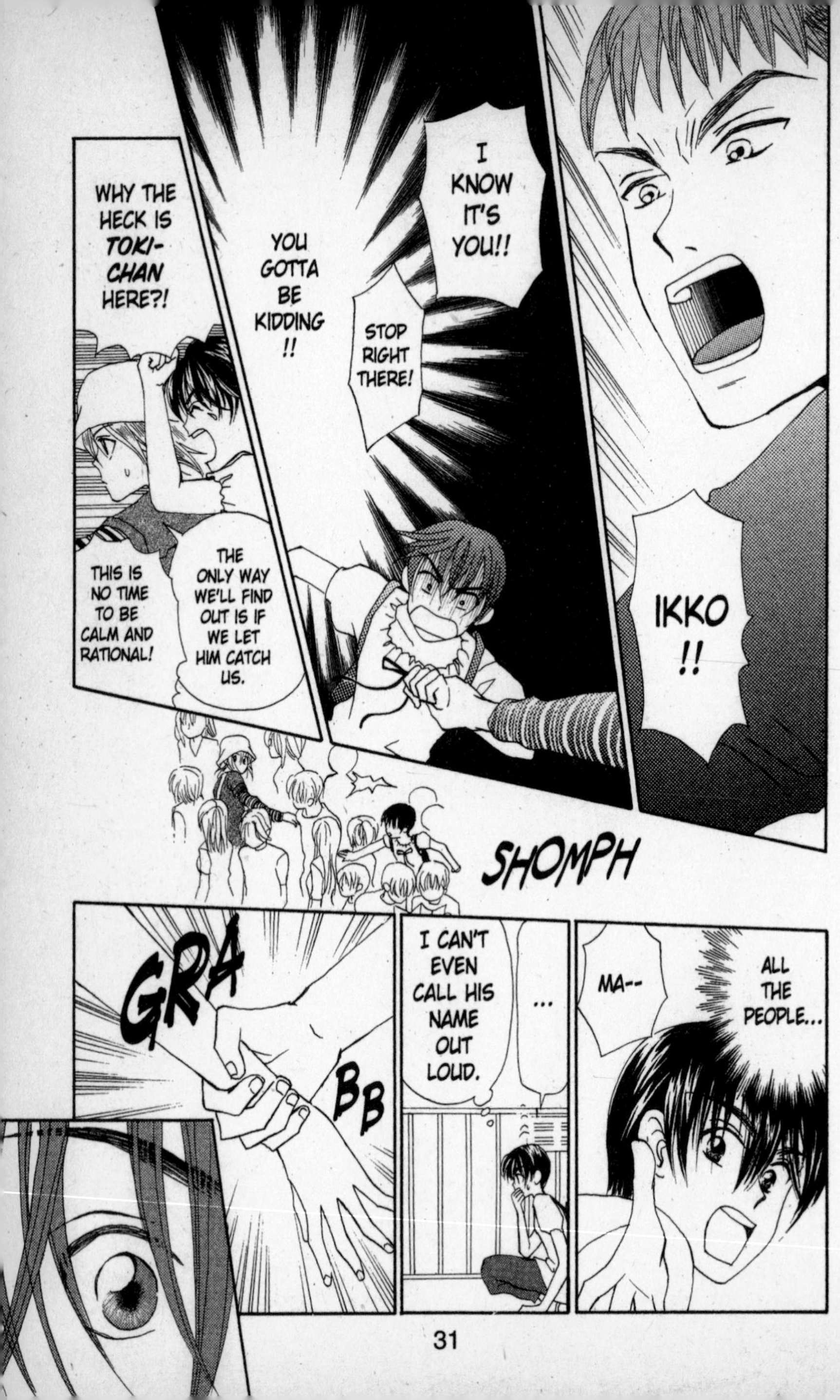
IKKO !!
I KNOW IT'S YOU!!
STOP RIGHT THERE!
YOU GOTTA BE KIDDING !!
WHY THE HECK IS TOKI-CHAN HERE?!
THE ONLY WAY WE'LL FIND OUT IS IF WE LET HIM CATCH US.
THIS IS NO TIME TO BE CALM AND RATIONAL!
SHOMPH
ALL THE PEOPLE...
MA--
...
I CAN'T EVEN CALL HIS NAME OUT LOUD.
GRA
BB

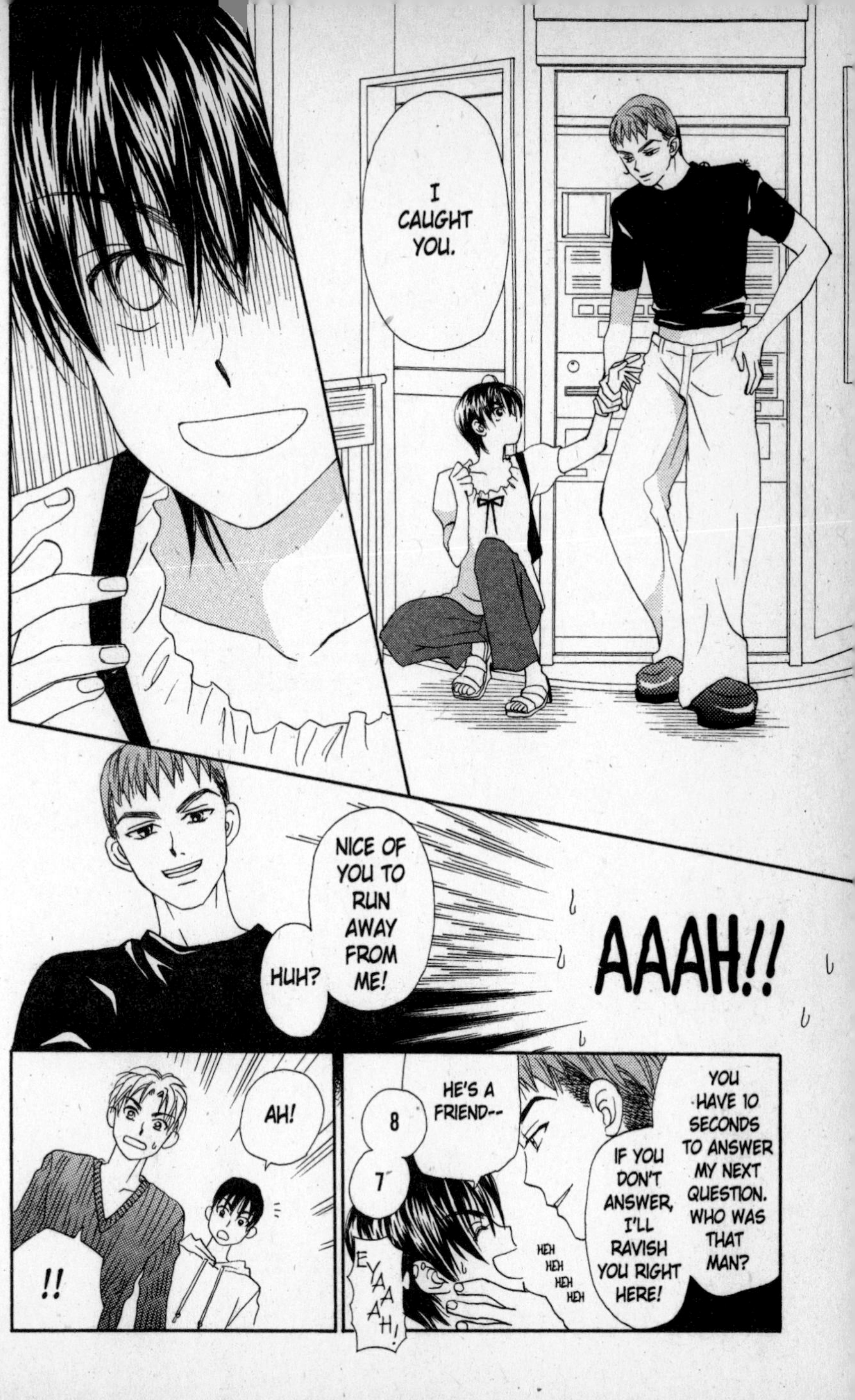
I CAUGHT YOU.
AAAH!!
NICE OF YOU TO RUN AWAY FROM ME!
HUH?
YOU HAVE 10 SECONDS TO ANSWER MY NEXT QUESTION. WHO WAS THAT MAN?
IF YOU DON'T ANSWER, I'LL RAVISH YOU RIGHT HERE!
HEH HEH HEH HEH
HE'S A FRIEND--
8
7
EYAAAAH!
AH!
!!

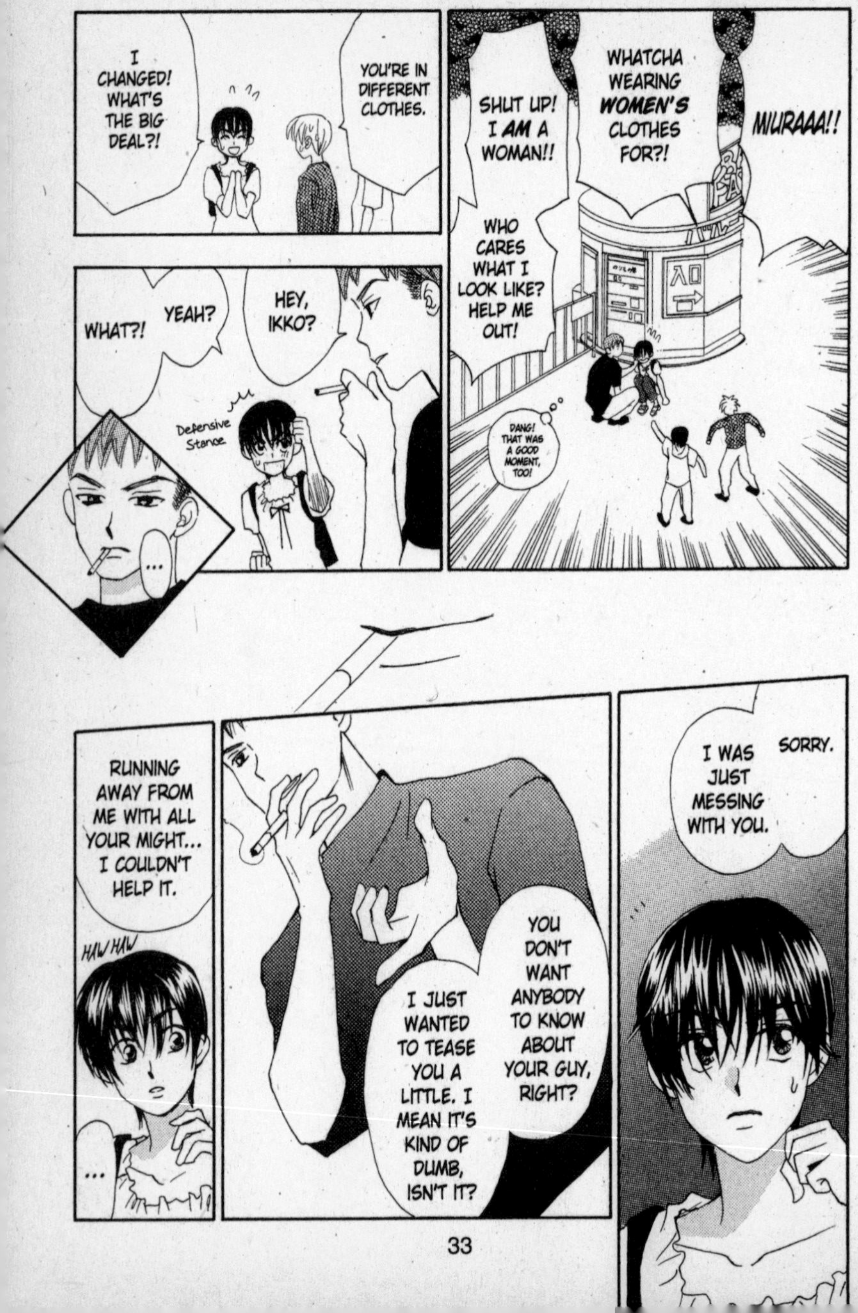
MIURAAA!!
WHATCHA WEARING *WOMEN'S* CLOTHES FOR?!
SHUT UP! I *AM* A WOMAN!!
WHO CARES WHAT I LOOK LIKE? HELP ME OUT!
DANG! THAT WAS A GOOD MOMENT, TOO!
YOU'RE IN DIFFERENT CLOTHES.
I CHANGED! WHAT'S THE BIG DEAL?!
HEY, IKKO?
YEAH?
WHAT?!
Defensive Stance
...
SORRY.
I WAS JUST MESSING WITH YOU.
YOU DON'T WANT ANYBODY TO KNOW ABOUT YOUR GUY, RIGHT?
I JUST WANTED TO TEASE YOU A LITTLE. I MEAN IT'S KIND OF DUMB, ISN'T IT?
RUNNING AWAY FROM ME WITH ALL YOUR MIGHT... I COULDN'T HELP IT.
HAW HAW
...

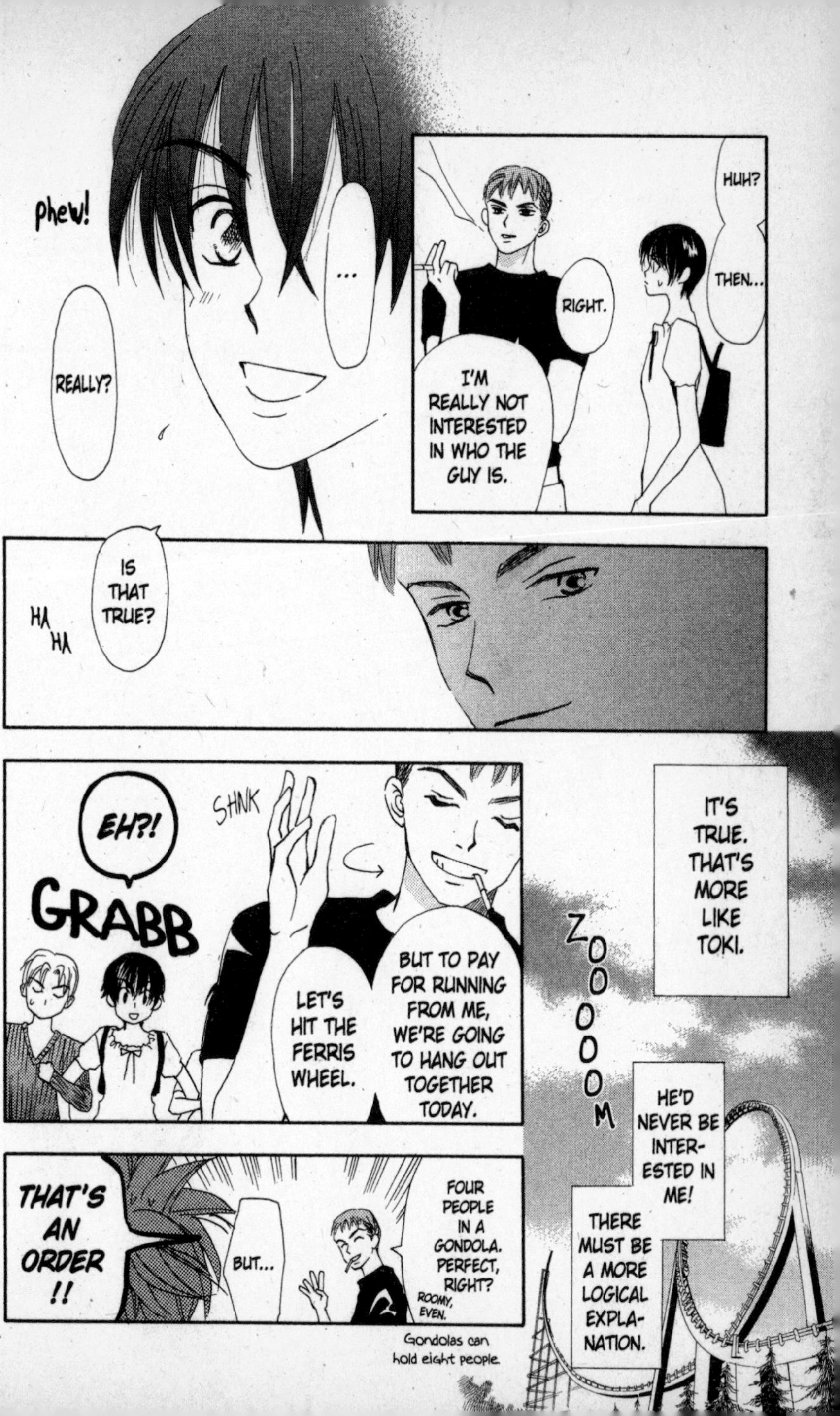
HUH?
THEN...
RIGHT.
I'M REALLY NOT INTERESTED IN WHO THE GUY IS.
...
REALLY?
phew!
IS THAT TRUE?
HA HA
IT'S TRUE. THAT'S MORE LIKE TOKI.
HE'D NEVER BE INTER-ESTED IN ME!
THERE MUST BE A MORE LOGICAL EXPLA-NATION.
ZOOOOOM
BUT TO PAY FOR RUNNING FROM ME, WE'RE GOING TO HANG OUT TOGETHER TODAY.
LET'S HIT THE FERRIS WHEEL.
SHNK
EH?!
GRABB
FOUR PEOPLE IN A GONDOLA. PERFECT, RIGHT?
ROOMY, EVEN.
BUT...
THAT'S AN ORDER!!
Gondolas can hold eight people.

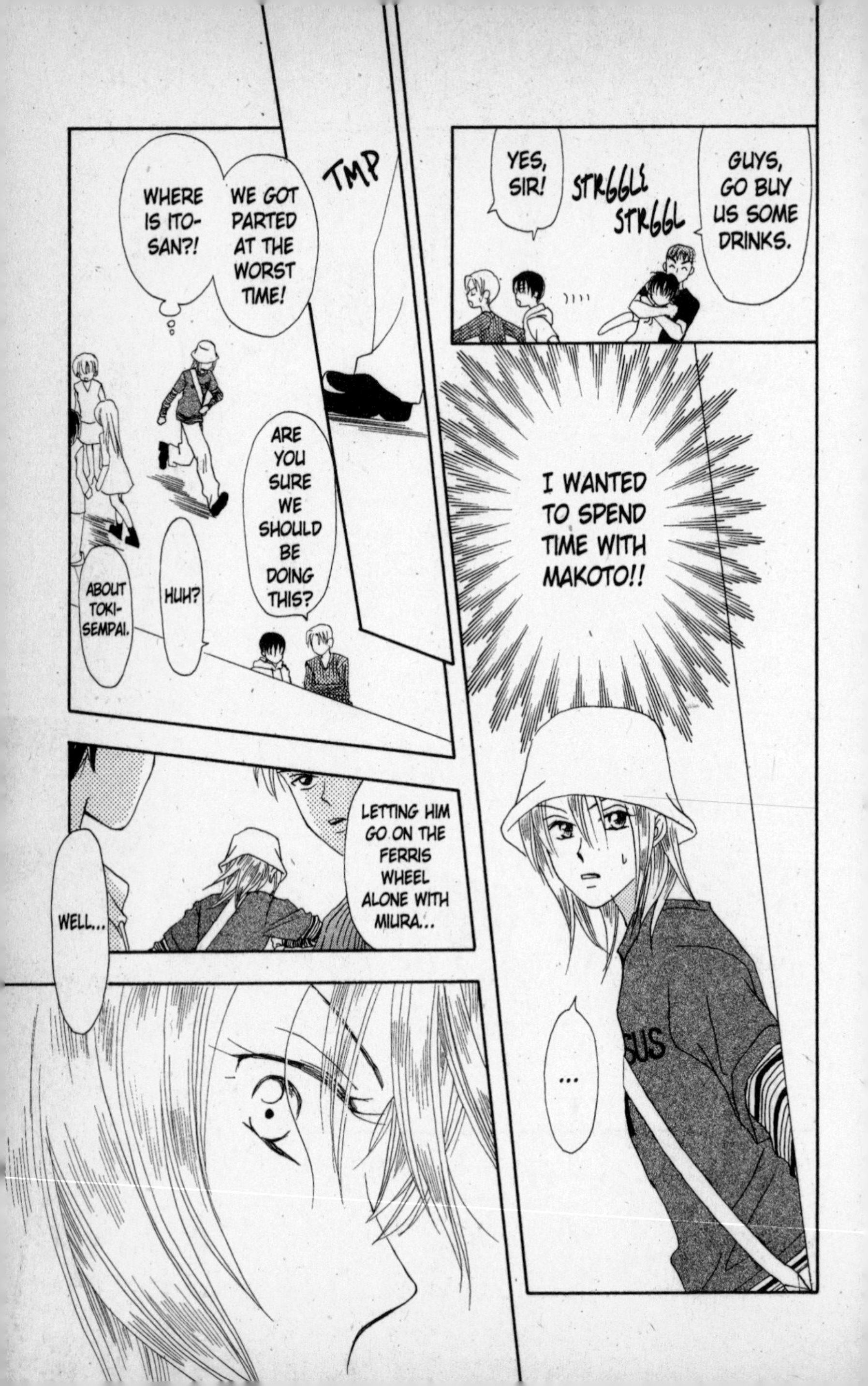
GUYS, GO BUY US SOME DRINKS.
YES, SIR!
STRGGLE STRGGL
WHERE IS ITO-SAN?!
WE GOT PARTED AT THE WORST TIME!
TMP
ARE YOU SURE WE SHOULD BE DOING THIS?
HUH?
ABOUT TOKI-SEMPAI.
I WANTED TO SPEND TIME WITH MAKOTO!!
...
LETTING HIM GO ON THE FERRIS WHEEL ALONE WITH MIURA...
WELL...

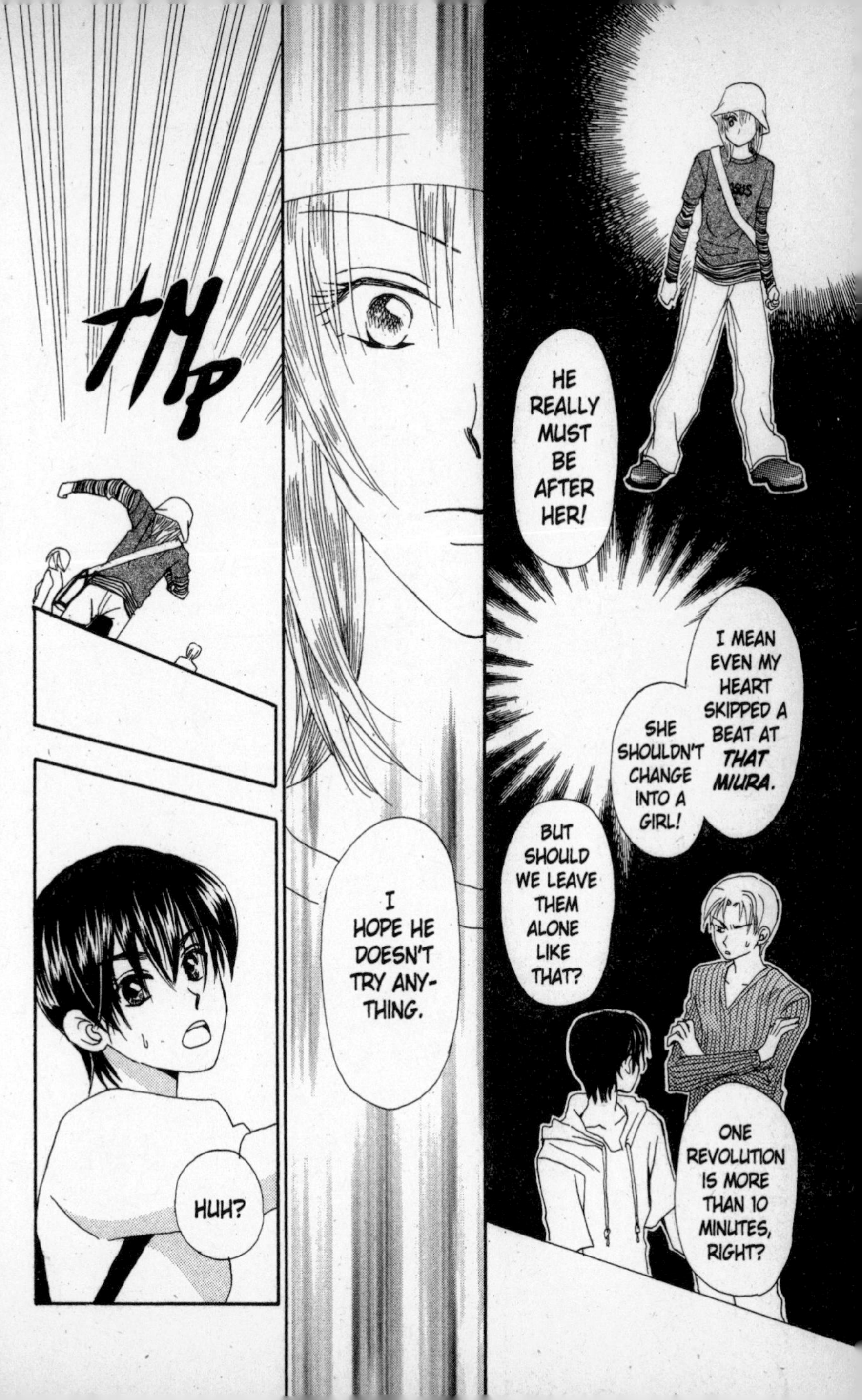
HE REALLY MUST BE AFTER HER!
I MEAN EVEN MY HEART SKIPPED A BEAT AT *THAT MIURA*.
SHE SHOULDN'T CHANGE INTO A GIRL!
BUT SHOULD WE LEAVE THEM ALONE LIKE THAT?
ONE REVOLUTION IS MORE THAN 10 MINUTES, RIGHT?
I HOPE HE DOESN'T TRY ANY-THING.
TMP
HUH?

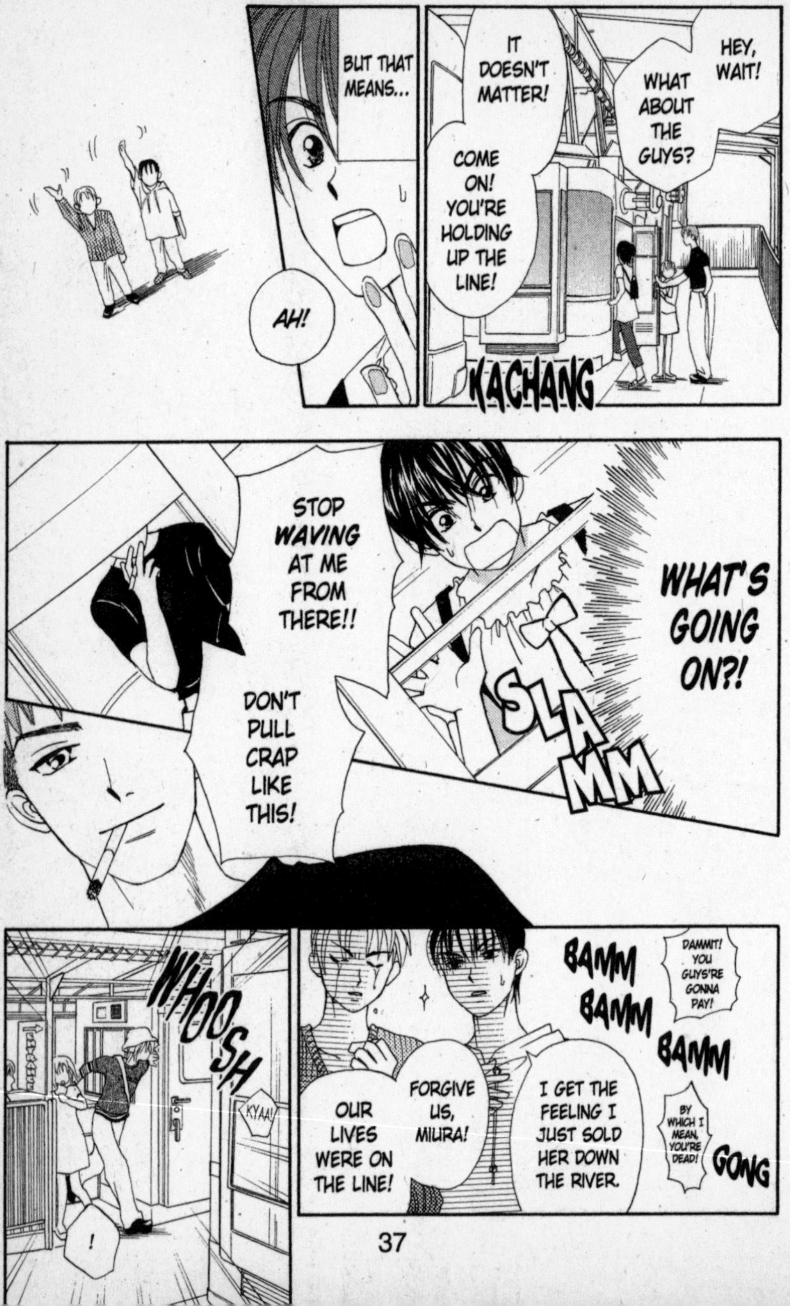
HEY, WAIT!
WHAT ABOUT THE GUYS?
IT DOESN'T MATTER!
COME ON! YOU'RE HOLDING UP THE LINE!
KACHANG
BUT THAT MEANS...
AH!
WHAT'S GOING ON?!
SLAMM
STOP WAVING AT ME FROM THERE!!
DON'T PULL CRAP LIKE THIS!
DAMMIT! YOU GUYS'RE GONNA PAY!
BAMM BAMM BAMM
BY WHICH I MEAN, YOU'RE DEAD!
GONG
I GET THE FEELING I JUST SOLD HER DOWN THE RIVER.
FORGIVE US, MIURA!
OUR LIVES WERE ON THE LINE!
WHOOSH
KYAA!
!

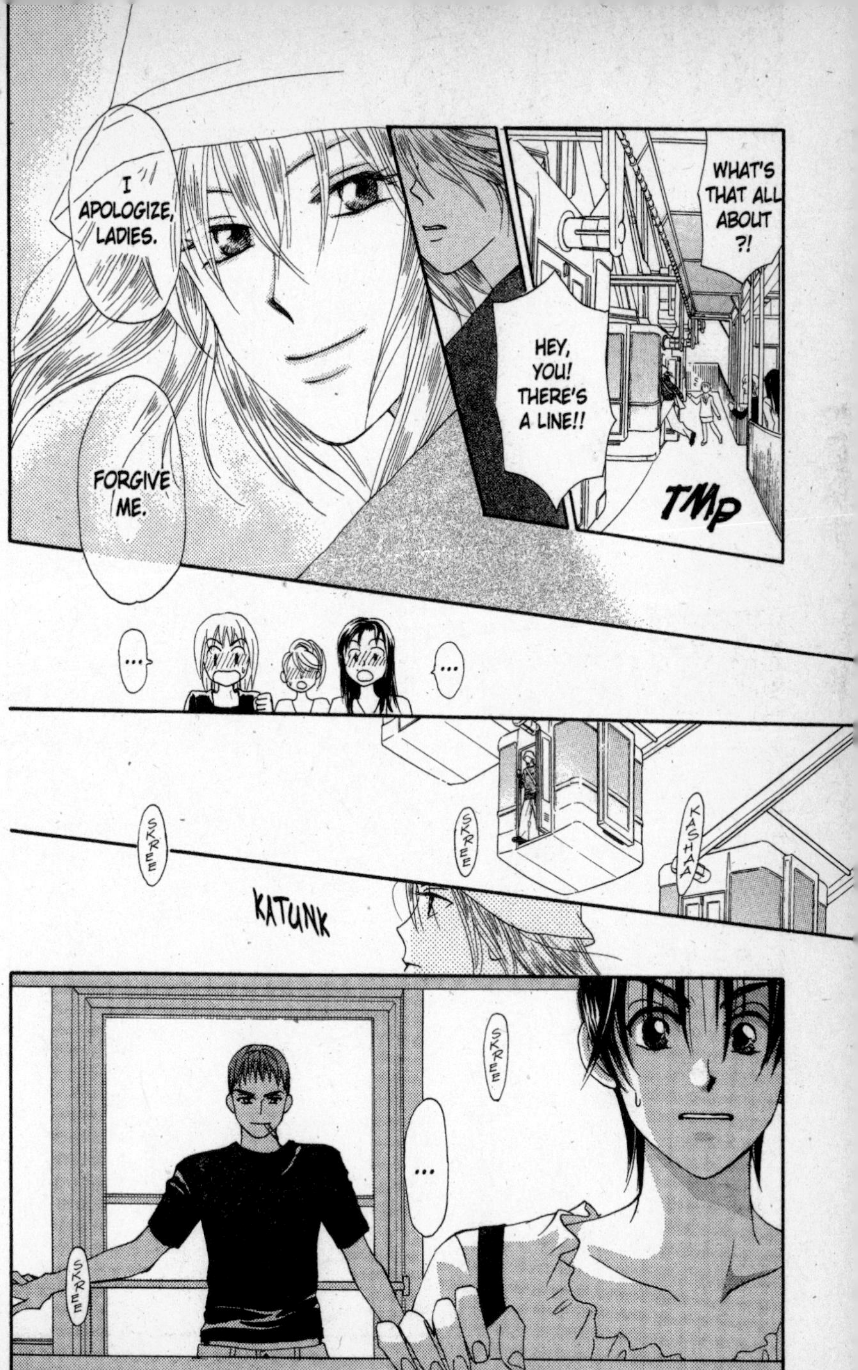
WHAT'S THAT ALL ABOUT ?!
HEY, YOU! THERE'S A LINE!!
TMP
I APOLOGIZE, LADIES.
FORGIVE ME.
...
...
KASHAA
SKREE
SKREE
KATUNK
SKREE
...
SKREE

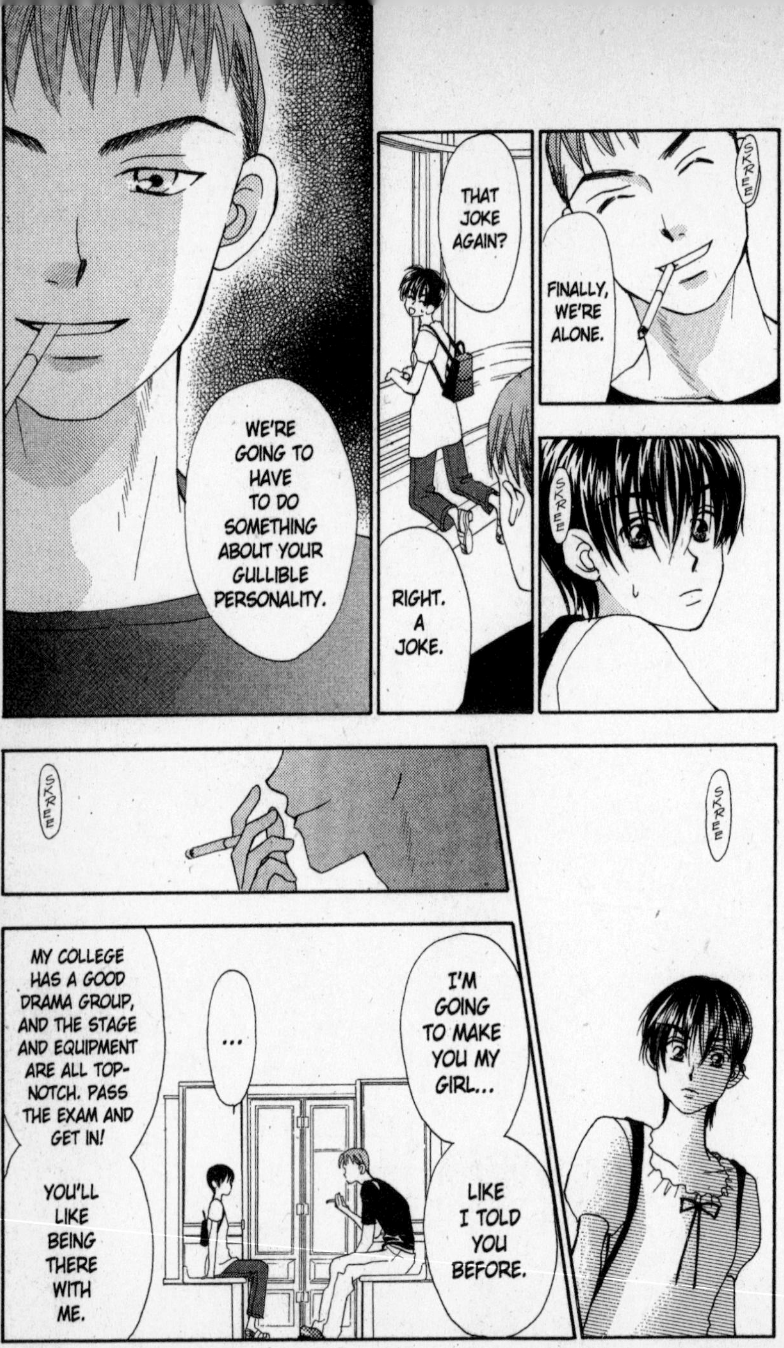
SKREE
FINALLY, WE'RE ALONE.
SKREE
THAT JOKE AGAIN?
RIGHT. A JOKE.
WE'RE GOING TO HAVE TO DO SOMETHING ABOUT YOUR GULLIBLE PERSONALITY.
SKREE
SKREE
I'M GOING TO MAKE YOU MY GIRL...
LIKE I TOLD YOU BEFORE.
...
MY COLLEGE HAS A GOOD DRAMA GROUP, AND THE STAGE AND EQUIPMENT ARE ALL TOP-NOTCH. PASS THE EXAM AND GET IN!
YOU'LL LIKE BEING THERE WITH ME.

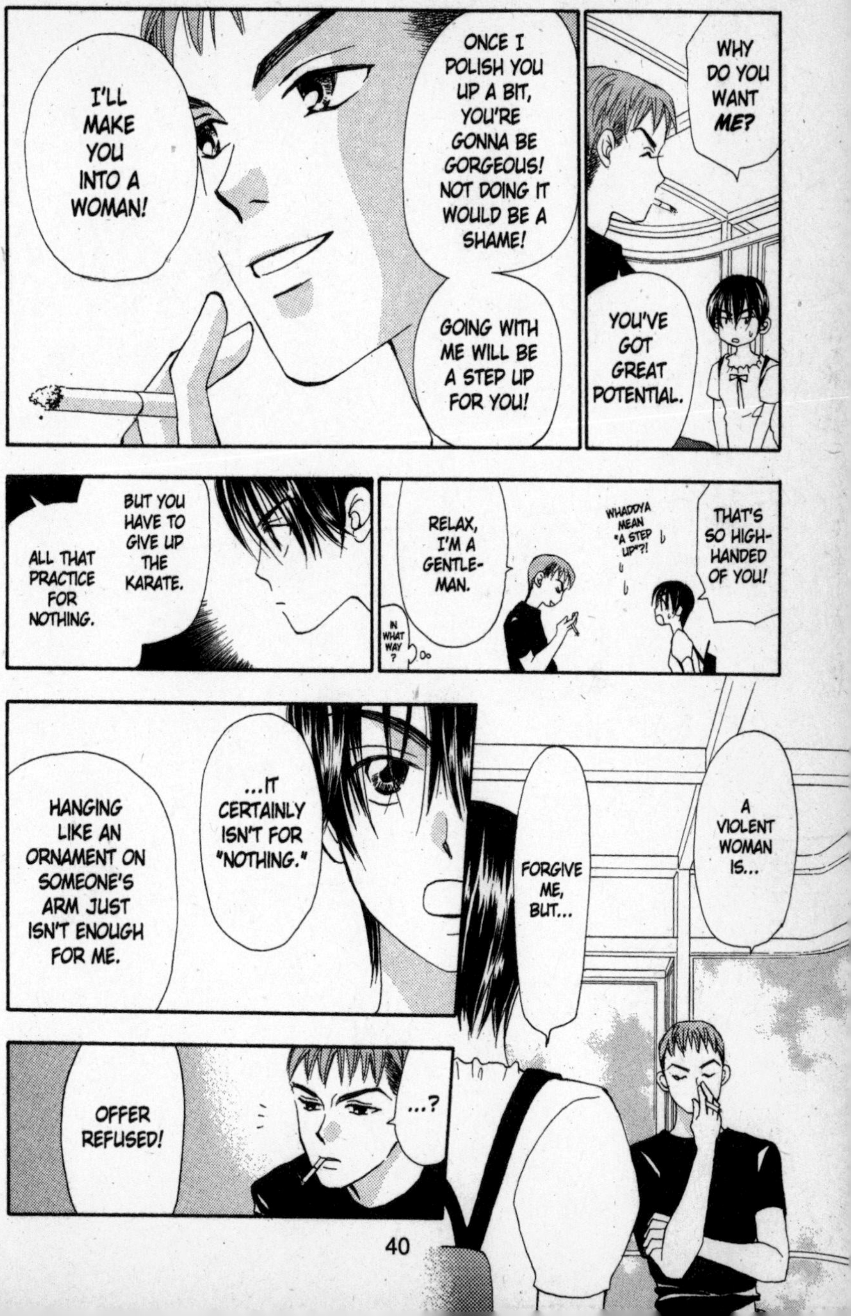
WHY DO YOU WANT *ME?*
YOU'VE GOT GREAT POTENTIAL.
ONCE I POLISH YOU UP A BIT, YOU'RE GONNA BE GORGEOUS! NOT DOING IT WOULD BE A SHAME!
GOING WITH ME WILL BE A STEP UP FOR YOU!
I'LL MAKE YOU INTO A WOMAN!
THAT'S SO HIGH-HANDED OF YOU!
WHADDYA MEAN "A STEP UP"?!
RELAX, I'M A GENTLE-MAN.
IN WHAT WAY?
BUT YOU HAVE TO GIVE UP THE KARATE.
ALL THAT PRACTICE FOR NOTHING.
A VIOLENT WOMAN IS...
FORGIVE ME, BUT...
...IT CERTAINLY ISN'T FOR "NOTHING."
HANGING LIKE AN ORNAMENT ON SOMEONE'S ARM JUST ISN'T ENOUGH FOR ME.
...?
OFFER REFUSED!

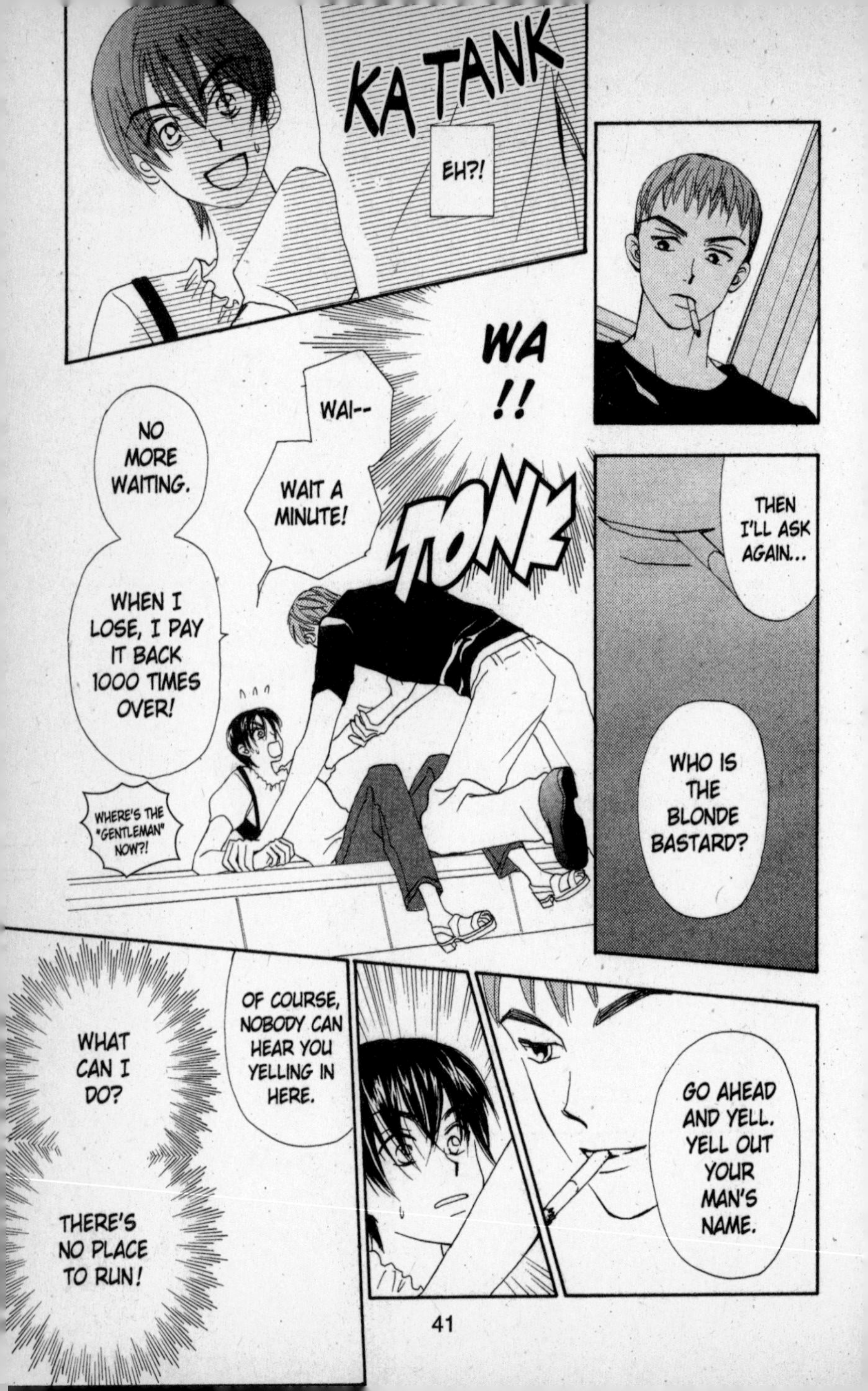
KA TANK
EH?!
THEN I'LL ASK AGAIN...
WHO IS THE BLONDE BASTARD?
WA!!
TONK
WAI--
WAIT A MINUTE!
NO MORE WAITING.
WHEN I LOSE, I PAY IT BACK 1000 TIMES OVER!
WHERE'S THE "GENTLEMAN" NOW?!
GO AHEAD AND YELL. YELL OUT YOUR MAN'S NAME.
OF COURSE, NOBODY CAN HEAR YOU YELLING IN HERE.
WHAT CAN I DO?
THERE'S NO PLACE TO RUN!

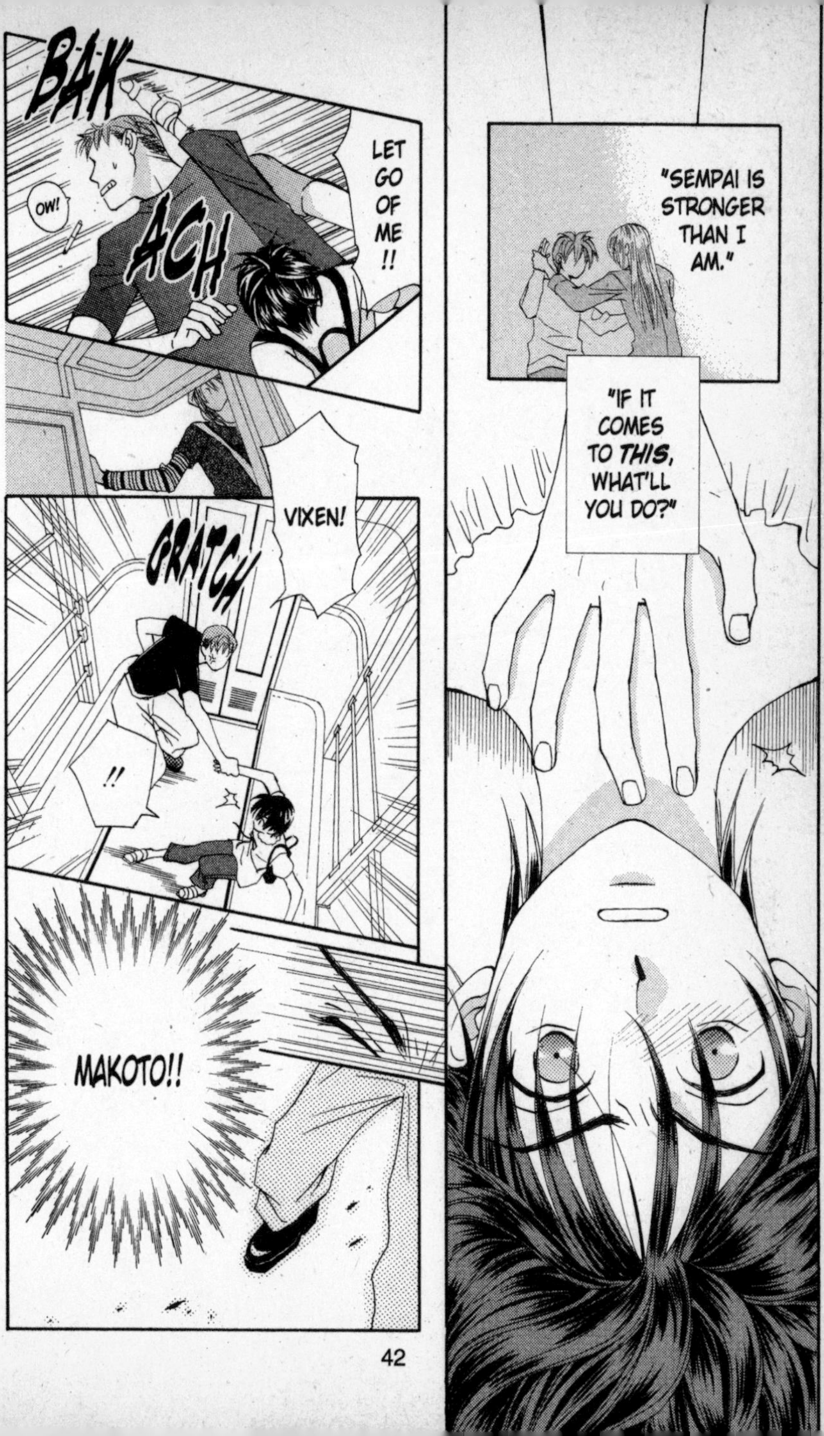
"SEMPAI IS STRONGER THAN I AM."
"IF IT COMES TO THIS, WHAT'LL YOU DO?"
LET GO OF ME!!
BAK
OW!
ACH
VIXEN!
GRATCH
!!
MAKOTO!!

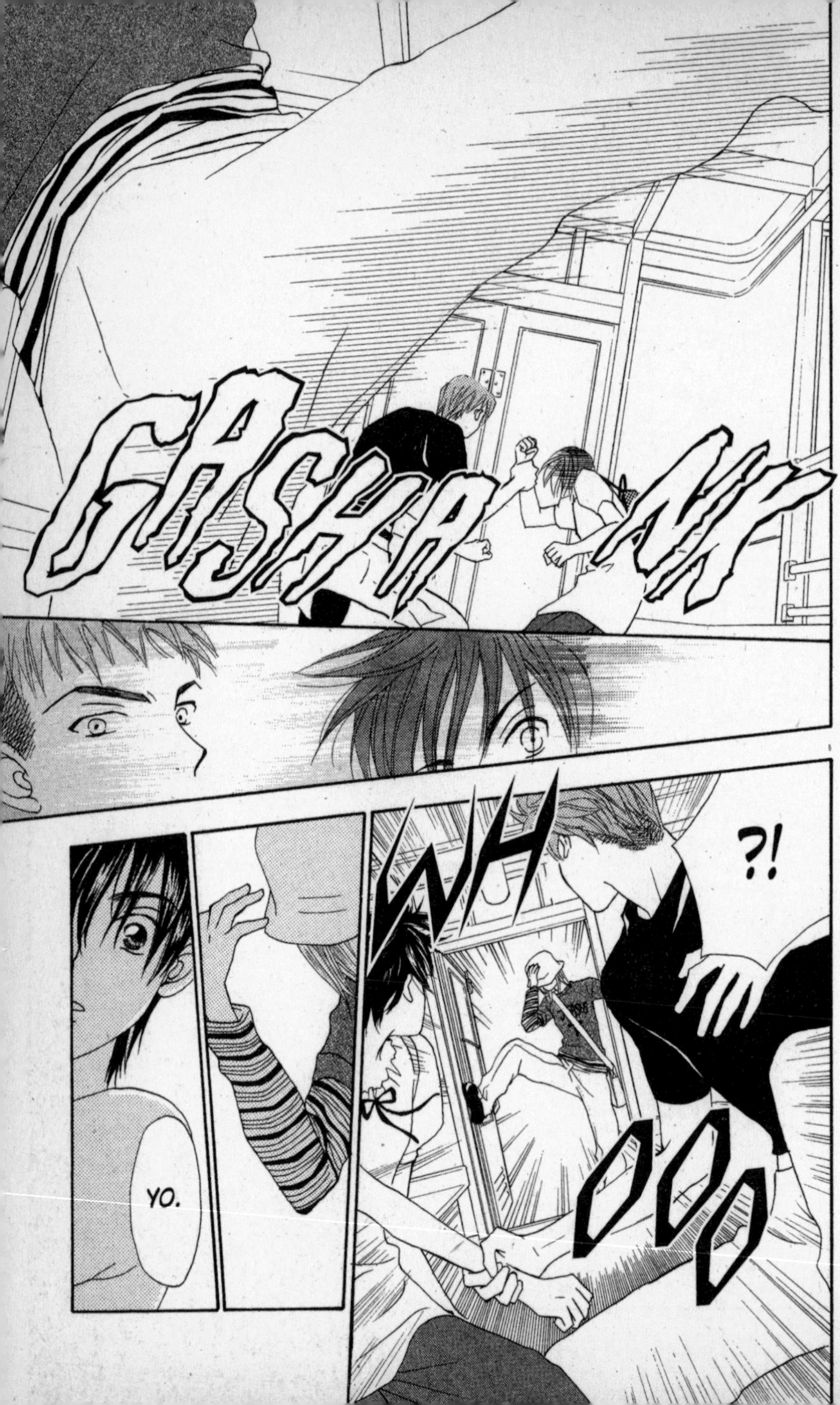
GASHAAK
?!
WH
OOO
YO.

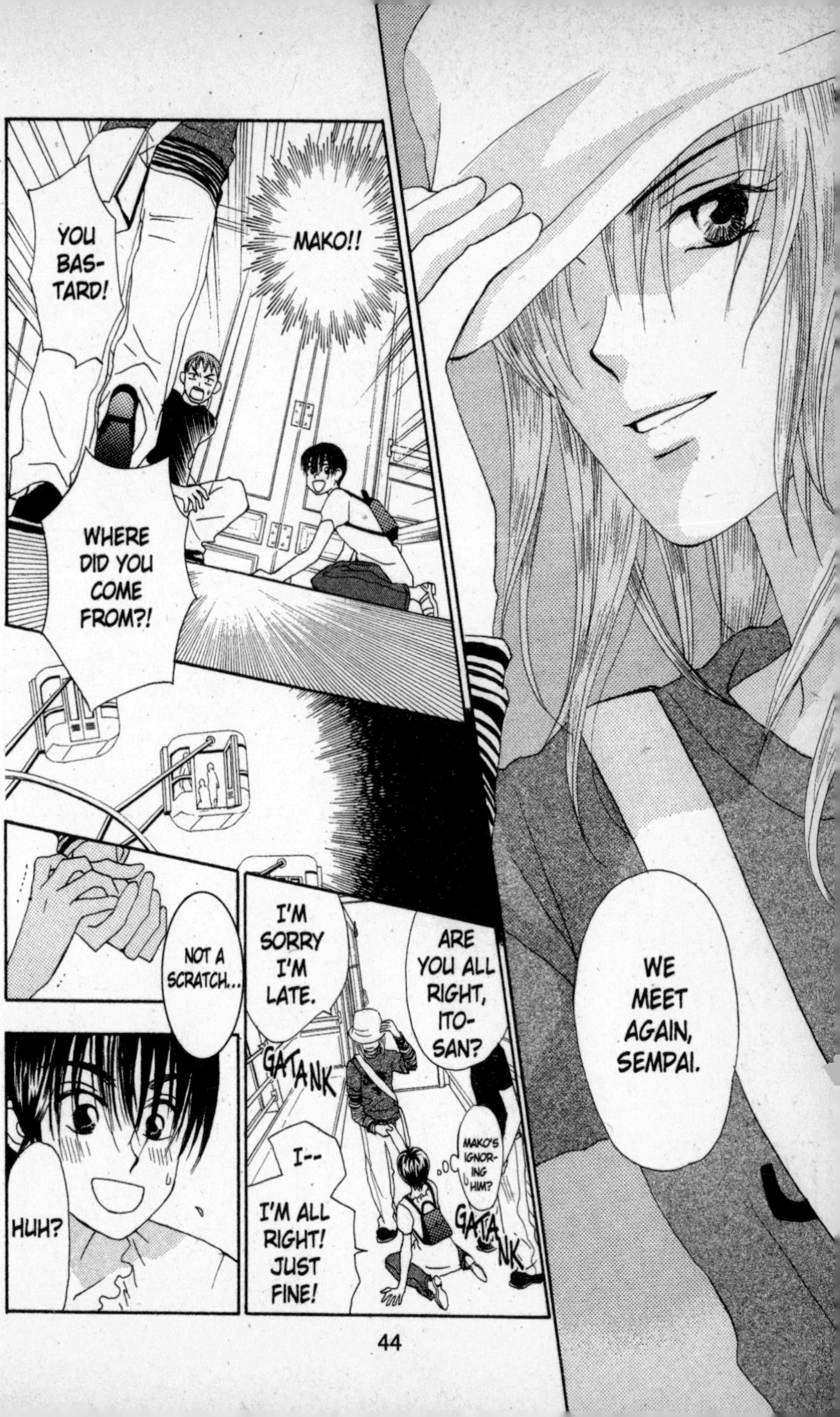

WE MEET AGAIN, SEMPAI.
MAKO!!
YOU BAS-TARD!
WHERE DID YOU COME FROM?!
ARE YOU ALL RIGHT, ITO-SAN?
I'M SORRY I'M LATE.
GATANK
MAKO'S IGNOR-ING HIM?
GATANK
I--
I'M ALL RIGHT! JUST FINE!
NOT A SCRATCH...
HUH?

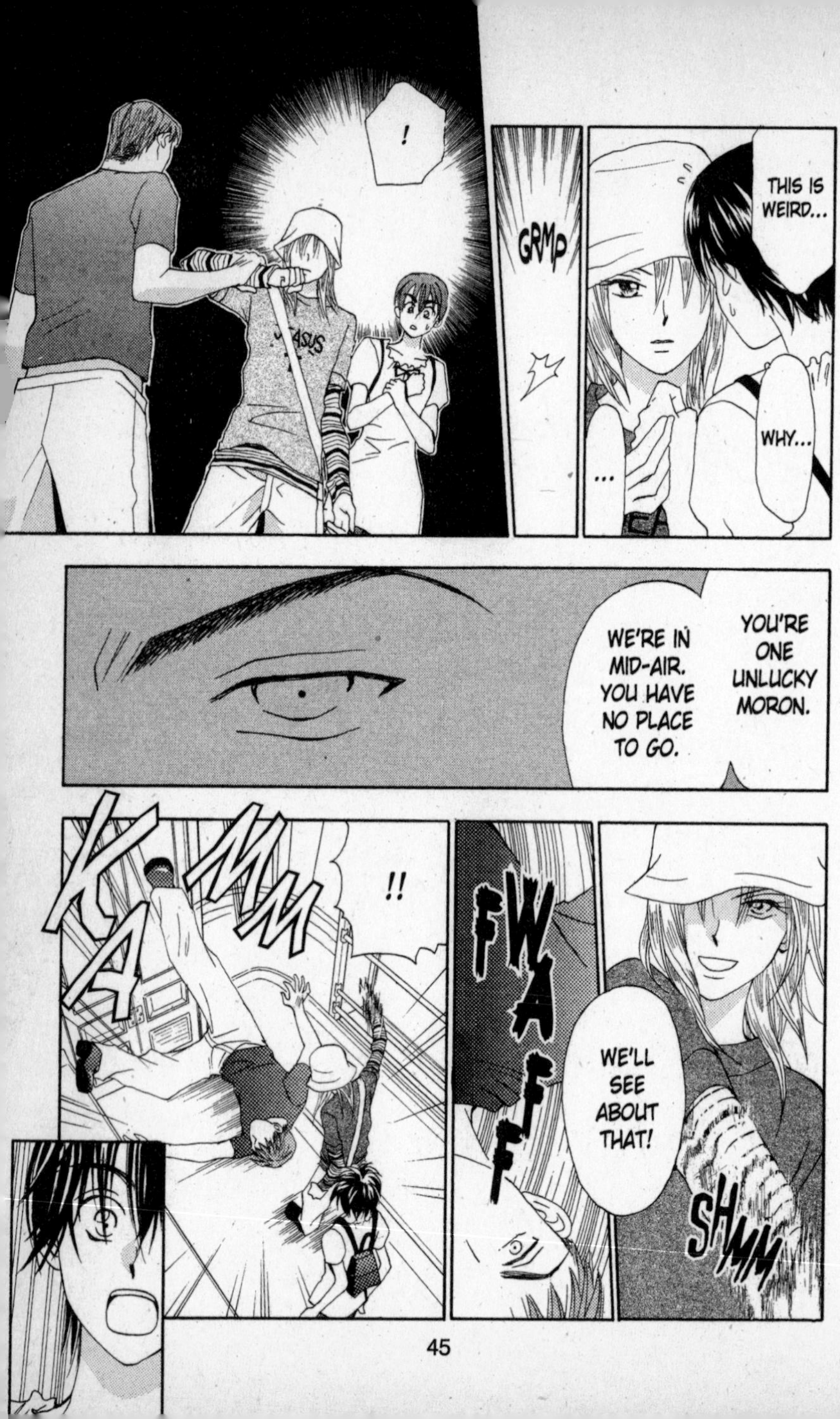
THIS IS WEIRD...
WHY...
...
GRMP
!
YOU'RE ONE UNLUCKY MORON.
WE'RE IN MID-AIR. YOU HAVE NO PLACE TO GO.
WE'LL SEE ABOUT THAT!
SHMM
FWAFF
!!
KAMMM

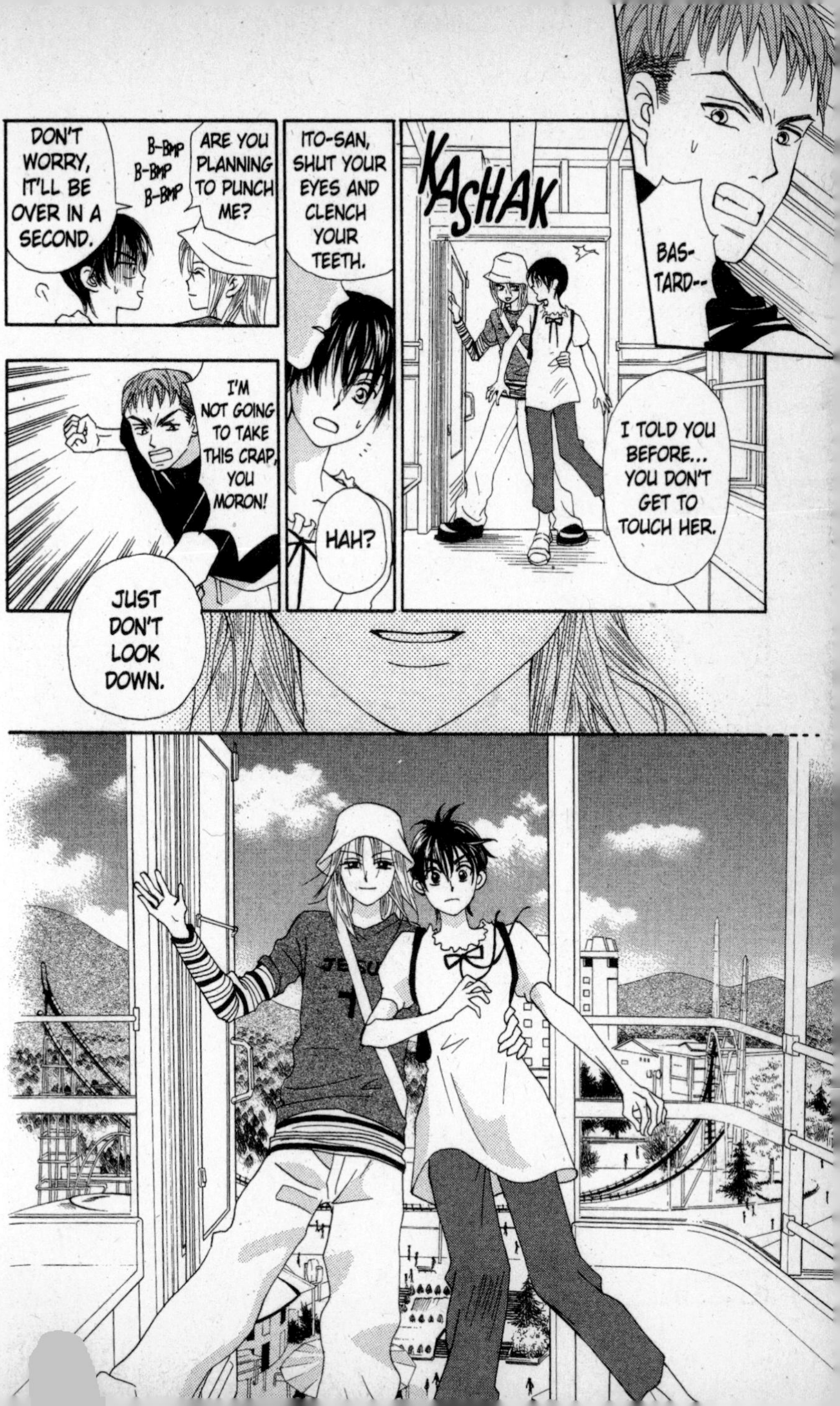
BAS-TARD--
KASHAK
I TOLD YOU BEFORE... YOU DON'T GET TO TOUCH HER.
ITO-SAN, SHUT YOUR EYES AND CLENCH YOUR TEETH.
HAH?
ARE YOU PLANNING TO PUNCH ME?
B-BMP B-BMP B-BMP
DON'T WORRY, IT'LL BE OVER IN A SECOND.
I'M NOT GOING TO TAKE THIS CRAP, YOU MORON!
JUST DON'T LOOK DOWN.
JESU

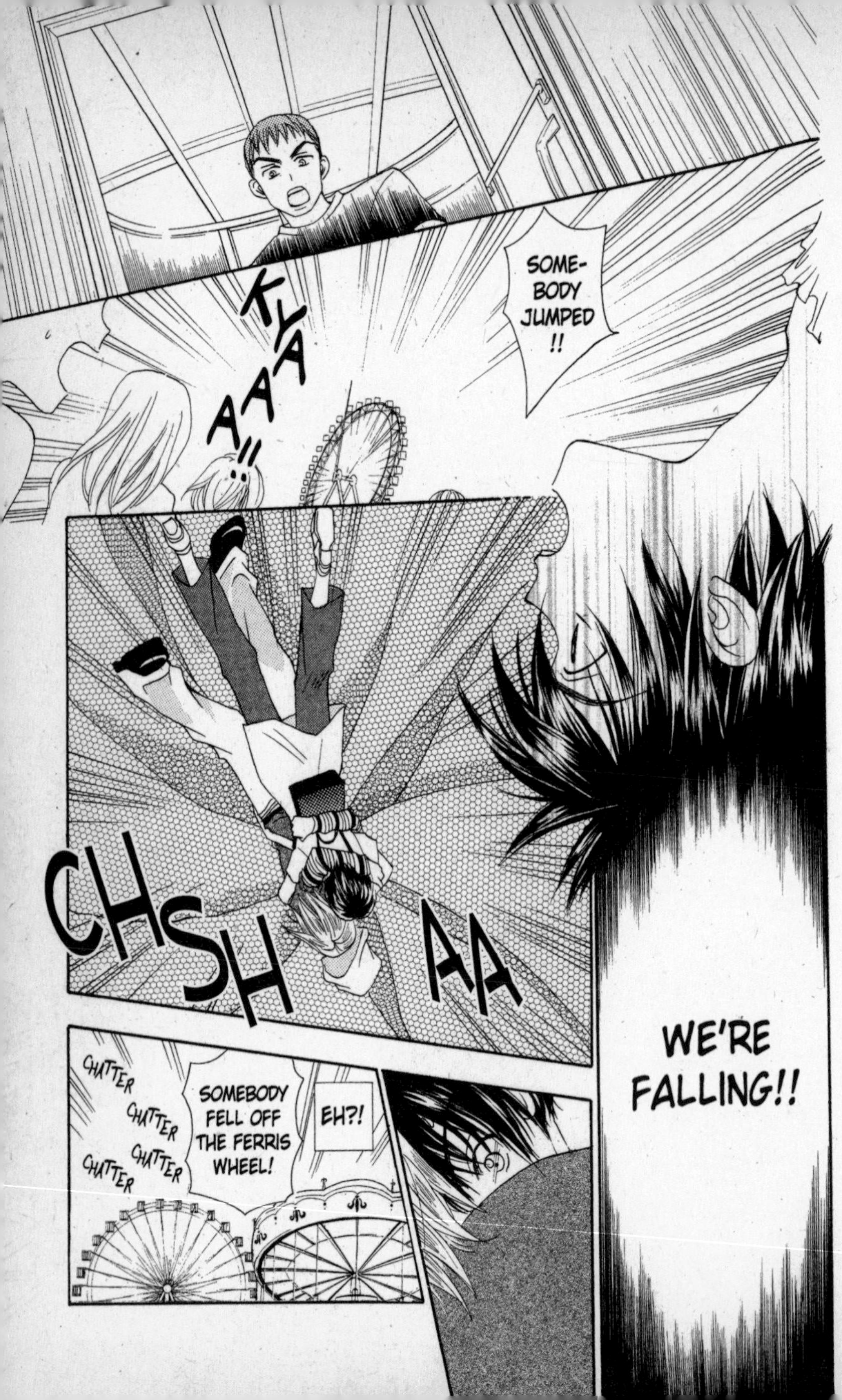
SOME-
BODY
JUMPED
!!
KYAAAA!!
WE'RE FALLING!!
CHSHAA
EH?!
SOMEBODY FELL OFF THE FERRIS WHEEL!
CHATTER
CHATTER
CHATTER
CHATTER

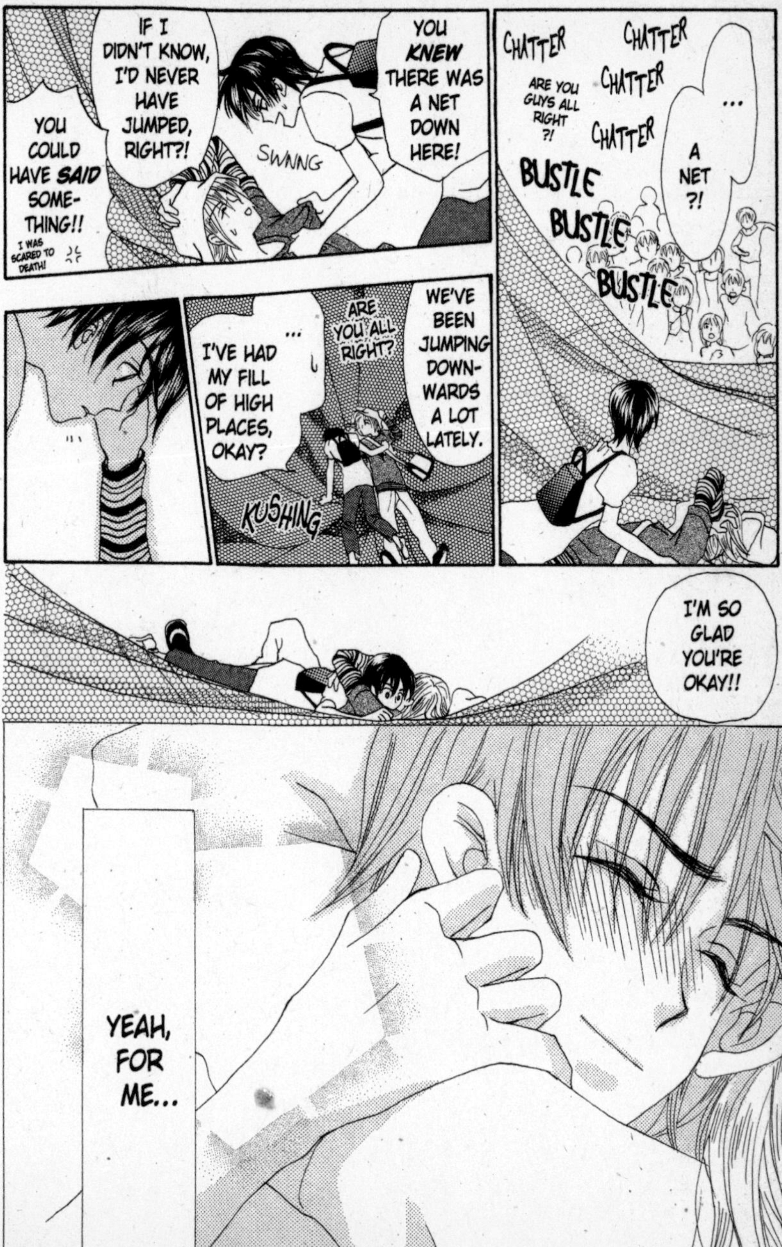
...
A NET ?!
CHATTER
CHATTER
CHATTER
ARE YOU GUYS ALL RIGHT ?!
CHATTER
BUSTLE
BUSTLE
BUSTLE
YOU KNEW THERE WAS A NET DOWN HERE!
SWNNG
IF I DIDN'T KNOW, I'D NEVER HAVE JUMPED, RIGHT?!
YOU COULD HAVE SAID SOMETHING!!
I WAS SCARED TO DEATH!
WE'VE BEEN JUMPING DOWNWARDS A LOT LATELY.
ARE YOU ALL RIGHT?
... I'VE HAD MY FILL OF HIGH PLACES, OKAY?
KUSHING
I'M SO GLAD YOU'RE OKAY!!
YEAH, FOR ME...

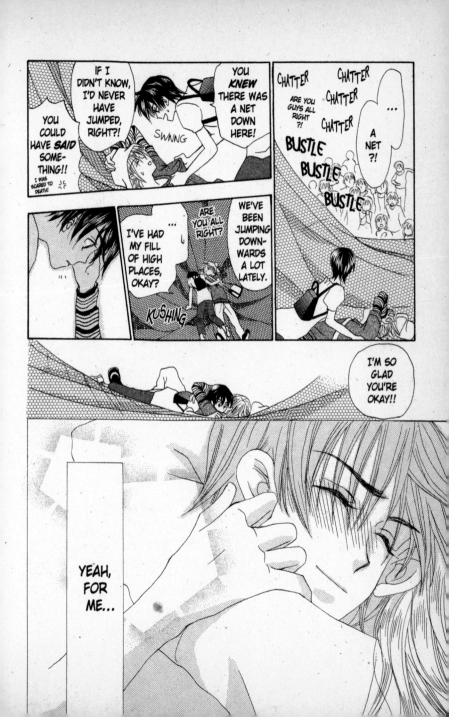

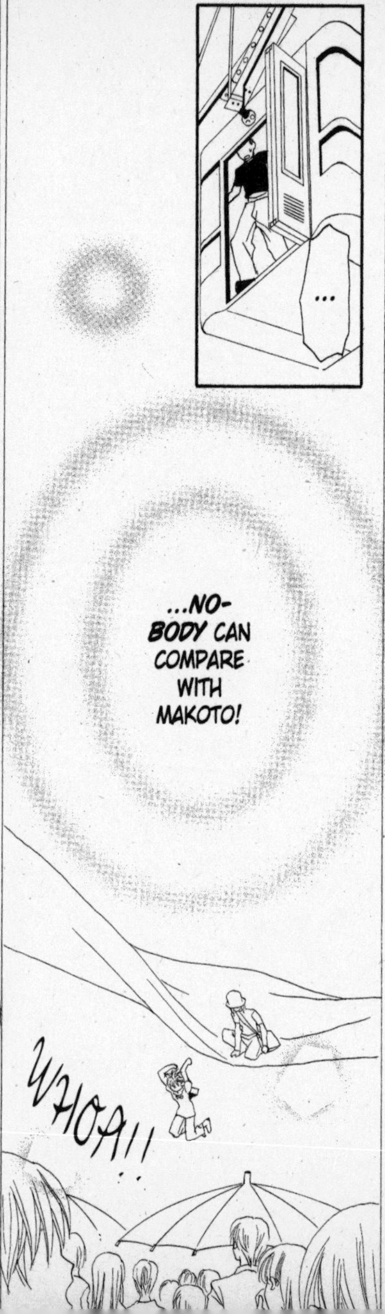
...
...NOBODY CAN COMPARE WITH MAKOTO!
WHOA!!

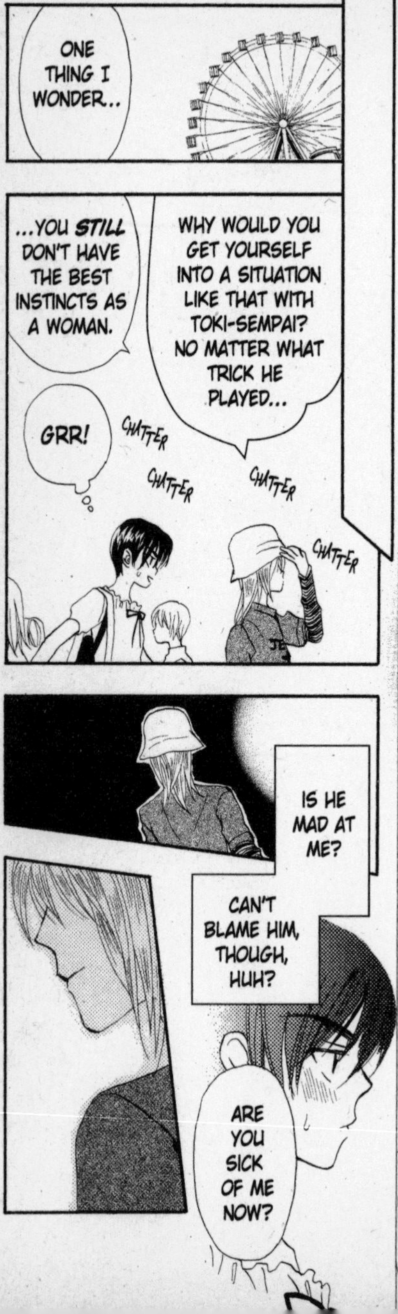
ONE THING I WONDER...
WHY WOULD YOU GET YOURSELF INTO A SITUATION LIKE THAT WITH TOKI-SEMPAI? NO MATTER WHAT TRICK HE PLAYED...
...YOU STILL DON'T HAVE THE BEST INSTINCTS AS A WOMAN.
GRR!
CHATTER
CHATTER
CHATTER
CHATTER
IS HE MAD AT ME?
CAN'T BLAME HIM, THOUGH, HUH?
ARE YOU SICK OF ME NOW?

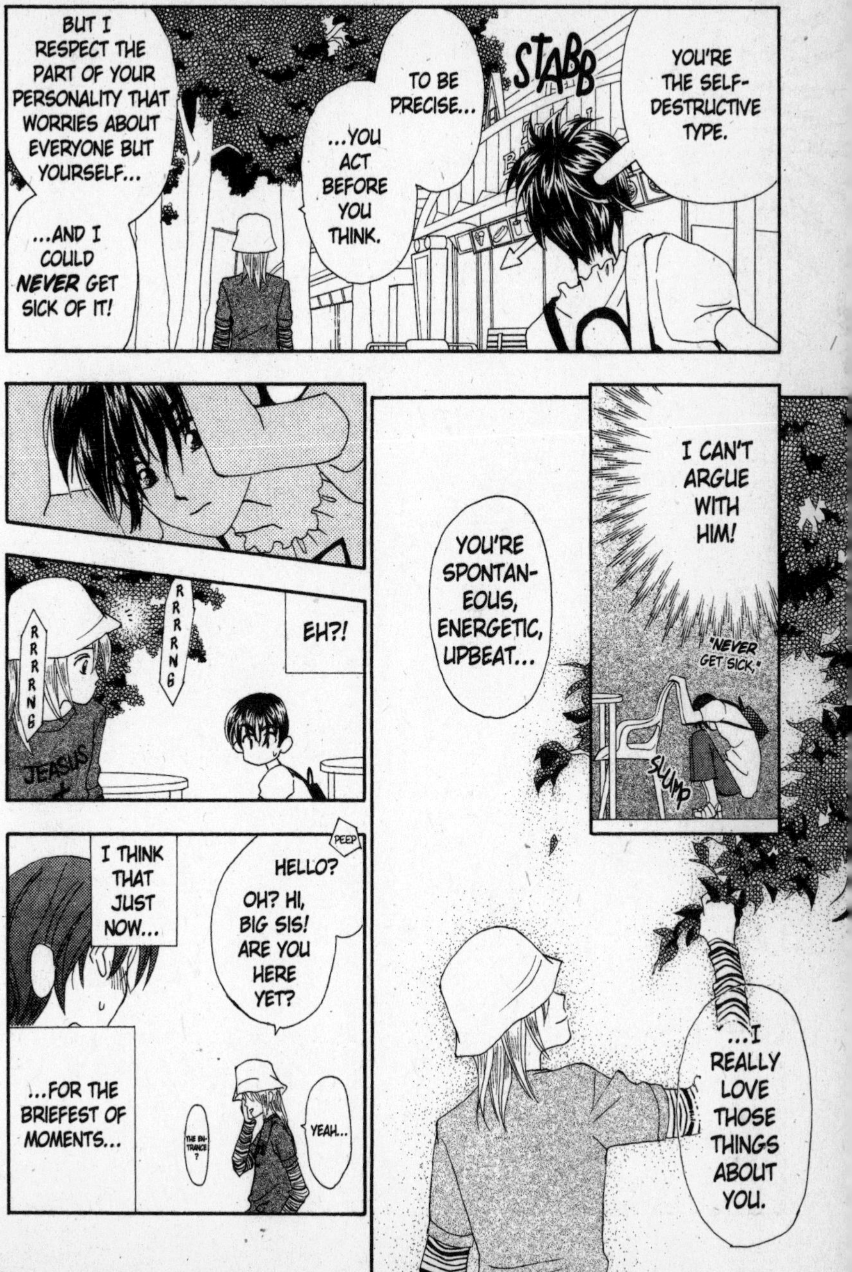
YOU'RE THE SELF-DESTRUCTIVE TYPE.
STABB
TO BE PRECISE...
...YOU ACT BEFORE YOU THINK.
BUT I RESPECT THE PART OF YOUR PERSONALITY THAT WORRIES ABOUT EVERYONE BUT YOURSELF...
...AND I COULD NEVER GET SICK OF IT!
I CAN'T ARGUE WITH HIM!
"NEVER GET SICK,"
SLUMP
YOU'RE SPONTANEOUS, ENERGETIC, UPBEAT...
...I REALLY LOVE THOSE THINGS ABOUT YOU.
EH?!
RRRRNG
RRRRNG
JEASUS
PEEP
I THINK THAT JUST NOW...
HELLO?
OH? HI, BIG SIS! ARE YOU HERE YET?
YEAH...
THE EN-TRANCE?
...FOR THE BRIEFEST OF MOMENTS...

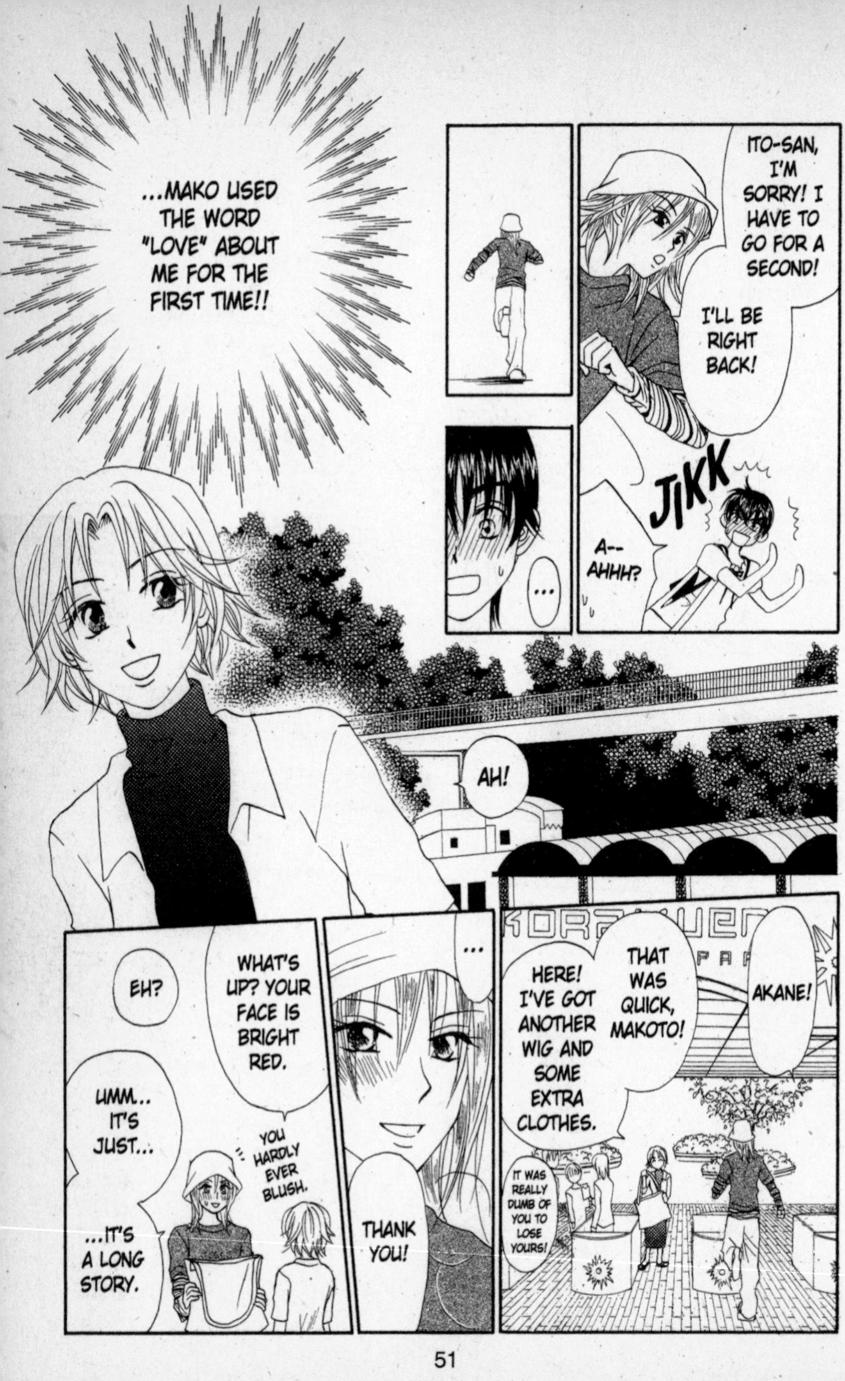
ITO-SAN, I'M SORRY! I HAVE TO GO FOR A SECOND!
I'LL BE RIGHT BACK!
JIKK
A-- AHHH?
...
...MAKO USED THE WORD "LOVE" ABOUT ME FOR THE FIRST TIME!!
AH!
AKANE!
THAT WAS QUICK, MAKOTO!
HERE! I'VE GOT ANOTHER WIG AND SOME EXTRA CLOTHES.
IT WAS REALLY DUMB OF YOU TO LOSE YOURS!
...
THANK YOU!
WHAT'S UP? YOUR FACE IS BRIGHT RED.
EH?
YOU HARDLY EVER BLUSH.
UMM... IT'S JUST...
...IT'S A LONG STORY.

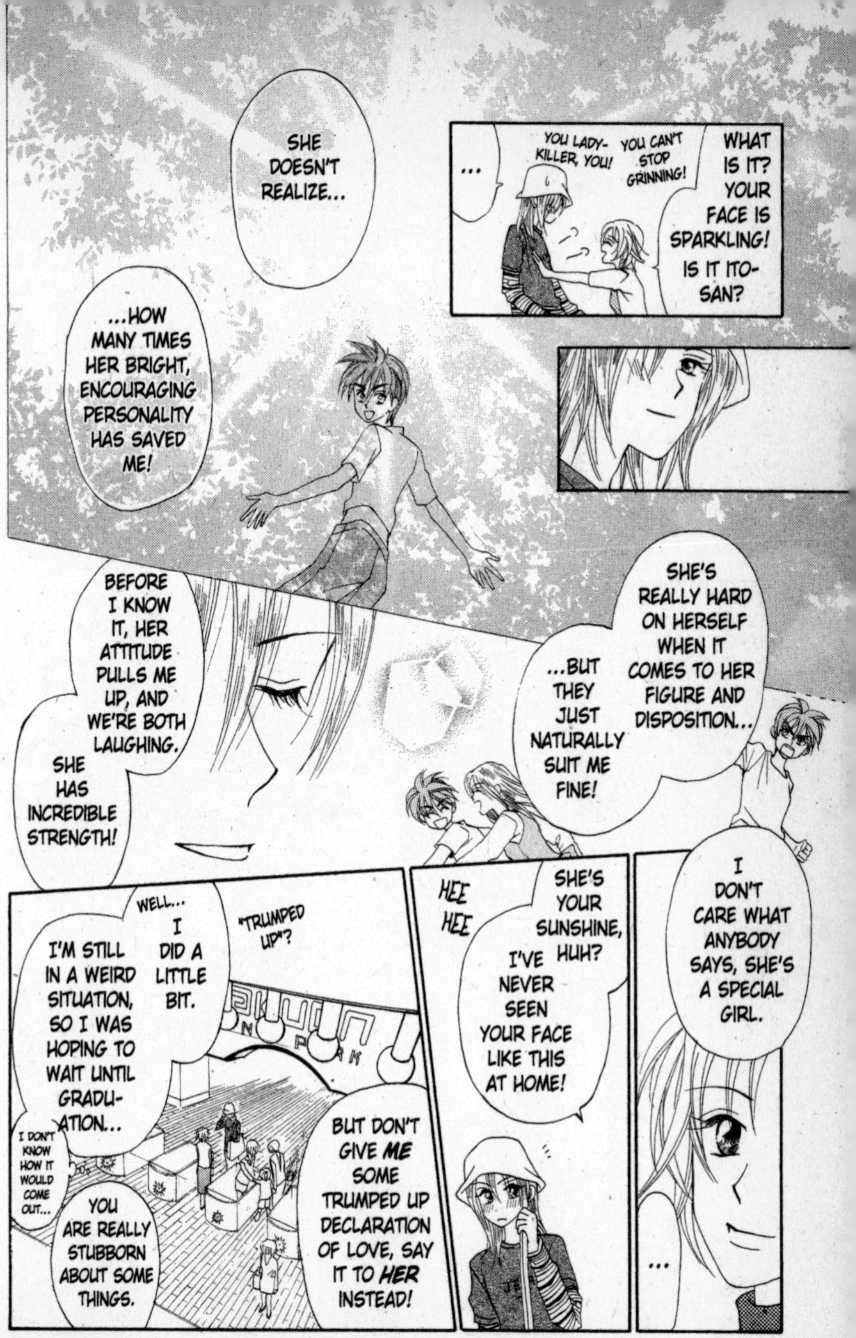
WHAT IS IT? YOUR FACE IS SPARKLING!
IS IT ITO-SAN?
YOU CAN'T STOP GRINNING!
YOU LADY-KILLER, YOU!
...
SHE DOESN'T REALIZE...
...HOW MANY TIMES HER BRIGHT, ENCOURAGING PERSONALITY HAS SAVED ME!
SHE'S REALLY HARD ON HERSELF WHEN IT COMES TO HER FIGURE AND DISPOSITION...
...BUT THEY JUST NATURALLY SUIT ME FINE!
BEFORE I KNOW IT, HER ATTITUDE PULLS ME UP, AND WE'RE BOTH LAUGHING.
SHE HAS INCREDIBLE STRENGTH!
I DON'T CARE WHAT ANYBODY SAYS, SHE'S A SPECIAL GIRL.
...
HEE HEE
SHE'S YOUR SUNSHINE, HUH?
I'VE NEVER SEEN YOUR FACE LIKE THIS AT HOME!
BUT DON'T GIVE *ME* SOME TRUMPED UP DECLARATION OF LOVE, SAY IT TO *HER* INSTEAD!
"TRUMPED UP"?
WELL...
I DID A LITTLE BIT.
I'M STILL IN A WEIRD SITUATION, SO I WAS HOPING TO WAIT UNTIL GRADUATION...
I DON'T KNOW HOW IT WOULD COME OUT...
YOU ARE REALLY STUBBORN ABOUT SOME THINGS.

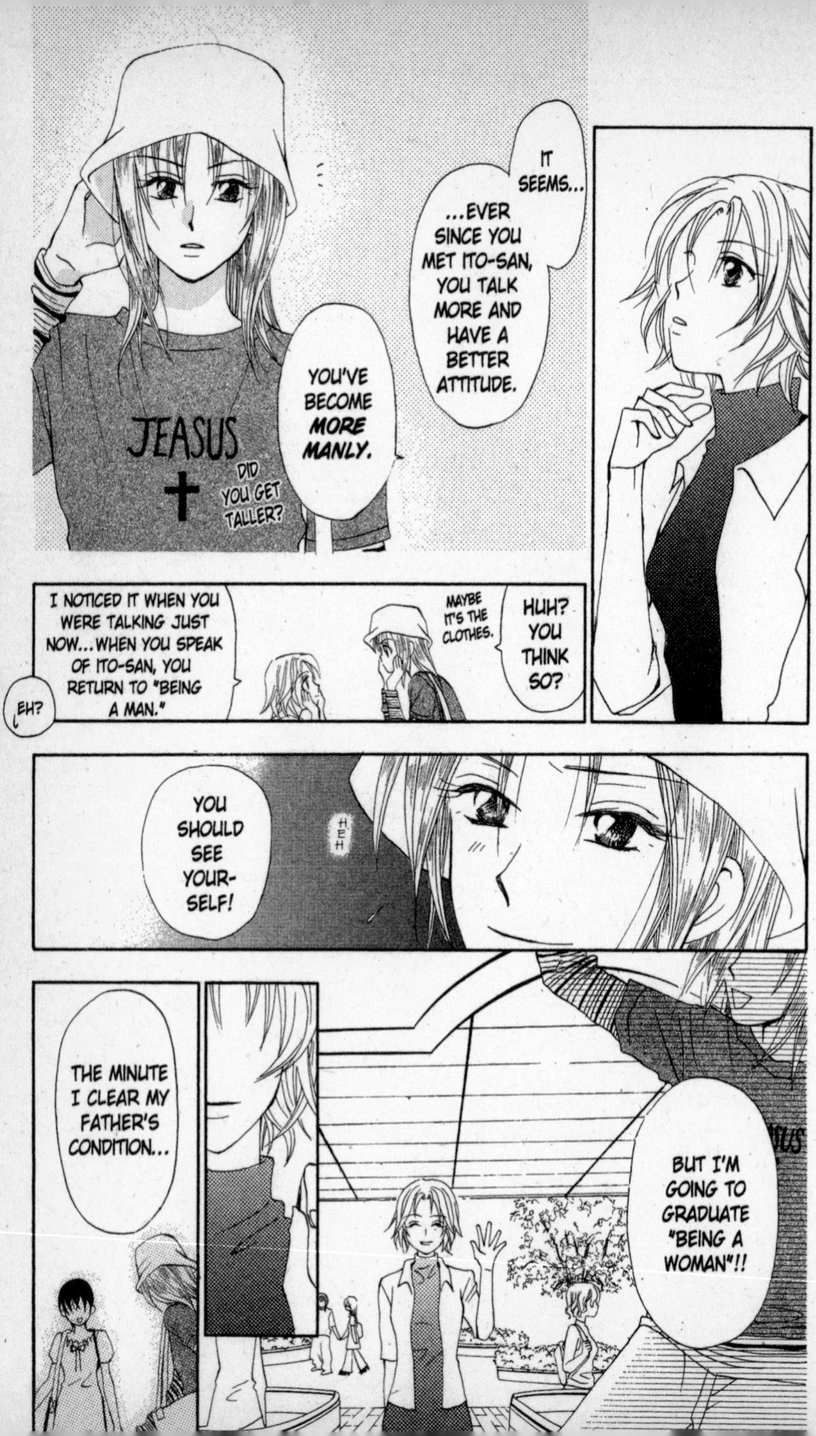
IT SEEMS...
...EVER SINCE YOU MET ITO-SAN, YOU TALK MORE AND HAVE A BETTER ATTITUDE.
YOU'VE BECOME ***MORE MANLY.***
JEASUS
DID YOU GET TALLER?
HUH? YOU THINK SO?
MAYBE IT'S THE CLOTHES.
I NOTICED IT WHEN YOU WERE TALKING JUST NOW...WHEN YOU SPEAK OF ITO-SAN, YOU RETURN TO "BEING A MAN."
EH?
HEH
YOU SHOULD SEE YOUR-SELF!
BUT I'M GOING TO GRADUATE "BEING A WOMAN"!!
THE MINUTE I CLEAR MY FATHER'S CONDITION...

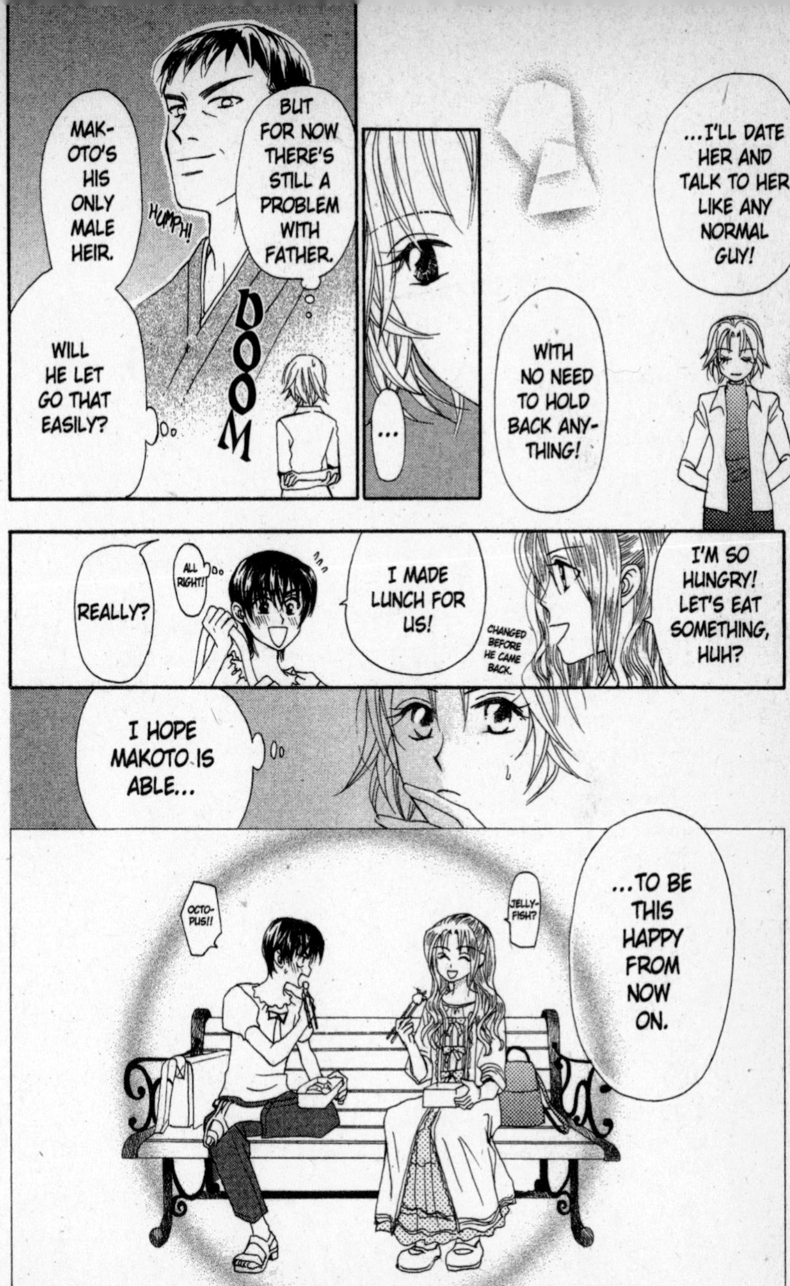
...I'LL DATE HER AND TALK TO HER LIKE ANY NORMAL GUY!
WITH NO NEED TO HOLD BACK ANYTHING!
...
BUT FOR NOW THERE'S STILL A PROBLEM WITH FATHER.
MAKOTO'S HIS ONLY MALE HEIR.
HUMPH!
DOOM
WILL HE LET GO THAT EASILY?
I'M SO HUNGRY! LET'S EAT SOMETHING, HUH?
CHANGED BEFORE HE CAME BACK.
I MADE LUNCH FOR US!
ALL RIGHT!
REALLY?
I HOPE MAKOTO IS ABLE...
...TO BE THIS HAPPY FROM NOW ON.
JELLY-FISH?
OCTO-PUS!!

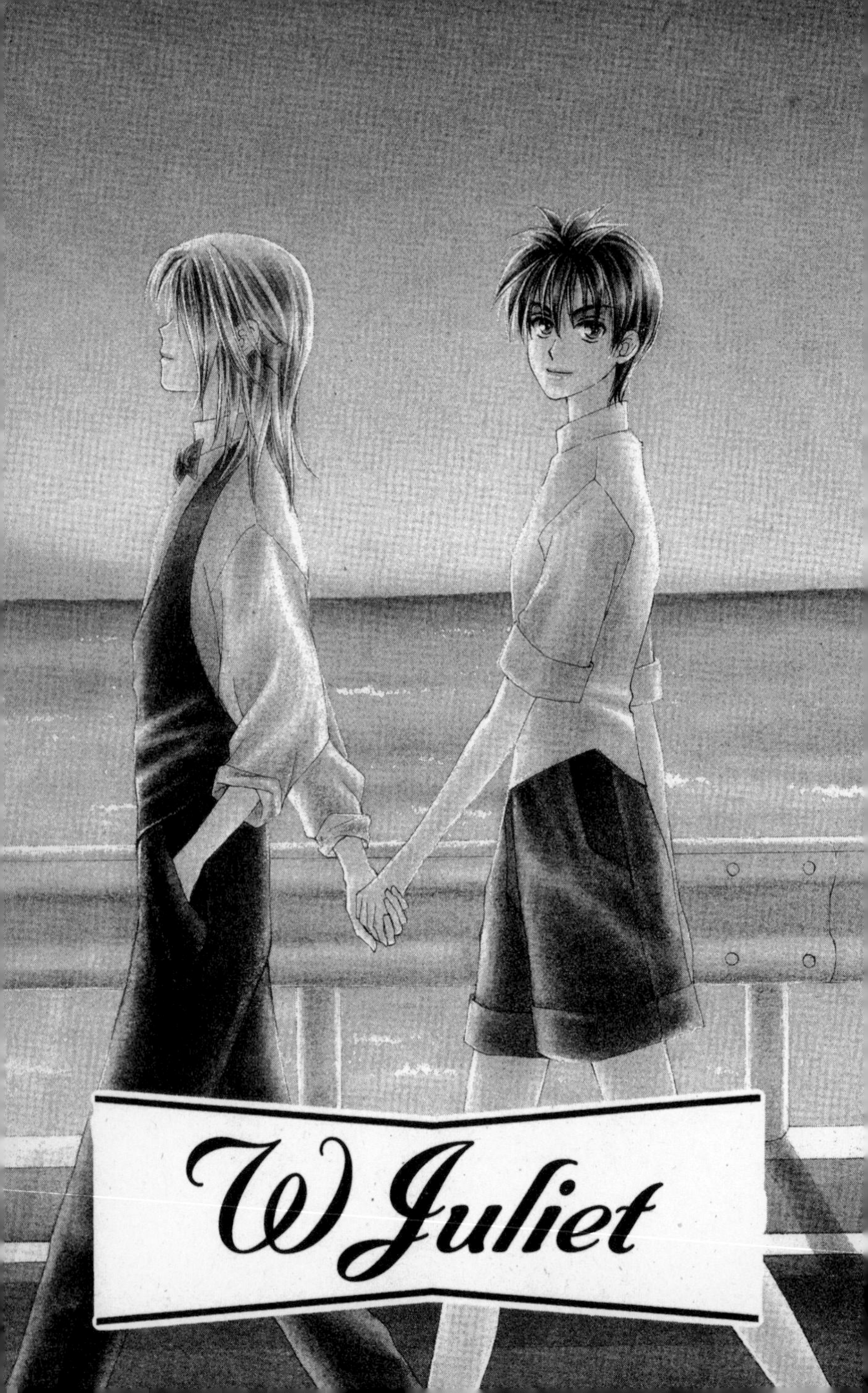
W Juliet

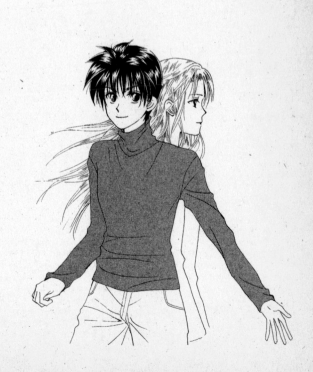

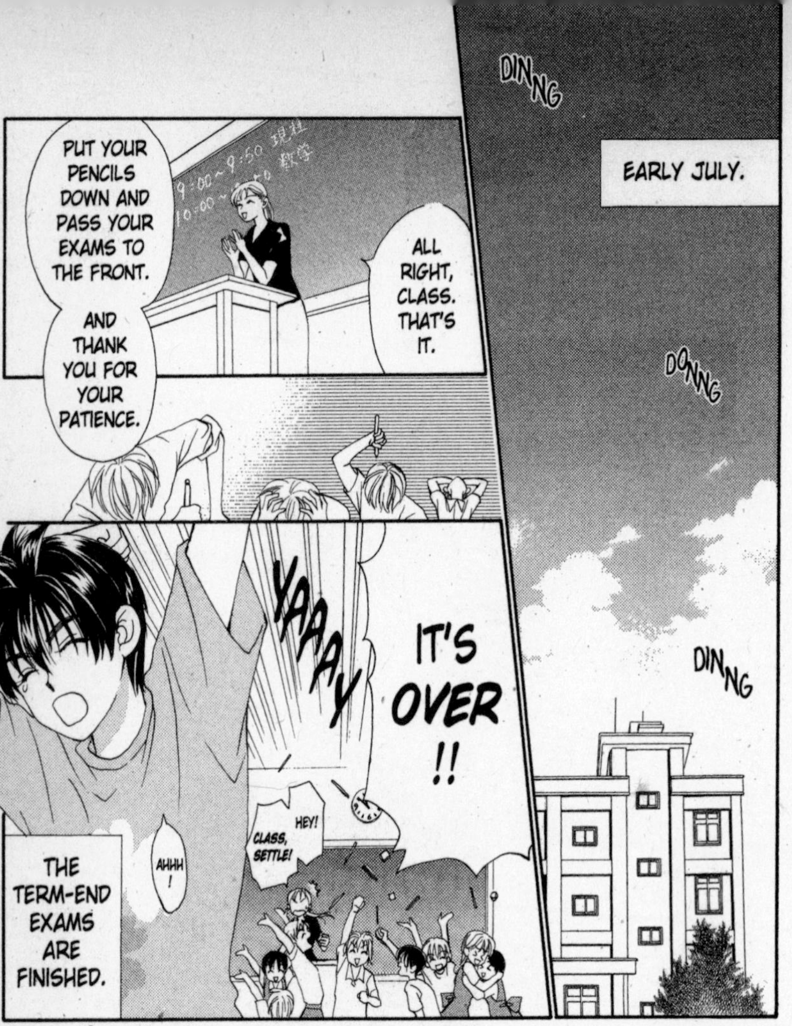
DINNG
EARLY JULY.
DONNG
DINNG
ALL RIGHT, CLASS. THAT'S IT.
PUT YOUR PENCILS DOWN AND PASS YOUR EXAMS TO THE FRONT.
AND THANK YOU FOR YOUR PATIENCE.
IT'S OVER !!
YAAAY
HEY!
CLASS, SETTLE!
AHHH !
THE TERM-END EXAMS ARE FINISHED.

-Behind the Scenes Story- ②

Ito and her friends live in a place that is about 45 minutes by foot and train from where I live. It's just a model for the town in the book! Just to get a feel for it! But I'm sure the people who know the place will understand what I'm talking about. I would often go driving with a female friend at night to a beach near there, and when I am ready to start drawing the series again, I go there with my sister to take pictures of the area. But ....

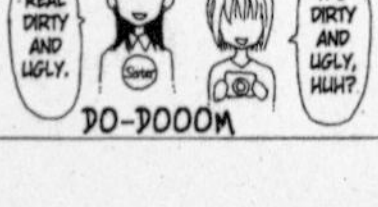
IT'S DIRTY AND UGLY, HUH?
REAL DIRTY AND UGLY.
DO-DOOOM

The water at the beach was **colored brown**... It really was brown. And there was foam swirling around on the surface. It was dark the first time I went there, but I went into the water in bare legs and played around in it! But when I draw it, it'll be clean and blue water! If I'm going to create a world, it'll be a pretty world!

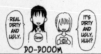

The water on the opposite shore was clean and blue!

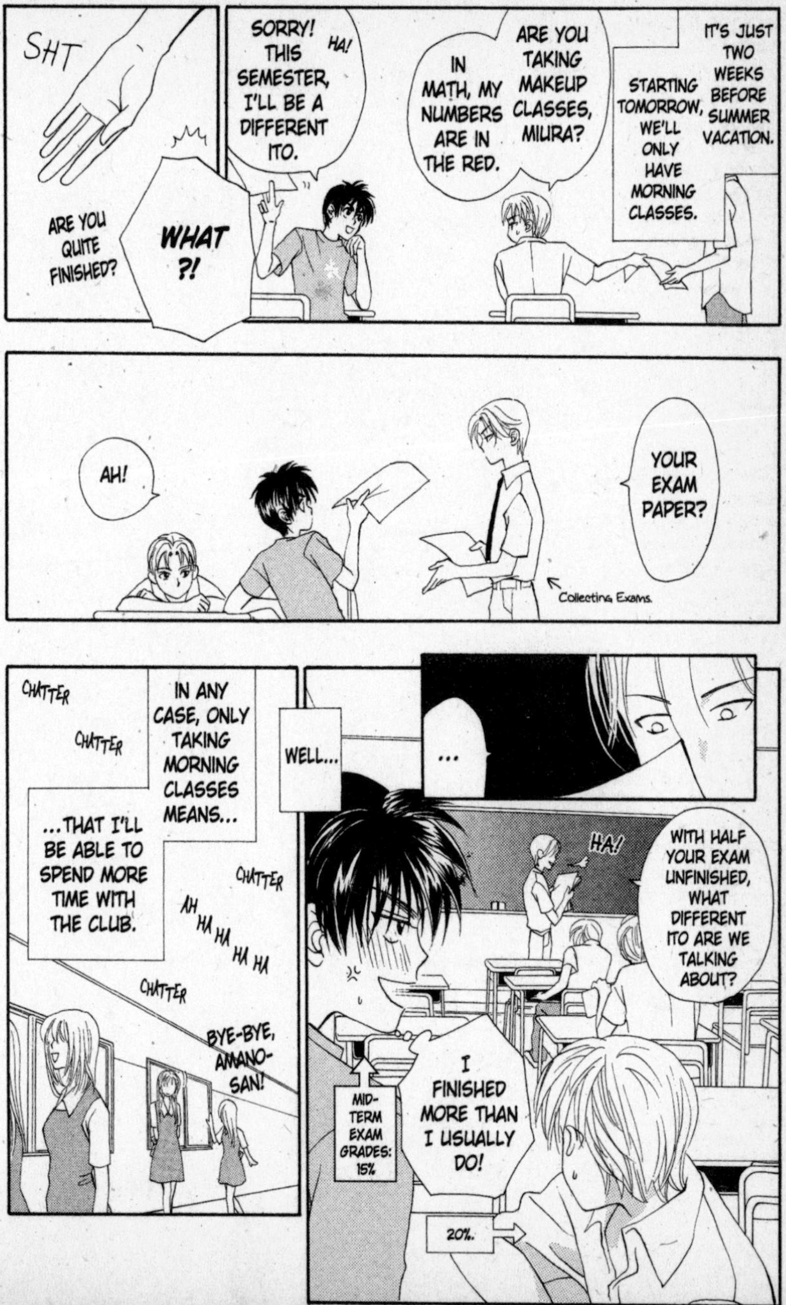
IT'S JUST TWO WEEKS BEFORE SUMMER VACATION.
STARTING TOMORROW, WE'LL ONLY HAVE MORNING CLASSES.
ARE YOU TAKING MAKEUP CLASSES, MIURA?
IN MATH, MY NUMBERS ARE IN THE RED.
SORRY! THIS SEMESTER, I'LL BE A DIFFERENT ITO.
HA!
SHT
WHAT ?!
ARE YOU QUITE FINISHED?
YOUR EXAM PAPER?
Collecting Exams.
AH!
...
WELL...
WITH HALF YOUR EXAM UNFINISHED, WHAT DIFFERENT ITO ARE WE TALKING ABOUT?
HA!
I FINISHED MORE THAN I USUALLY DO!
MID-TERM EXAM GRADES: 15%
20%.
IN ANY CASE, ONLY TAKING MORNING CLASSES MEANS...
CHATTER
CHATTER
...THAT I'LL BE ABLE TO SPEND MORE TIME WITH THE CLUB.
CHATTER
AH HA HA HA HA
CHATTER
BYE-BYE, AMANO-SAN!

ABOUT MAKOTO

In a column in Volume Two, I wrote that Makoto and Ito were "way out in first place." And so a ton of letters came in that say, "I'm an Ito fan!" But there were a lot of, "I love Makoto!" letters too. The main character, Ito, can generate a massive amount of attention, but the two really are about the same in popularity. The "I like them both!" faction is very powerful, so powerful that it's really hard to tell who's first. But the thing that finally put Makoto on top was the amusement park story in this volume. That story generated an unbelievable amount of mail... I guess the content of the story was pretty unbelievable, too. My editor said:

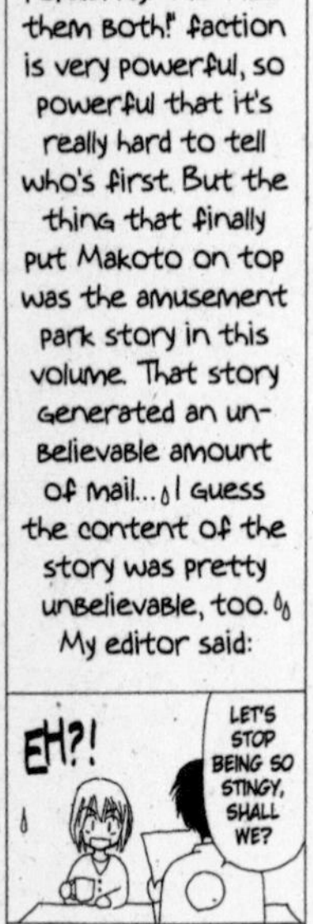
LET'S STOP BEING SO STINGY, SHALL WE?
EH?!

And since he said that at the meeting (he could still say it, huh?), all of my more recent stories have featured a lot of male Makoto...

Is that a good thing?

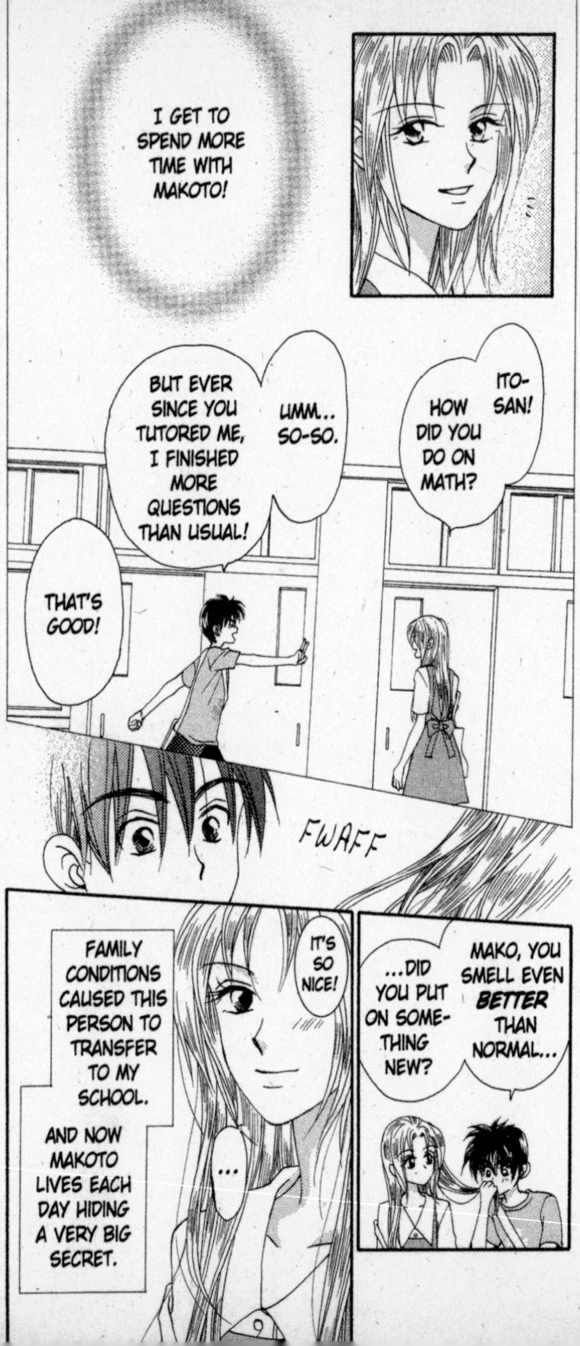
I GET TO SPEND MORE TIME WITH MAKOTO!
ITO-SAN!
HOW DID YOU DO ON MATH?
UMM... SO-SO.
BUT EVER SINCE YOU TUTORED ME, I FINISHED MORE QUESTIONS THAN USUAL!
THAT'S GOOD!
FWAFF
MAKO, YOU SMELL EVEN BETTER THAN NORMAL...
...DID YOU PUT ON SOMETHING NEW?
IT'S SO NICE!
FAMILY CONDITIONS CAUSED THIS PERSON TO TRANSFER TO MY SCHOOL.
AND NOW MAKOTO LIVES EACH DAY HIDING A VERY BIG SECRET.
...

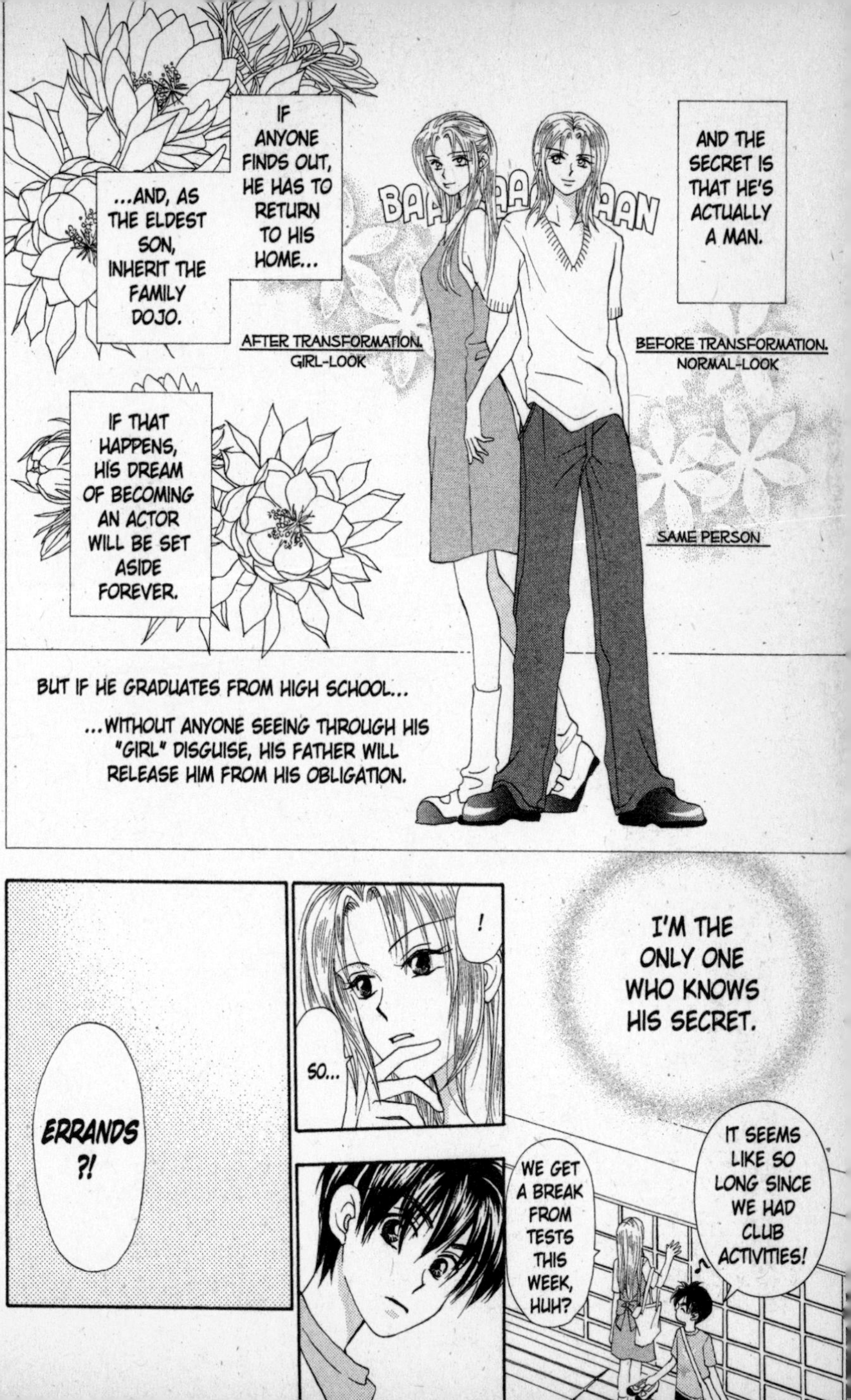
AND THE SECRET IS THAT HE'S ACTUALLY A MAN.
BAAAAAAN
BEFORE TRANSFORMATION. NORMAL-LOOK
AFTER TRANSFORMATION. GIRL-LOOK
SAME PERSON
IF ANYONE FINDS OUT, HE HAS TO RETURN TO HIS HOME...
...AND, AS THE ELDEST SON, INHERIT THE FAMILY DOJO.
IF THAT HAPPENS, HIS DREAM OF BECOMING AN ACTOR WILL BE SET ASIDE FOREVER.
BUT IF HE GRADUATES FROM HIGH SCHOOL...
...WITHOUT ANYONE SEEING THROUGH HIS "GIRL" DISGUISE, HIS FATHER WILL RELEASE HIM FROM HIS OBLIGATION.
I'M THE ONLY ONE WHO KNOWS HIS SECRET.
IT SEEMS LIKE SO LONG SINCE WE HAD CLUB ACTIVITIES!
WE GET A BREAK FROM TESTS THIS WEEK, HUH?
!
SO...
ERRANDS ?!

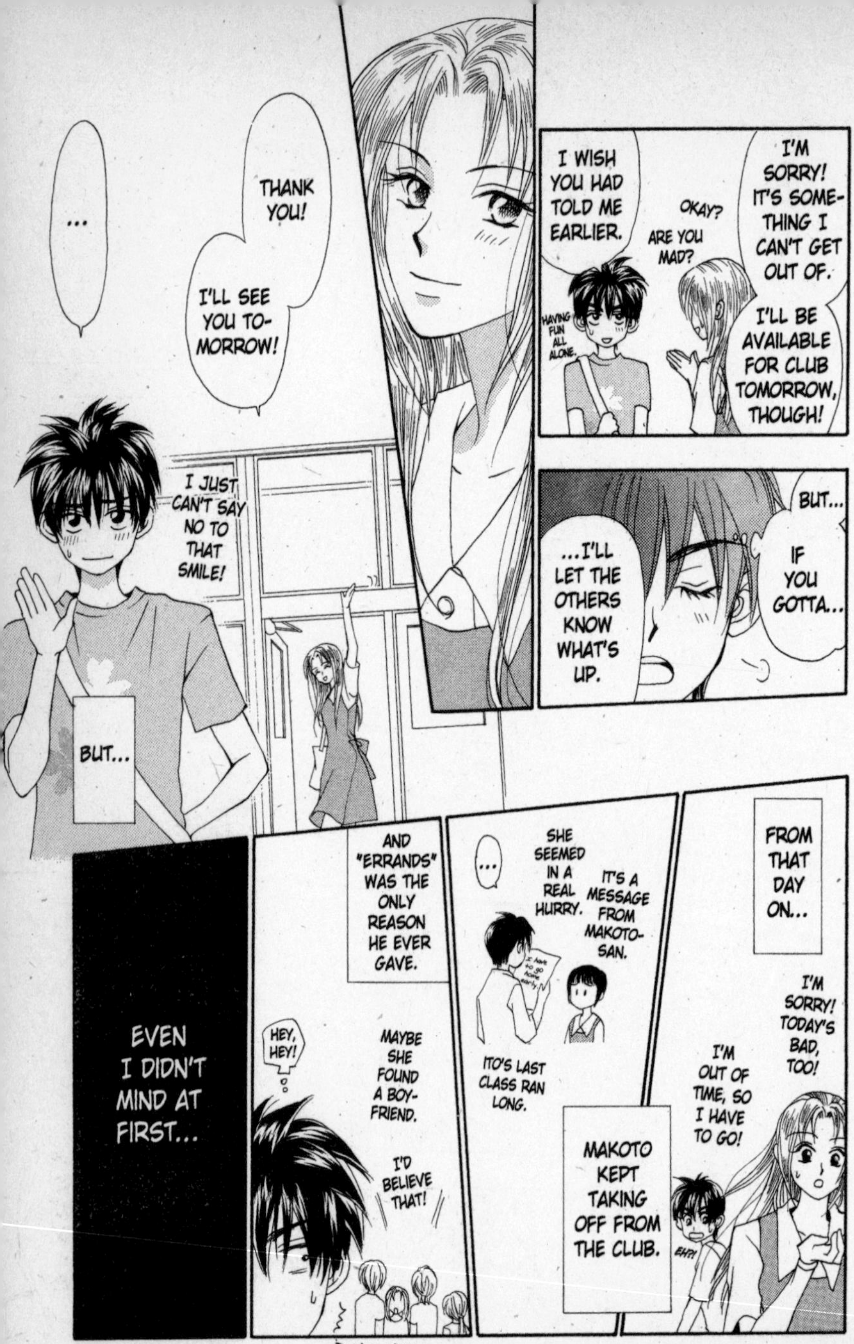

I'M SORRY! IT'S SOMETHING I CAN'T GET OUT OF.
I WISH YOU HAD TOLD ME EARLIER.
OKAY? ARE YOU MAD?
I'LL BE AVAILABLE FOR CLUB TOMORROW, THOUGH!
HAVING FUN ALL ALONE.
BUT... IF YOU GOTTA...
...I'LL LET THE OTHERS KNOW WHAT'S UP.
THANK YOU!
I'LL SEE YOU TO-MORROW!
...
I JUST CAN'T SAY NO TO THAT SMILE!
BUT...
FROM THAT DAY ON...
I'M SORRY! TODAY'S BAD, TOO!
I'M OUT OF TIME, SO I HAVE TO GO!
EH?!
MAKOTO KEPT TAKING OFF FROM THE CLUB.
IT'S A MESSAGE FROM MAKOTO-SAN.
SHE SEEMED IN A REAL HURRY.
...
ITO'S LAST CLASS RAN LONG.
AND "ERRANDS" WAS THE ONLY REASON HE EVER GAVE.
MAYBE SHE FOUND A BOY-FRIEND.
HEY, HEY!
I'D BELIEVE THAT!
EVEN I DIDN'T MIND AT FIRST...

During club rehearsal.

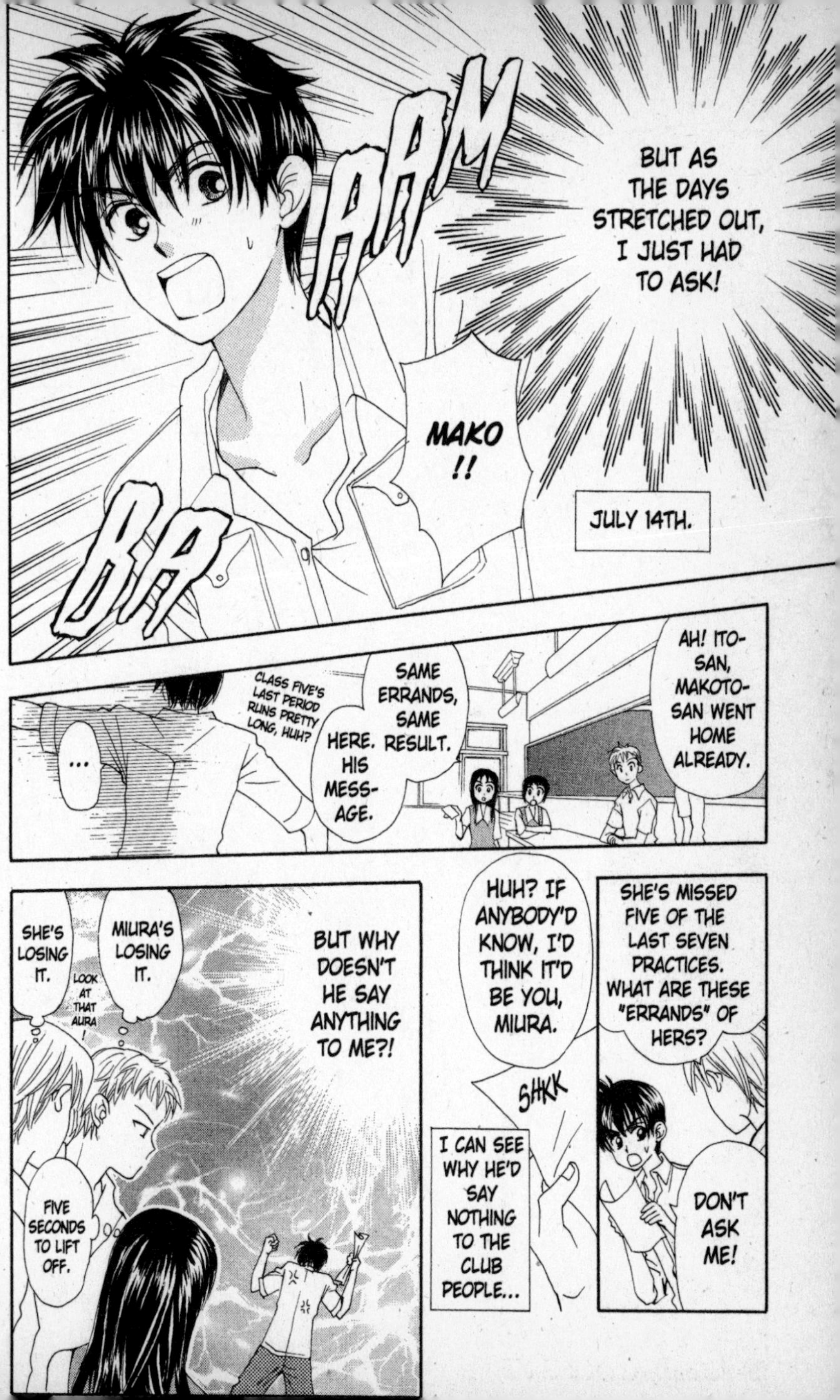
BUT AS THE DAYS STRETCHED OUT, I JUST HAD TO ASK!
AAM
MAKO !!
JULY 14TH.
BA
AH! ITO-SAN, MAKOTO-SAN WENT HOME ALREADY.
SAME ERRANDS, SAME RESULT.
HERE. HIS MESS-AGE.
CLASS FIVE'S LAST PERIOD RUNS PRETTY LONG, HUH?
...
SHE'S MISSED FIVE OF THE LAST SEVEN PRACTICES. WHAT ARE THESE "ERRANDS" OF HERS?
HUH? IF ANYBODY'D KNOW, I'D THINK IT'D BE YOU, MIURA.
DON'T ASK ME!
SHKK
I CAN SEE WHY HE'D SAY NOTHING TO THE CLUB PEOPLE...
BUT WHY DOESN'T HE SAY ANYTHING TO ME?!
MIURA'S LOSING IT.
LOOK AT THAT AURA!
SHE'S LOSING IT.
FIVE SECONDS TO LIFT OFF.

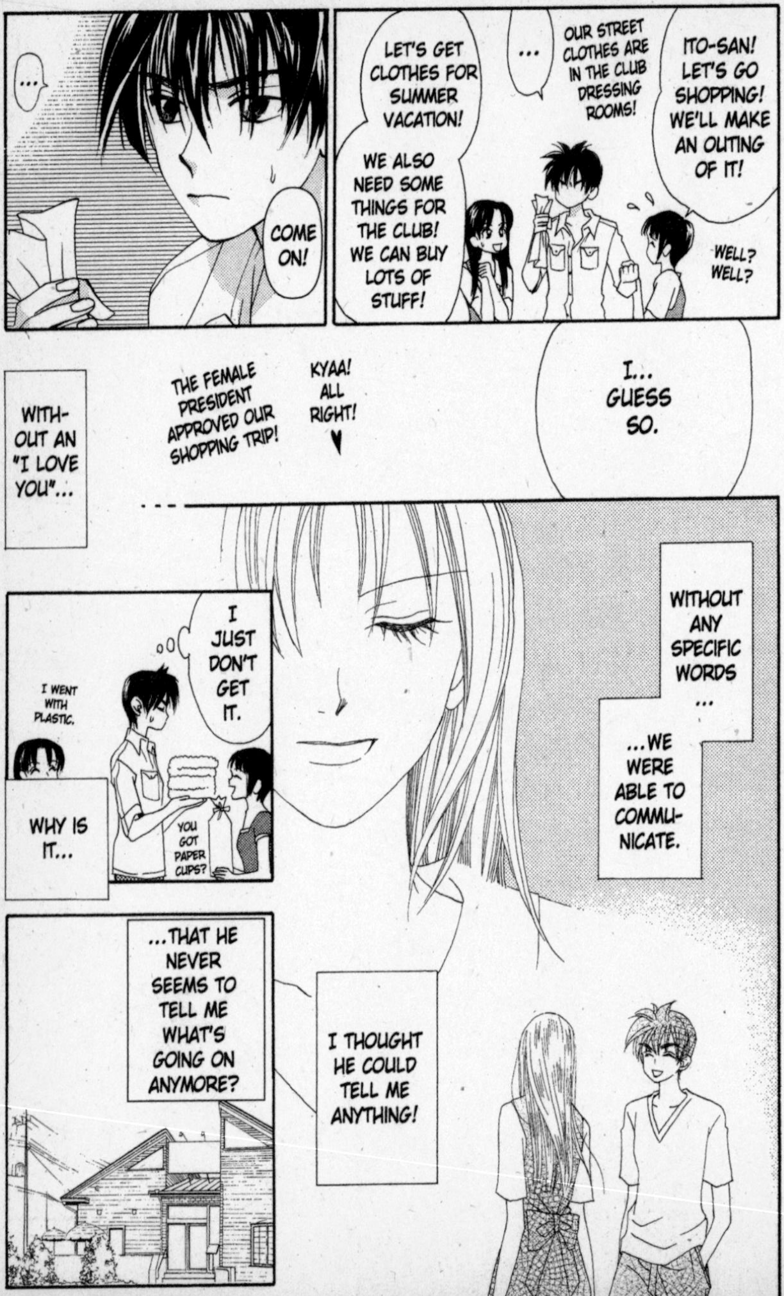
ITO-SAN! LET'S GO SHOPPING! WE'LL MAKE AN OUTING OF IT!
WELL? WELL?
OUR STREET CLOTHES ARE IN THE CLUB DRESSING ROOMS!
...
LET'S GET CLOTHES FOR SUMMER VACATION!
WE ALSO NEED SOME THINGS FOR THE CLUB! WE CAN BUY LOTS OF STUFF!
COME ON!
...
I... GUESS SO.
KYAA! ALL RIGHT! ♥
THE FEMALE PRESIDENT APPROVED OUR SHOPPING TRIP!
WITH-OUT AN "I LOVE YOU"...
WITHOUT ANY SPECIFIC WORDS ...
...WE WERE ABLE TO COMMUNI-NICATE.
I JUST DON'T GET IT.
I WENT WITH PLASTIC.
YOU GOT PAPER CUPS?
WHY IS IT...
...THAT HE NEVER SEEMS TO TELL ME WHAT'S GOING ON ANYMORE?
I THOUGHT HE COULD TELL ME ANYTHING!

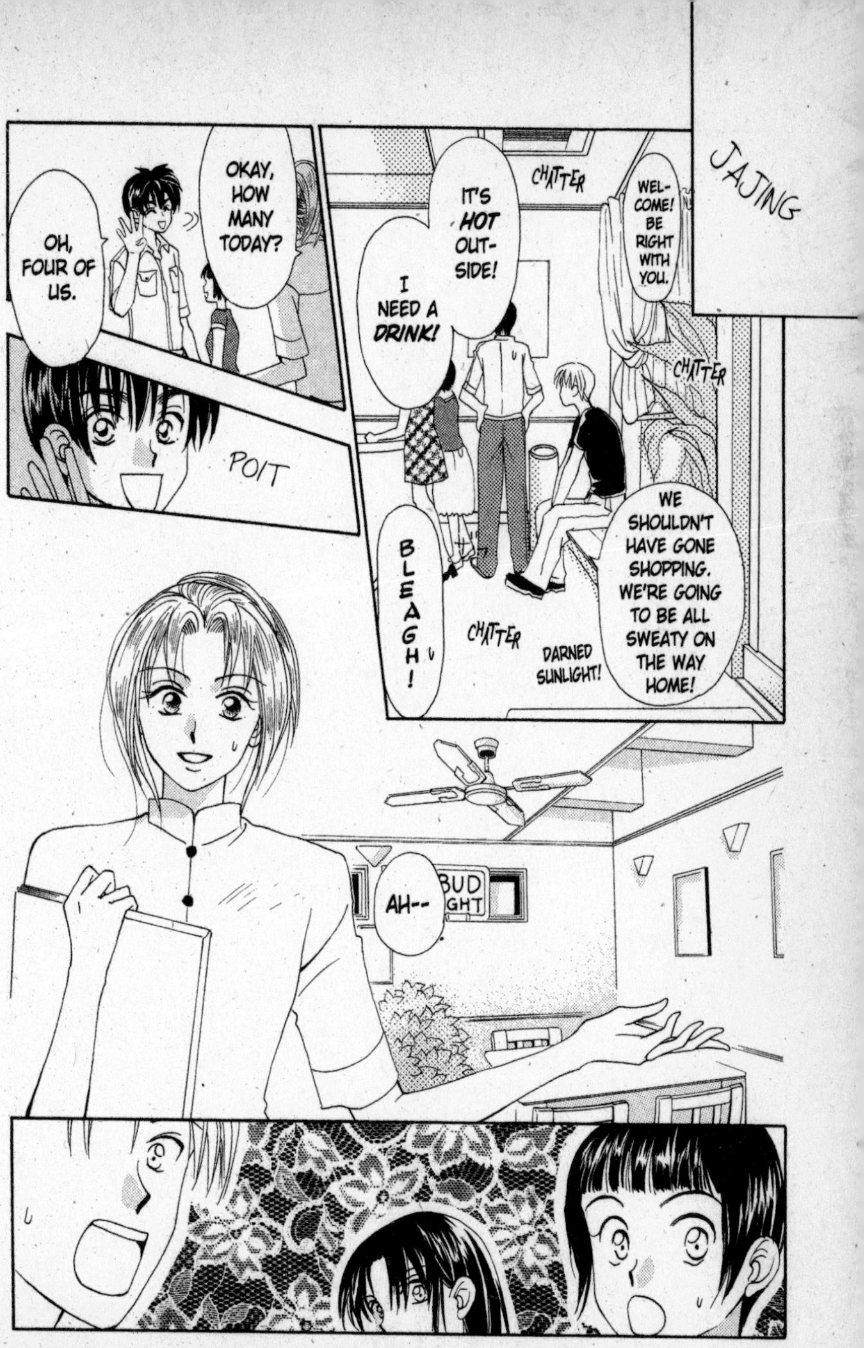
JAJING
WELCOME! BE RIGHT WITH YOU.
CHATTER
IT'S HOT OUTSIDE!
I NEED A DRINK!
CHATTER
WE SHOULDN'T HAVE GONE SHOPPING. WE'RE GOING TO BE ALL SWEATY ON THE WAY HOME!
DARNED SUNLIGHT!
CHATTER
BLEAGH!
OKAY, HOW MANY TODAY?
OH, FOUR OF US.
POIT
BUD
AH--

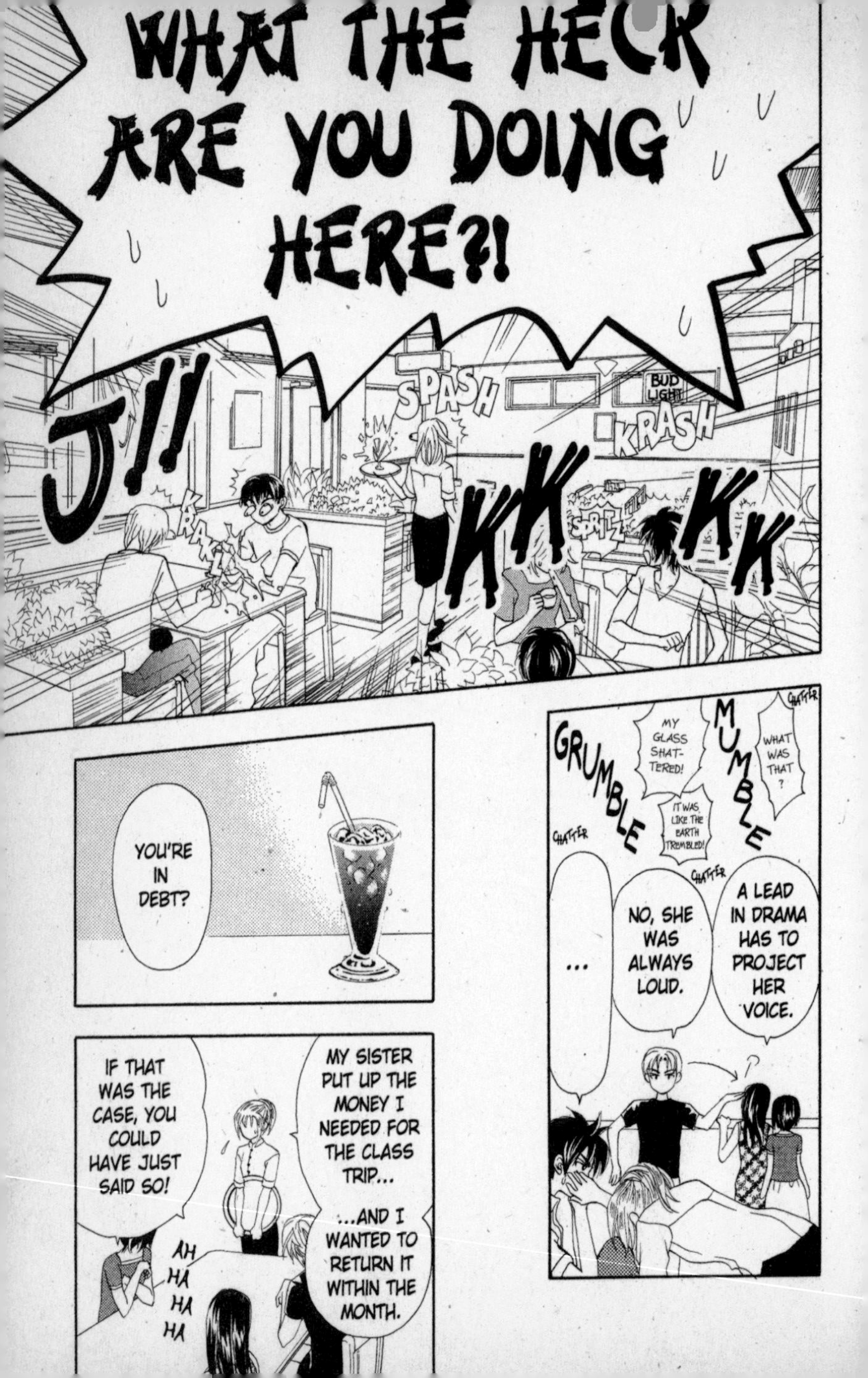
WHAT THE HECK ARE YOU DOING HERE?!
KK
KRASH
SPASH
KK
J!!
CHATTER
WHAT WAS THAT?
MUMBLE
MY GLASS SHAT-TERED!
IT WAS LIKE THE EARTH TREMBLED!
GRUMBLE
CHATTER
A LEAD IN DRAMA HAS TO PROJECT HER VOICE.
CHATTER
NO, SHE WAS ALWAYS LOUD.
...
YOU'RE IN DEBT?
MY SISTER PUT UP THE MONEY I NEEDED FOR THE CLASS TRIP...
...AND I WANTED TO RETURN IT WITHIN THE MONTH.
IF THAT WAS THE CASE, YOU COULD HAVE JUST SAID SO!
AH HA HA HA

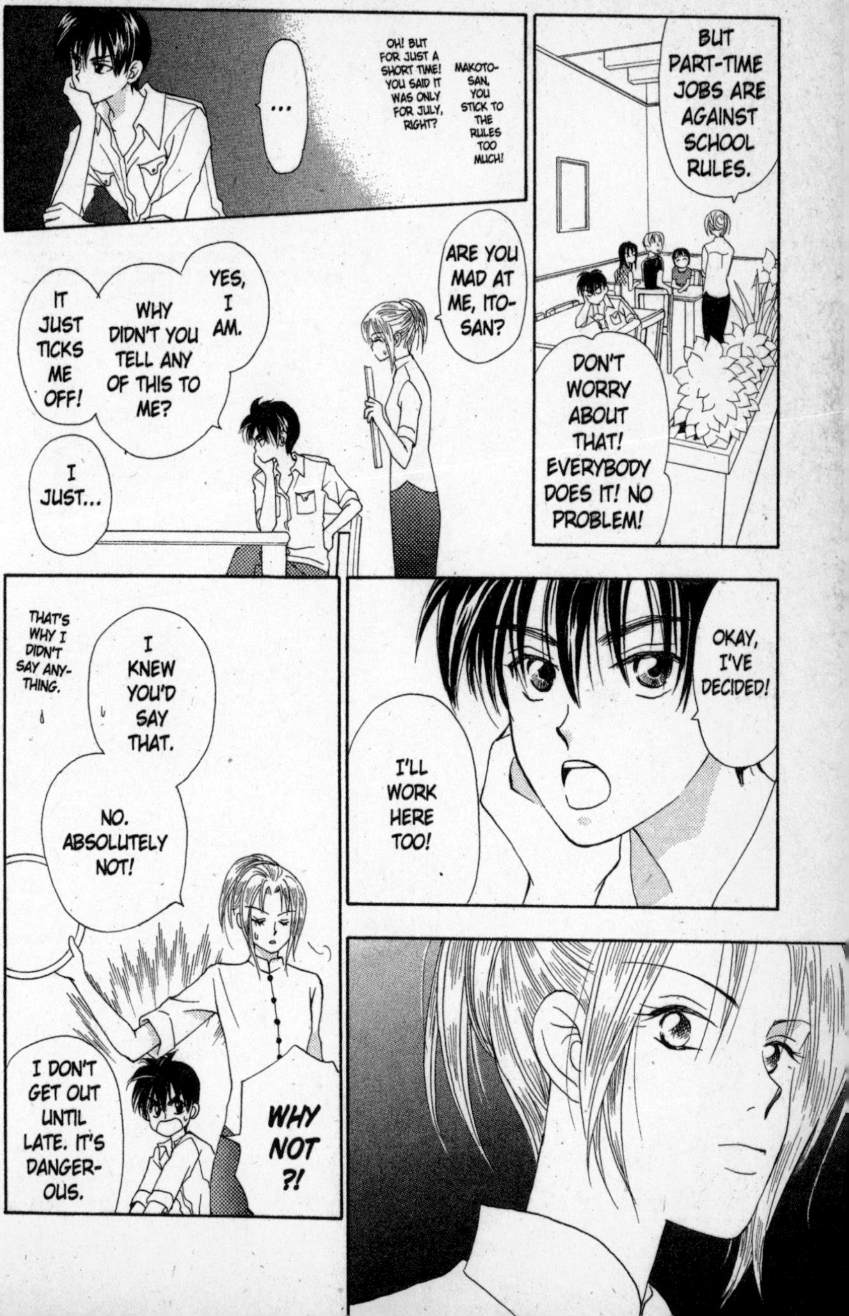
BUT PART-TIME JOBS ARE AGAINST SCHOOL RULES.
DON'T WORRY ABOUT THAT! EVERYBODY DOES IT! NO PROBLEM!
MAKOTO-SAN, YOU STICK TO THE RULES TOO MUCH!
OH! BUT FOR JUST A SHORT TIME! YOU SAID IT WAS ONLY FOR JULY, RIGHT?
...
ARE YOU MAD AT ME, ITO-SAN?
YES, I AM.
WHY DIDN'T YOU TELL ANY OF THIS TO ME?
IT JUST TICKS ME OFF!
I JUST...
OKAY, I'VE DECIDED!
I'LL WORK HERE TOO!
I KNEW YOU'D SAY THAT.
THAT'S WHY I DIDN'T SAY ANY-THING.
NO. ABSOLUTELY NOT!
WHY NOT ?!
I DON'T GET OUT UNTIL LATE. IT'S DANGER-OUS.

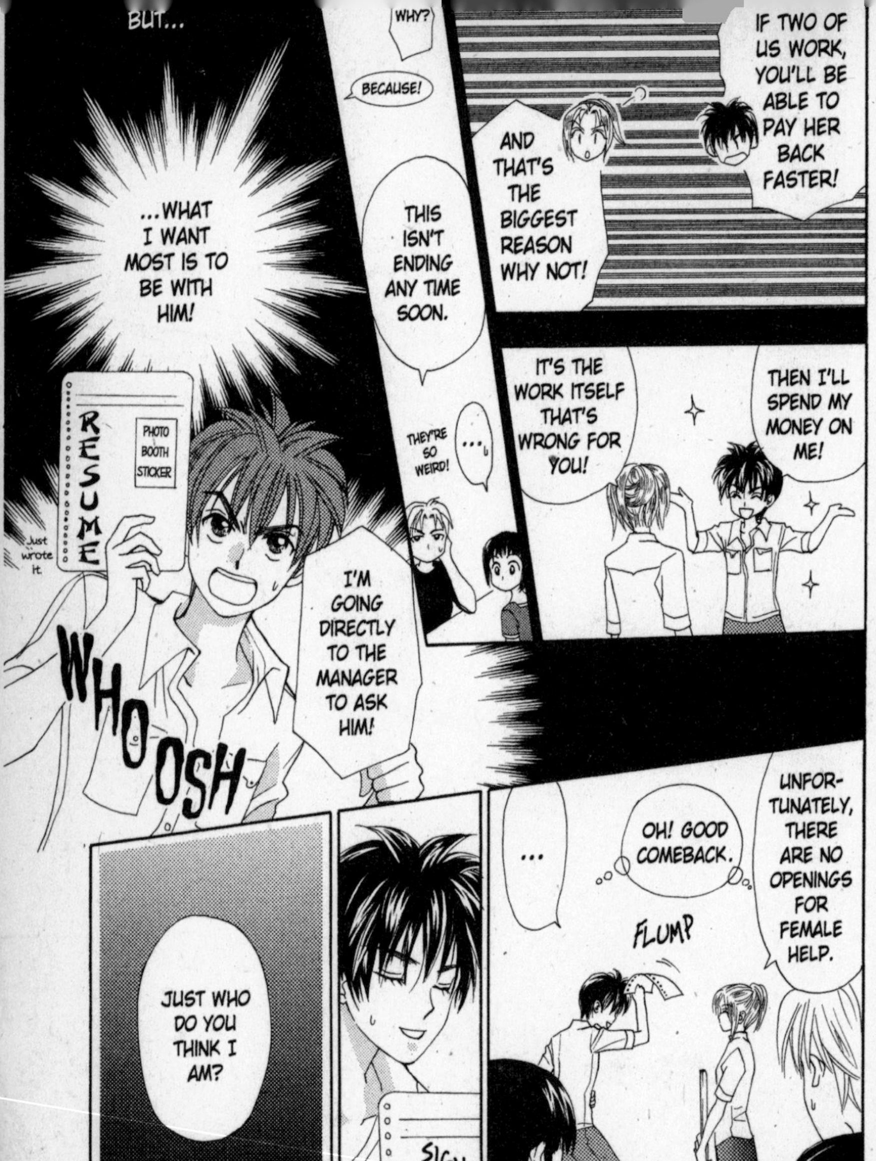
IF TWO OF US WORK, YOU'LL BE ABLE TO PAY HER BACK FASTER!
AND THAT'S THE BIGGEST REASON WHY NOT!
THEN I'LL SPEND MY MONEY ON ME!
IT'S THE WORK ITSELF THAT'S WRONG FOR YOU!
WHY?
BECAUSE!
THIS ISN'T ENDING ANY TIME SOON.
...
THEY'RE SO WEIRD!
BUT...
...WHAT I WANT MOST IS TO BE WITH HIM!
RESUME
PHOTO BOOTH STICKER
Just wrote it.
I'M GOING DIRECTLY TO THE MANAGER TO ASK HIM!
WHOOSH
UNFORTUNATELY, THERE ARE NO OPENINGS FOR FEMALE HELP.
OH! GOOD COMEBACK.
...
FLUMP
SIGH
JUST WHO DO YOU THINK I AM?

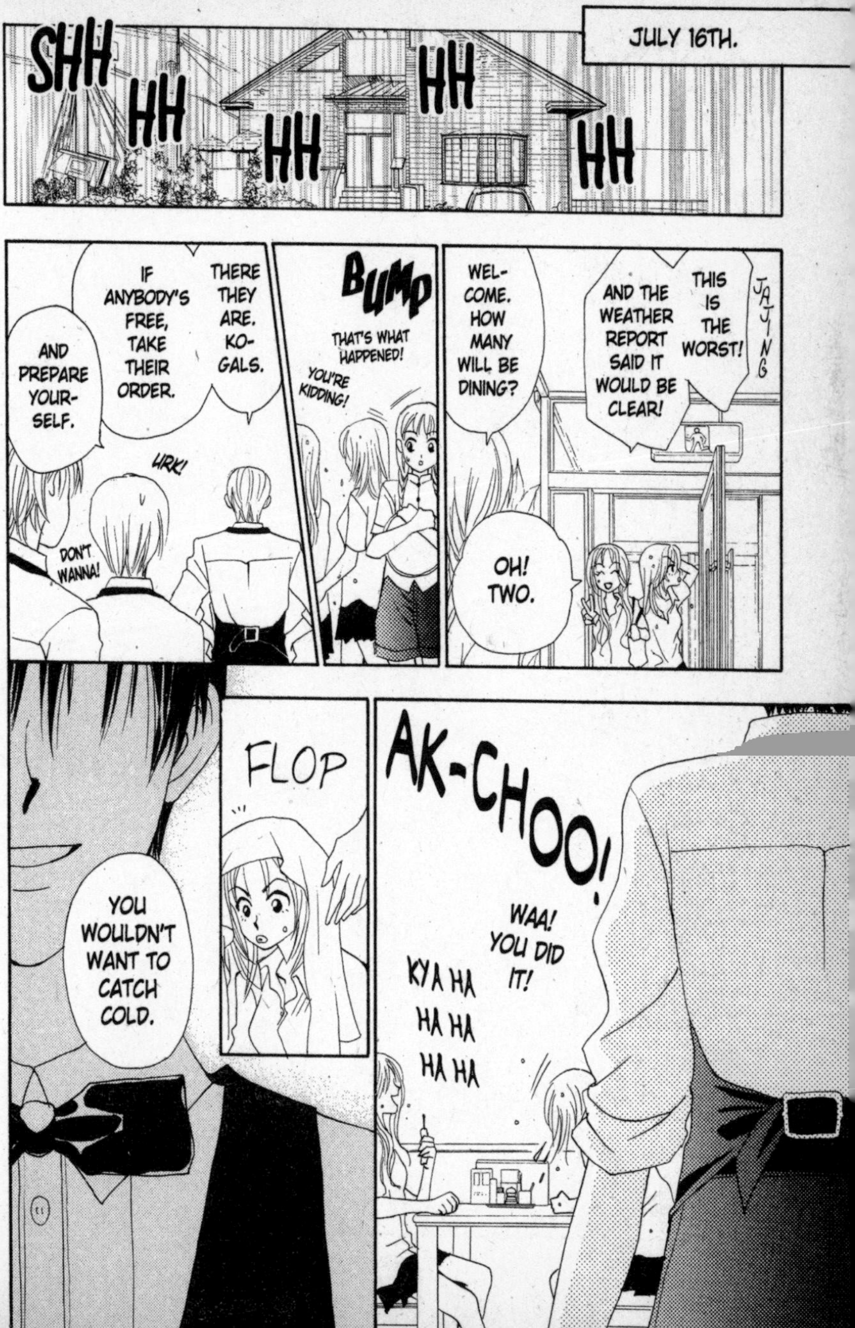
JULY 16TH.
SHHHHHHHHHHHH
JAJING
THIS IS THE WORST!
AND THE WEATHER REPORT SAID IT WOULD BE CLEAR!
WEL-COME. HOW MANY WILL BE DINING?
OH! TWO.
BUMP
THAT'S WHAT HAPPENED!
YOU'RE KIDDING!
THERE THEY ARE. KO-GALS.
IF ANYBODY'S FREE, TAKE THEIR ORDER.
AND PREPARE YOUR-SELF.
URK!
DON'T WANNA!
AK-CHOO!
WAA! YOU DID IT!
KYA HA HA HA HA HA
FLOP
YOU WOULDN'T WANT TO CATCH COLD.

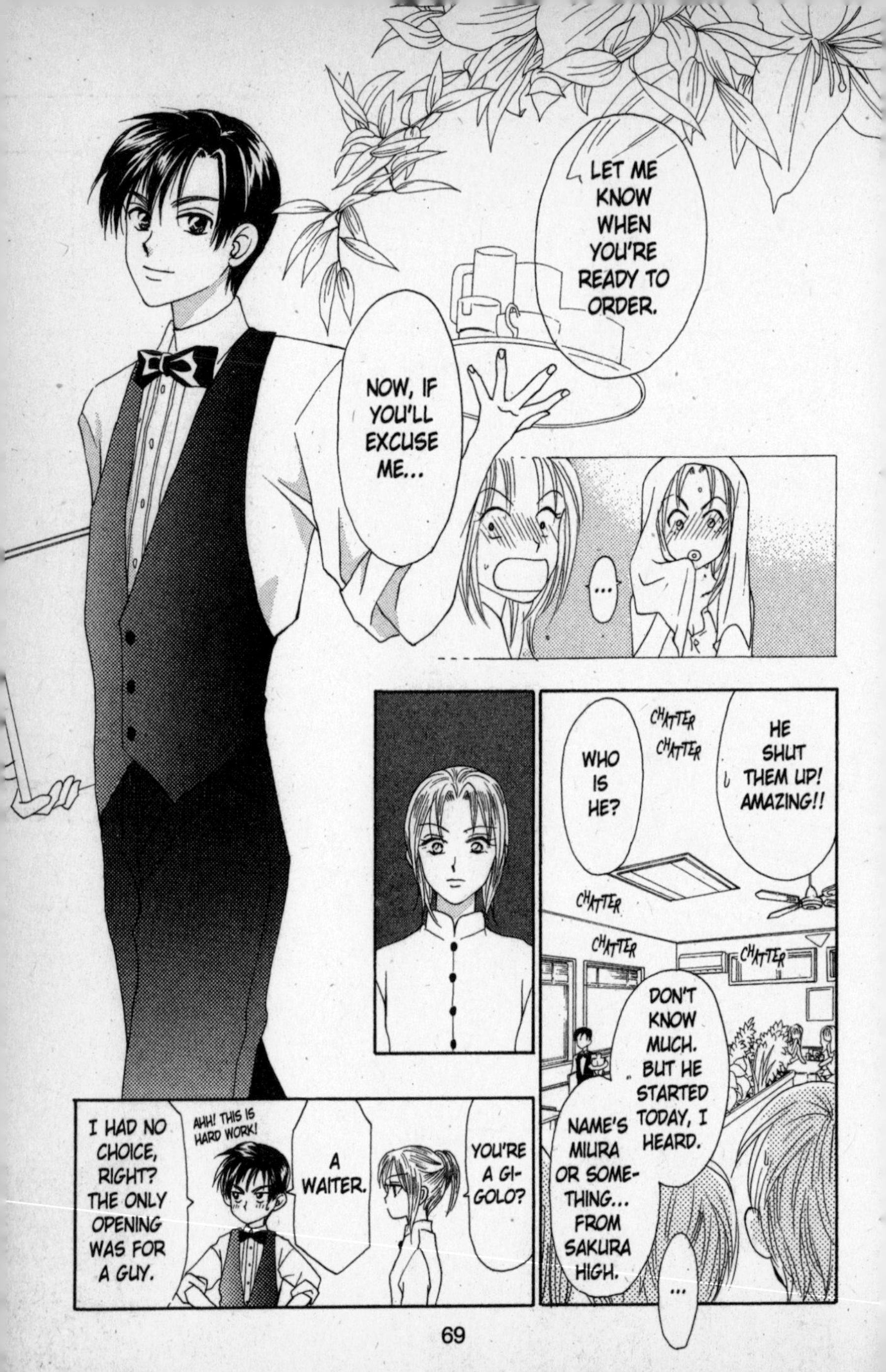
LET ME KNOW WHEN YOU'RE READY TO ORDER.
NOW, IF YOU'LL EXCUSE ME...
...
HE SHUT THEM UP! AMAZING!!
CHATTER CHATTER
WHO IS HE?
CHATTER
CHATTER
CHATTER
DON'T KNOW MUCH. BUT HE STARTED TODAY, I HEARD.
NAME'S MIURA OR SOME-THING... FROM SAKURA HIGH.
...
YOU'RE A GI-GOLO?
A WAITER.
AHH! THIS IS HARD WORK!
I HAD NO CHOICE, RIGHT? THE ONLY OPENING WAS FOR A GUY.

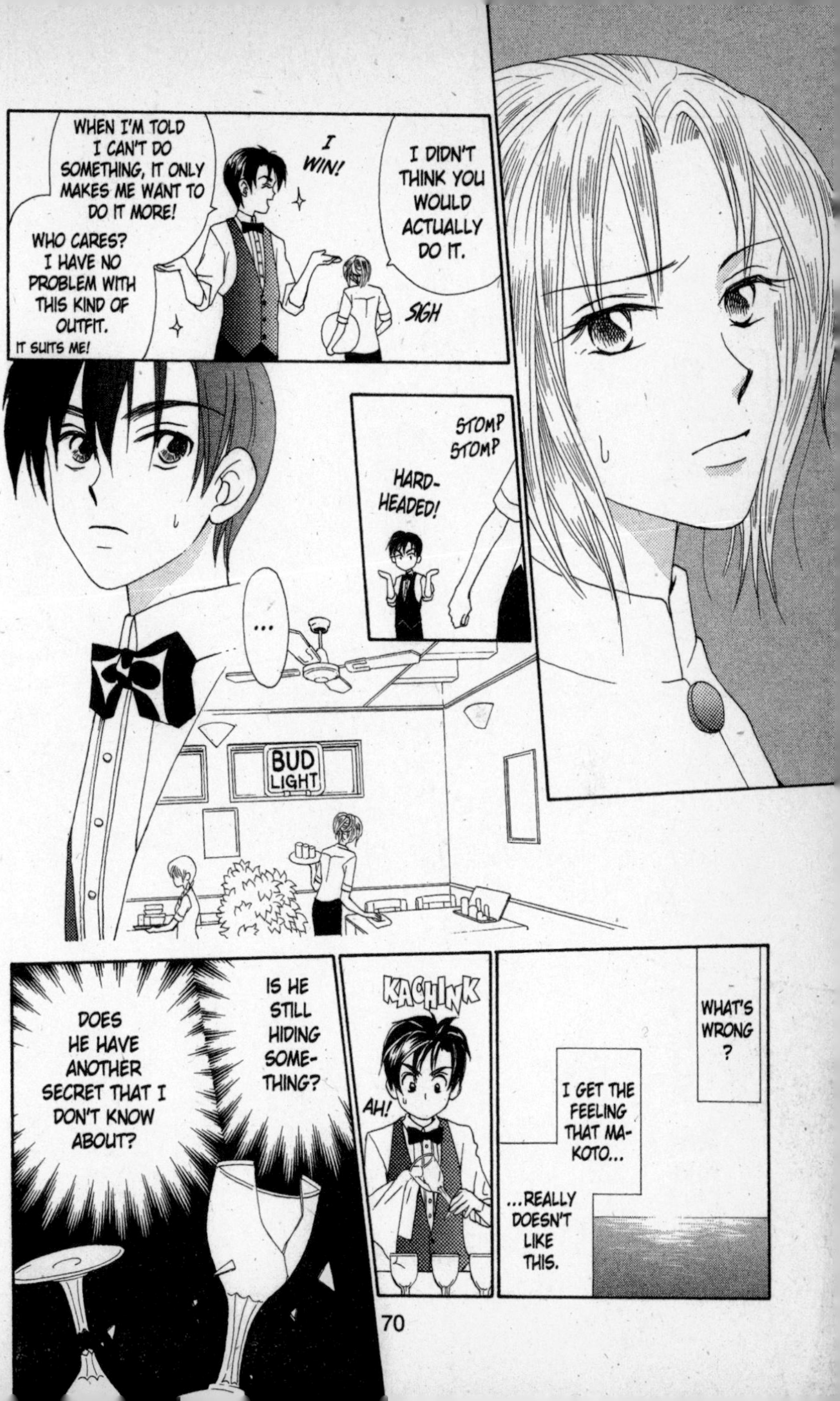
I DIDN'T THINK YOU WOULD ACTUALLY DO IT.
SIGH
I WIN!
WHEN I'M TOLD I CAN'T DO SOMETHING, IT ONLY MAKES ME WANT TO DO IT MORE!
WHO CARES? I HAVE NO PROBLEM WITH THIS KIND OF OUTFIT.
IT SUITS ME!
STOMP STOMP
HARD-HEADED!
...
WHAT'S WRONG?
I GET THE FEELING THAT MA-KOTO...
...REALLY DOESN'T LIKE THIS.
KACHINK
AH!
IS HE STILL HIDING SOME-THING?
DOES HE HAVE ANOTHER SECRET THAT I DON'T KNOW ABOUT?

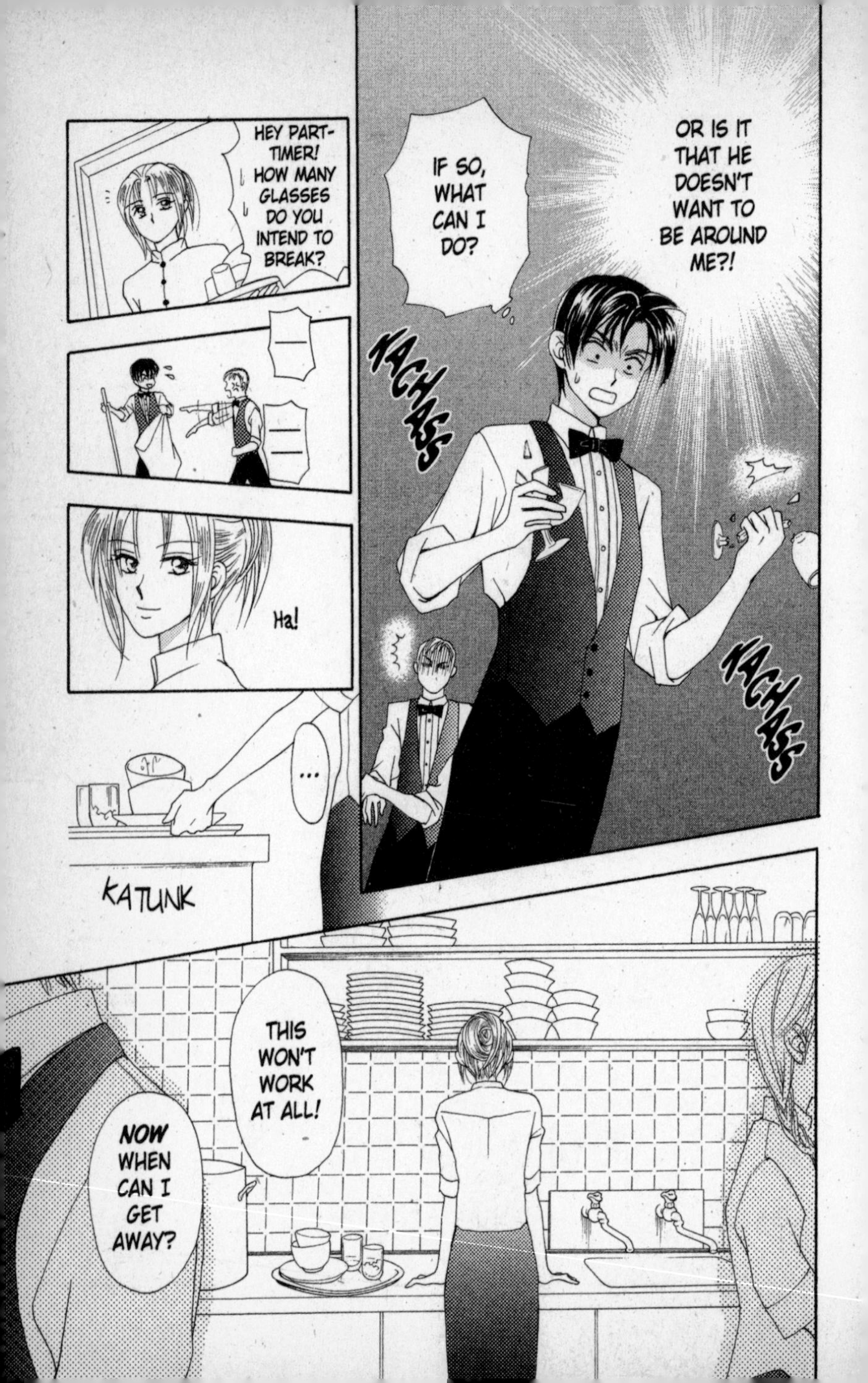
OR IS IT THAT HE DOESN'T WANT TO BE AROUND ME?!
IF SO, WHAT CAN I DO?
KACHASS
KACHASS
HEY PART-TIMER! HOW MANY GLASSES DO YOU INTEND TO BREAK?
——
——
Ha!
...
KATUNK
THIS WON'T WORK AT ALL!
NOW WHEN CAN I GET AWAY?

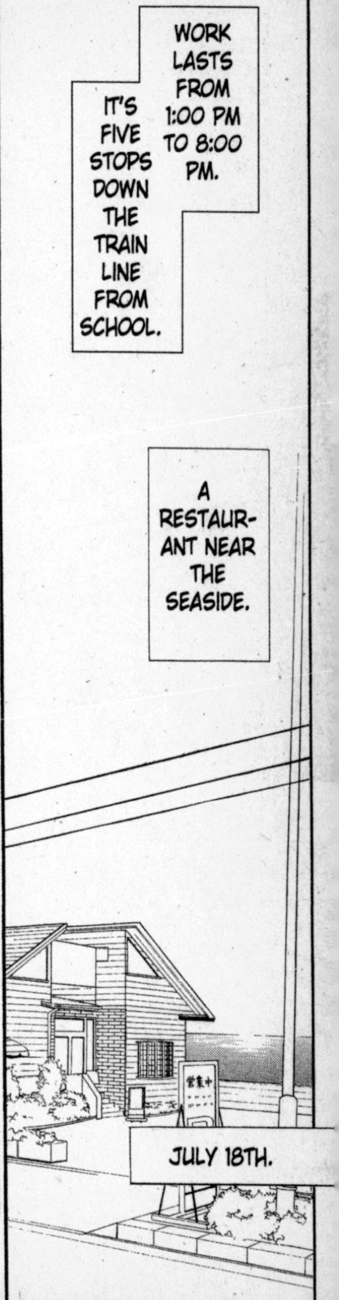
WORK LASTS FROM 1:00 PM TO 8:00 PM.
IT'S FIVE STOPS DOWN THE TRAIN LINE FROM SCHOOL.
A RESTAURANT NEAR THE SEASIDE.
JULY 18TH.

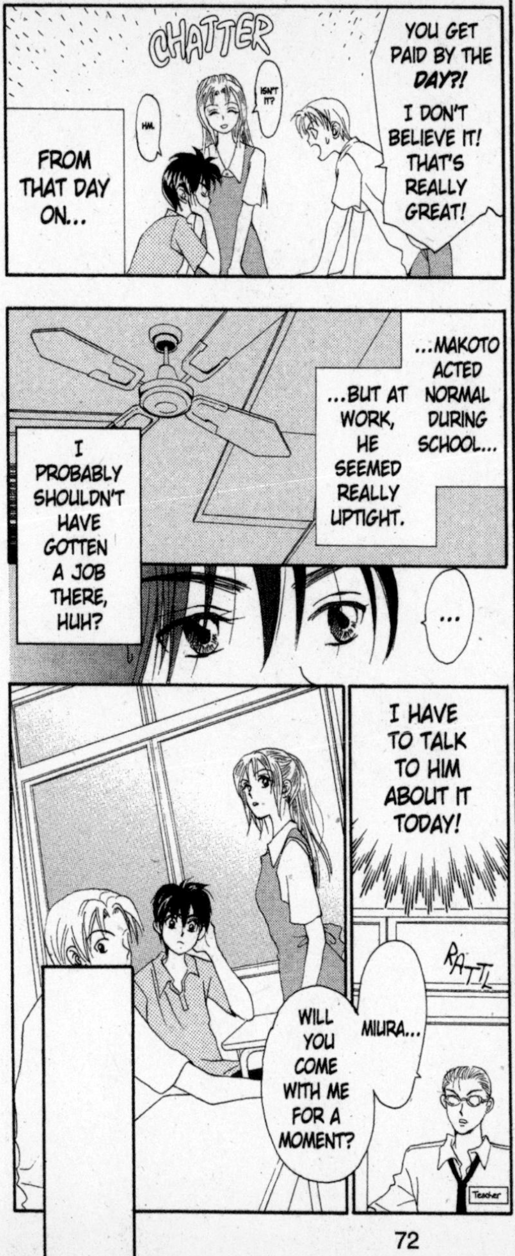
YOU GET PAID BY THE *DAY?!* I DON'T BELIEVE IT! THAT'S REALLY GREAT!
CHATTER
ISN'T IT?
HM.
FROM THAT DAY ON...
...MAKOTO ACTED NORMAL DURING SCHOOL...
...BUT AT WORK, HE SEEMED REALLY UPTIGHT.
I PROBABLY SHOULDN'T HAVE GOTTEN A JOB THERE, HUH?
...
I HAVE TO TALK TO HIM ABOUT IT TODAY!
RATTL
MIURA...
WILL YOU COME WITH ME FOR A MOMENT?
Teacher

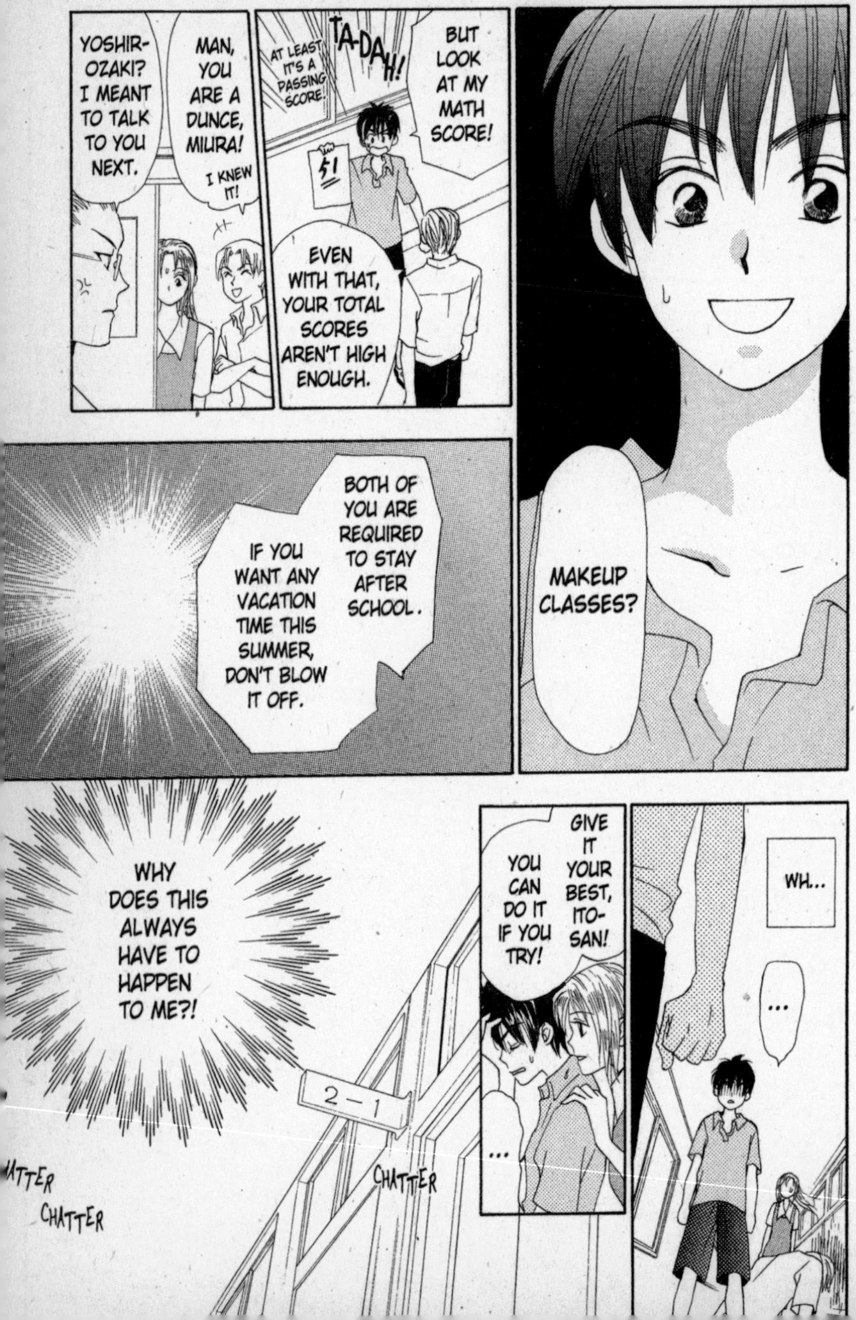
MAKEUP CLASSES?
BUT LOOK AT MY MATH SCORE!
TA-DAH!
AT LEAST IT'S A PASSING SCORE!
EVEN WITH THAT, YOUR TOTAL SCORES AREN'T HIGH ENOUGH.
MAN, YOU ARE A DUNCE, MIURA!
I KNEW IT!
YOSHIR-OZAKI? I MEANT TO TALK TO YOU NEXT.
BOTH OF YOU ARE REQUIRED TO STAY AFTER SCHOOL.
IF YOU WANT ANY VACATION TIME THIS SUMMER, DON'T BLOW IT OFF.
WH...
...
GIVE IT YOUR BEST, ITO-SAN!
YOU CAN DO IT IF YOU TRY!
...
CHATTER
2-1
WHY DOES THIS ALWAYS HAVE TO HAPPEN TO ME?!
CHATTER
CHATTER

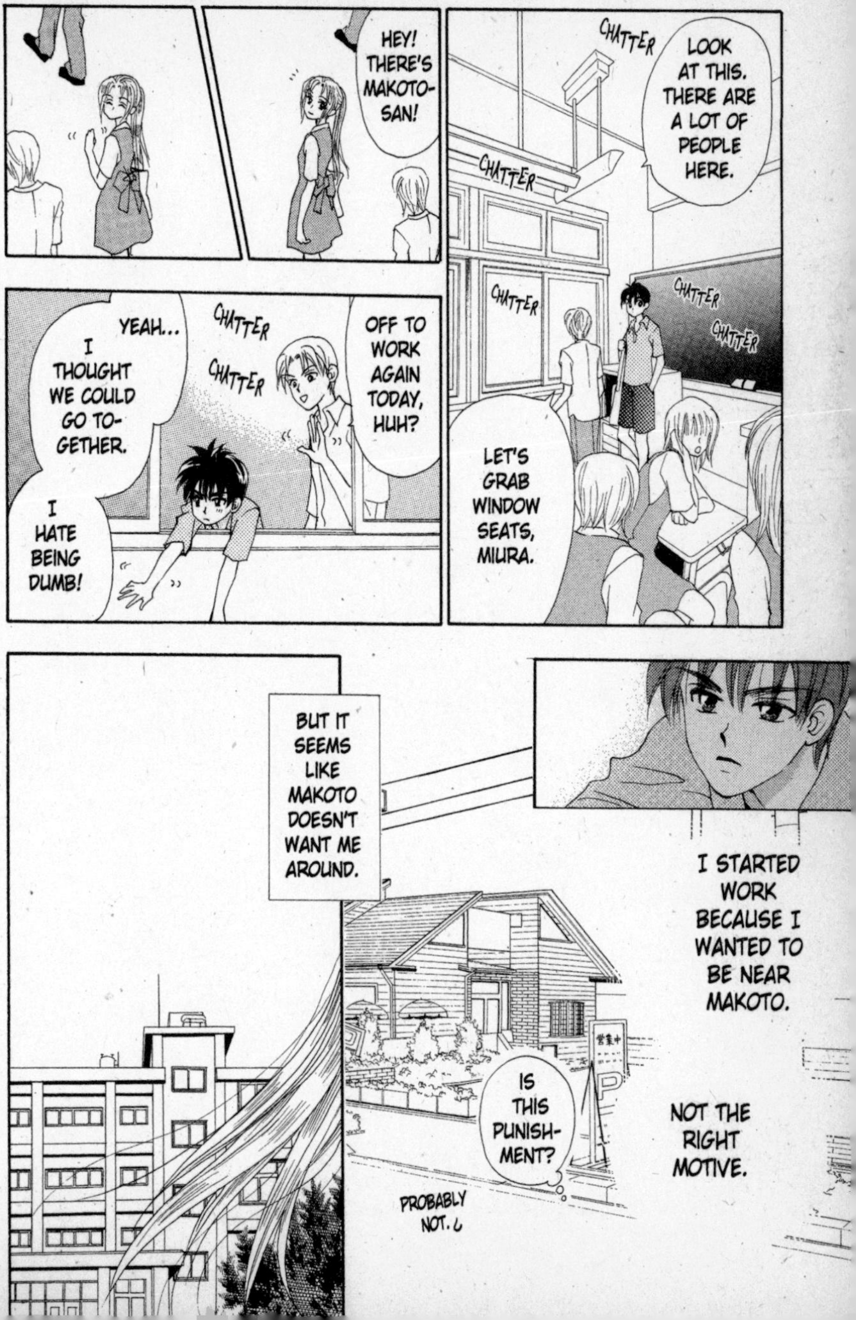
CHATTER
LOOK AT THIS. THERE ARE A LOT OF PEOPLE HERE.
CHATTER
CHATTER
CHATTER
CHATTER
LET'S GRAB WINDOW SEATS, MIURA.
HEY! THERE'S MAKOTO-SAN!
OFF TO WORK AGAIN TODAY, HUH?
CHATTER
CHATTER
YEAH... I THOUGHT WE COULD GO TO-GETHER.
I HATE BEING DUMB!
I STARTED WORK BECAUSE I WANTED TO BE NEAR MAKOTO.
NOT THE RIGHT MOTIVE.
営業中
IS THIS PUNISHMENT?
PROBABLY NOT.
BUT IT SEEMS LIKE MAKOTO DOESN'T WANT ME AROUND.

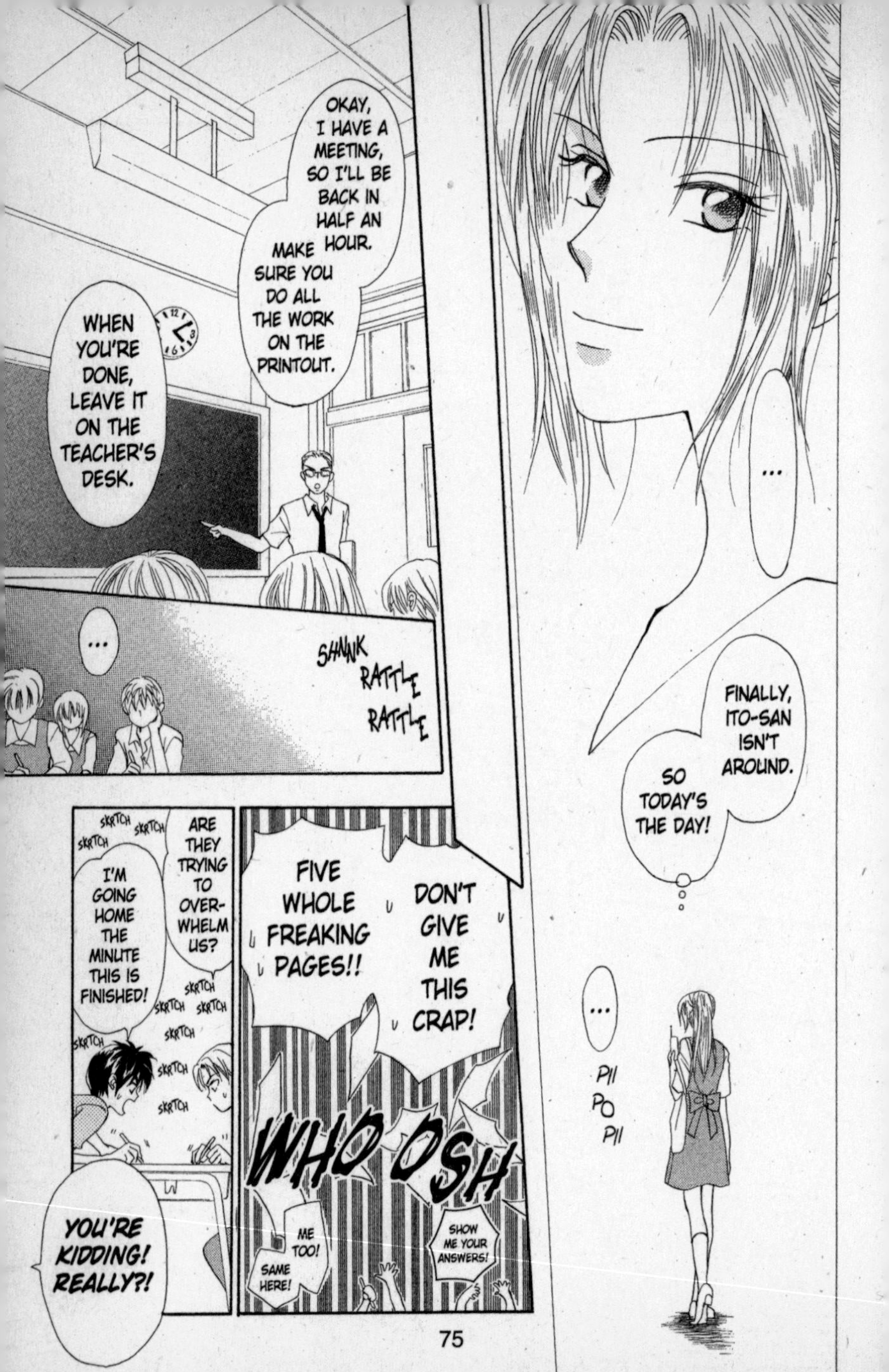
...
FINALLY, ITO-SAN ISN'T AROUND.
SO TODAY'S THE DAY!
...
PII PO PII
OKAY, I HAVE A MEETING, SO I'LL BE BACK IN HALF AN HOUR.
MAKE SURE YOU DO ALL THE WORK ON THE PRINTOUT.
WHEN YOU'RE DONE, LEAVE IT ON THE TEACHER'S DESK.
SHNNK RATTLE RATTLE
...
DON'T GIVE ME THIS CRAP!
FIVE WHOLE FREAKING PAGES!!
WHOOSH
SHOW ME YOUR ANSWERS!
ME TOO!
SAME HERE!
ARE THEY TRYING TO OVERWHELM US?
SKRTCH SKRTCH SKRTCH
I'M GOING HOME THE MINUTE THIS IS FINISHED!
SKRTCH SKRTCH SKRTCH SKRTCH SKRTCH SKRTCH SKRTCH
YOU'RE KIDDING! REALLY?!

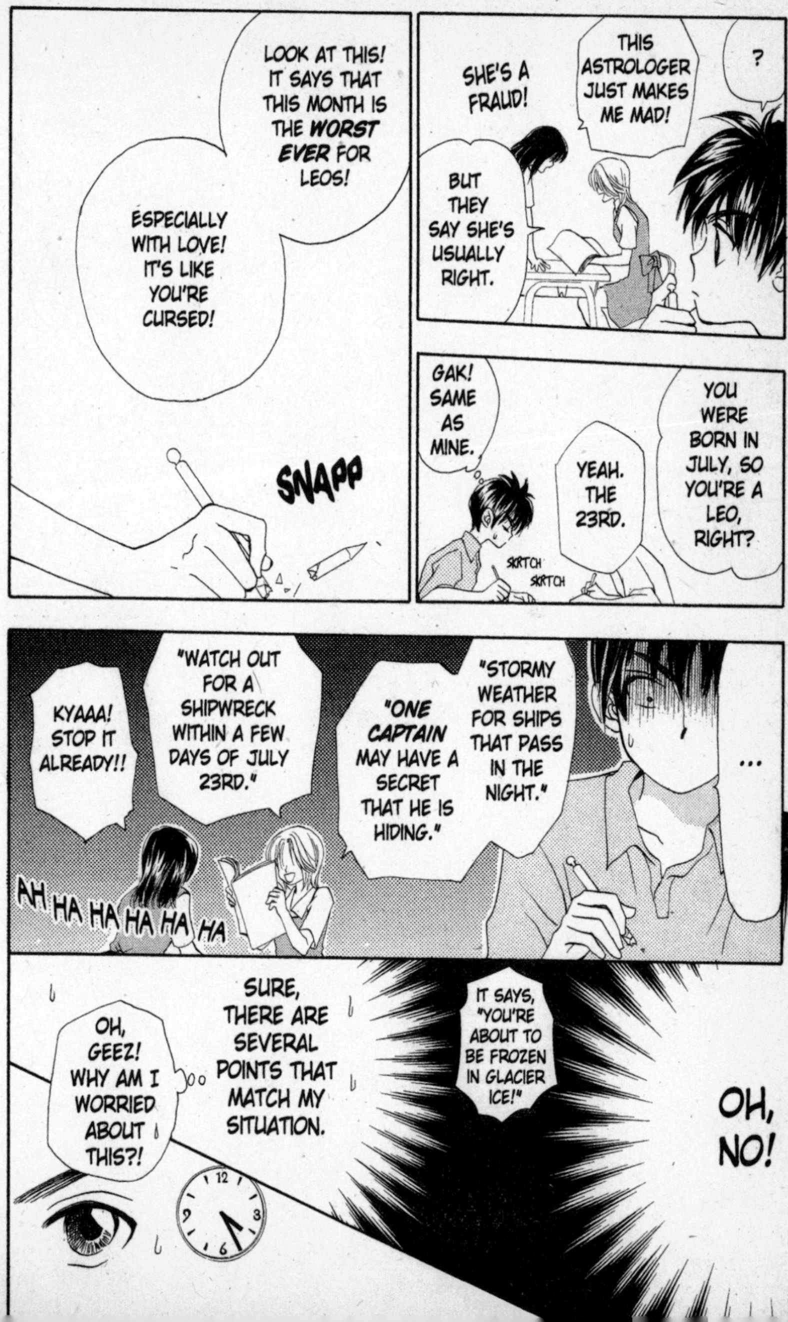
?
THIS ASTROLOGER JUST MAKES ME MAD!
SHE'S A FRAUD!
BUT THEY SAY SHE'S USUALLY RIGHT.
YOU WERE BORN IN JULY, SO YOU'RE A LEO, RIGHT?
YEAH. THE 23RD.
GAK! SAME AS MINE.
SKRTCH
SKRTCH
LOOK AT THIS! IT SAYS THAT THIS MONTH IS THE WORST EVER FOR LEOS!
ESPECIALLY WITH LOVE! IT'S LIKE YOU'RE CURSED!
SNAPP
...
"STORMY WEATHER FOR SHIPS THAT PASS IN THE NIGHT."
"ONE CAPTAIN MAY HAVE A SECRET THAT HE IS HIDING."
"WATCH OUT FOR A SHIPWRECK WITHIN A FEW DAYS OF JULY 23RD."
KYAAA! STOP IT ALREADY!!
AH HA HA HA HA HA
OH, NO!
IT SAYS, "YOU'RE ABOUT TO BE FROZEN IN GLACIER ICE!"
SURE, THERE ARE SEVERAL POINTS THAT MATCH MY SITUATION.
OH, GEEZ! WHY AM I WORRIED ABOUT THIS?!

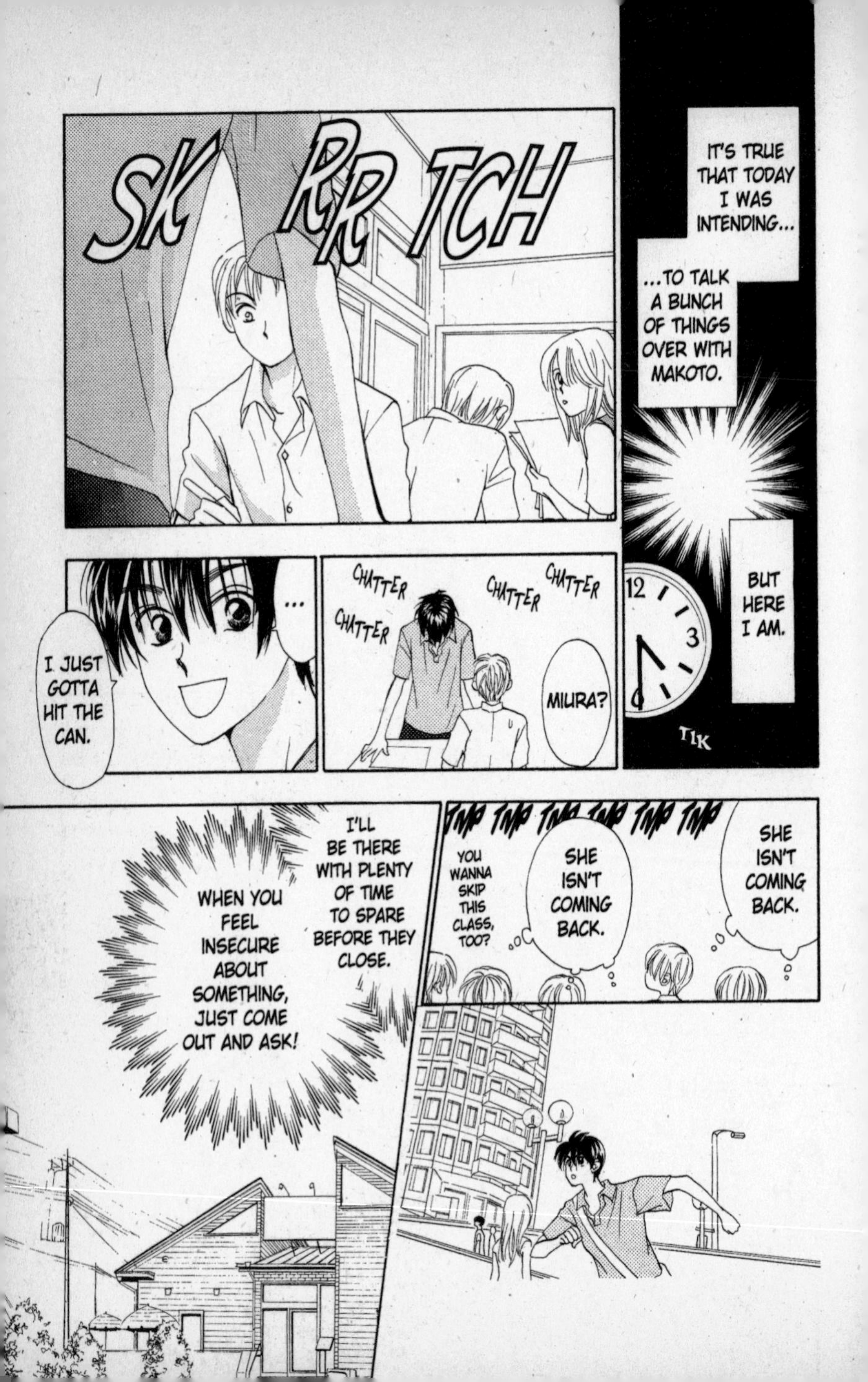
IT'S TRUE THAT TODAY I WAS INTENDING...
...TO TALK A BUNCH OF THINGS OVER WITH MAKOTO.
BUT HERE I AM.
TIK
SK RR TCH
CHATTER
CHATTER
CHATTER
CHATTER
MIURA?
...
I JUST GOTTA HIT THE CAN.
TMP TMP TMP TMP TMP TMP
SHE ISN'T COMING BACK.
SHE ISN'T COMING BACK.
YOU WANNA SKIP THIS CLASS, TOO?
I'LL BE THERE WITH PLENTY OF TIME TO SPARE BEFORE THEY CLOSE.
WHEN YOU FEEL INSECURE ABOUT SOMETHING, JUST COME OUT AND ASK!

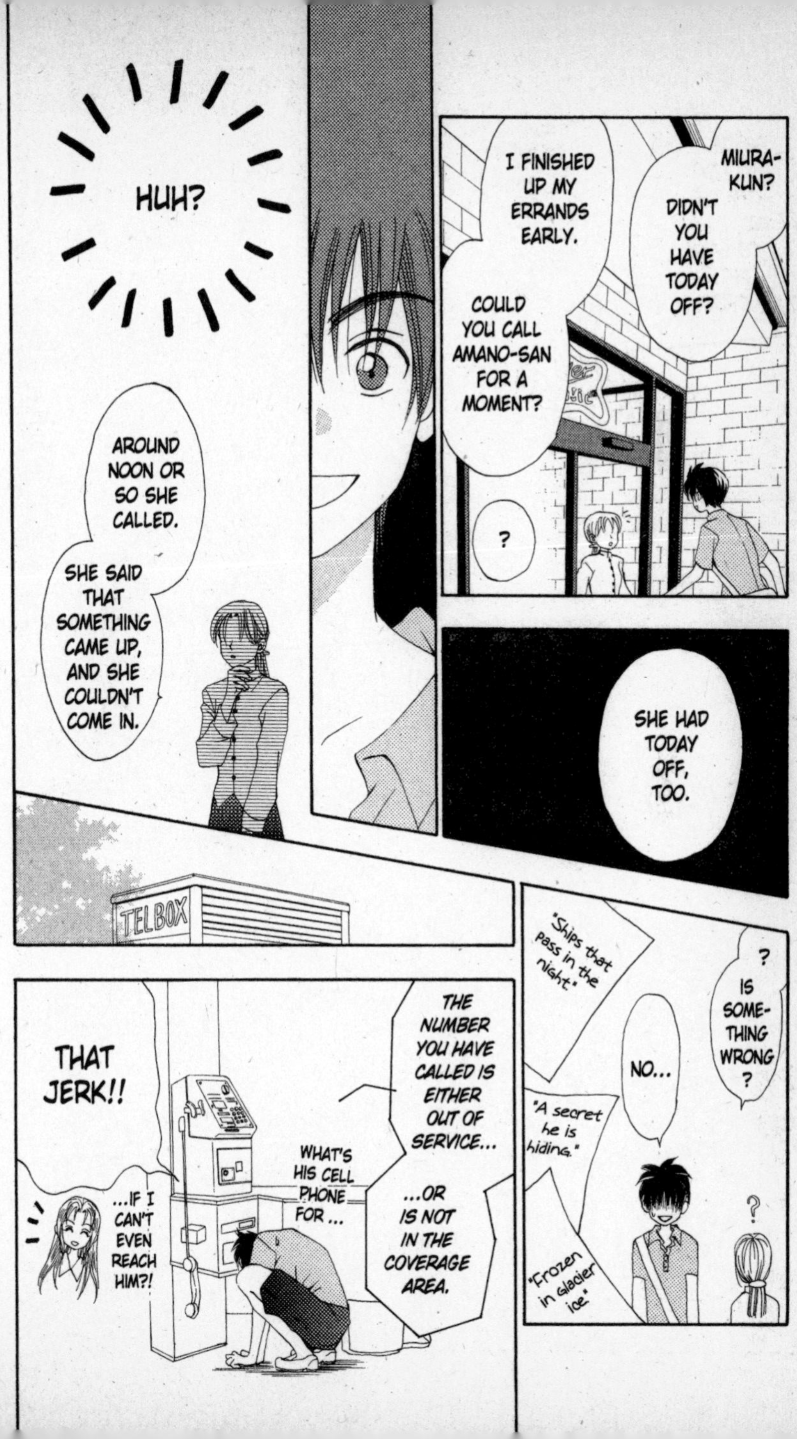
MIURA-KUN?
DIDN'T YOU HAVE TODAY OFF?
I FINISHED UP MY ERRANDS EARLY.
COULD YOU CALL AMANO-SAN FOR A MOMENT?
?
SHE HAD TODAY OFF, TOO.
HUH?
AROUND NOON OR SO SHE CALLED.
SHE SAID THAT SOMETHING CAME UP, AND SHE COULDN'T COME IN.
TELBOX
?
IS SOMETHING WRONG?
NO...
"Ships that pass in the night."
"A secret he is hiding."
"Frozen in glacier ice."
?
THE NUMBER YOU HAVE CALLED IS EITHER OUT OF SERVICE...
...OR IS NOT IN THE COVERAGE AREA.
WHAT'S HIS CELL PHONE FOR...
...IF I CAN'T EVEN REACH HIM?!
THAT JERK!!

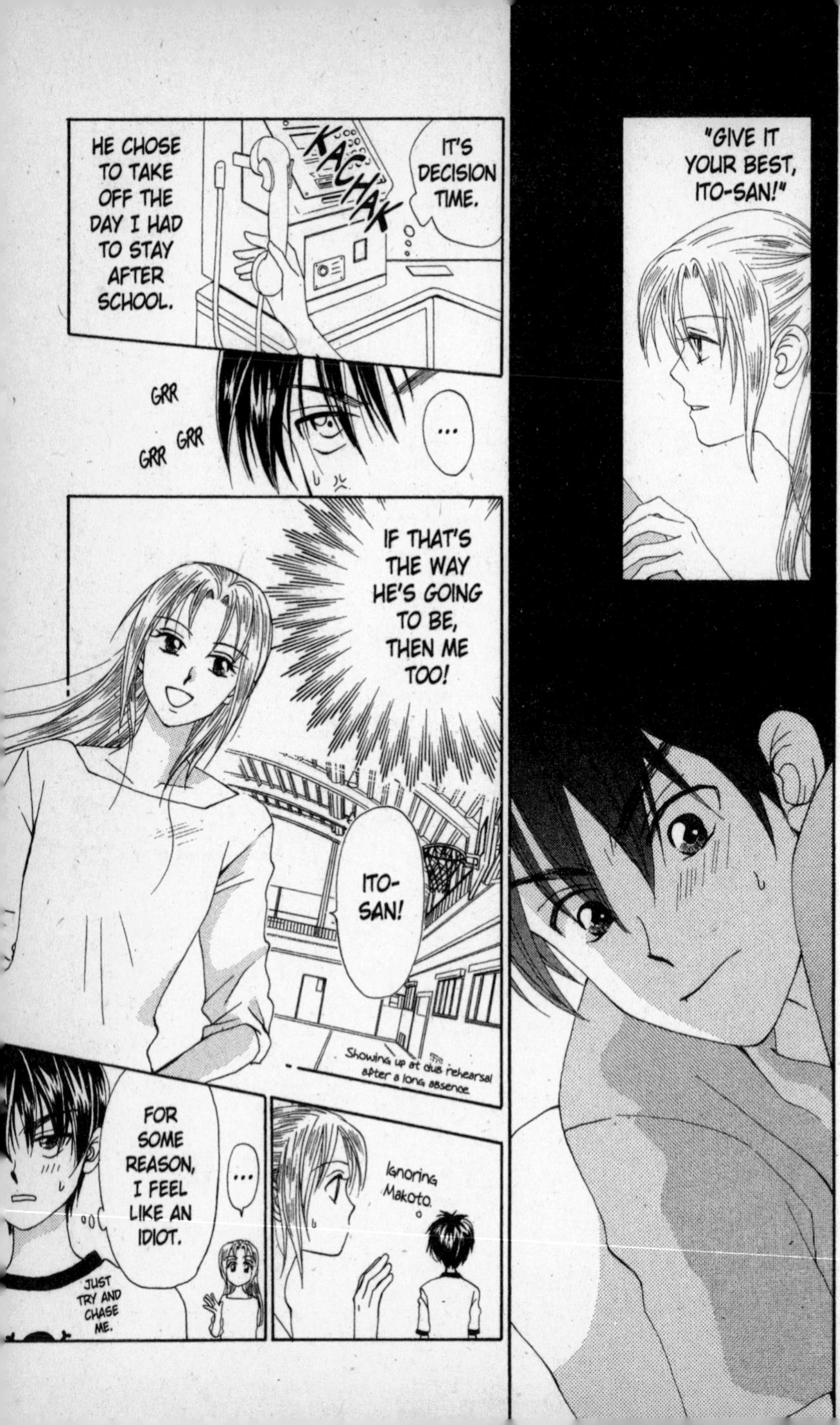
"GIVE IT YOUR BEST, ITO-SAN!"
IT'S DECISION TIME.
KACHAK
HE CHOSE TO TAKE OFF THE DAY I HAD TO STAY AFTER SCHOOL.
...
GRR
GRR GRR
IF THAT'S THE WAY HE'S GOING TO BE, THEN ME TOO!
ITO-SAN!
Showing up at club rehearsal after a long absence.
Ignoring Makoto.
...
FOR SOME REASON, I FEEL LIKE AN IDIOT.
JUST TRY AND CHASE ME.

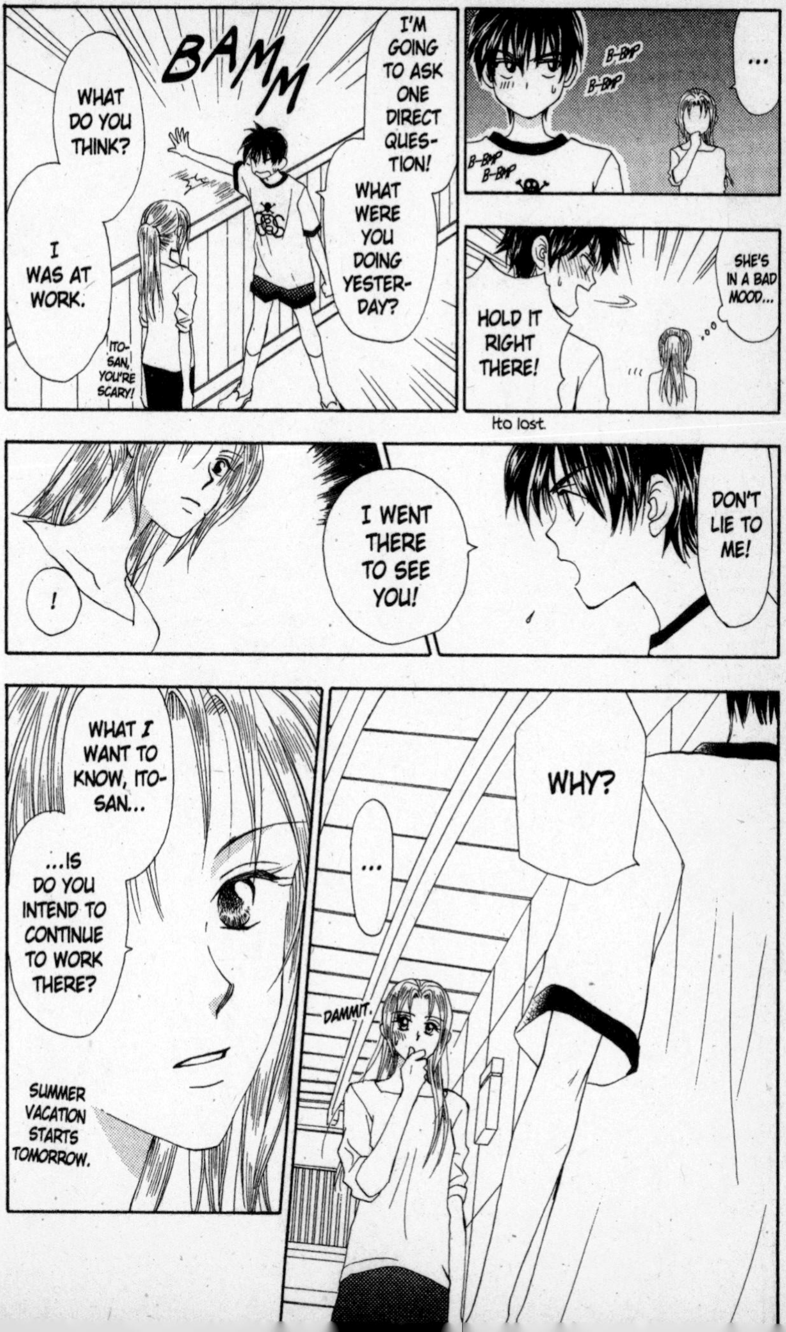

B-BMP
B-BMP
...
B-BMP
B-BMP
SHE'S IN A BAD MOOD...
HOLD IT RIGHT THERE!
BAMM
I'M GOING TO ASK ONE DIRECT QUESTION!
WHAT WERE YOU DOING YESTERDAY?
WHAT DO YOU THINK?
I WAS AT WORK.
ITO-SAN, YOU'RE SCARY!
Ito lost.
DON'T LIE TO ME!
I WENT THERE TO SEE YOU!
!
WHY?
...
DAMMIT.
WHAT I WANT TO KNOW, ITO-SAN...
...IS DO YOU INTEND TO CONTINUE TO WORK THERE?
SUMMER VACATION STARTS TOMORROW.

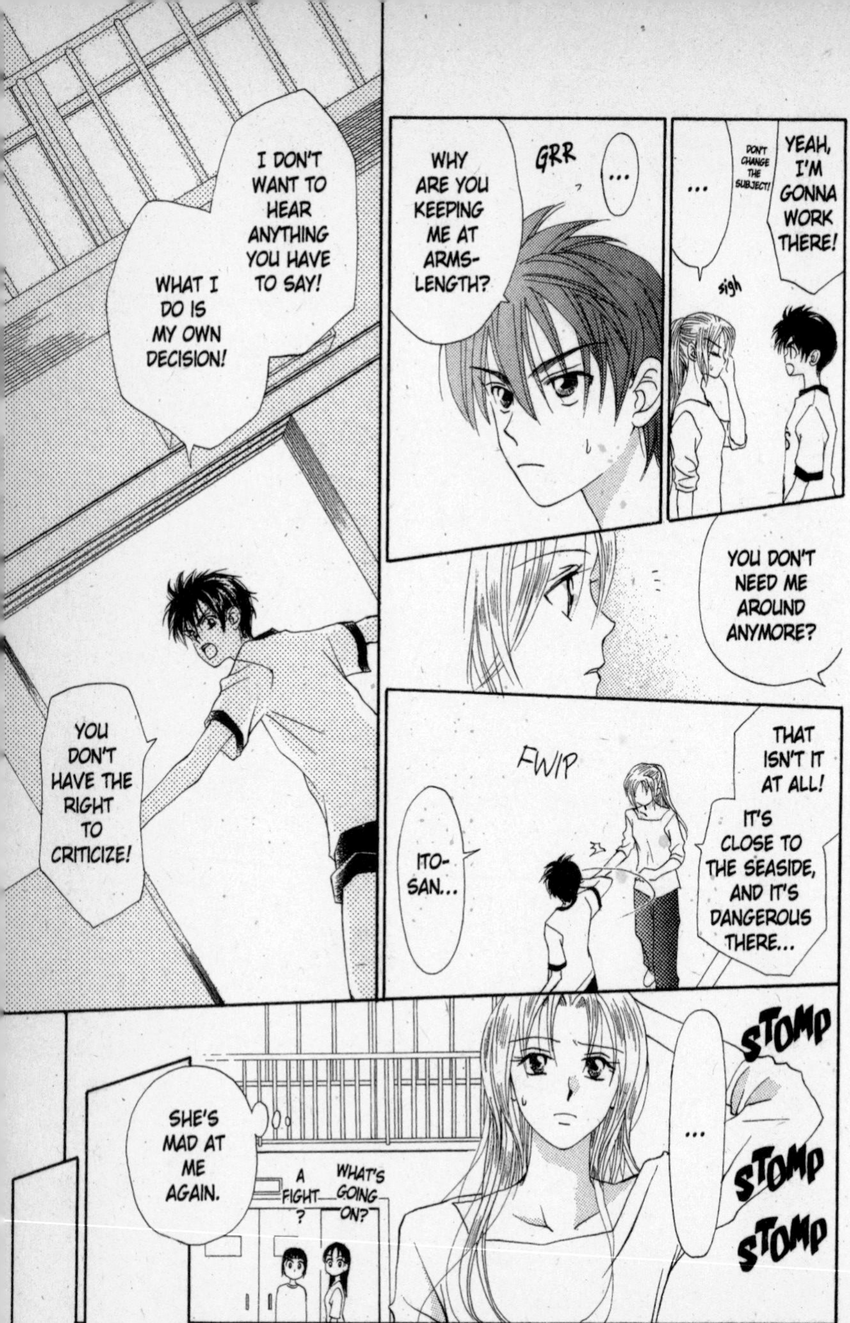
YEAH, I'M GONNA WORK THERE!
DON'T CHANGE THE SUBJECT!
...
sigh
...
GRR
WHY ARE YOU KEEPING ME AT ARMS-LENGTH?
YOU DON'T NEED ME AROUND ANYMORE?
THAT ISN'T IT AT ALL!
IT'S CLOSE TO THE SEASIDE, AND IT'S DANGEROUS THERE...
FWIP
ITO-SAN...
I DON'T WANT TO HEAR ANYTHING YOU HAVE TO SAY!
WHAT I DO IS MY OWN DECISION!
YOU DON'T HAVE THE RIGHT TO CRITICIZE!
STOMP
STOMP
STOMP
...
SHE'S MAD AT ME AGAIN.
WHAT'S GOING ON?
A FIGHT?

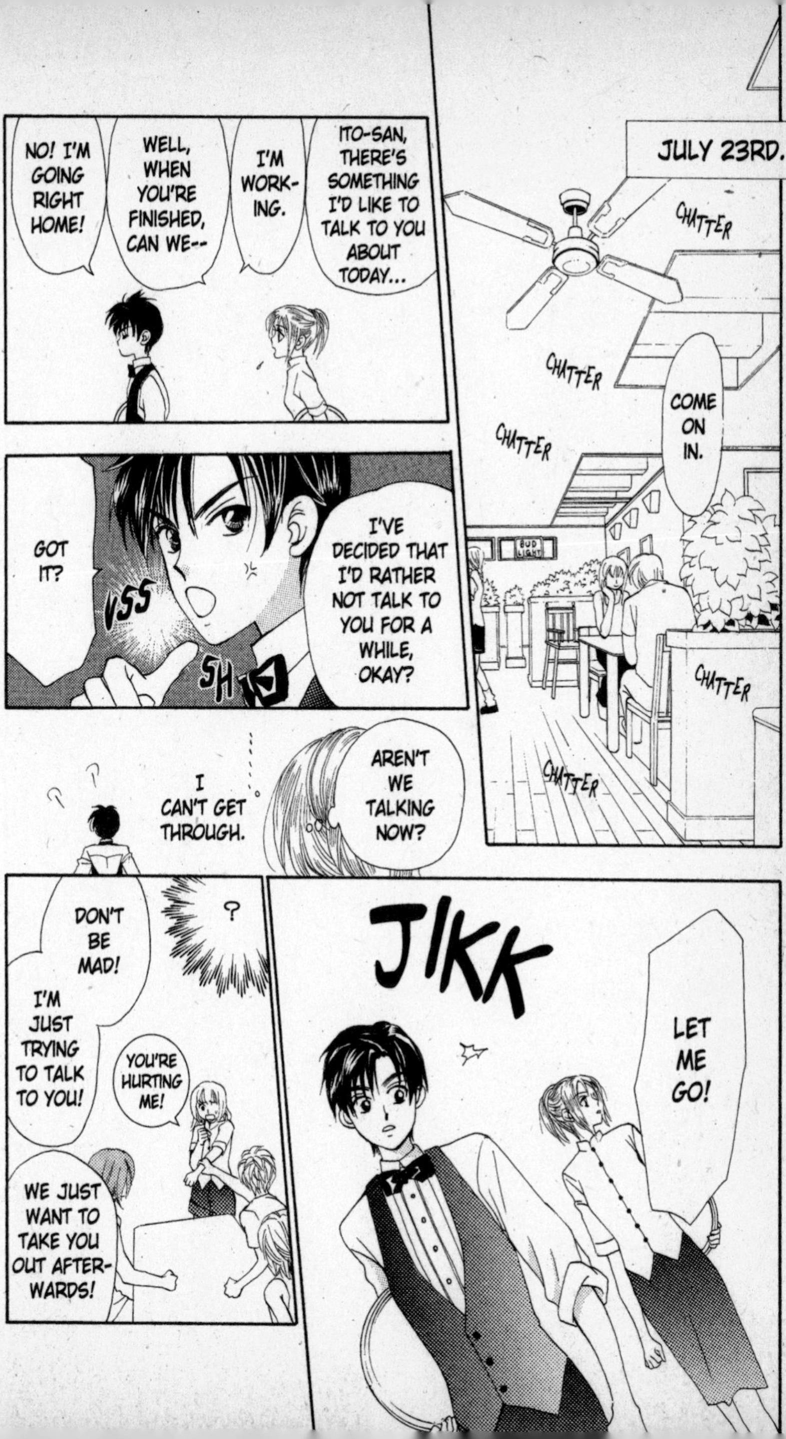
JULY 23RD.
CHATTER
CHATTER
CHATTER
COME ON IN.
CHATTER
CHATTER
ITO-SAN, THERE'S SOMETHING I'D LIKE TO TALK TO YOU ABOUT TODAY...
I'M WORKING.
WELL, WHEN YOU'RE FINISHED, CAN WE--
NO! I'M GOING RIGHT HOME!
I'VE DECIDED THAT I'D RATHER NOT TALK TO YOU FOR A WHILE, OKAY?
GOT IT?
VSS
SH
AREN'T WE TALKING NOW?
I CAN'T GET THROUGH.
JIKK
LET ME GO!
DON'T BE MAD!
?
I'M JUST TRYING TO TALK TO YOU!
YOU'RE HURTING ME!
WE JUST WANT TO TAKE YOU OUT AFTERWARDS!

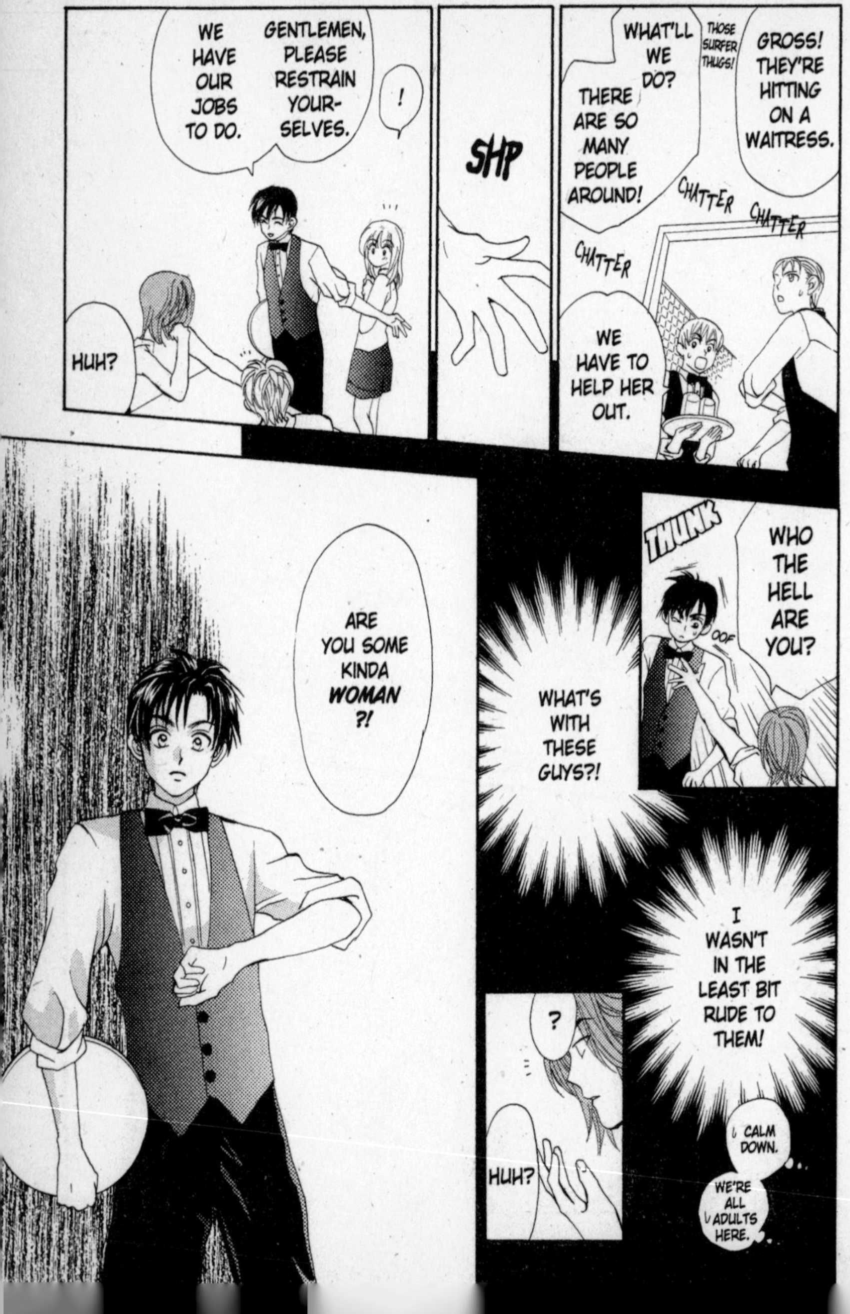
GROSS! THEY'RE HITTING ON A WAITRESS.
THOSE SURFER THUGS!
WHAT'LL WE DO?
THERE ARE SO MANY PEOPLE AROUND!
CHATTER
CHATTER
CHATTER
WE HAVE TO HELP HER OUT.
SHP
!
GENTLEMEN, PLEASE RESTRAIN YOUR-SELVES.
WE HAVE OUR JOBS TO DO.
HUH?
THUNK
WHO THE HELL ARE YOU?
OOF
WHAT'S WITH THESE GUYS?!
I WASN'T IN THE LEAST BIT RUDE TO THEM!
CALM DOWN.
WE'RE ALL ADULTS HERE.
?
HUH?
ARE YOU SOME KINDA WOMAN?!

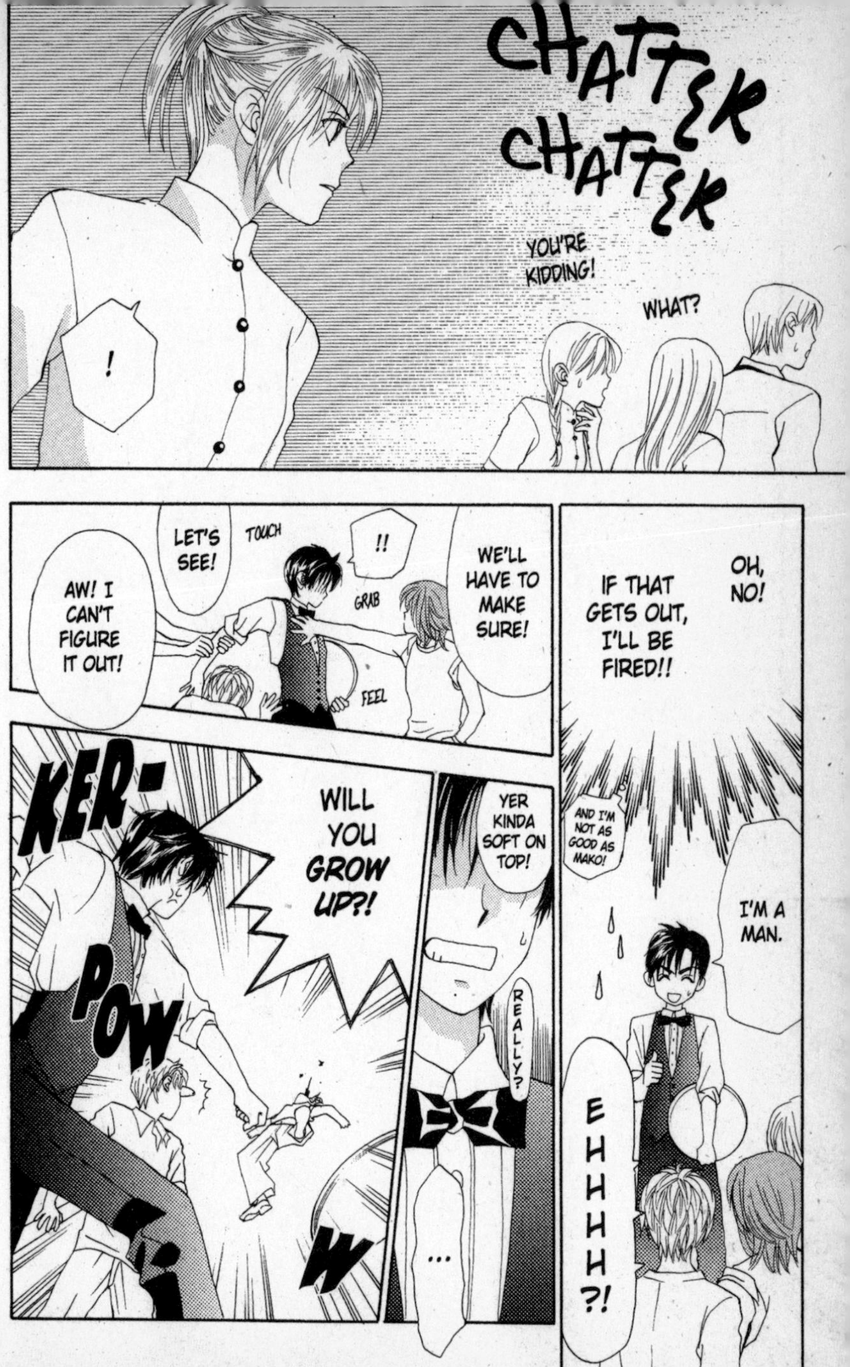
CHATTER CHATTER
YOU'RE KIDDING!
WHAT?
!
OH, NO!
IF THAT GETS OUT, I'LL BE FIRED!!
AND I'M NOT AS GOOD AS MAKO!
I'M A MAN.
EHHHHH?!
WE'LL HAVE TO MAKE SURE!
!!
TOUCH
LET'S SEE!
GRAB
FEEL
AW! I CAN'T FIGURE IT OUT!
YER KINDA SOFT ON TOP!
REALLY?
...
WILL YOU GROW UP?!
KER-POW

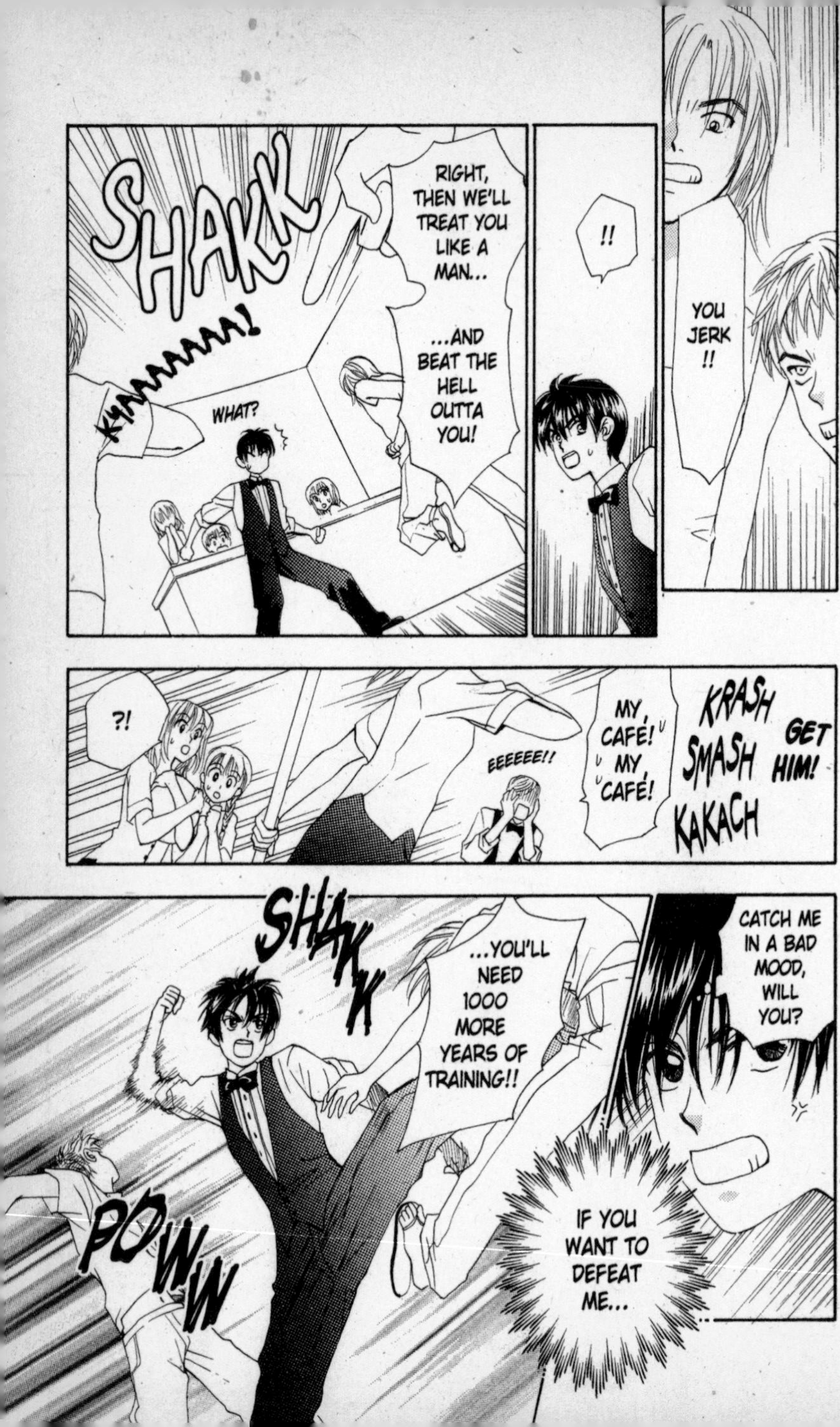
YOU JERK !!
!!
RIGHT, THEN WE'LL TREAT YOU LIKE A MAN...
...AND BEAT THE HELL OUTTA YOU!
SHAKK
KYAAAAAAA!
WHAT?
GET HIM!
KRASH
SMASH
KAKACH
MY, CAFÉ! MY, CAFÉ!
EEEEEE!!
?!
CATCH ME IN A BAD MOOD, WILL YOU?
IF YOU WANT TO DEFEAT ME...
...YOU'LL NEED 1000 MORE YEARS OF TRAINING!!
SHAKK
POWW

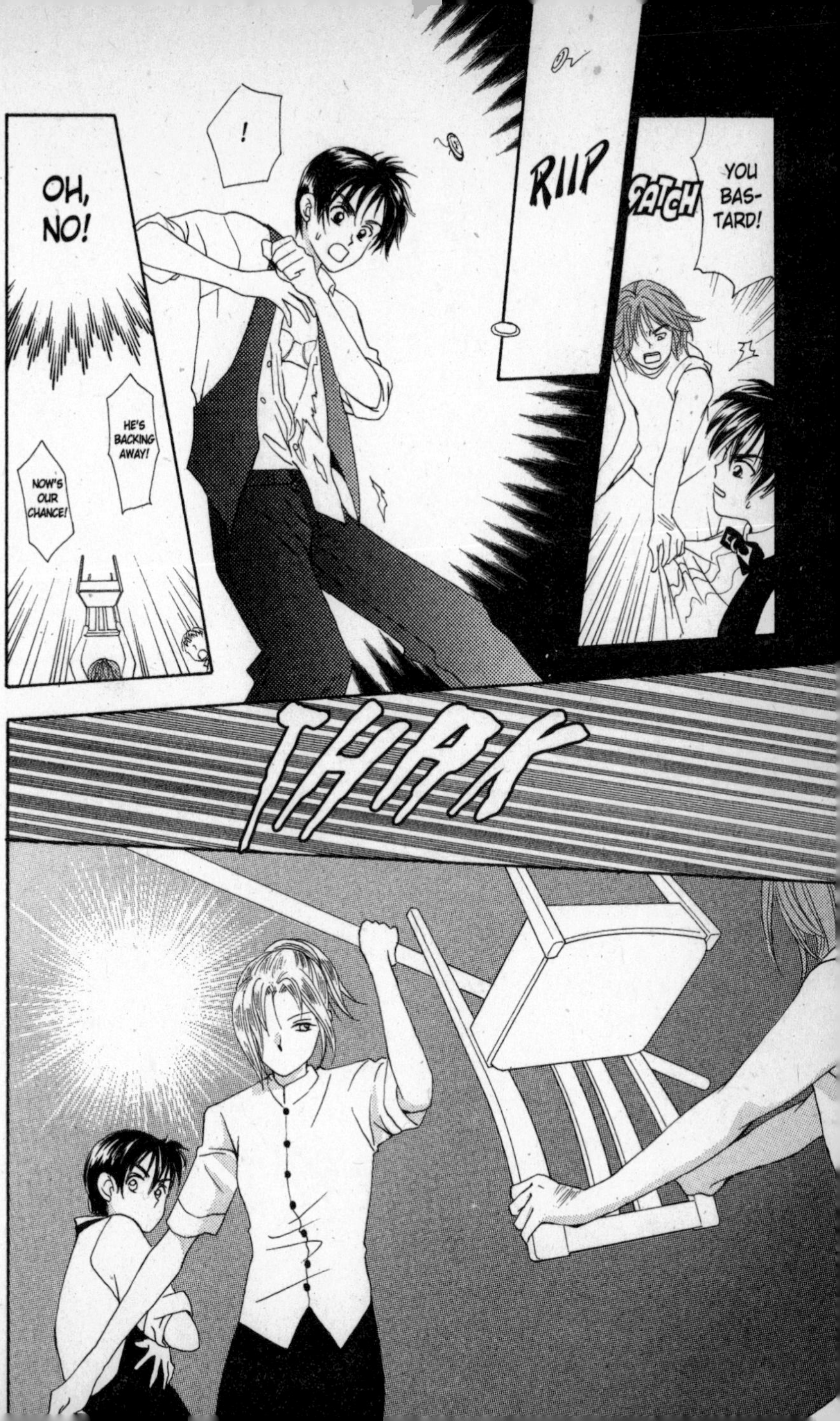
YOU BAS-TARD!
SNATCH
RIIP
!
OH, NO!
HE'S BACKING AWAY!
NOW'S OUR CHANCE!
THRK

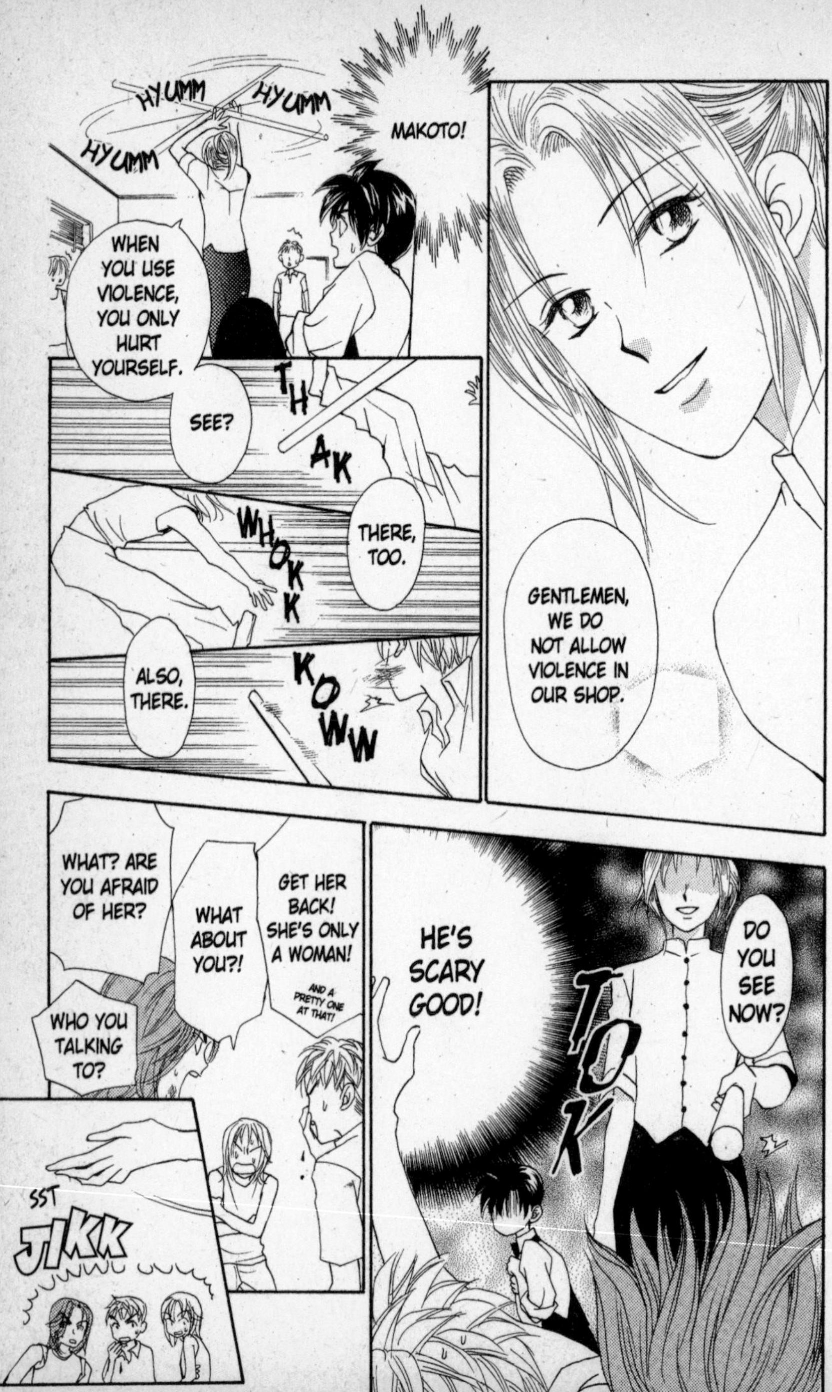
GENTLEMEN, WE DO NOT ALLOW VIOLENCE IN OUR SHOP.
MAKOTO!
HYUMM HYUMM
HYUMM
WHEN YOU USE VIOLENCE, YOU ONLY HURT YOURSELF.
THAK
SEE?
THERE, TOO.
WHOKK
ALSO, THERE.
KOWW
DO YOU SEE NOW?
TOK
HE'S SCARY GOOD!
GET HER BACK! SHE'S ONLY A WOMAN!
AND A PRETTY ONE AT THAT!
WHAT ABOUT YOU?!
WHAT? ARE YOU AFRAID OF HER?
WHO YOU TALKING TO?
SST
JIKK

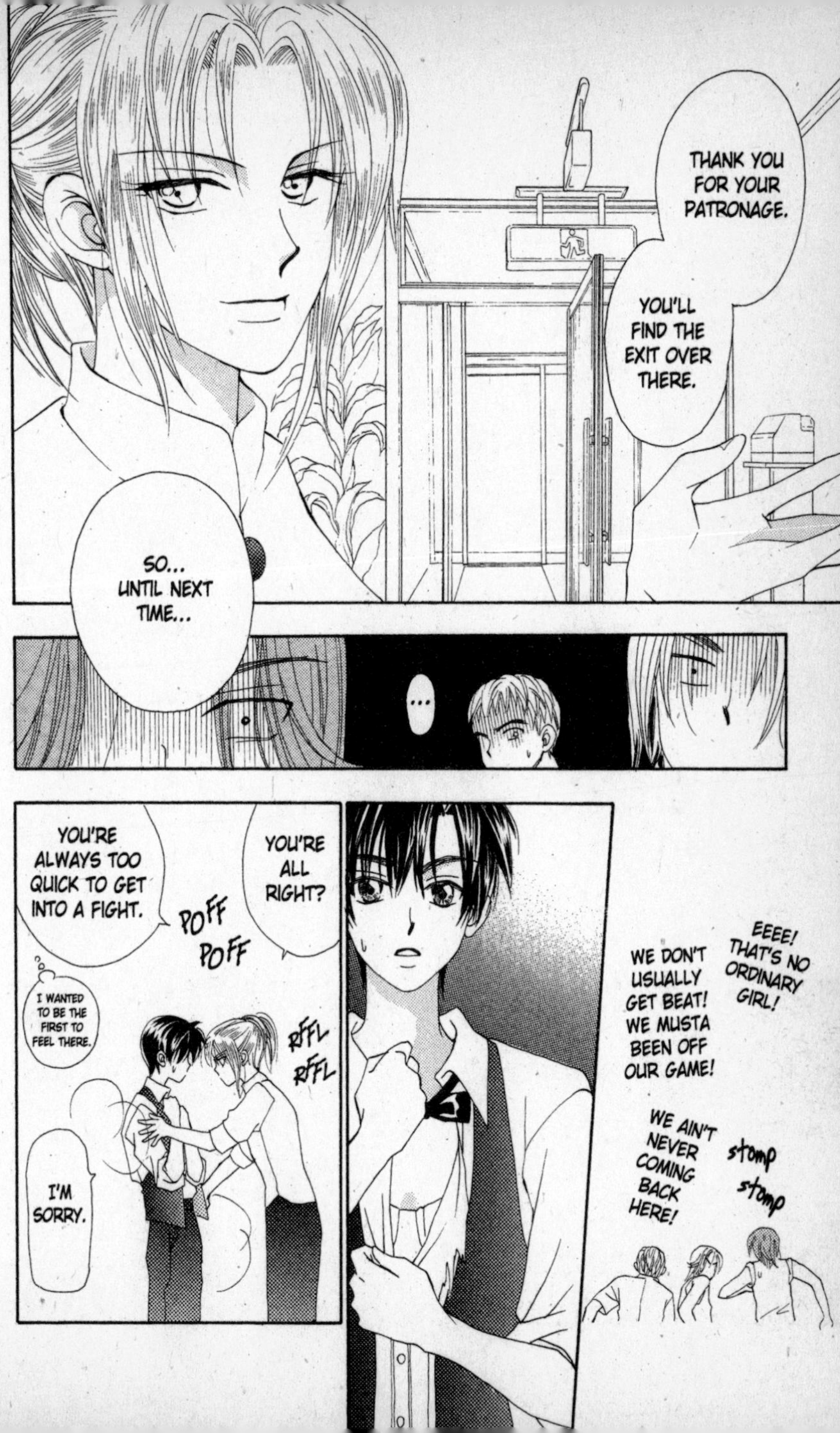
THANK YOU FOR YOUR PATRONAGE.
YOU'LL FIND THE EXIT OVER THERE.
SO... UNTIL NEXT TIME...
...
EEEE! THAT'S NO ORDINARY GIRL!
WE DON'T USUALLY GET BEAT! WE MUSTA BEEN OFF OUR GAME!
WE AIN'T NEVER COMING BACK HERE!
stomp stomp
YOU'RE ALL RIGHT?
POFF POFF
YOU'RE ALWAYS TOO QUICK TO GET INTO A FIGHT.
I WANTED TO BE THE FIRST TO FEEL THERE.
RFFL RFFL
I'M SORRY.

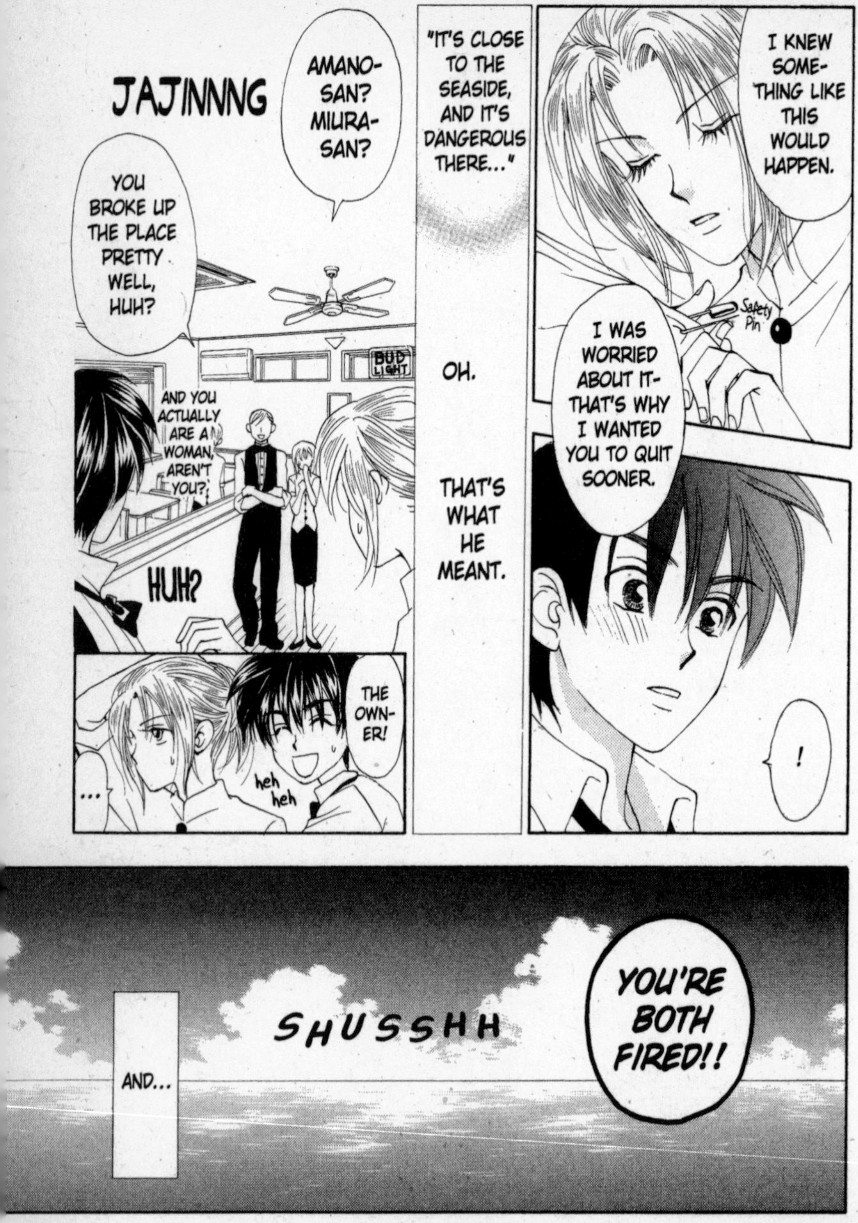
I KNEW SOMETHING LIKE THIS WOULD HAPPEN.
Safety Pin
I WAS WORRIED ABOUT IT- THAT'S WHY I WANTED YOU TO QUIT SOONER.
!
"IT'S CLOSE TO THE SEASIDE, AND IT'S DANGEROUS THERE..."
OH.
THAT'S WHAT HE MEANT.
AMANO-SAN? MIURA-SAN?
JAJINNNG
YOU BROKE UP THE PLACE PRETTY WELL, HUH?
BUD LIGHT
AND YOU ACTUALLY ARE A WOMAN, AREN'T YOU?
HUH?
THE OWNER!
heh heh
...
YOU'RE BOTH FIRED!!
SHUSSHH
AND...

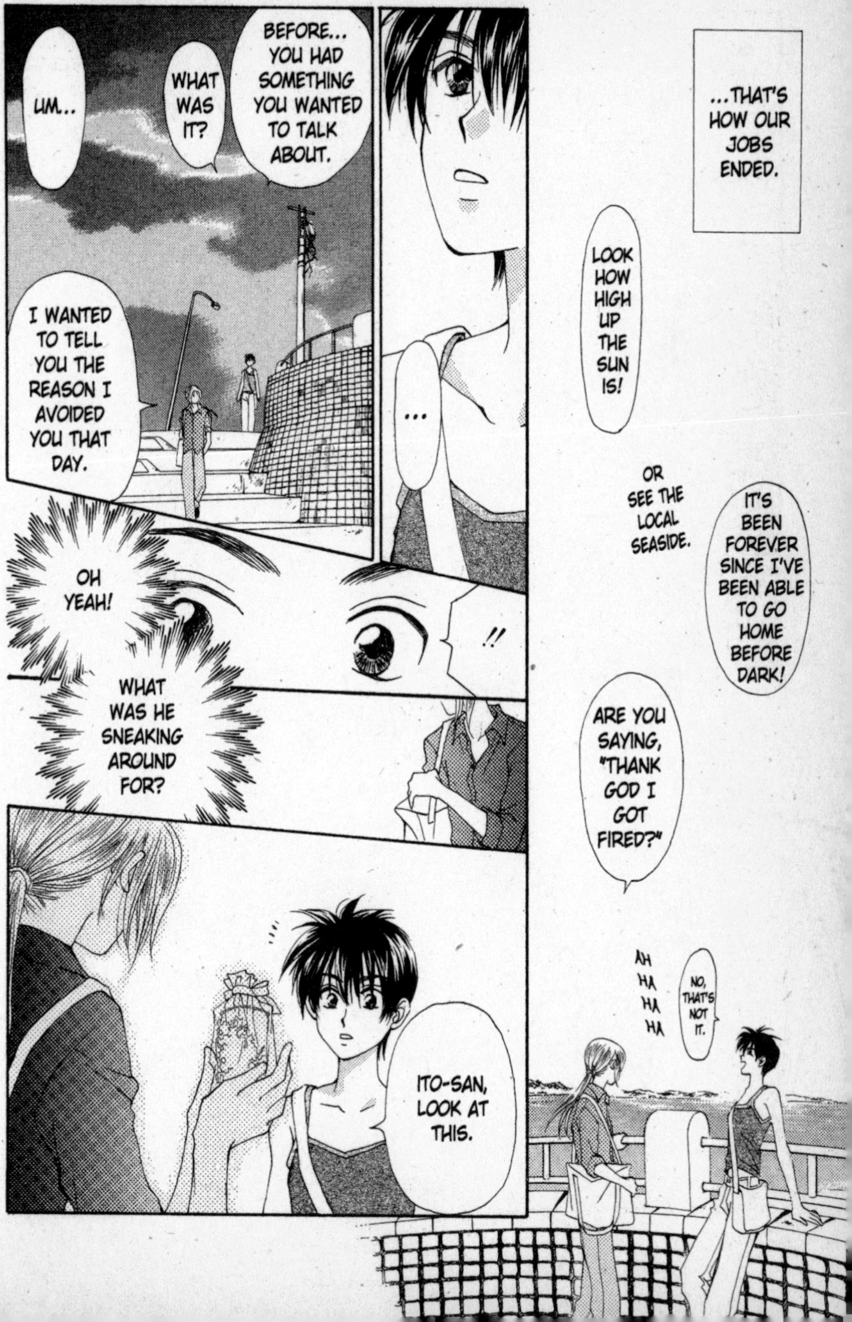
...THAT'S HOW OUR JOBS ENDED.
LOOK HOW HIGH UP THE SUN IS!
IT'S BEEN FOREVER SINCE I'VE BEEN ABLE TO GO HOME BEFORE DARK!
OR SEE THE LOCAL SEASIDE.
ARE YOU SAYING, "THANK GOD I GOT FIRED?"
NO, THAT'S NOT IT.
AH HA HA HA
...
BEFORE... YOU HAD SOMETHING YOU WANTED TO TALK ABOUT.
WHAT WAS IT?
UM...
I WANTED TO TELL YOU THE REASON I AVOIDED YOU THAT DAY.
!!
OH YEAH!
WHAT WAS HE SNEAKING AROUND FOR?
ITO-SAN, LOOK AT THIS.

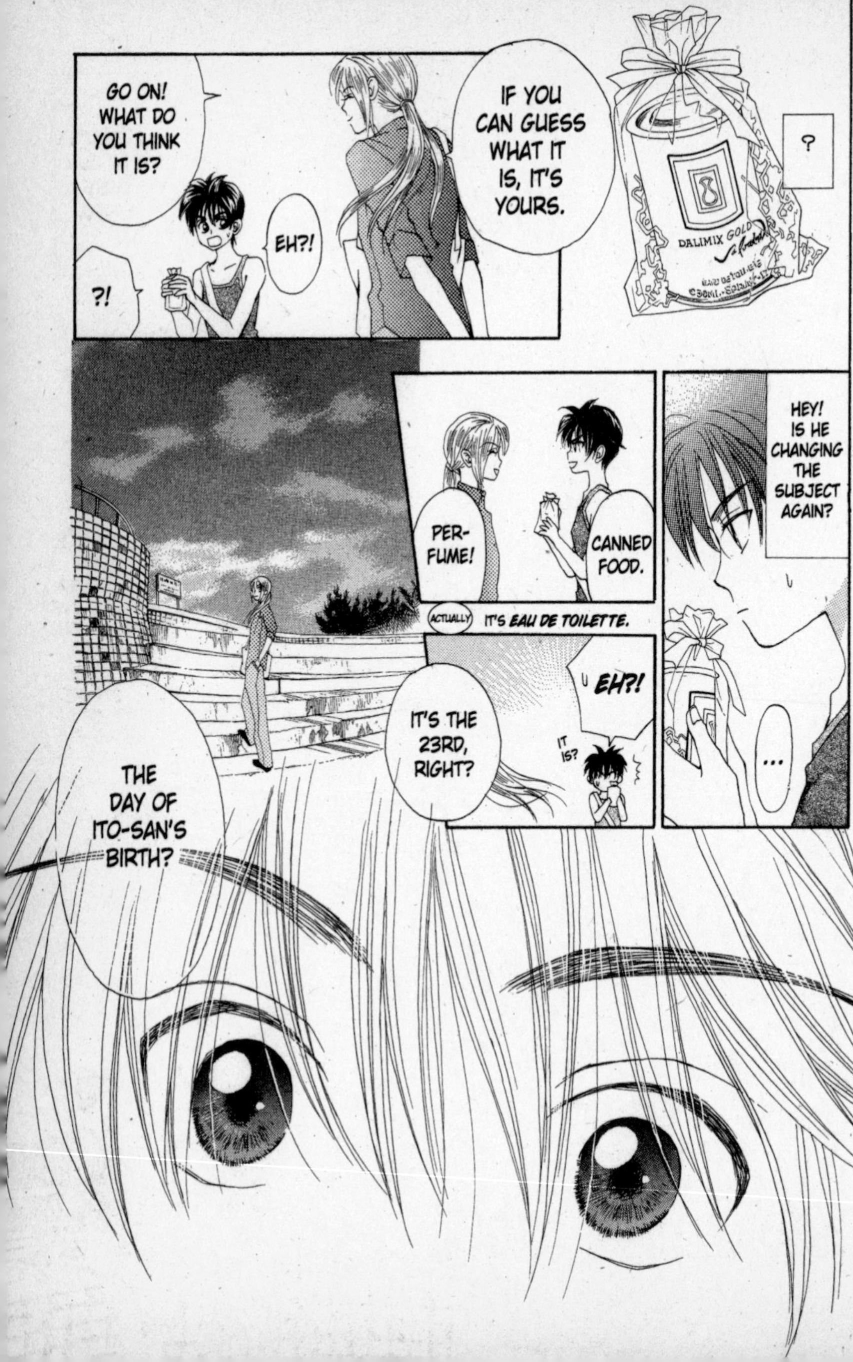
?
DALIMIX GOLD
IF YOU CAN GUESS WHAT IT IS, IT'S YOURS.
GO ON! WHAT DO YOU THINK IT IS?
EH?!
?!
HEY! IS HE CHANGING THE SUBJECT AGAIN?
...
CANNED FOOD.
PER-FUME!
ACTUALLY IT'S EAU DE TOILETTE.
EH?!
IT IS?
IT'S THE 23RD, RIGHT?
THE DAY OF ITO-SAN'S BIRTH?

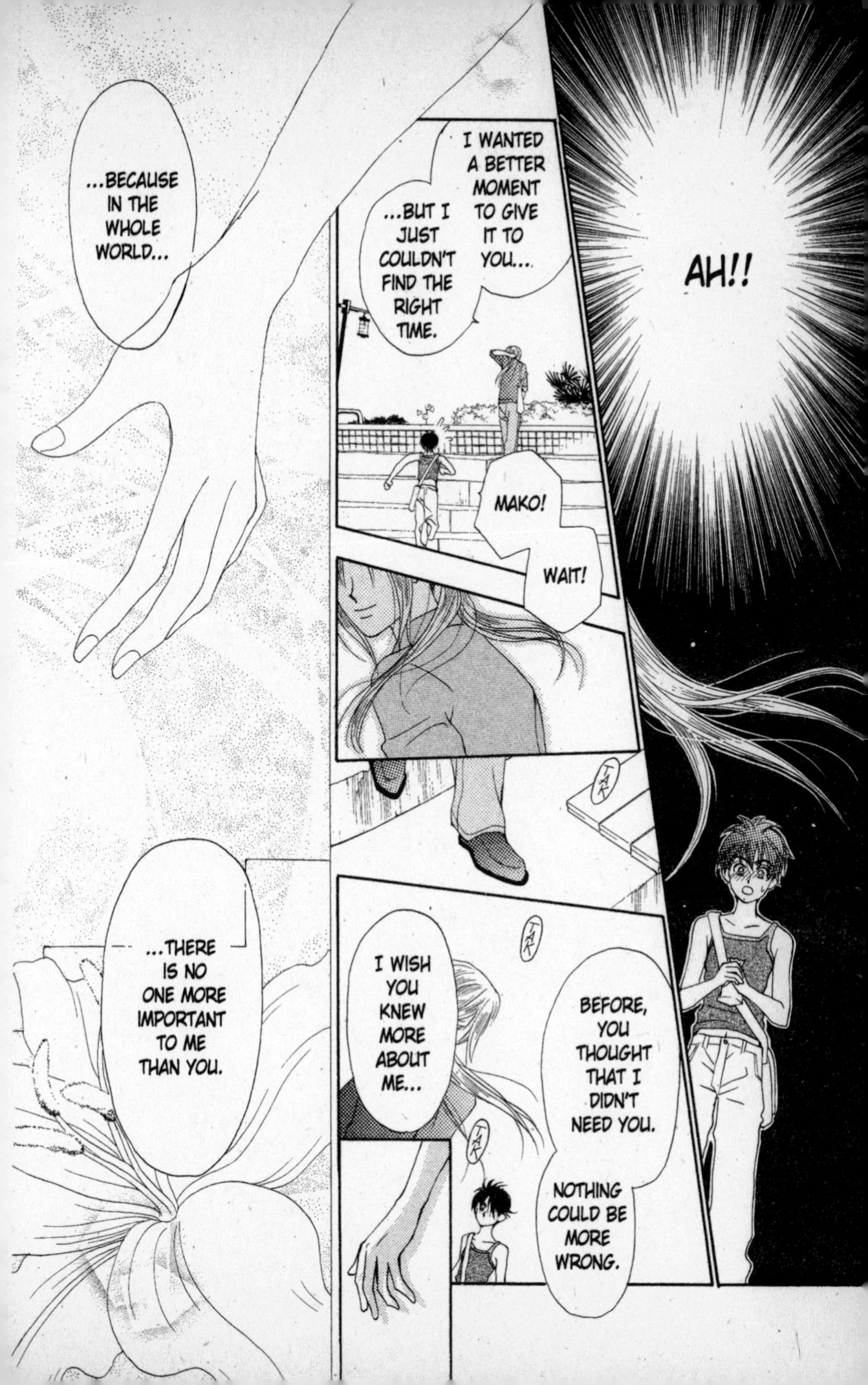
AH!!
I WANTED A BETTER MOMENT TO GIVE IT TO YOU...
...BUT I JUST COULDN'T FIND THE RIGHT TIME.
MAKO!
WAIT!
TAK
TAK
BEFORE, YOU THOUGHT THAT I DIDN'T NEED YOU.
NOTHING COULD BE MORE WRONG.
I WISH YOU KNEW MORE ABOUT ME...
TAK
...BECAUSE IN THE WHOLE WORLD...
...THERE IS NO ONE MORE IMPORTANT TO ME THAN YOU.

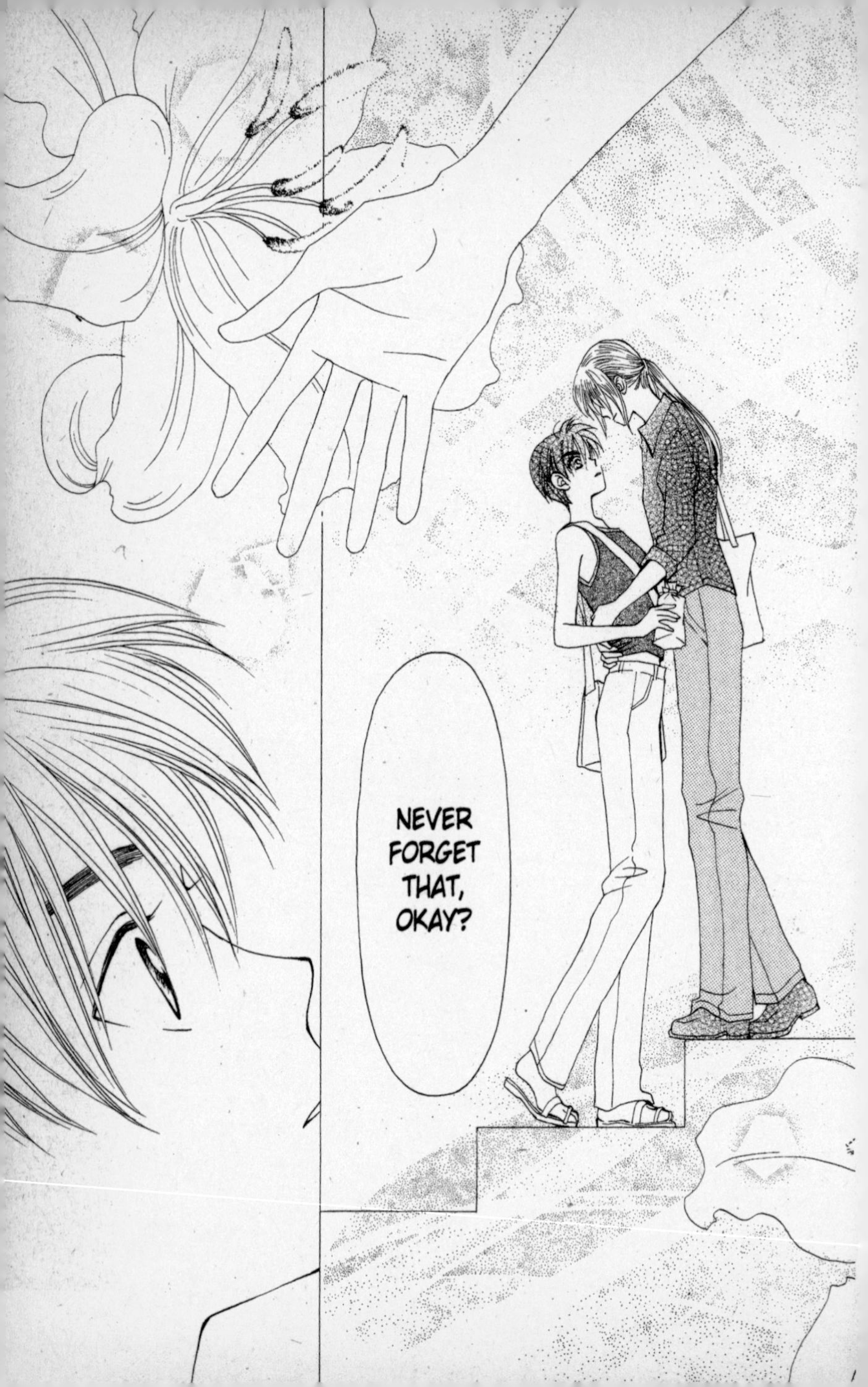
NEVER FORGET THAT, OKAY?

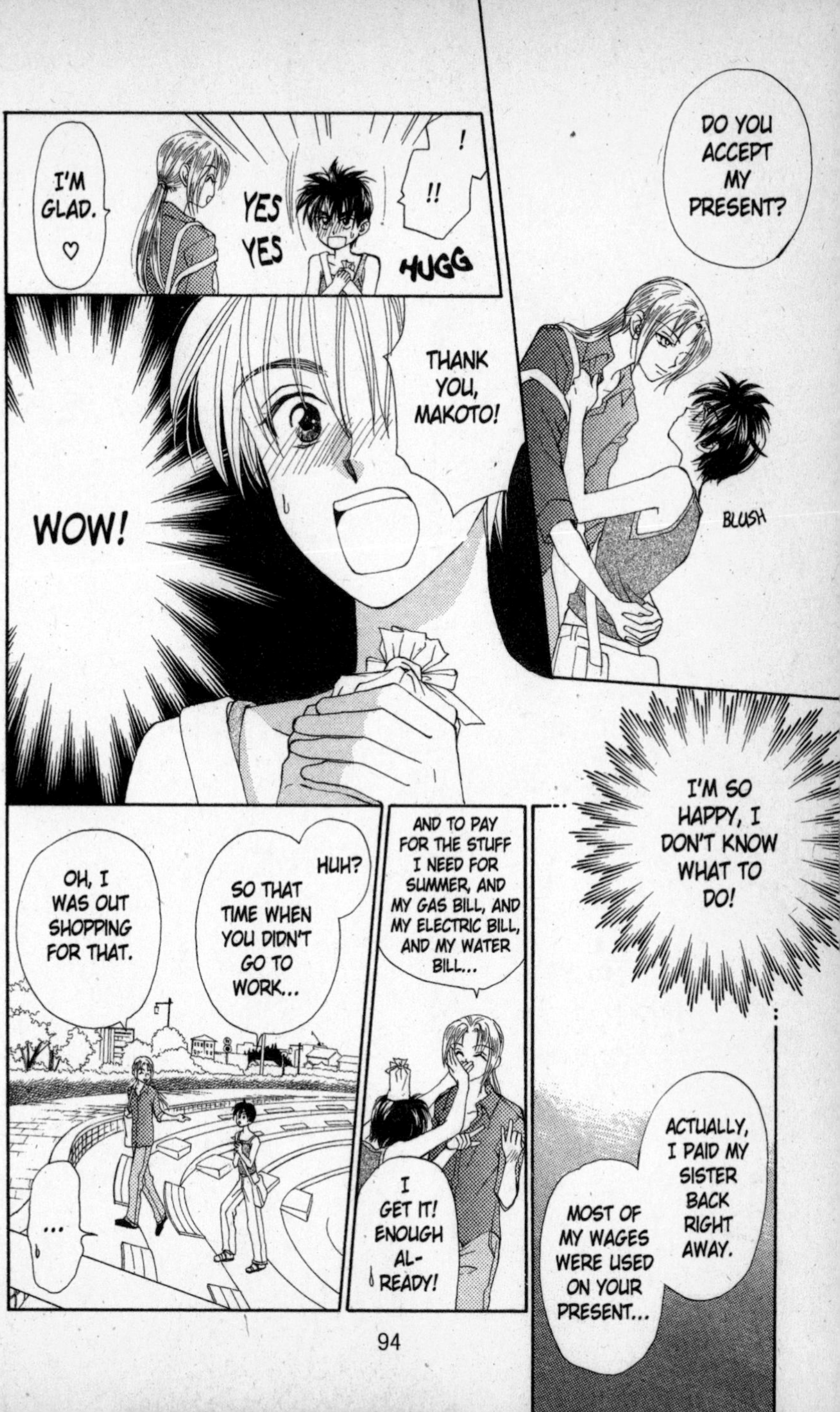

DO YOU ACCEPT MY PRESENT?
BLUSH
!
!!
HUGG
YES YES
I'M GLAD. ♡
THANK YOU, MAKOTO!
WOW!
I'M SO HAPPY, I DON'T KNOW WHAT TO DO!
ACTUALLY, I PAID MY SISTER BACK RIGHT AWAY.
MOST OF MY WAGES WERE USED ON YOUR PRESENT...
AND TO PAY FOR THE STUFF I NEED FOR SUMMER, AND MY GAS BILL, AND MY ELECTRIC BILL, AND MY WATER BILL...
I GET IT! ENOUGH AL-READY!
HUH?
SO THAT TIME WHEN YOU DIDN'T GO TO WORK...
OH, I WAS OUT SHOPPING FOR THAT.
...

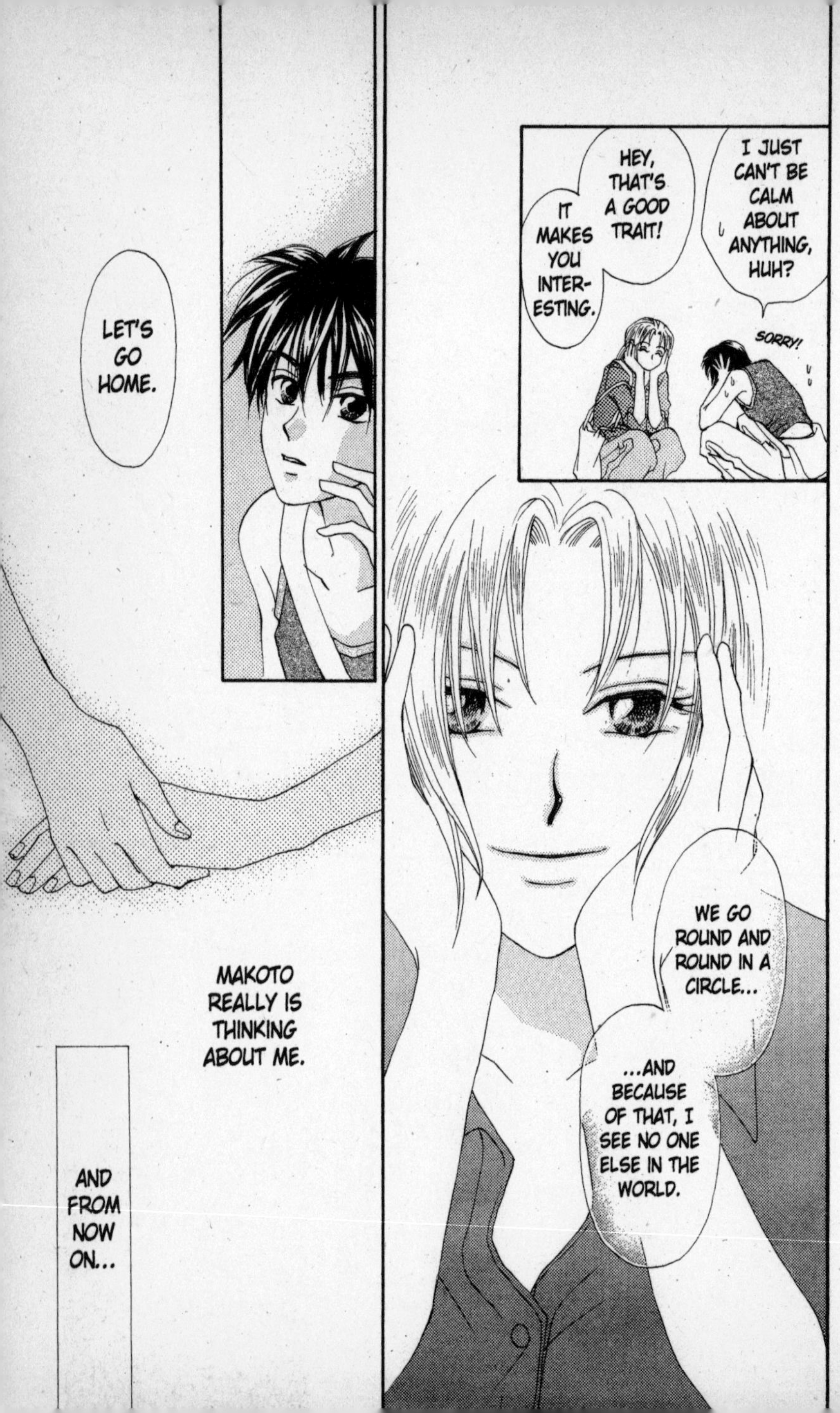
I JUST CAN'T BE CALM ABOUT ANYTHING, HUH?
SORRY!
HEY, THAT'S A GOOD TRAIT!
IT MAKES YOU INTER-ESTING.
WE GO ROUND AND ROUND IN A CIRCLE...
...AND BECAUSE OF THAT, I SEE NO ONE ELSE IN THE WORLD.
LET'S GO HOME.
MAKOTO REALLY IS THINKING ABOUT ME.
AND FROM NOW ON...

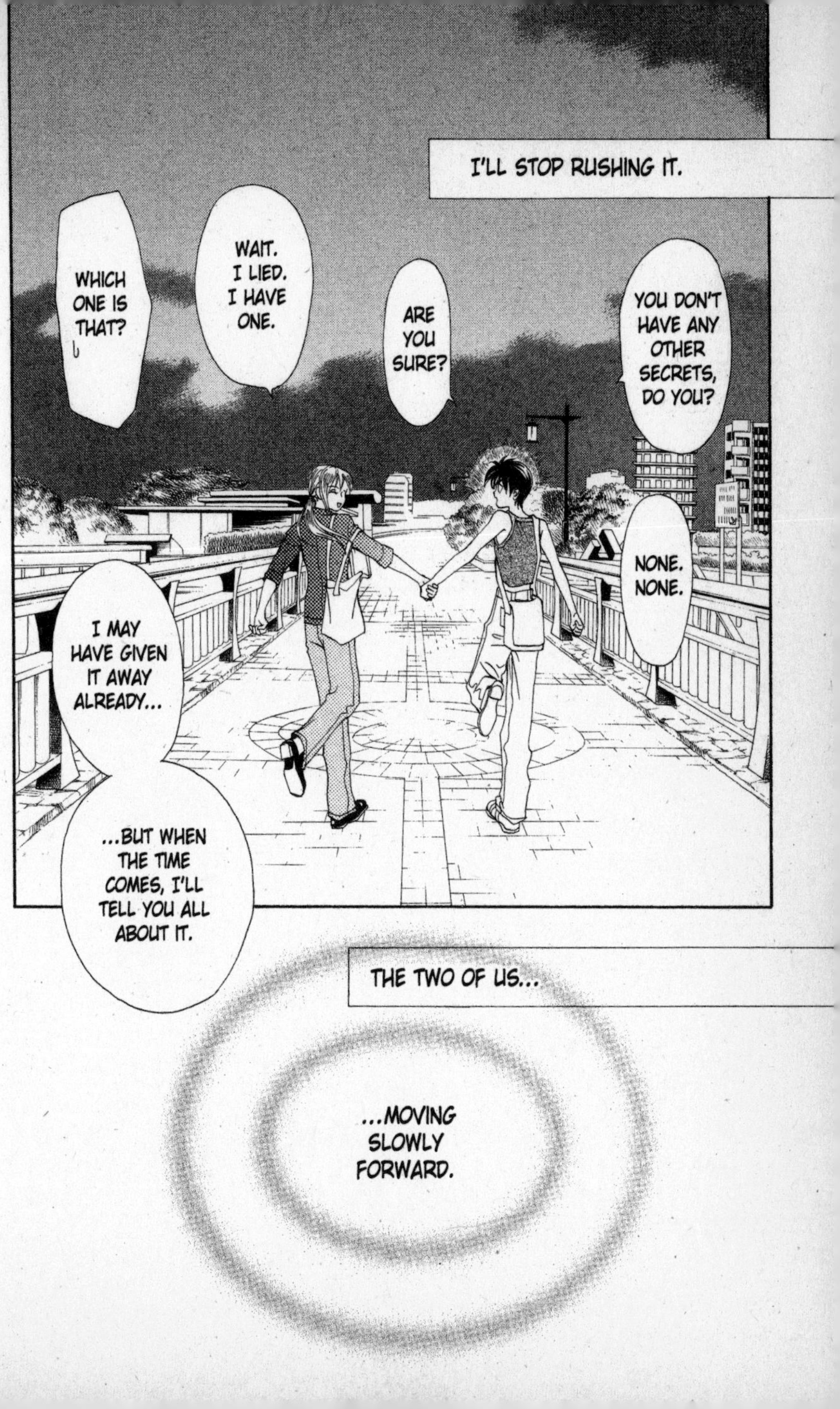
I'LL STOP RUSHING IT.
YOU DON'T HAVE ANY OTHER SECRETS, DO YOU?
NONE. NONE.
ARE YOU SURE?
WAIT. I LIED. I HAVE ONE.
WHICH ONE IS THAT?
I MAY HAVE GIVEN IT AWAY ALREADY...
...BUT WHEN THE TIME COMES, I'LL TELL YOU ALL ABOUT IT.
THE TWO OF US...
...MOVING SLOWLY FORWARD.

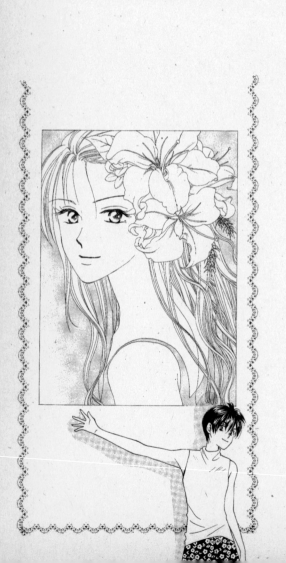

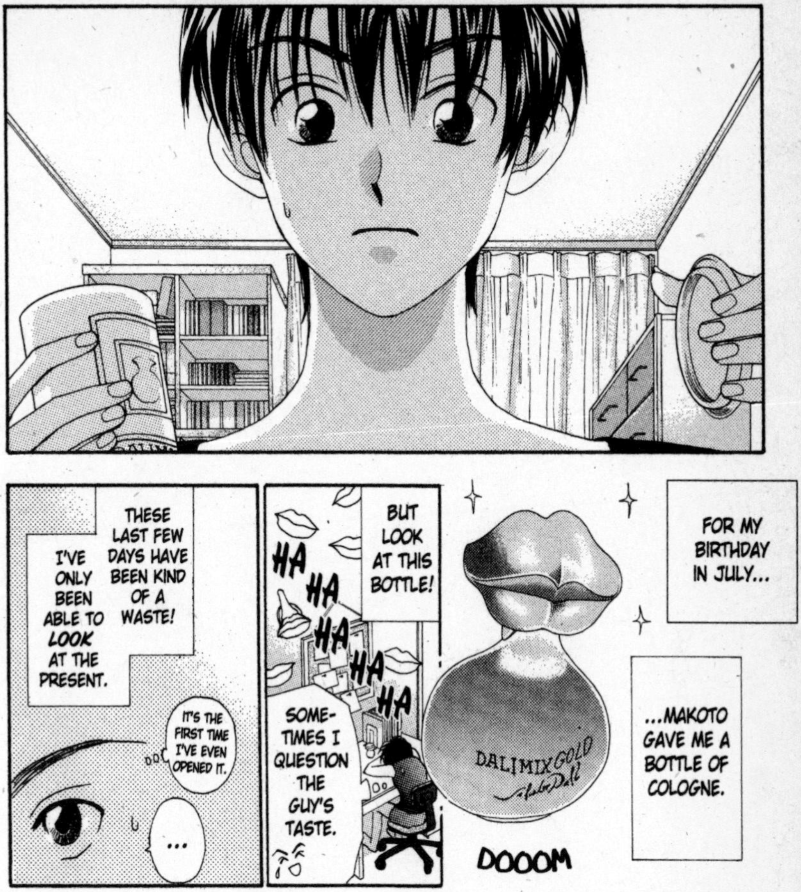
FOR MY BIRTHDAY IN JULY...
...MAKOTO GAVE ME A BOTTLE OF COLOGNE.
DALIMIX GOLD
DOOOM
BUT LOOK AT THIS BOTTLE!
HA HA HA HA HA HA
SOME-TIMES I QUESTION THE GUY'S TASTE.
THESE LAST FEW DAYS HAVE BEEN KIND OF A WASTE!
I'VE ONLY BEEN ABLE TO LOOK AT THE PRESENT.
IT'S THE FIRST TIME I'VE EVEN OPENED IT.
...

-Behind the Scenes Story- ③

When I first came up with the idea of Kô-chan, the image I had of him was a younger version of Takky (Hideaki Takizawa)! But if you ask what happened... Well, now his face is different. But I really have fun drawing him! I love cute young guys! In fact, in the future, I plan to draw more easy-for-Emura-to-draw faces like Kô-chan and Nobuko! They may be easy to draw, or they may just be less stressful to draw... Anyway they are faces that I just draw a lot! For guys, faces like Ito's and Yoshirô's are classic easy-to-draw types. Although Ito is a girl... But since faces tend to change over the course of a manga series, their faces won't always be the same.

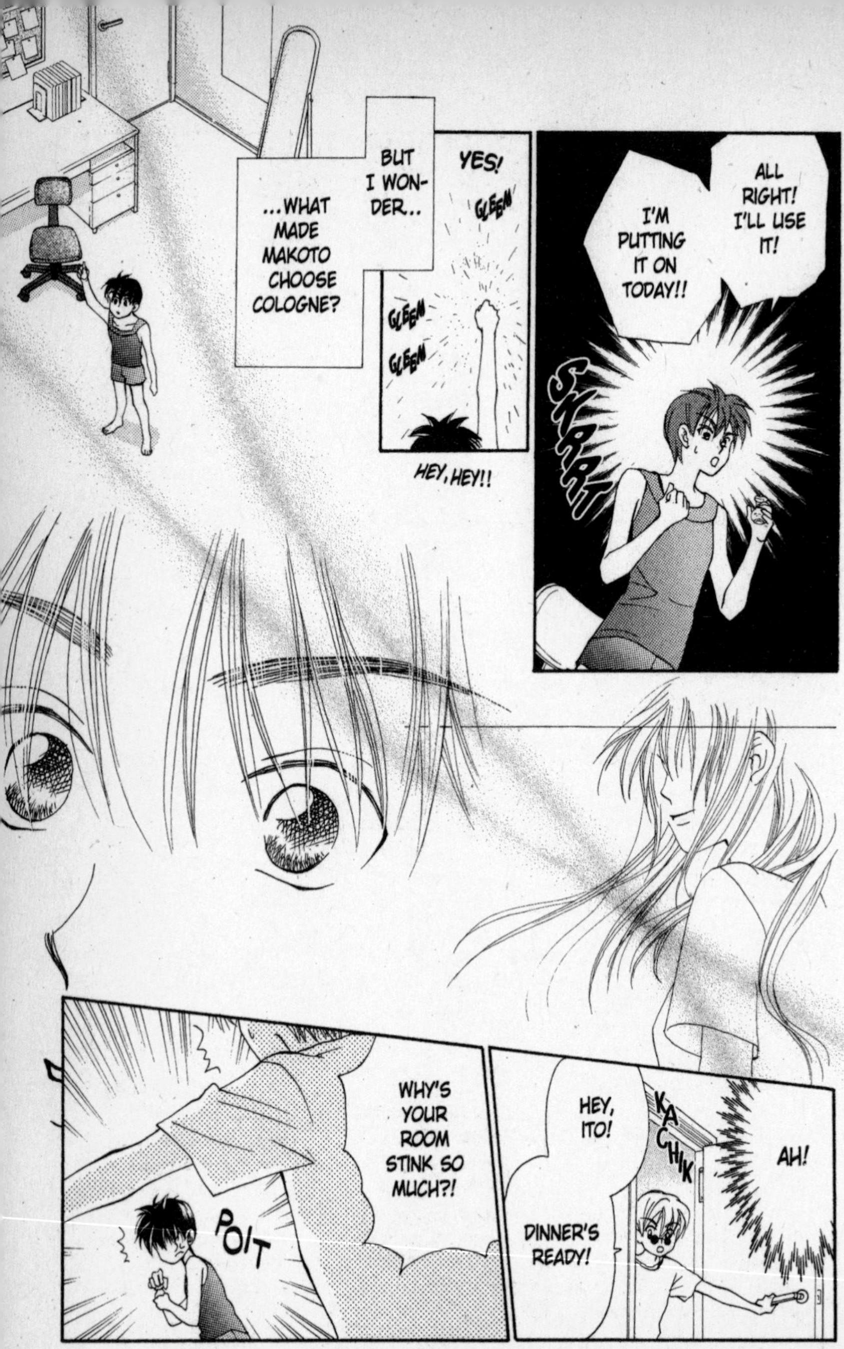
ALL RIGHT! I'LL USE IT!
I'M PUTTING IT ON TODAY!!
SKRAT
YES!
GLEEM
GLEEM
GLEEM
HEY, HEY!!
BUT I WON-DER...
...WHAT MADE MAKOTO CHOOSE COLOGNE?
AH!
KACHIK
HEY, ITO!
DINNER'S READY!
WHY'S YOUR ROOM STINK SO MUCH?!
POIT

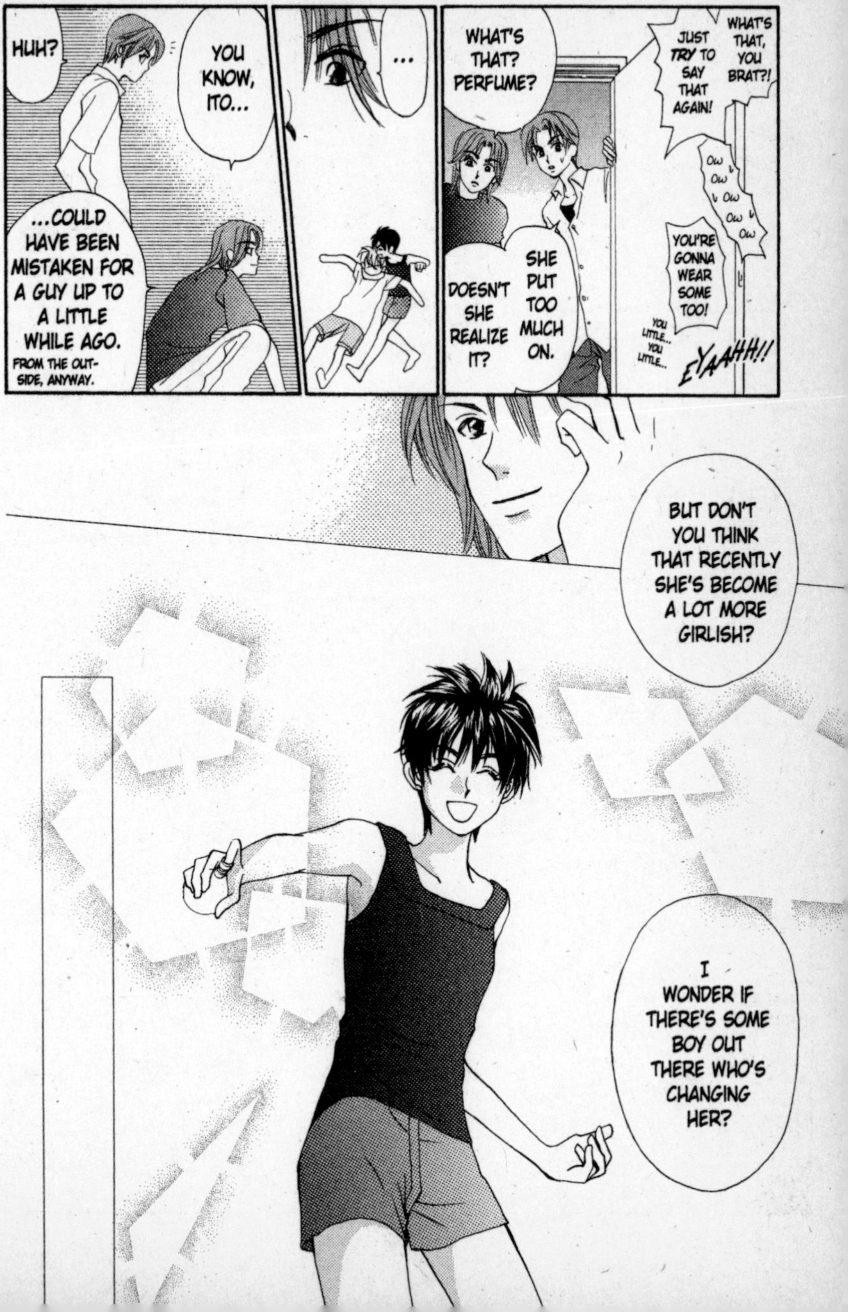
WHAT'S THAT, YOU BRAT?!
JUST TRY TO SAY THAT AGAIN!
WHAT'S THAT? PERFUME?
OW OW OW OW OW
YOU'RE GONNA WEAR SOME TOO!
SHE PUT TOO MUCH ON.
DOESN'T SHE REALIZE IT?
EYAAHH!!
YOU LITTLE... YOU LITTLE...
...
YOU KNOW, ITO...
HUH?
...COULD HAVE BEEN MISTAKEN FOR A GUY UP TO A LITTLE WHILE AGO.
FROM THE OUT-SIDE, ANYWAY.
BUT DON'T YOU THINK THAT RECENTLY SHE'S BECOME A LOT MORE GIRLISH?
I WONDER IF THERE'S SOME BOY OUT THERE WHO'S CHANGING HER?

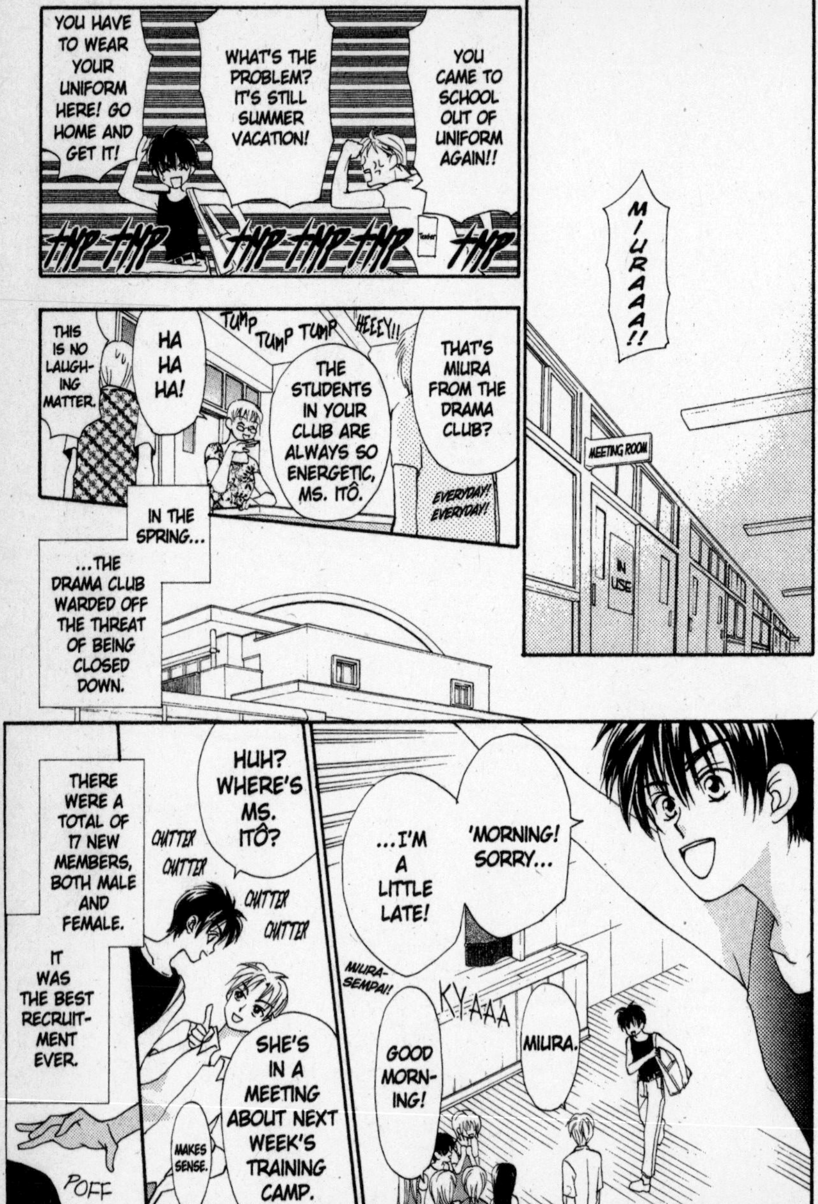
MIURAAAA!!
MEETING ROOM
IN USE
YOU CAME TO SCHOOL OUT OF UNIFORM AGAIN!!
WHAT'S THE PROBLEM? IT'S STILL SUMMER VACATION!
YOU HAVE TO WEAR YOUR UNIFORM HERE! GO HOME AND GET IT!
THP THP THP THP THP THP THP
Teacher
HEEEY!!
THAT'S MIURA FROM THE DRAMA CLUB?
EVERYDAY! EVERYDAY!
TUMP TUMP TUMP
THE STUDENTS IN YOUR CLUB ARE ALWAYS SO ENERGETIC, MS. ITÔ.
HA HA HA!
THIS IS NO LAUGHING MATTER.
IN THE SPRING...
...THE DRAMA CLUB WARDED OFF THE THREAT OF BEING CLOSED DOWN.
'MORNING! SORRY...
...I'M A LITTLE LATE!
MIURA.
KYAAA
MIURA-SEMPAI!
GOOD MORNING!
HUH? WHERE'S MS. ITÔ?
CHATTER CHATTER
CHATTER CHATTER
SHE'S IN A MEETING ABOUT NEXT WEEK'S TRAINING CAMP.
MAKES SENSE.
THERE WERE A TOTAL OF 17 NEW MEMBERS, BOTH MALE AND FEMALE.
IT WAS THE BEST RECRUITMENT EVER.
POFF

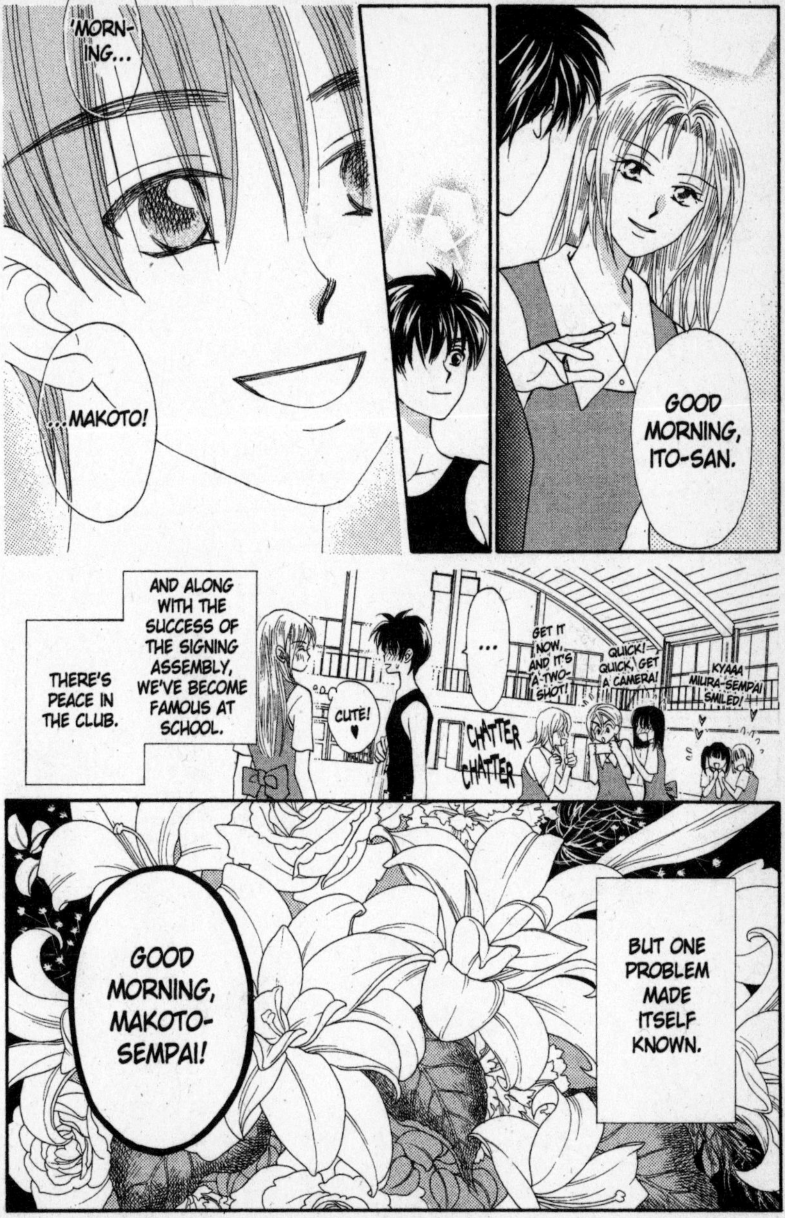
GOOD MORNING, ITO-SAN.
'MORNING...
...MAKOTO!
KYAAA MIURA-SEMPAI SMILED!
QUICK! QUICK, GET A CAMERA!
GET IT NOW, AND IT'S A TWO-SHOT!
...
CHATTER CHATTER
CUTE!
THERE'S PEACE IN THE CLUB.
AND ALONG WITH THE SUCCESS OF THE SIGNING ASSEMBLY, WE'VE BECOME FAMOUS AT SCHOOL.
BUT ONE PROBLEM MADE ITSELF KNOWN.
GOOD MORNING, MAKOTO-SEMPAI!

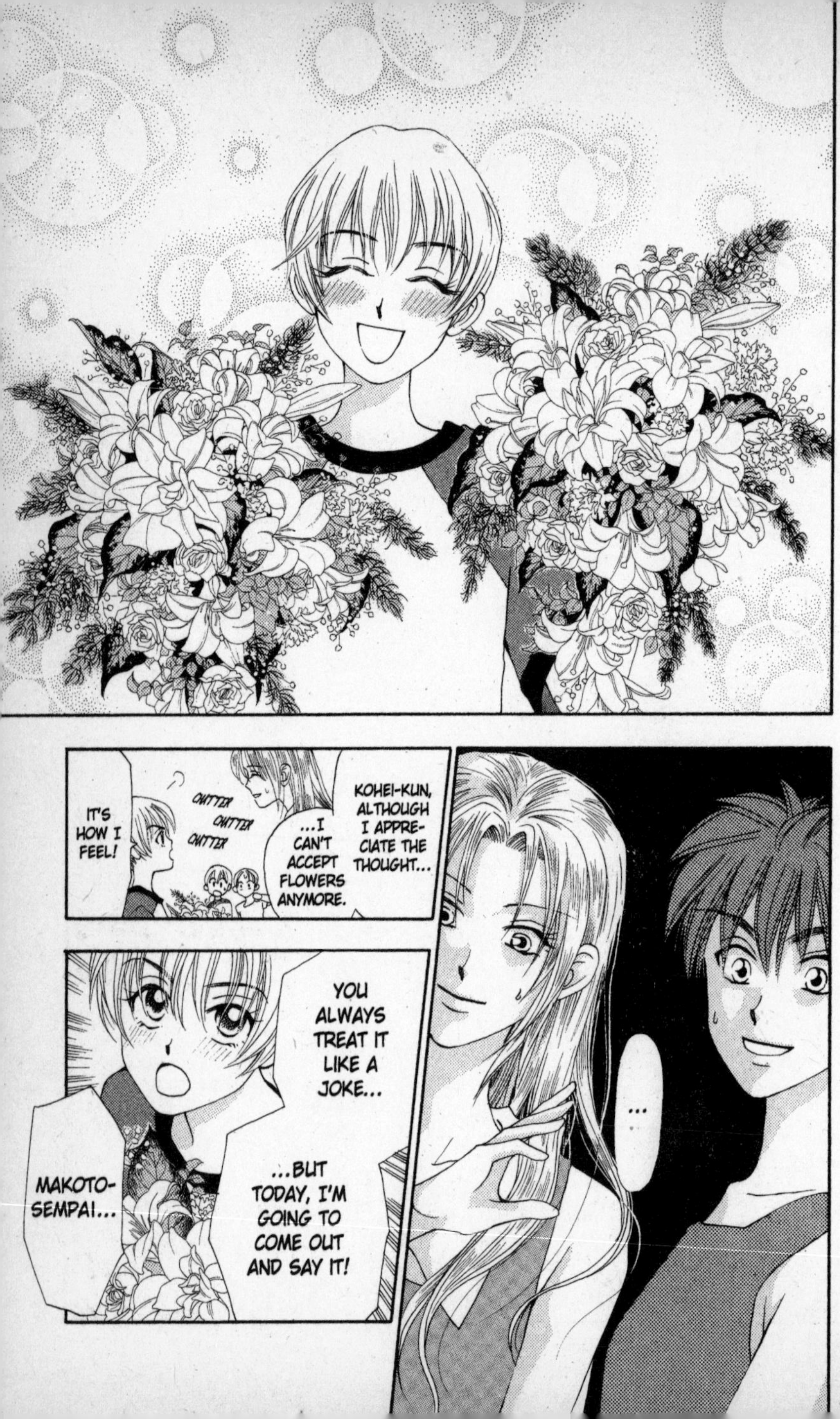
...
KOHEI-KUN, ALTHOUGH I APPRECIATE THE THOUGHT...
...I CAN'T ACCEPT FLOWERS ANYMORE.
CHATTER CHATTER CHATTER
IT'S HOW I FEEL!
YOU ALWAYS TREAT IT LIKE A JOKE...
...BUT TODAY, I'M GOING TO COME OUT AND SAY IT!
MAKOTO-SEMPAI...

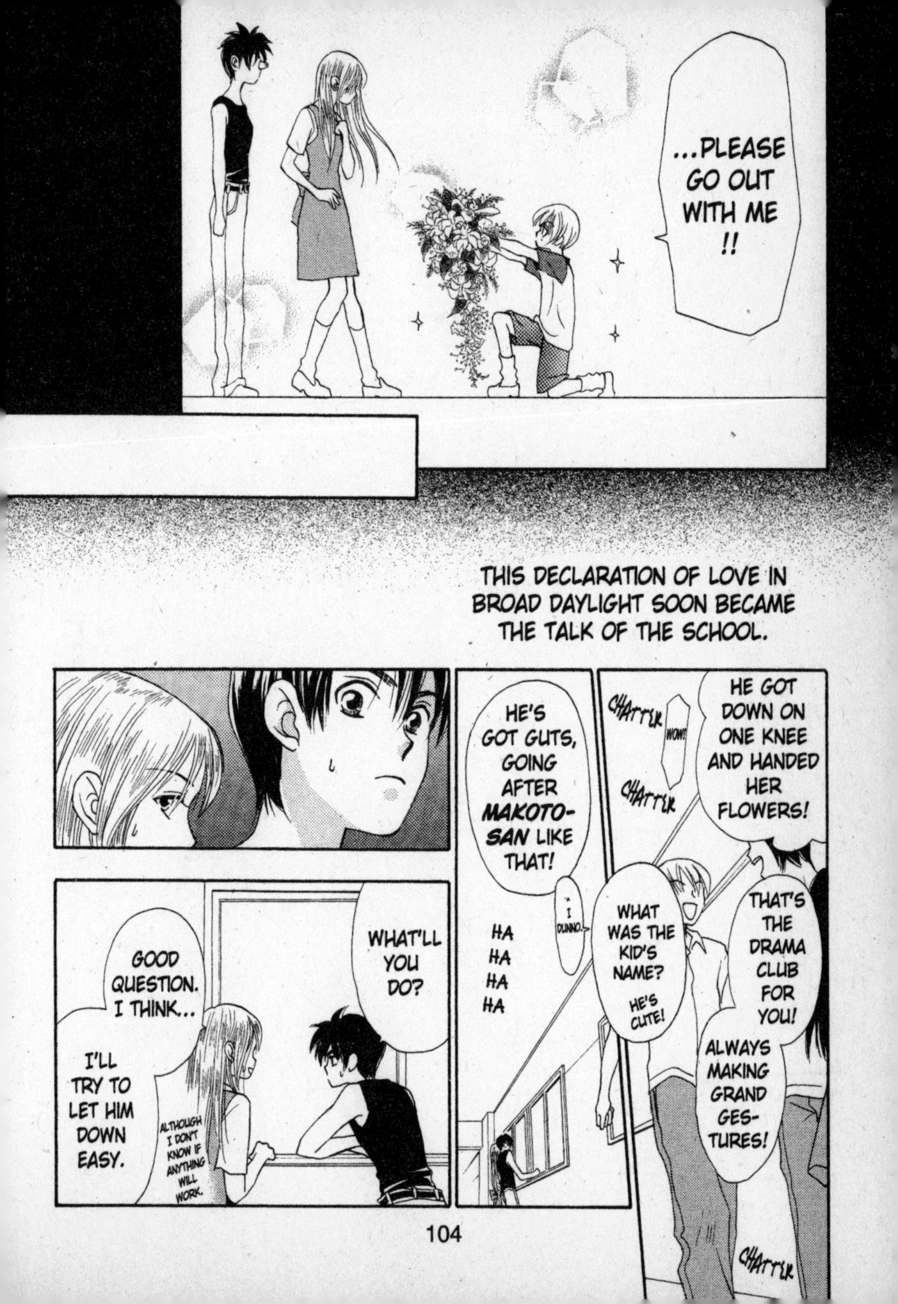
...PLEASE GO OUT WITH ME !!
THIS DECLARATION OF LOVE IN BROAD DAYLIGHT SOON BECAME THE TALK OF THE SCHOOL.
HE GOT DOWN ON ONE KNEE AND HANDED HER FLOWERS!
CHATTER
WOW!
CHATTER
HE'S GOT GUTS, GOING AFTER MAKOTO-SAN LIKE THAT!
THAT'S THE DRAMA CLUB FOR YOU!
ALWAYS MAKING GRAND GES-TURES!
WHAT WAS THE KID'S NAME?
HE'S CUTE!
I DUNNO.
HA HA HA HA
CHATTER
WHAT'LL YOU DO?
GOOD QUESTION. I THINK...
I'LL TRY TO LET HIM DOWN EASY.
ALTHOUGH I DON'T KNOW IF ANYTHING WILL WORK.

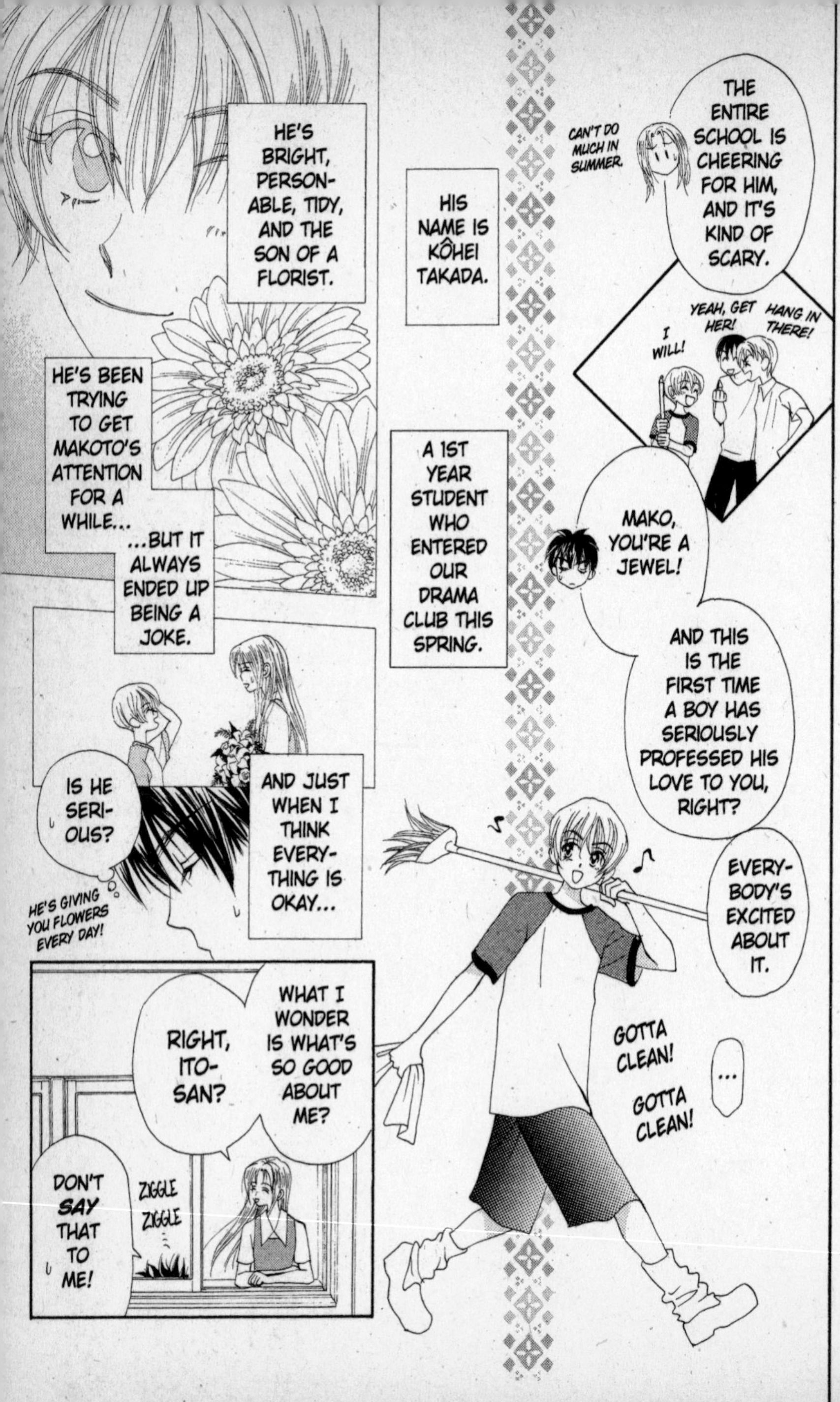
CAN'T DO MUCH IN SUMMER.
THE ENTIRE SCHOOL IS CHEERING FOR HIM, AND IT'S KIND OF SCARY.
HANG IN THERE!
YEAH, GET HER!
I WILL!
MAKO, YOU'RE A JEWEL!
AND THIS IS THE FIRST TIME A BOY HAS SERIOUSLY PROFESSED HIS LOVE TO YOU, RIGHT?
EVERYBODY'S EXCITED ABOUT IT.
GOTTA CLEAN!
GOTTA CLEAN!
...
HIS NAME IS KÔHEI TAKADA.
A 1ST YEAR STUDENT WHO ENTERED OUR DRAMA CLUB THIS SPRING.
HE'S BRIGHT, PERSON-ABLE, TIDY, AND THE SON OF A FLORIST.
HE'S BEEN TRYING TO GET MAKOTO'S ATTENTION FOR A WHILE...
...BUT IT ALWAYS ENDED UP BEING A JOKE.
AND JUST WHEN I THINK EVERY-THING IS OKAY...
IS HE SERI-OUS?
HE'S GIVING YOU FLOWERS EVERY DAY!
WHAT I WONDER IS WHAT'S SO GOOD ABOUT ME?
RIGHT, ITO-SAN?
ZIGGLE ZIGGLE
DON'T SAY THAT TO ME!

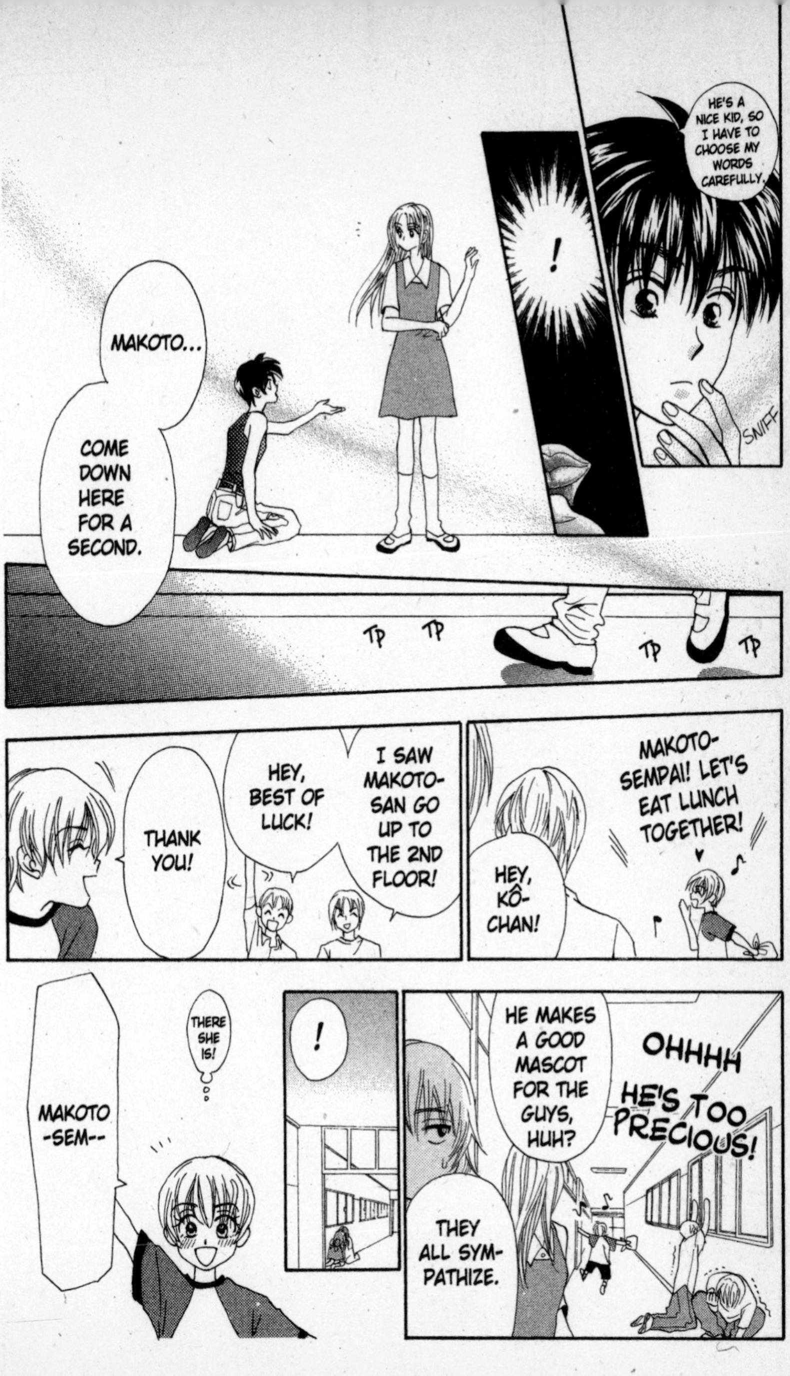
HE'S A NICE KID, SO I HAVE TO CHOOSE MY WORDS CAREFULLY.
SNIFF
!
MAKOTO...
COME DOWN HERE FOR A SECOND.
TP TP TP TP
MAKOTO-SEMPAI! LET'S EAT LUNCH TOGETHER!
HEY, KÔ-CHAN!
I SAW MAKOTO-SAN GO UP TO THE 2ND FLOOR!
HEY, BEST OF LUCK!
THANK YOU!
OHHHH
HE'S TOO PRECIOUS!
HE MAKES A GOOD MASCOT FOR THE GUYS, HUH?
THEY ALL SYMPATHIZE.
!
THERE SHE IS!
MAKOTO -SEM--

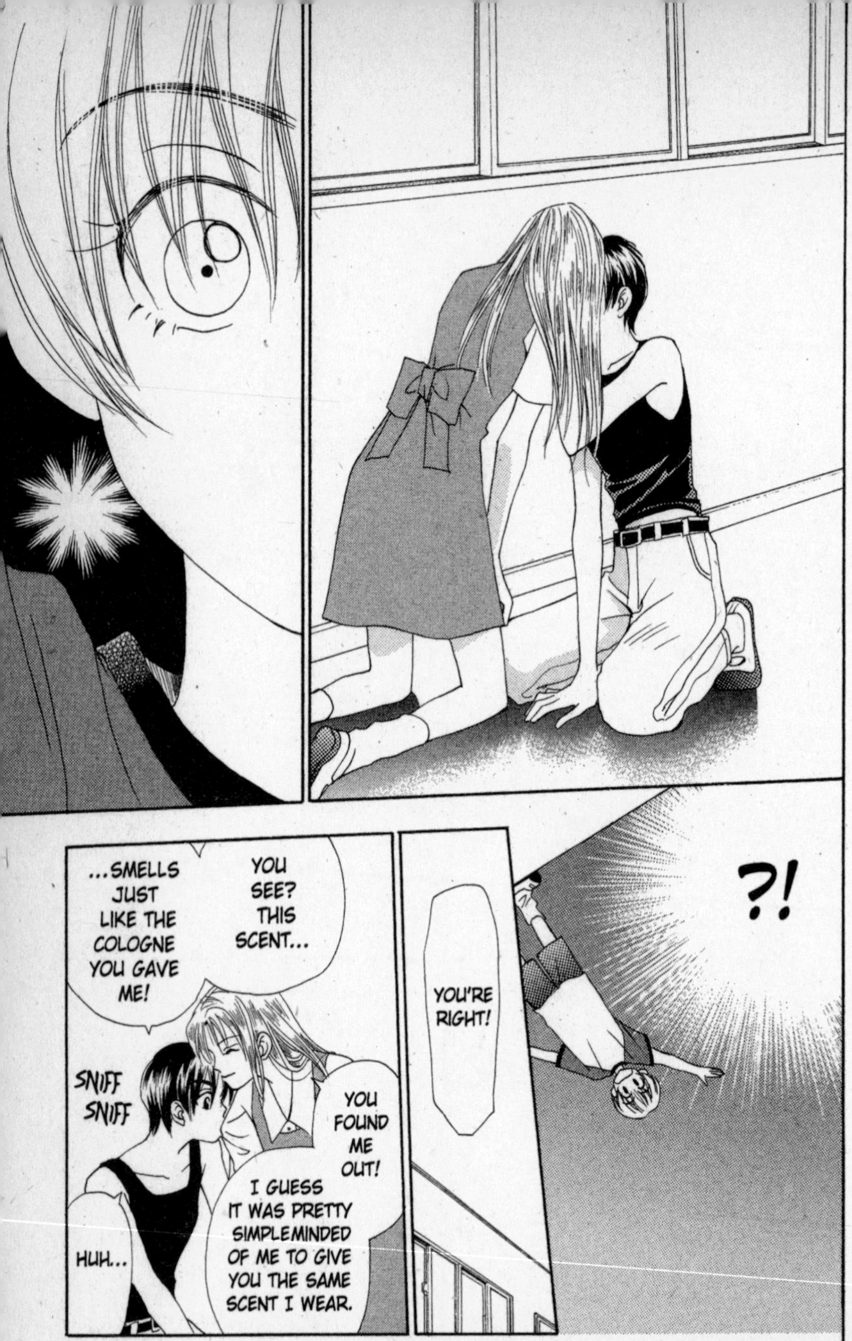
?!
YOU'RE RIGHT!
YOU SEE? THIS SCENT...
...SMELLS JUST LIKE THE COLOGNE YOU GAVE ME!
SNIFF SNIFF
YOU FOUND ME OUT!
I GUESS IT WAS PRETTY SIMPLEMINDED OF ME TO GIVE YOU THE SAME SCENT I WEAR.
HUH...

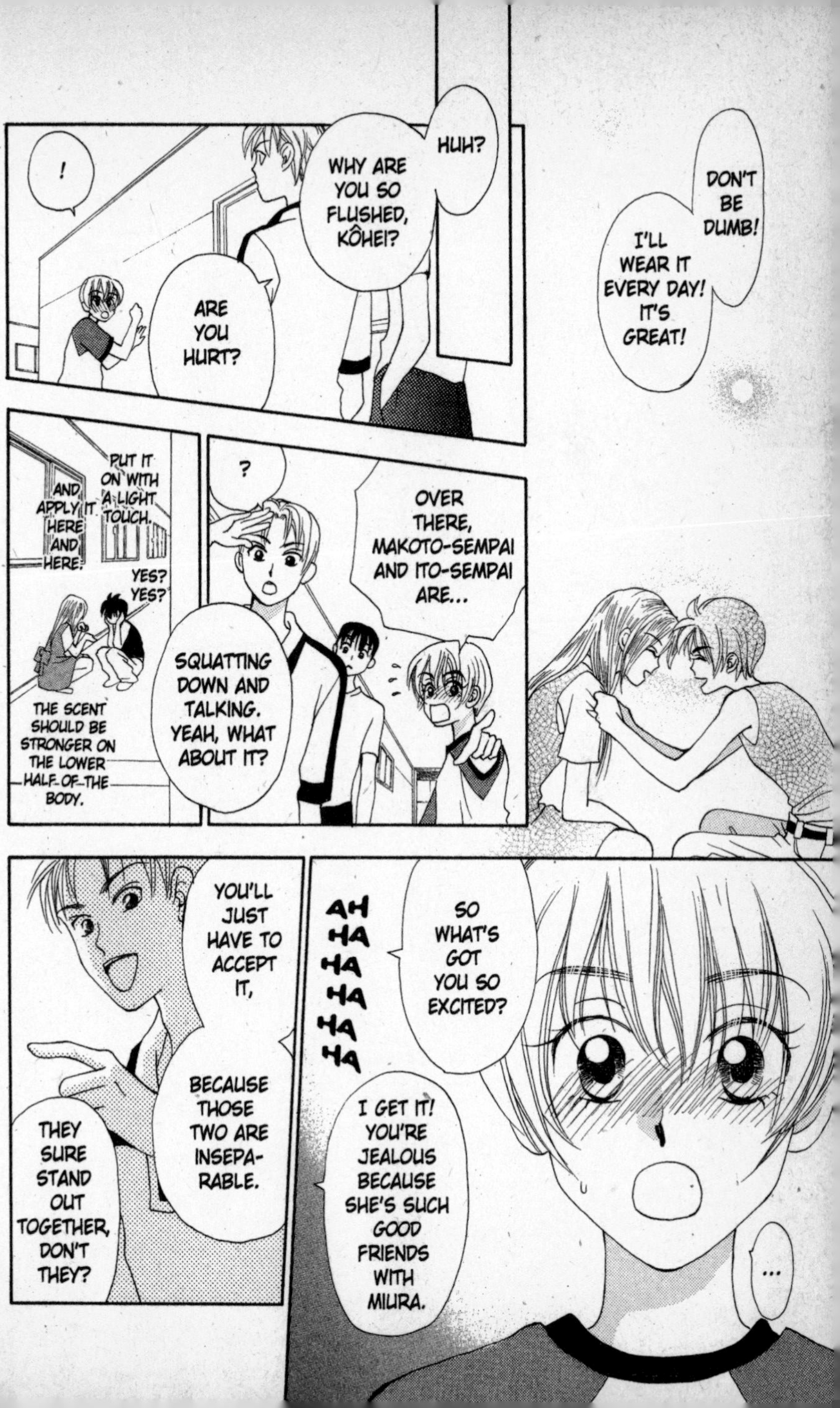

DON'T BE DUMB!
I'LL WEAR IT EVERY DAY! IT'S GREAT!
HUH?
WHY ARE YOU SO FLUSHED, KÔHEI?
ARE YOU HURT?
!
?
OVER THERE, MAKOTO-SEMPAI AND ITO-SEMPAI ARE...
SQUATTING DOWN AND TALKING. YEAH, WHAT ABOUT IT?
PUT IT ON WITH A LIGHT TOUCH.
AND APPLY IT HERE AND HERE.
YES? YES?
THE SCENT SHOULD BE STRONGER ON THE LOWER HALF OF THE BODY.
SO WHAT'S GOT YOU SO EXCITED?
AH HA HA HA HA HA
I GET IT! YOU'RE JEALOUS BECAUSE SHE'S SUCH GOOD FRIENDS WITH MIURA.
...
YOU'LL JUST HAVE TO ACCEPT IT,
BECAUSE THOSE TWO ARE INSEPA-RABLE.
THEY SURE STAND OUT TOGETHER, DON'T THEY?

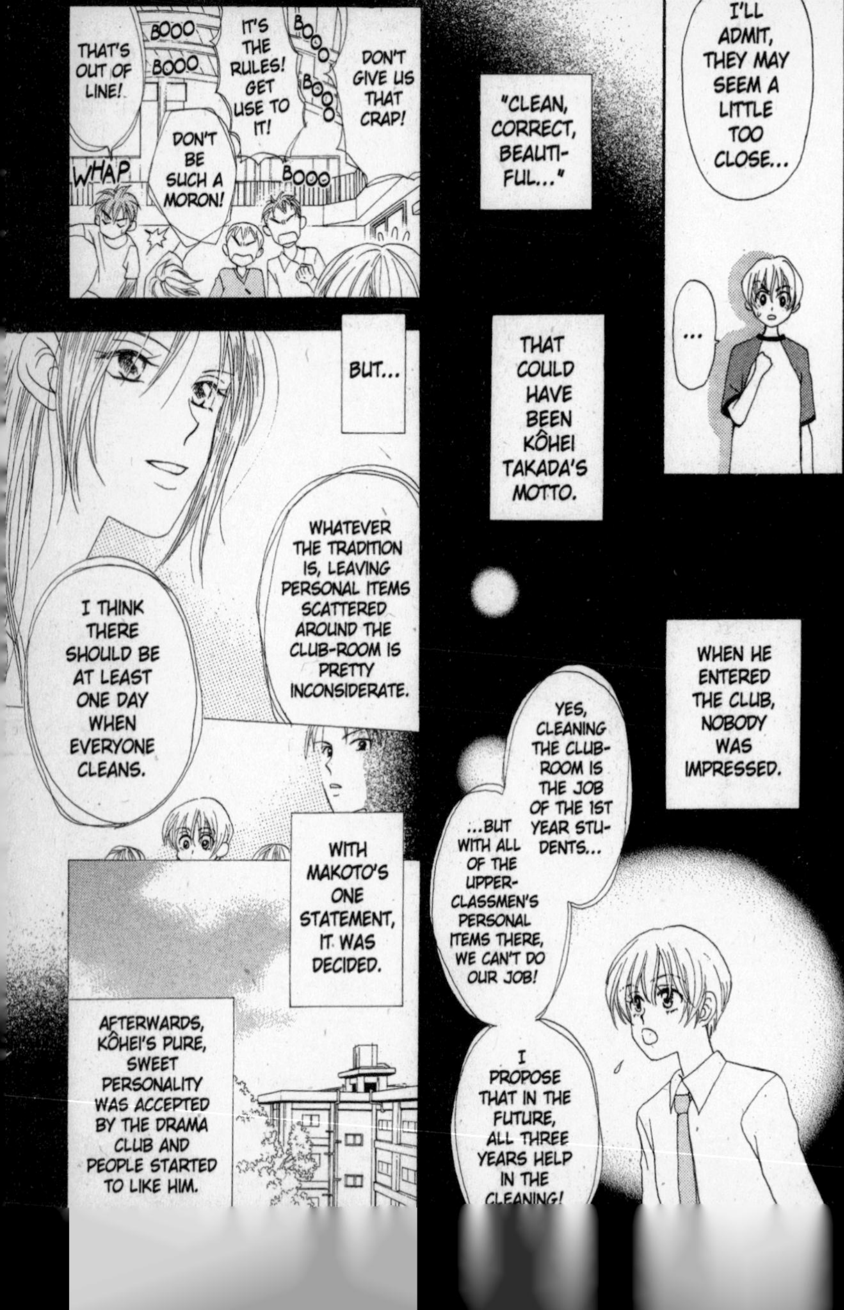
I'LL ADMIT, THEY MAY SEEM A LITTLE TOO CLOSE...
...
"CLEAN, CORRECT, BEAUTI-FUL..."
THAT COULD HAVE BEEN KÔHEI TAKADA'S MOTTO.
WHEN HE ENTERED THE CLUB, NOBODY WAS IMPRESSED.
YES, CLEANING THE CLUB-ROOM IS THE JOB OF THE 1ST YEAR STU-DENTS...
...BUT WITH ALL OF THE UPPER-CLASSMEN'S PERSONAL ITEMS THERE, WE CAN'T DO OUR JOB!
I PROPOSE THAT IN THE FUTURE, ALL THREE YEARS HELP IN THE CLEANING!
DON'T GIVE US THAT CRAP!
BOOO BOOO
IT'S THE RULES! GET USE TO IT!
BOOO
DON'T BE SUCH A MORON!
BOOO BOOO
THAT'S OUT OF LINE!
WHAP
BUT...
WHATEVER THE TRADITION IS, LEAVING PERSONAL ITEMS SCATTERED AROUND THE CLUB-ROOM IS PRETTY INCONSIDERATE.
I THINK THERE SHOULD BE AT LEAST ONE DAY WHEN EVERYONE CLEANS.
WITH MAKOTO'S ONE STATEMENT, IT WAS DECIDED.
AFTERWARDS, KÔHEI'S PURE, SWEET PERSONALITY WAS ACCEPTED BY THE DRAMA CLUB AND PEOPLE STARTED TO LIKE HIM.

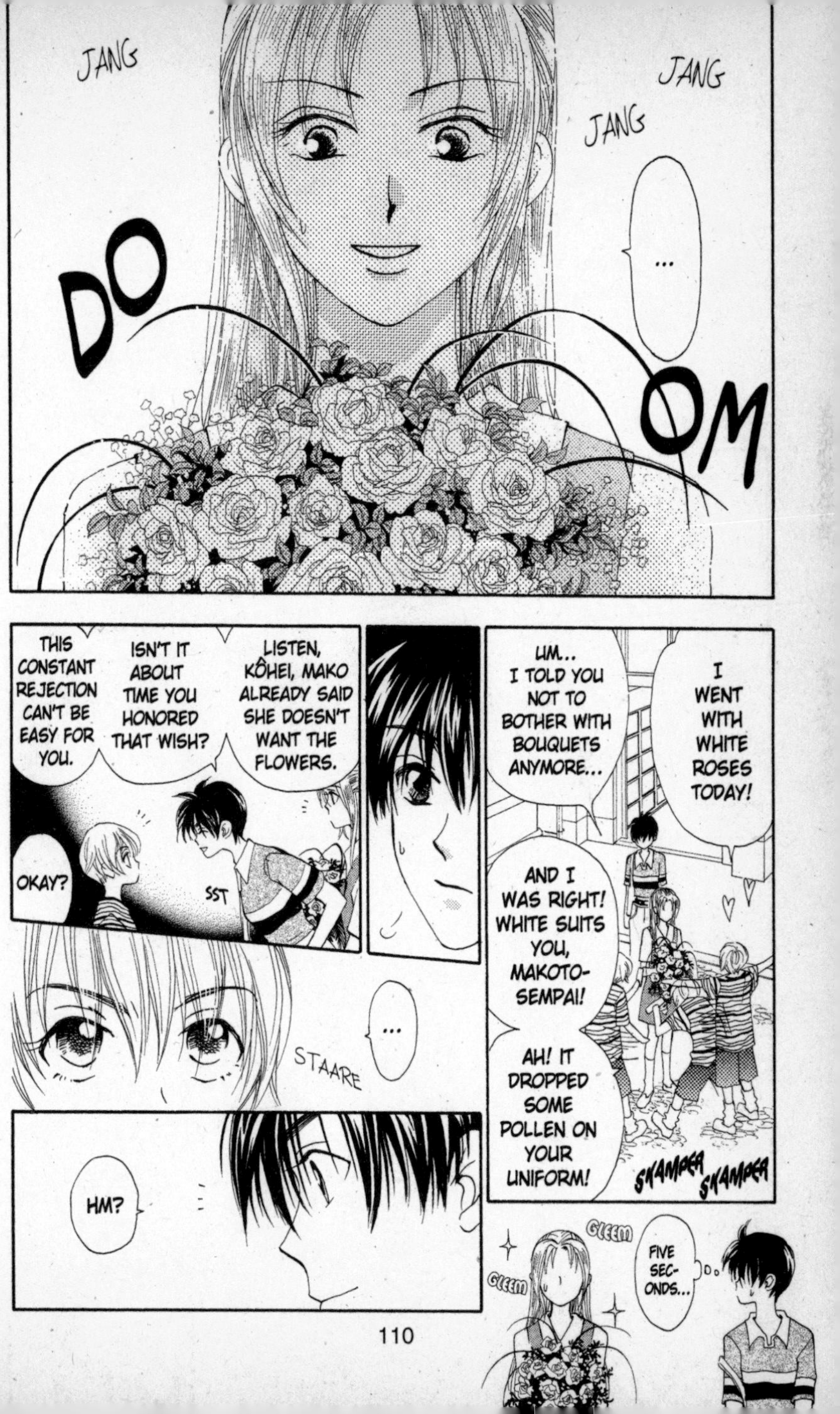
JANG
JANG
JANG
...
DO
OM
I WENT WITH WHITE ROSES TODAY!
UM.. I TOLD YOU NOT TO BOTHER WITH BOUQUETS ANYMORE...
AND I WAS RIGHT! WHITE SUITS YOU, MAKOTO-SEMPAI!
AH! IT DROPPED SOME POLLEN ON YOUR UNIFORM!
SKAMPER SKAMPER
LISTEN, KÔHEI, MAKO ALREADY SAID SHE DOESN'T WANT THE FLOWERS.
ISN'T IT ABOUT TIME YOU HONORED THAT WISH?
THIS CONSTANT REJECTION CAN'T BE EASY FOR YOU.
SST
OKAY?
...
STAARE
HM?
GLEEM
FIVE SEC-ONDS...
GLEEM

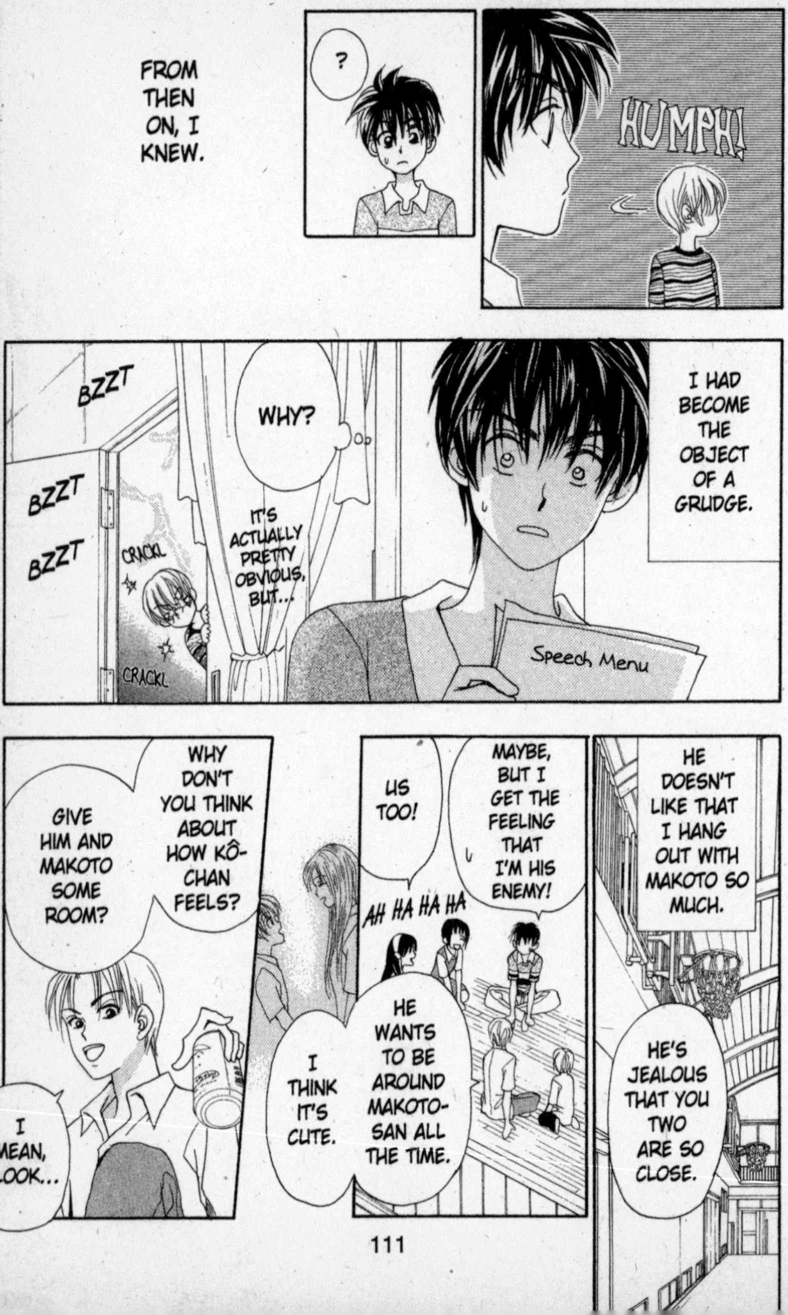
HUMPH!
?
FROM THEN ON, I KNEW.
I HAD BECOME THE OBJECT OF A GRUDGE.
WHY?
IT'S ACTUALLY PRETTY OBVIOUS, BUT...
BZZT
BZZT
BZZT
CRACKL
CRACKL
Speech Menu
HE DOESN'T LIKE THAT I HANG OUT WITH MAKOTO SO MUCH.
HE'S JEALOUS THAT YOU TWO ARE SO CLOSE.
MAYBE, BUT I GET THE FEELING THAT I'M HIS ENEMY!
US TOO!
AH HA HA HA
HE WANTS TO BE AROUND MAKOTO-SAN ALL THE TIME.
I THINK IT'S CUTE.
WHY DON'T YOU THINK ABOUT HOW KÔ-CHAN FEELS?
GIVE HIM AND MAKOTO SOME ROOM?
I MEAN, LOOK...

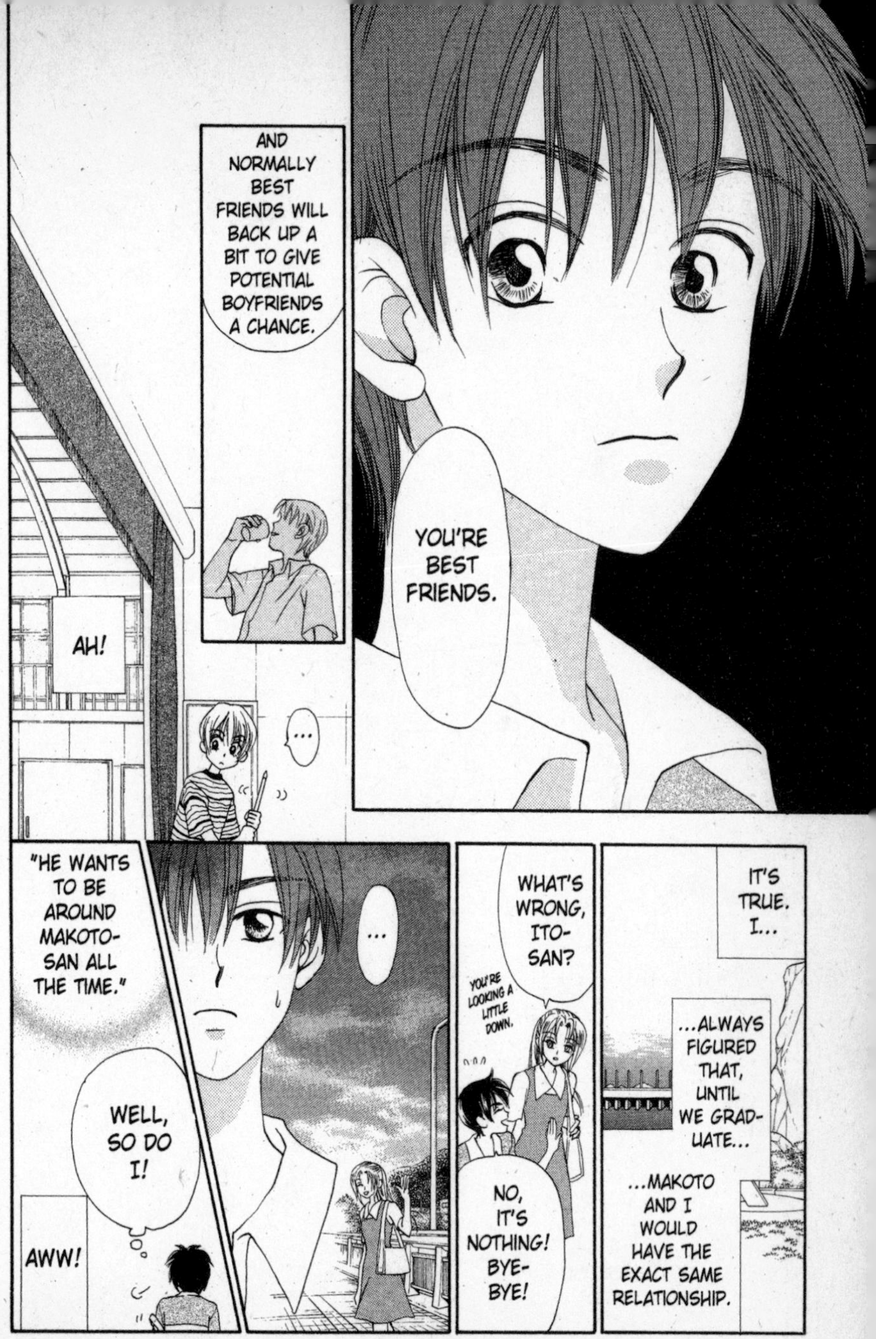
YOU'RE BEST FRIENDS.
AND NORMALLY BEST FRIENDS WILL BACK UP A BIT TO GIVE POTENTIAL BOYFRIENDS A CHANCE.
AH!
...
IT'S TRUE. I...
...ALWAYS FIGURED THAT, UNTIL WE GRADUATE...
...MAKOTO AND I WOULD HAVE THE EXACT SAME RELATIONSHIP.
WHAT'S WRONG, ITO-SAN?
YOU'RE LOOKING A LITTLE DOWN.
NO, IT'S NOTHING! BYE-BYE!
...
"HE WANTS TO BE AROUND MAKOTO-SAN ALL THE TIME."
WELL, SO DO I!
AWW!

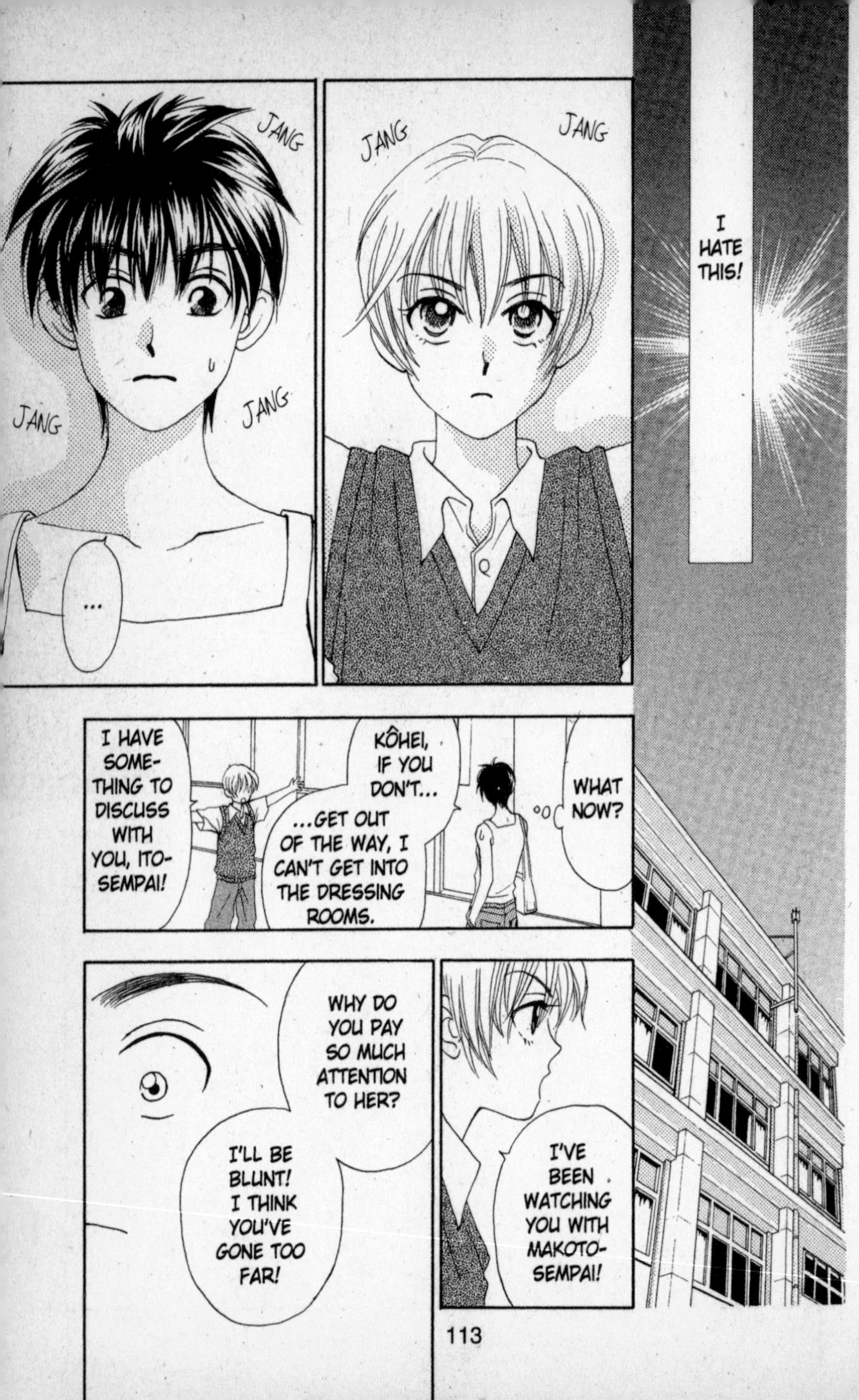
I HATE THIS!
JANG
JANG
JANG
JANG
JANG
JANG
...
WHAT NOW?
KÔHEI, IF YOU DON'T...
...GET OUT OF THE WAY, I CAN'T GET INTO THE DRESSING ROOMS.
I HAVE SOMETHING TO DISCUSS WITH YOU, ITO-SEMPAI!
I'VE BEEN WATCHING YOU WITH MAKOTO-SEMPAI!
WHY DO YOU PAY SO MUCH ATTENTION TO HER?
I'LL BE BLUNT! I THINK YOU'VE GONE TOO FAR!

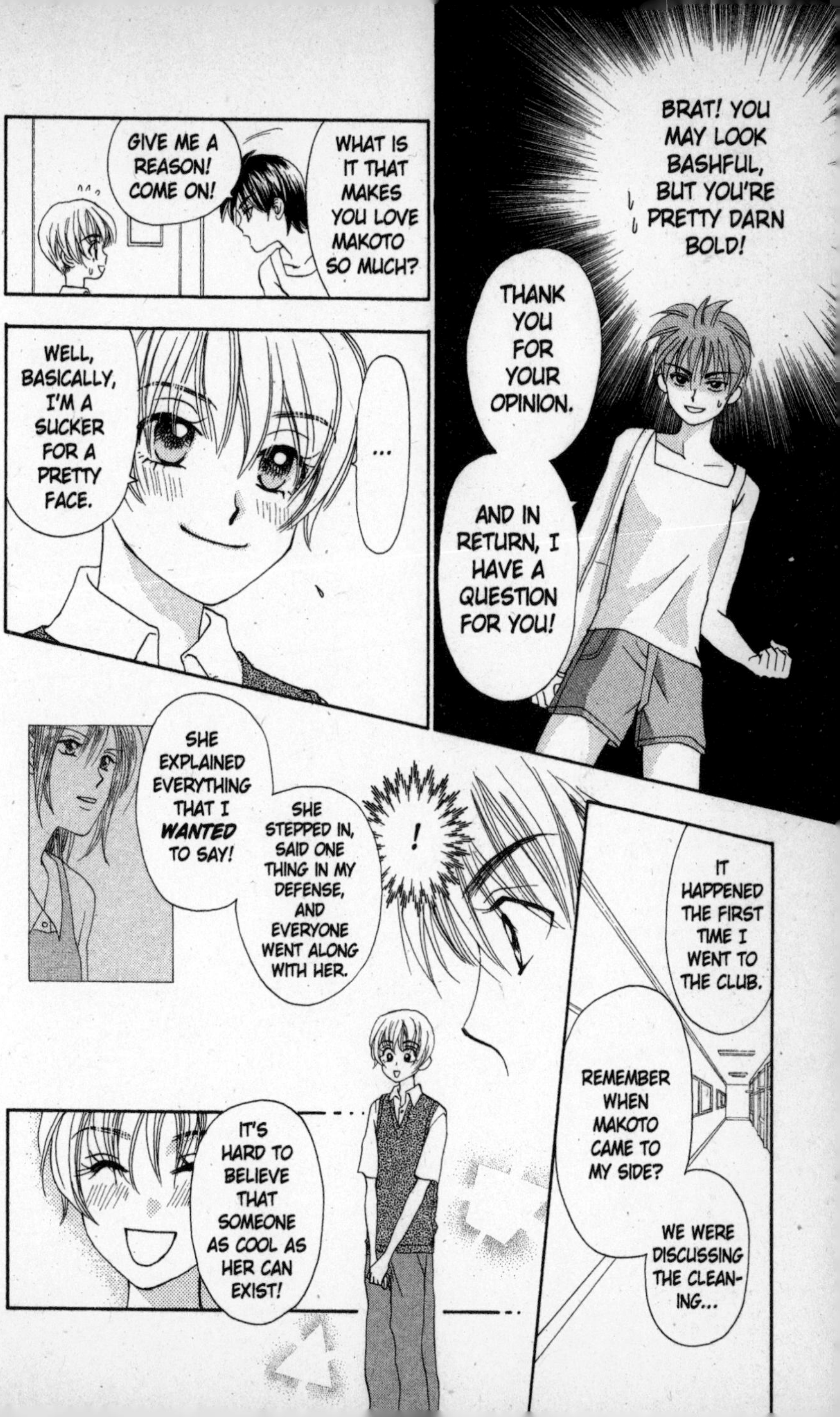
BRAT! YOU MAY LOOK BASHFUL, BUT YOU'RE PRETTY DARN BOLD!
THANK YOU FOR YOUR OPINION.
AND IN RETURN, I HAVE A QUESTION FOR YOU!
WHAT IS IT THAT MAKES YOU LOVE MAKOTO SO MUCH?
GIVE ME A REASON! COME ON!
...
WELL, BASICALLY, I'M A SUCKER FOR A PRETTY FACE.
IT HAPPENED THE FIRST TIME I WENT TO THE CLUB.
REMEMBER WHEN MAKOTO CAME TO MY SIDE?
WE WERE DISCUSSING THE CLEAN-ING...
!
SHE STEPPED IN, SAID ONE THING IN MY DEFENSE, AND EVERYONE WENT ALONG WITH HER.
SHE EXPLAINED EVERYTHING THAT I *WANTED* TO SAY!
IT'S HARD TO BELIEVE THAT SOMEONE AS COOL AS HER CAN EXIST!

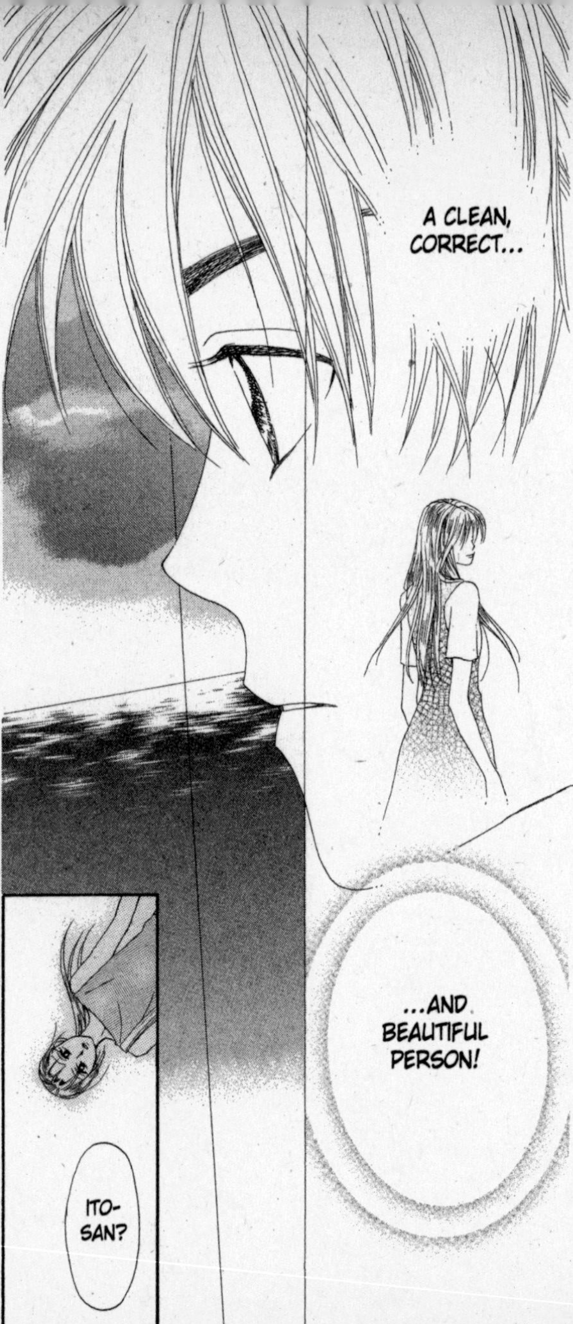
A CLEAN, CORRECT...
...AND BEAUTIFUL PERSON!
ITO-SAN?

COMPLETE IN ONE EPISODE

Okay, the story in Volume Two was a long continuing story, but in this volume and for the foreseeable future, the stories are pretty well completed (?) within the confines of the installments... There are a lot of reasons for it... It just turned out this way! Even though I wanted to do continuing stories!! SNIFF SNIFF

Part of it could be the fact that I'm going at a 40 page per installment pace. Thirty pages seems like such a tight space that I have to shave off parts of my episodes through my tears! (The Camp Episode.) I'm sorry that my stories all come out to be similar! (My parents are always saying that.) But the deadlines come up on me so fast, that I have to write them that way! I knew there'd be difficulties being a pro. I'm just not a good enough manga artist yet!

BOOM BOOM

But every now and again I'd like to... pull out a page and... ...churn out a good action scene!!

My ambition!

To learn the Continuing Story Technique!

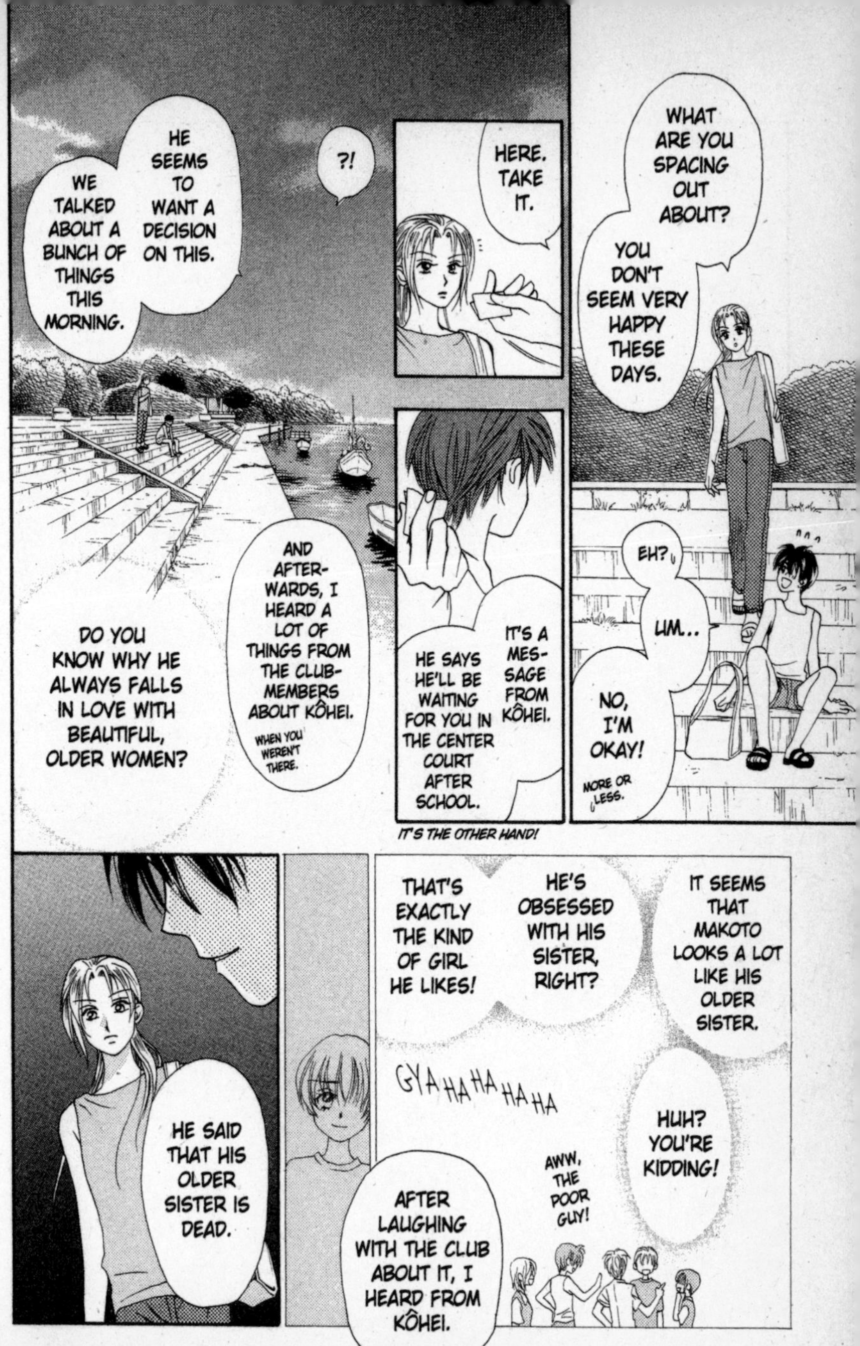
WHAT ARE YOU SPACING OUT ABOUT?
YOU DON'T SEEM VERY HAPPY THESE DAYS.
EH?
UM...
NO, I'M OKAY!
MORE OR LESS.
HERE. TAKE IT.
IT'S A MESSAGE FROM KÔHEI.
HE SAYS HE'LL BE WAITING FOR YOU IN THE CENTER COURT AFTER SCHOOL.
IT'S THE OTHER HAND!
?!
HE SEEMS TO WANT A DECISION ON THIS.
WE TALKED ABOUT A BUNCH OF THINGS THIS MORNING.
AND AFTERWARDS, I HEARD A LOT OF THINGS FROM THE CLUB-MEMBERS ABOUT KÔHEI.
WHEN YOU WEREN'T THERE.
DO YOU KNOW WHY HE ALWAYS FALLS IN LOVE WITH BEAUTIFUL, OLDER WOMEN?
IT SEEMS THAT MAKOTO LOOKS A LOT LIKE HIS OLDER SISTER.
HE'S OBSESSED WITH HIS SISTER, RIGHT?
THAT'S EXACTLY THE KIND OF GIRL HE LIKES!
GYAHAHAHAHAHA
HUH? YOU'RE KIDDING!
AWW, THE POOR GUY!
AFTER LAUGHING WITH THE CLUB ABOUT IT, I HEARD FROM KÔHEI.
HE SAID THAT HIS OLDER SISTER IS DEAD.

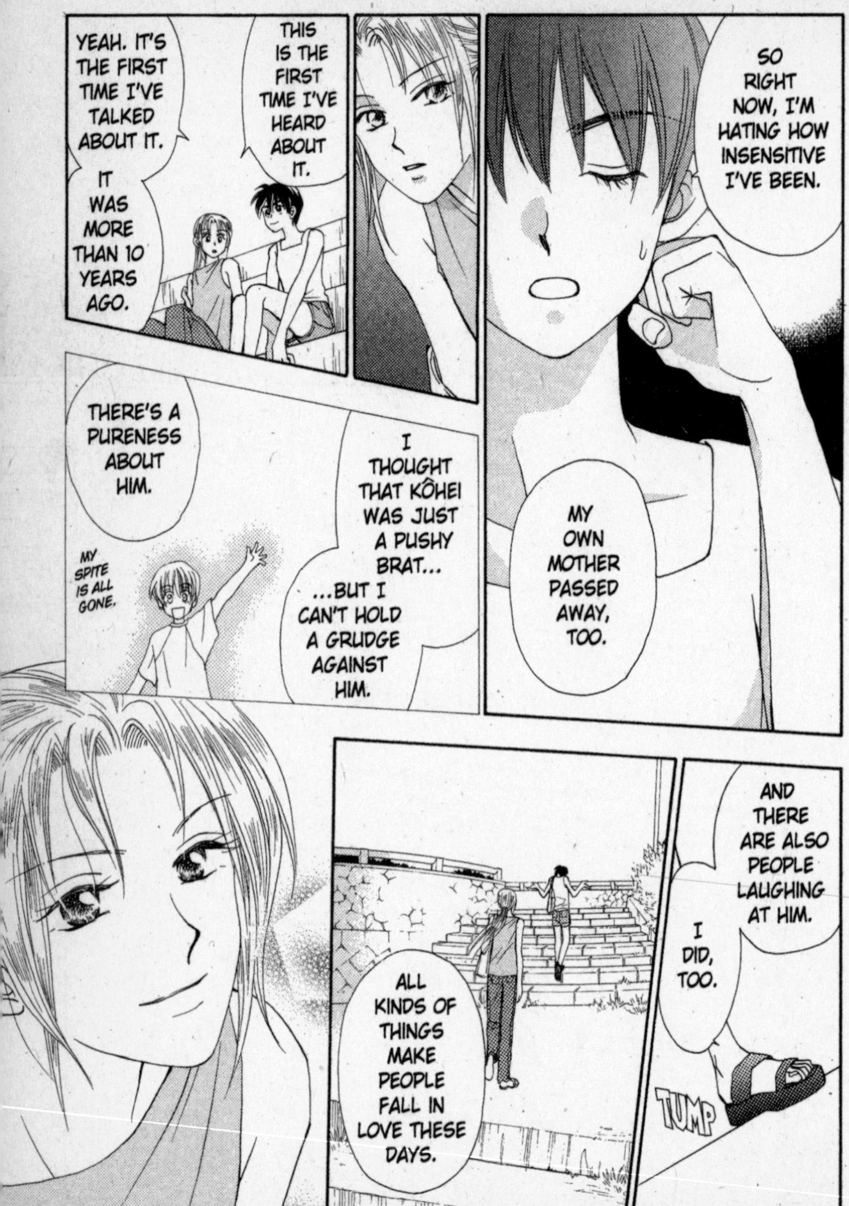
SO RIGHT NOW, I'M HATING HOW INSENSITIVE I'VE BEEN.
MY OWN MOTHER PASSED AWAY, TOO.
THIS IS THE FIRST TIME I'VE HEARD ABOUT IT.
YEAH. IT'S THE FIRST TIME I'VE TALKED ABOUT IT.
IT WAS MORE THAN 10 YEARS AGO.
I THOUGHT THAT KÔHEI WAS JUST A PUSHY BRAT...
...BUT I CAN'T HOLD A GRUDGE AGAINST HIM.
THERE'S A PURENESS ABOUT HIM.
MY SPITE IS ALL GONE.
AND THERE ARE ALSO PEOPLE LAUGHING AT HIM.
I DID, TOO.
TUMP
ALL KINDS OF THINGS MAKE PEOPLE FALL IN LOVE THESE DAYS.

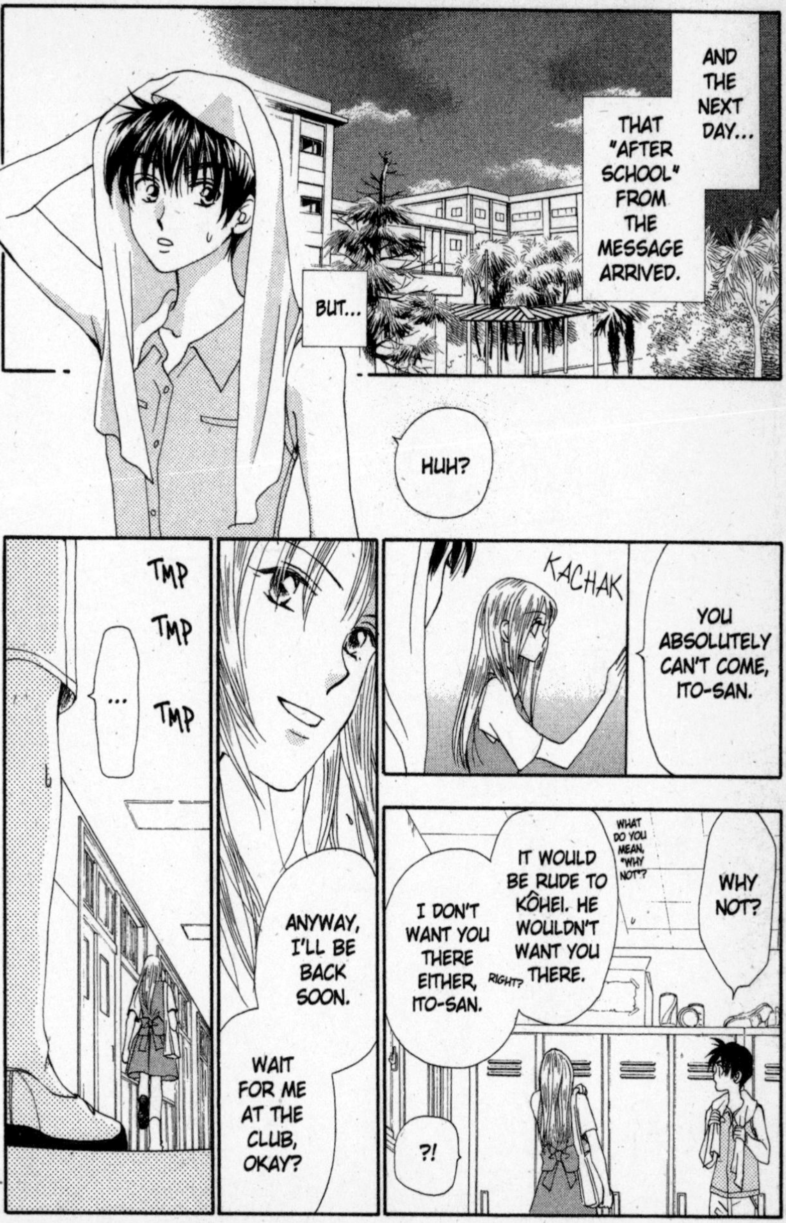
AND THE NEXT DAY...
THAT "AFTER SCHOOL" FROM THE MESSAGE ARRIVED.
BUT...
HUH?
KACHAK
YOU ABSOLUTELY CAN'T COME, ITO-SAN.
WHY NOT?
WHAT DO YOU MEAN, "WHY NOT"?
IT WOULD BE RUDE TO KÔHEI. HE WOULDN'T WANT YOU THERE.
RIGHT?
I DON'T WANT YOU THERE EITHER, ITO-SAN.
?!
ANYWAY, I'LL BE BACK SOON.
WAIT FOR ME AT THE CLUB, OKAY?
TMP
TMP
TMP
...

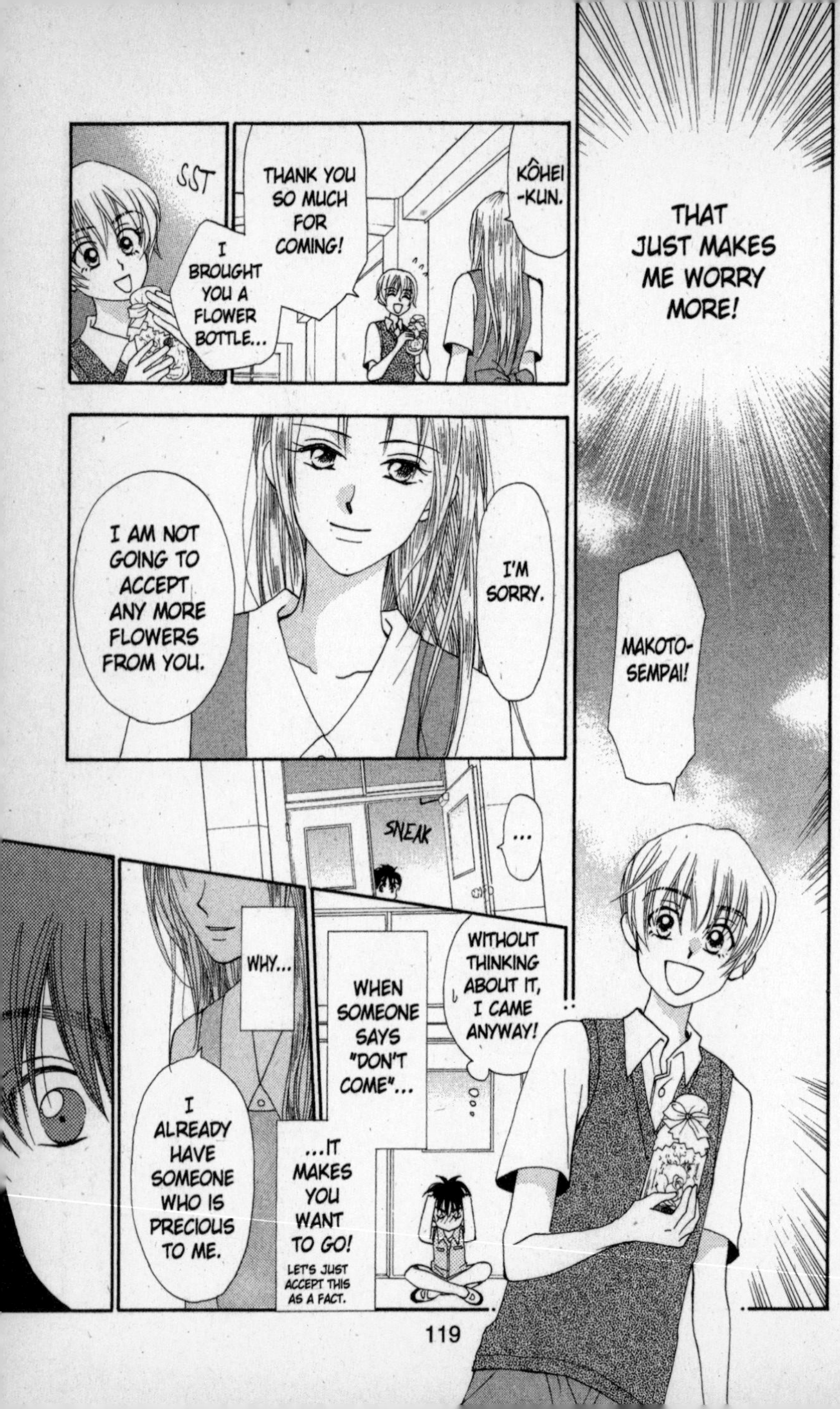
THAT JUST MAKES ME WORRY MORE!
MAKOTO-SEMPAI!
WITHOUT THINKING ABOUT IT, I CAME ANYWAY!
KÔHEI -KUN.
THANK YOU SO MUCH FOR COMING!
I BROUGHT YOU A FLOWER BOTTLE...
SST
I'M SORRY.
I AM NOT GOING TO ACCEPT ANY MORE FLOWERS FROM YOU.
...
SNEAK
WHEN SOMEONE SAYS "DON'T COME"...
...IT MAKES YOU WANT TO GO!
LET'S JUST ACCEPT THIS AS A FACT.
WHY...
I ALREADY HAVE SOMEONE WHO IS PRECIOUS TO ME.

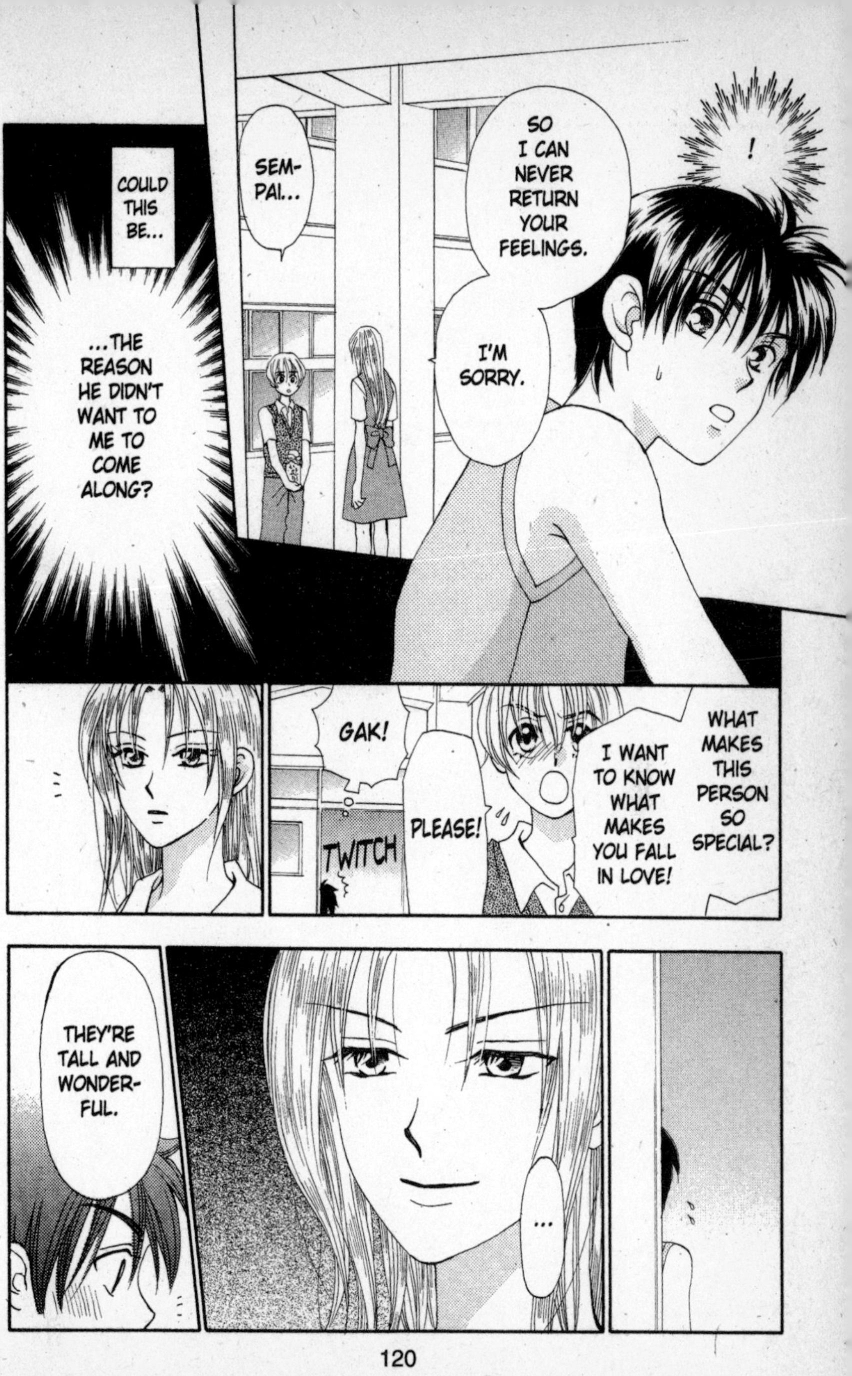
!
SO I CAN NEVER RETURN YOUR FEELINGS.
I'M SORRY.
SEM-PAI...
COULD THIS BE...
...THE REASON HE DIDN'T WANT TO ME TO COME ALONG?
WHAT MAKES THIS PERSON SO SPECIAL?
I WANT TO KNOW WHAT MAKES YOU FALL IN LOVE!
PLEASE!
GAK!
TWITCH
...
THEY'RE TALL AND WONDER-FUL.

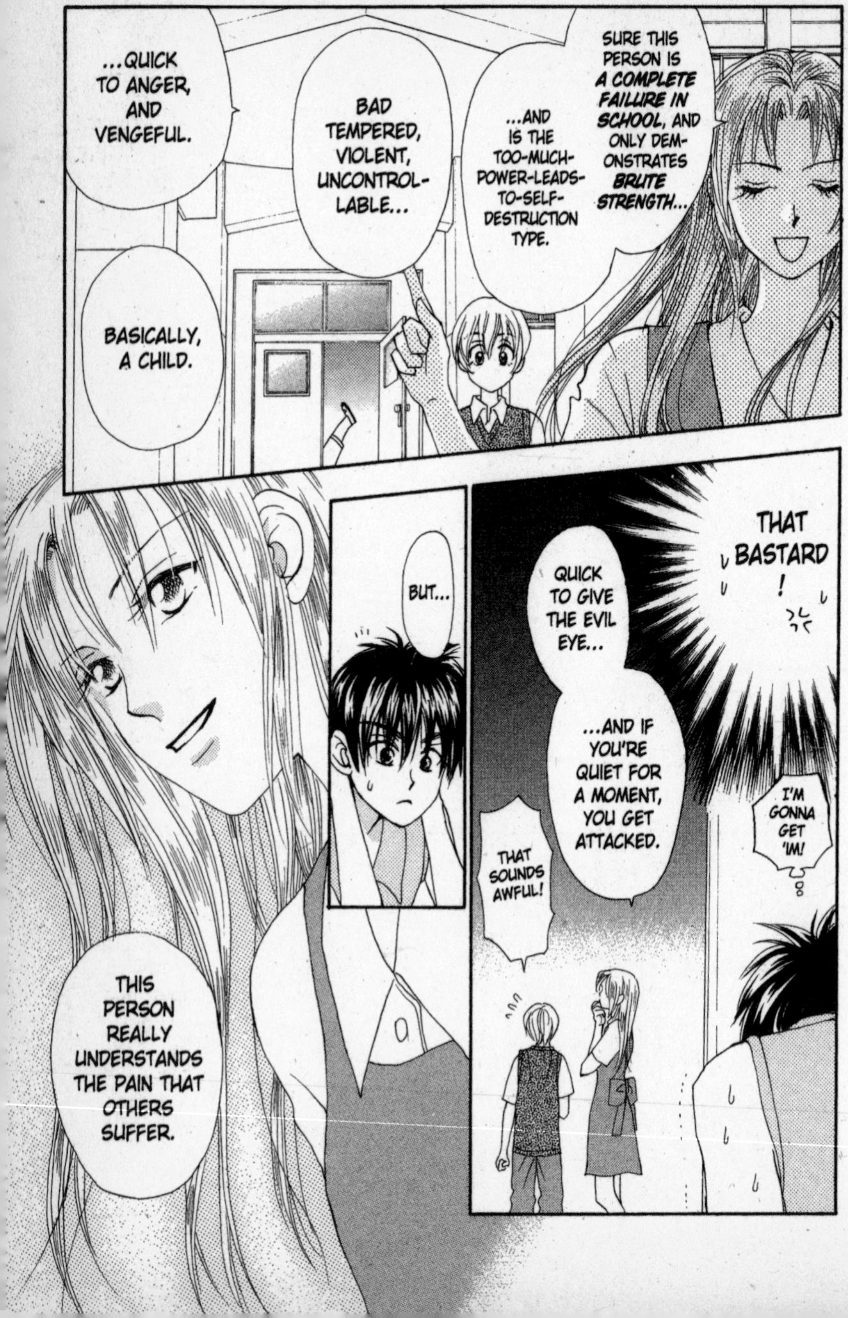
SURE THIS PERSON IS A COMPLETE FAILURE IN SCHOOL, AND ONLY DEMONSTRATES BRUTE STRENGTH...
...AND IS THE TOO-MUCH-POWER-LEADS-TO-SELF-DESTRUCTION TYPE.
BAD TEMPERED, VIOLENT, UNCONTROLLABLE...
...QUICK TO ANGER, AND VENGEFUL.
BASICALLY, A CHILD.
THAT BASTARD!
QUICK TO GIVE THE EVIL EYE...
...AND IF YOU'RE QUIET FOR A MOMENT, YOU GET ATTACKED.
I'M GONNA GET 'IM!
THAT SOUNDS AWFUL!
BUT...
THIS PERSON REALLY UNDERSTANDS THE PAIN THAT OTHERS SUFFER.

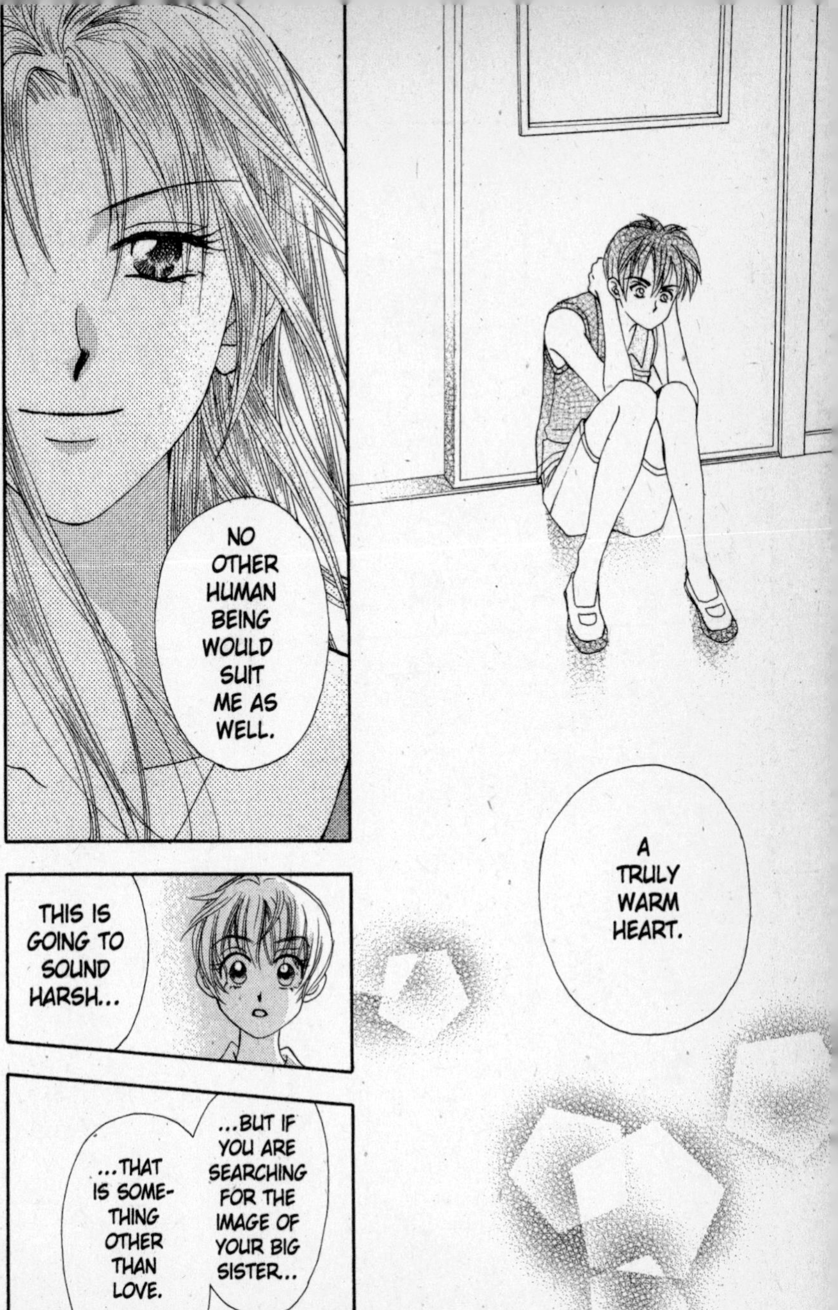
A TRULY WARM HEART.
NO OTHER HUMAN BEING WOULD SUIT ME AS WELL.
THIS IS GOING TO SOUND HARSH...
...BUT IF YOU ARE SEARCHING FOR THE IMAGE OF YOUR BIG SISTER...
...THAT IS SOME-THING OTHER THAN LOVE.

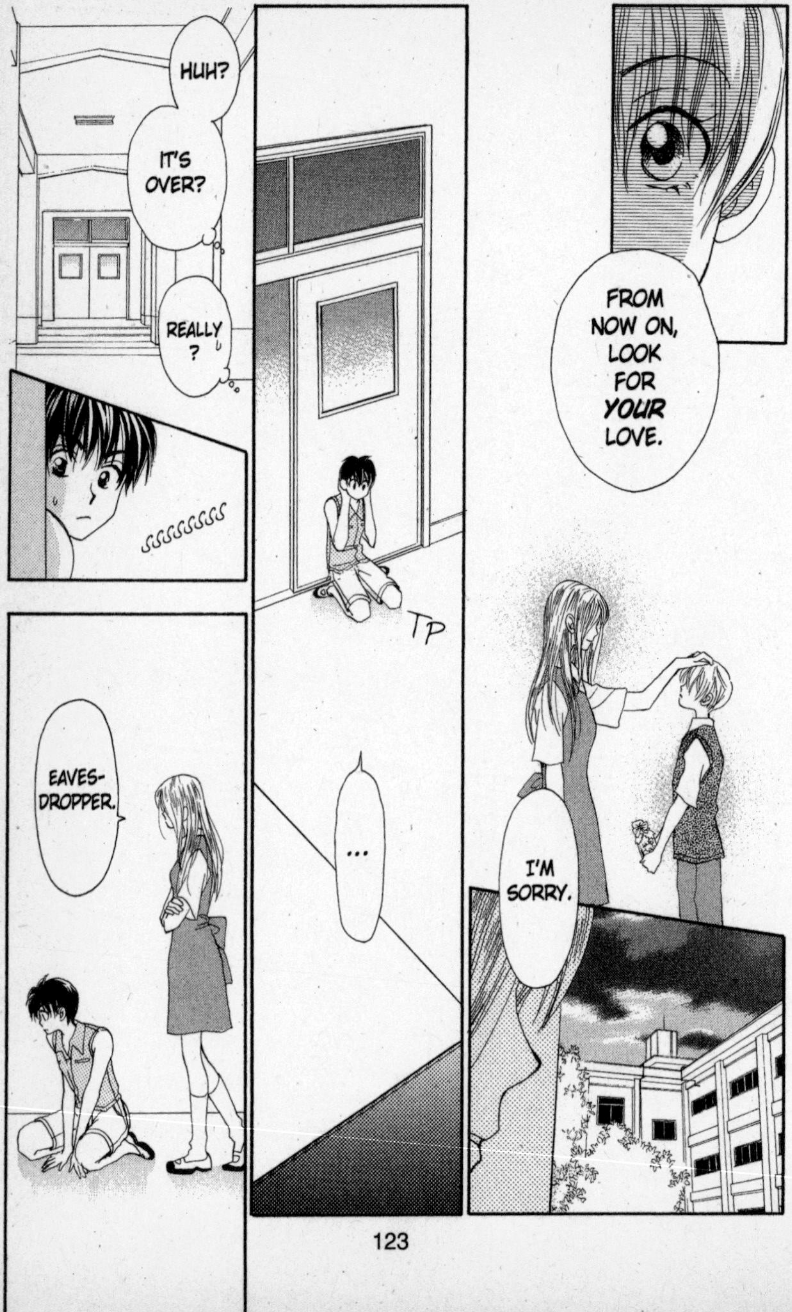
FROM NOW ON, LOOK FOR YOUR LOVE.
I'M SORRY.
TP
...
HUH?
IT'S OVER?
REALLY?
SSSSSSSSS
EAVES-DROPPER.

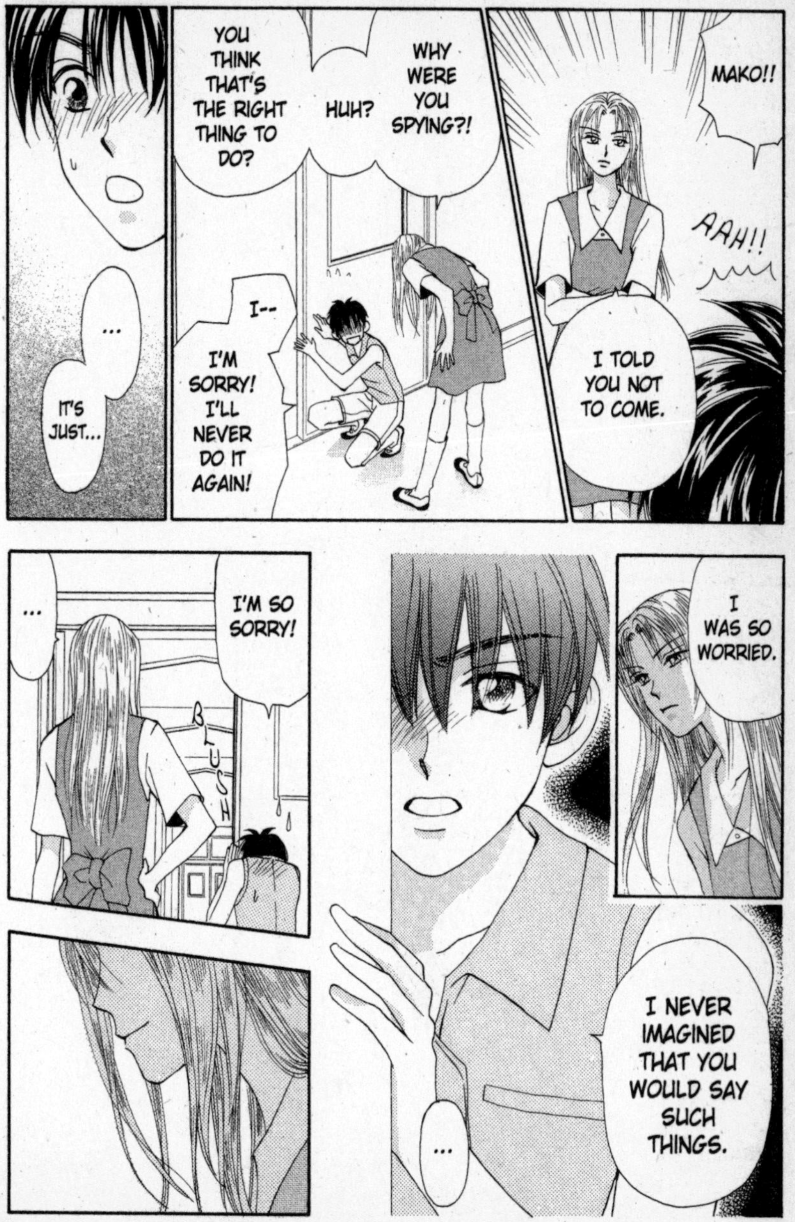
MAKO!!
AAH!!
I TOLD YOU NOT TO COME.
WHY WERE YOU SPYING?!
HUH?
YOU THINK THAT'S THE RIGHT THING TO DO?
I--
I'M SORRY! I'LL NEVER DO IT AGAIN!
...
IT'S JUST...
I WAS SO WORRIED.
I NEVER IMAGINED THAT YOU WOULD SAY SUCH THINGS.
...
I'M SO SORRY!
...
BLUSH

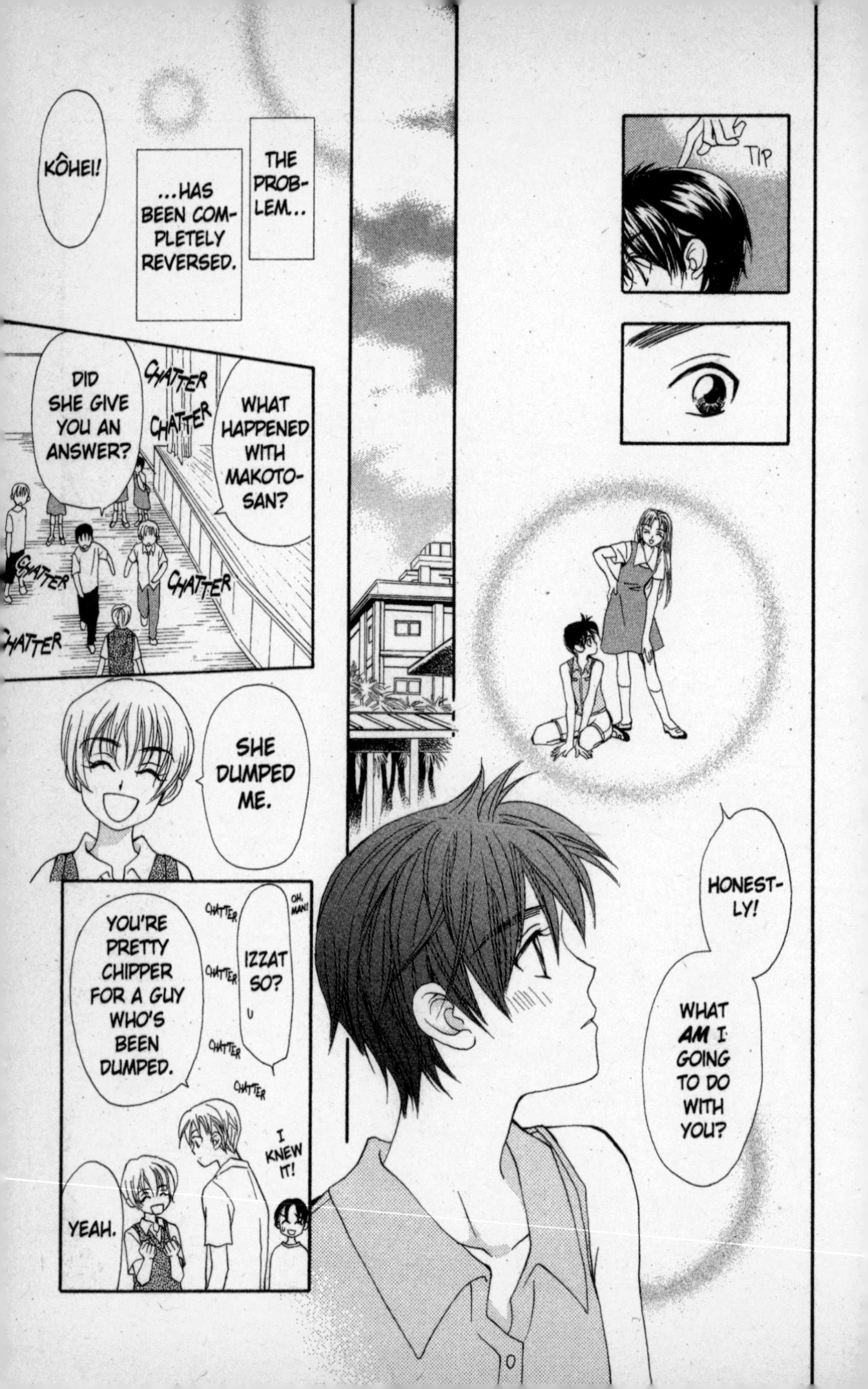

TIP
HONEST-LY!
WHAT AM I GOING TO DO WITH YOU?
THE PROB-LEM...
...HAS BEEN COM-PLETELY REVERSED.
KÔHEI!
WHAT HAPPENED WITH MAKOTO-SAN?
CHATTER
CHATTER
DID SHE GIVE YOU AN ANSWER?
CHATTER
CHATTER
CHATTER
SHE DUMPED ME.
OH, MAN!
IZZAT SO?
CHATTER
CHATTER
CHATTER
CHATTER
YOU'RE PRETTY CHIPPER FOR A GUY WHO'S BEEN DUMPED.
I KNEW IT!
YEAH.

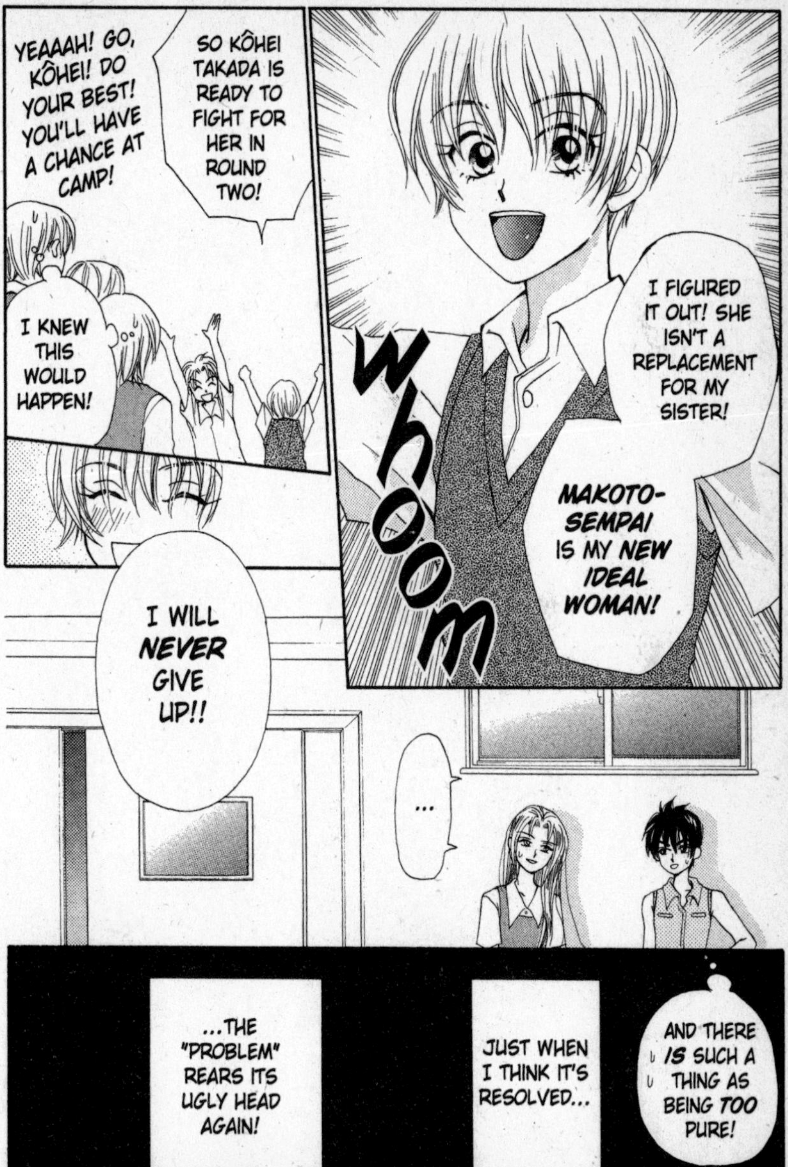
I FIGURED IT OUT! SHE ISN'T A REPLACEMENT FOR MY SISTER!
MAKOTO-SEMPAI IS MY NEW IDEAL WOMAN!
WHOOM
SO KÔHEI TAKADA IS READY TO FIGHT FOR HER IN ROUND TWO!
YEAAAH! GO, KÔHEI! DO YOUR BEST! YOU'LL HAVE A CHANCE AT CAMP!
I KNEW THIS WOULD HAPPEN!
I WILL NEVER GIVE UP!!
...
AND THERE IS SUCH A THING AS BEING TOO PURE!
JUST WHEN I THINK IT'S RESOLVED...
...THE "PROBLEM" REARS ITS UGLY HEAD AGAIN!

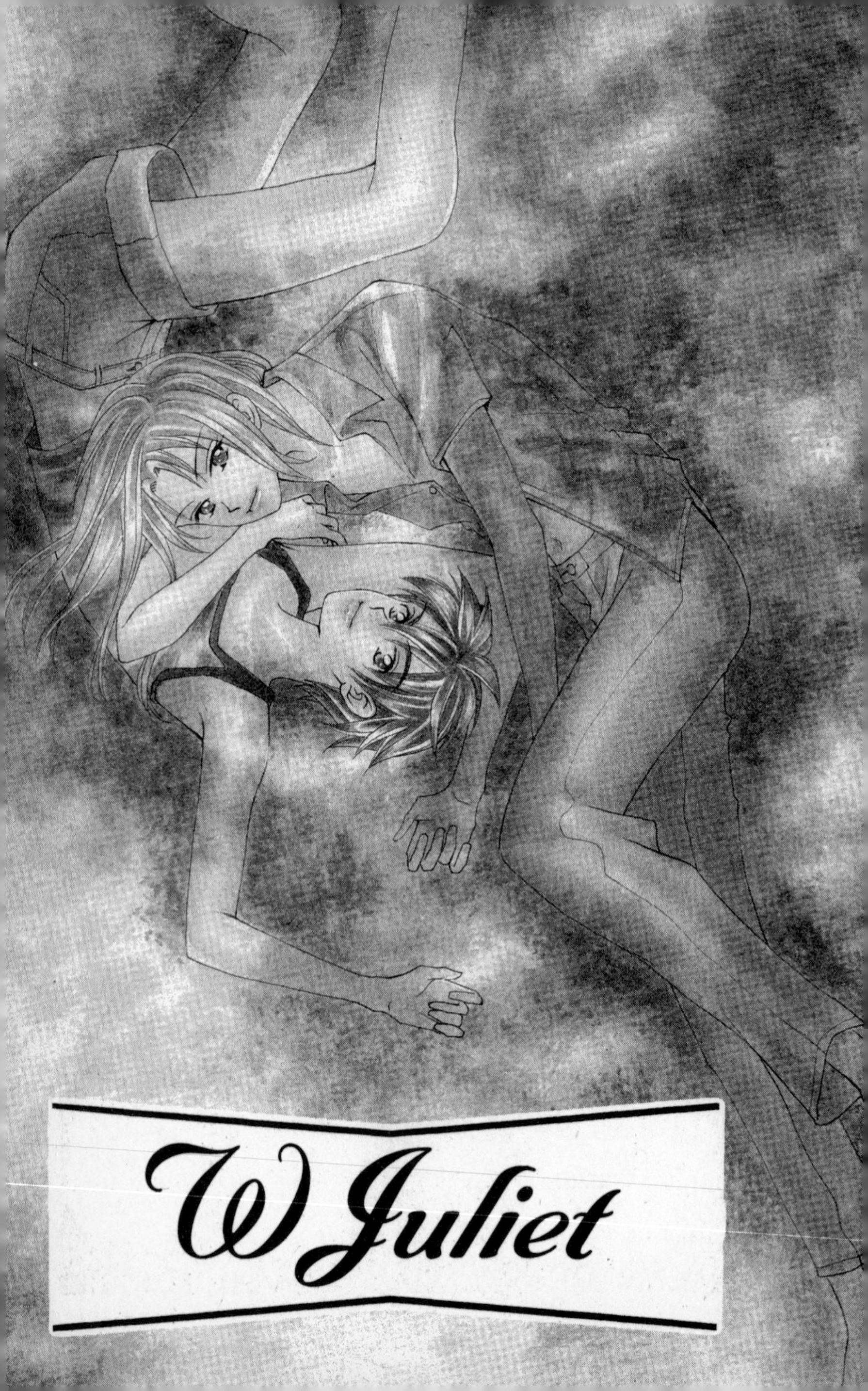
W Juliet

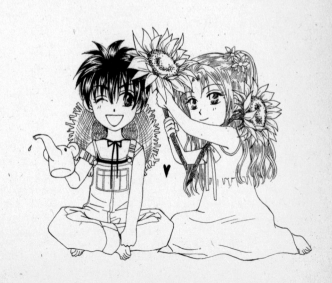

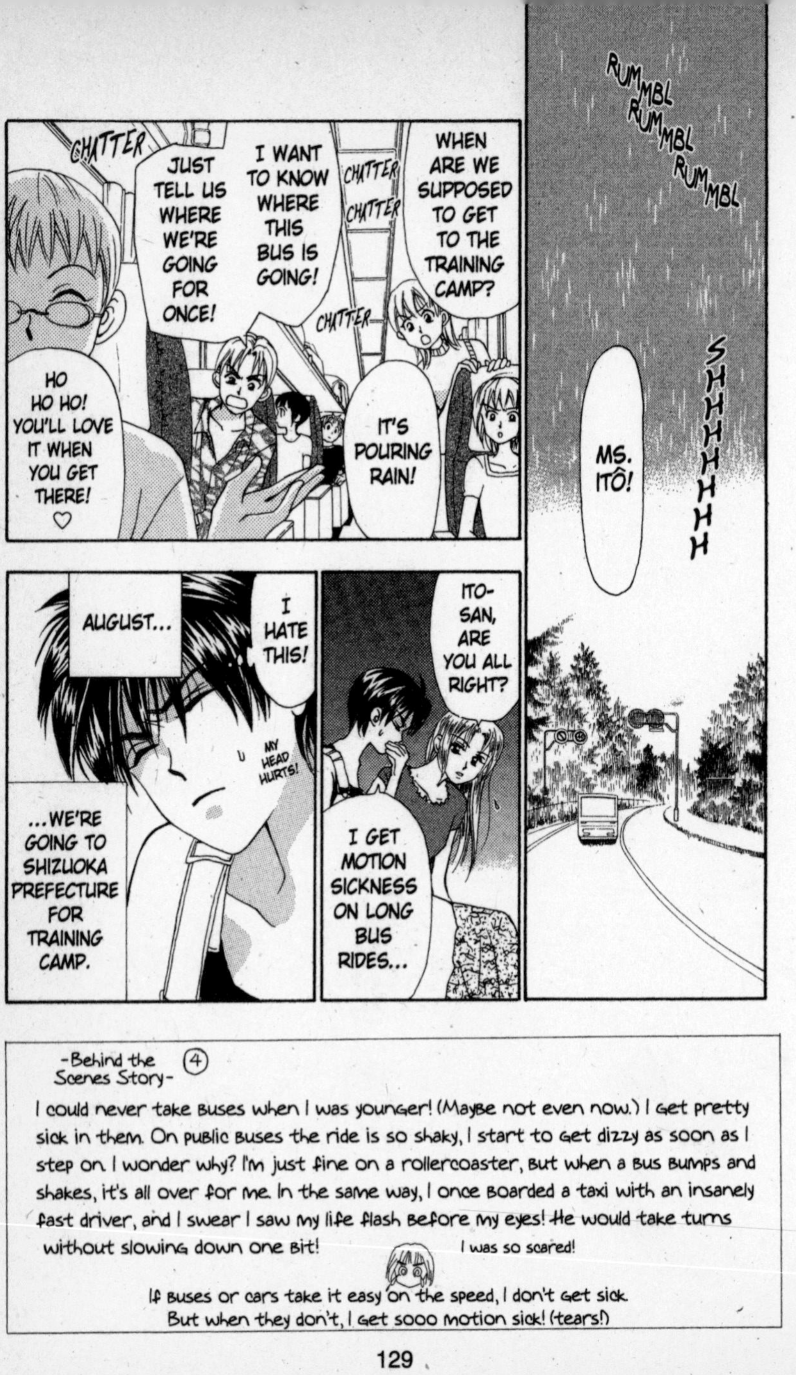
RUMMBL RUMMBL RUMMBL
SHHHHHHHH
MS. ITÔ!
WHEN ARE WE SUPPOSED TO GET TO THE TRAINING CAMP?
CHATTER
CHATTER
I WANT TO KNOW WHERE THIS BUS IS GOING!
CHATTER
JUST TELL US WHERE WE'RE GOING FOR ONCE!
CHATTER
IT'S POURING RAIN!
HO HO HO! YOU'LL LOVE IT WHEN YOU GET THERE! ♡
ITO-SAN, ARE YOU ALL RIGHT?
I GET MOTION SICKNESS ON LONG BUS RIDES...
I HATE THIS!
AUGUST...
MY HEAD HURTS!
...WE'RE GOING TO SHIZUOKA PREFECTURE FOR TRAINING CAMP.

-Behind the Scenes Story- ④

I could never take buses when I was younger! (Maybe not even now.) I get pretty sick in them. On public buses the ride is so shaky, I start to get dizzy as soon as I step on. I wonder why? I'm just fine on a rollercoaster, but when a bus bumps and shakes, it's all over for me. In the same way, I once boarded a taxi with an insanely fast driver, and I swear I saw my life flash before my eyes! He would take turns without slowing down one bit! I was so scared!

If buses or cars take it easy on the speed, I don't get sick. But when they don't, I get sooo motion sick! (tears!)

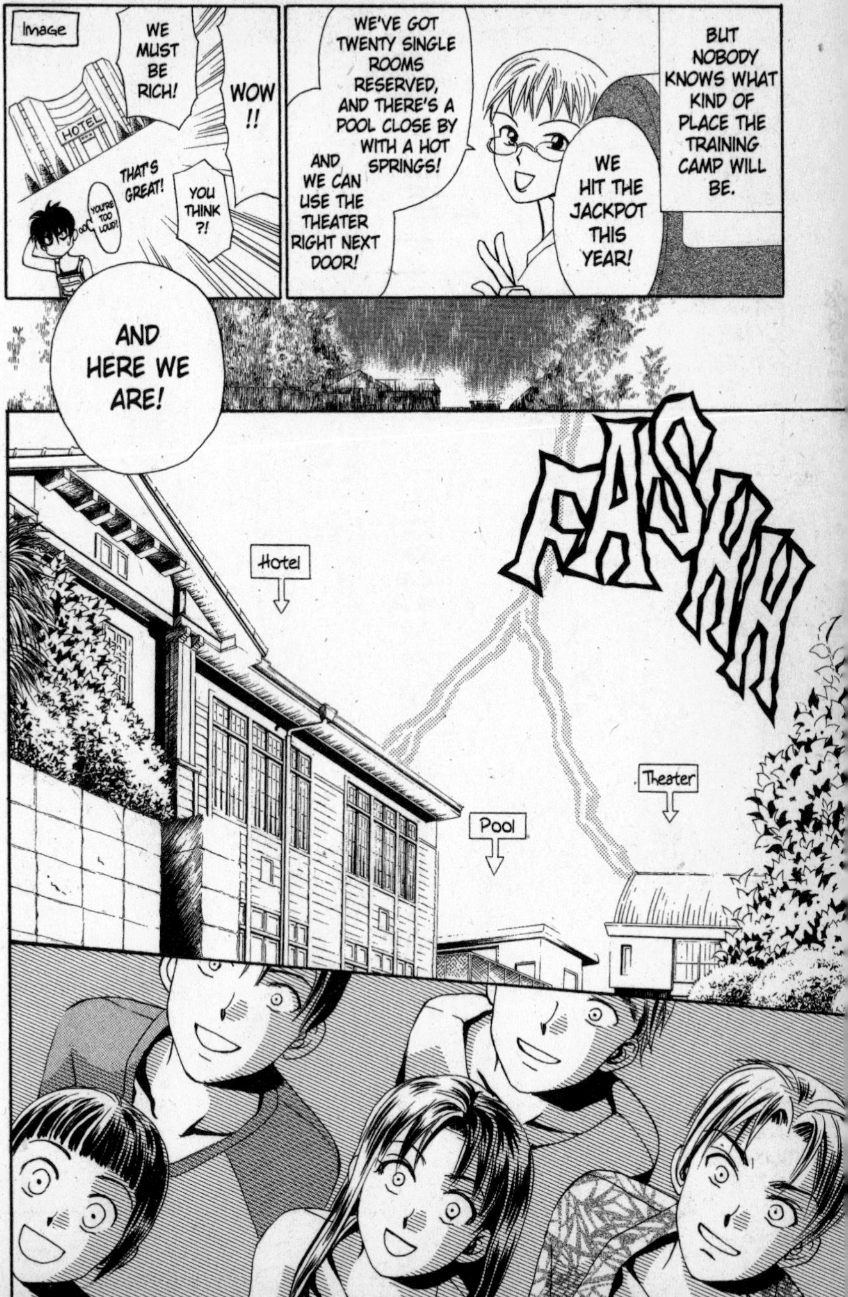
BUT NOBODY KNOWS WHAT KIND OF PLACE THE TRAINING CAMP WILL BE.
WE HIT THE JACKPOT THIS YEAR!
WE'VE GOT TWENTY SINGLE ROOMS RESERVED, AND THERE'S A POOL CLOSE BY WITH A HOT SPRINGS!
AND WE CAN USE THE THEATER RIGHT NEXT DOOR!
Image
WOW!!
WE MUST BE RICH!
HOTEL
YOU THINK?!
THAT'S GREAT!
YOU'RE TOO LOUD!
AND HERE WE ARE!
FASHH
Hotel
Theater
Pool

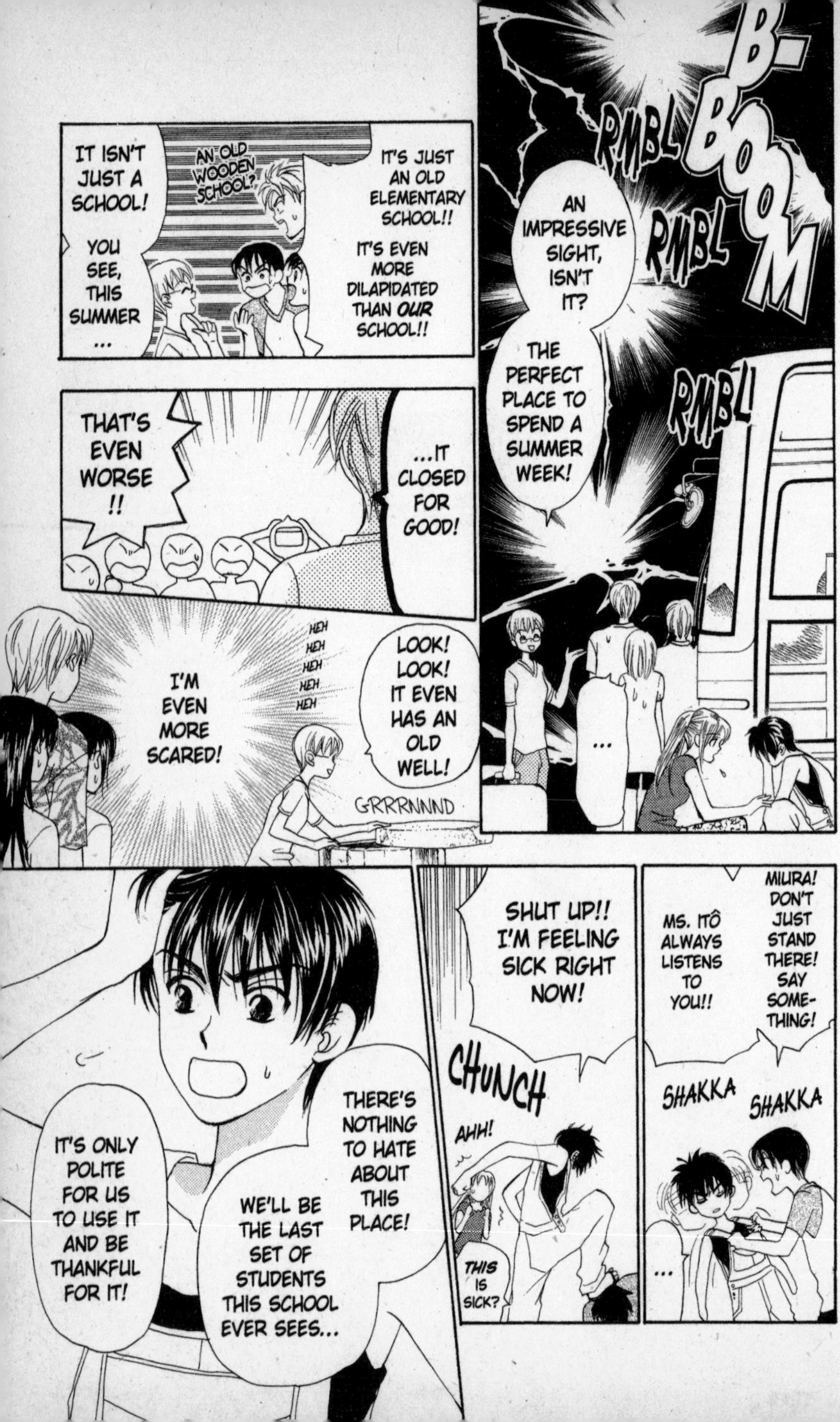
RMBL
B-BOOOM
RMBL
AN IMPRESSIVE SIGHT, ISN'T IT?
THE PERFECT PLACE TO SPEND A SUMMER WEEK!
RMBL
...
IT'S JUST AN OLD ELEMENTARY SCHOOL!!
IT'S EVEN MORE DILAPIDATED THAN *OUR* SCHOOL!!
AN OLD WOODEN SCHOOL?
IT ISN'T JUST A SCHOOL!
YOU SEE, THIS SUMMER ...
...IT CLOSED FOR GOOD!
THAT'S EVEN WORSE !!
LOOK! LOOK! IT EVEN HAS AN OLD WELL!
HEH HEH HEH HEH HEH
GRRRNNND
I'M EVEN MORE SCARED!
MIURA! DON'T JUST STAND THERE! SAY SOME-THING!
MS. ITÔ ALWAYS LISTENS TO YOU!!
SHAKKA
SHAKKA
...
SHUT UP!! I'M FEELING SICK RIGHT NOW!
CHUNCH
AHH!
THIS IS SICK?
THERE'S NOTHING TO HATE ABOUT THIS PLACE!
WE'LL BE THE LAST SET OF STUDENTS THIS SCHOOL EVER SEES...
IT'S ONLY POLITE FOR US TO USE IT AND BE THANKFUL FOR IT!

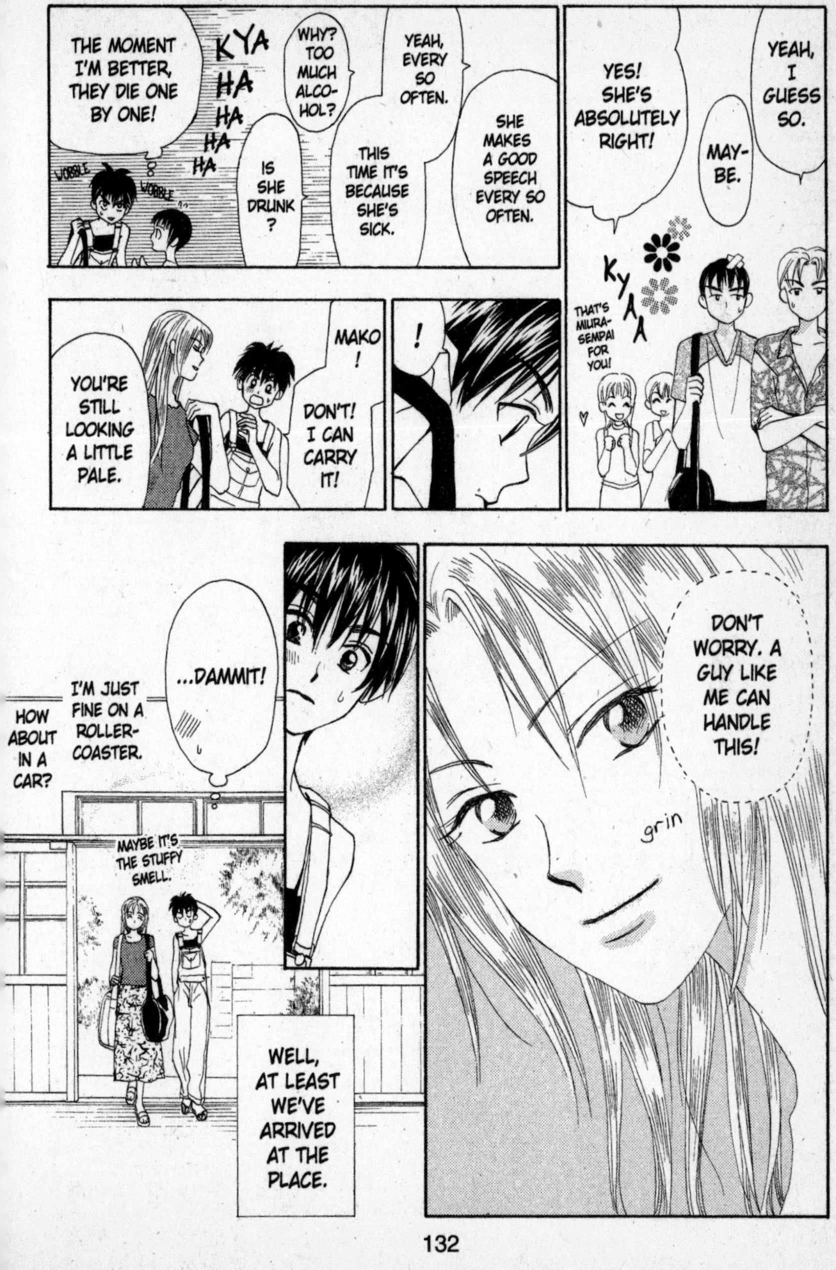
YEAH, I GUESS SO.
YES! SHE'S ABSOLUTELY RIGHT!
MAY-BE.
KYAA
THAT'S MIURA-SEMPAI FOR YOU!
SHE MAKES A GOOD SPEECH EVERY SO OFTEN.
YEAH, EVERY SO OFTEN.
THIS TIME IT'S BECAUSE SHE'S SICK.
WHY? TOO MUCH ALCO-HOL?
IS SHE DRUNK?
KYA HA HA HA HA HA
THE MOMENT I'M BETTER, THEY DIE ONE BY ONE!
WOBBLE
WOBBLE
!
MAKO!
DON'T! I CAN CARRY IT!
YOU'RE STILL LOOKING A LITTLE PALE.
DON'T WORRY. A GUY LIKE ME CAN HANDLE THIS!
grin
...DAMMIT!
I'M JUST FINE ON A ROLLER-COASTER.
HOW ABOUT IN A CAR?
MAYBE IT'S THE STUFFY SMELL.
WELL, AT LEAST WE'VE ARRIVED AT THE PLACE.

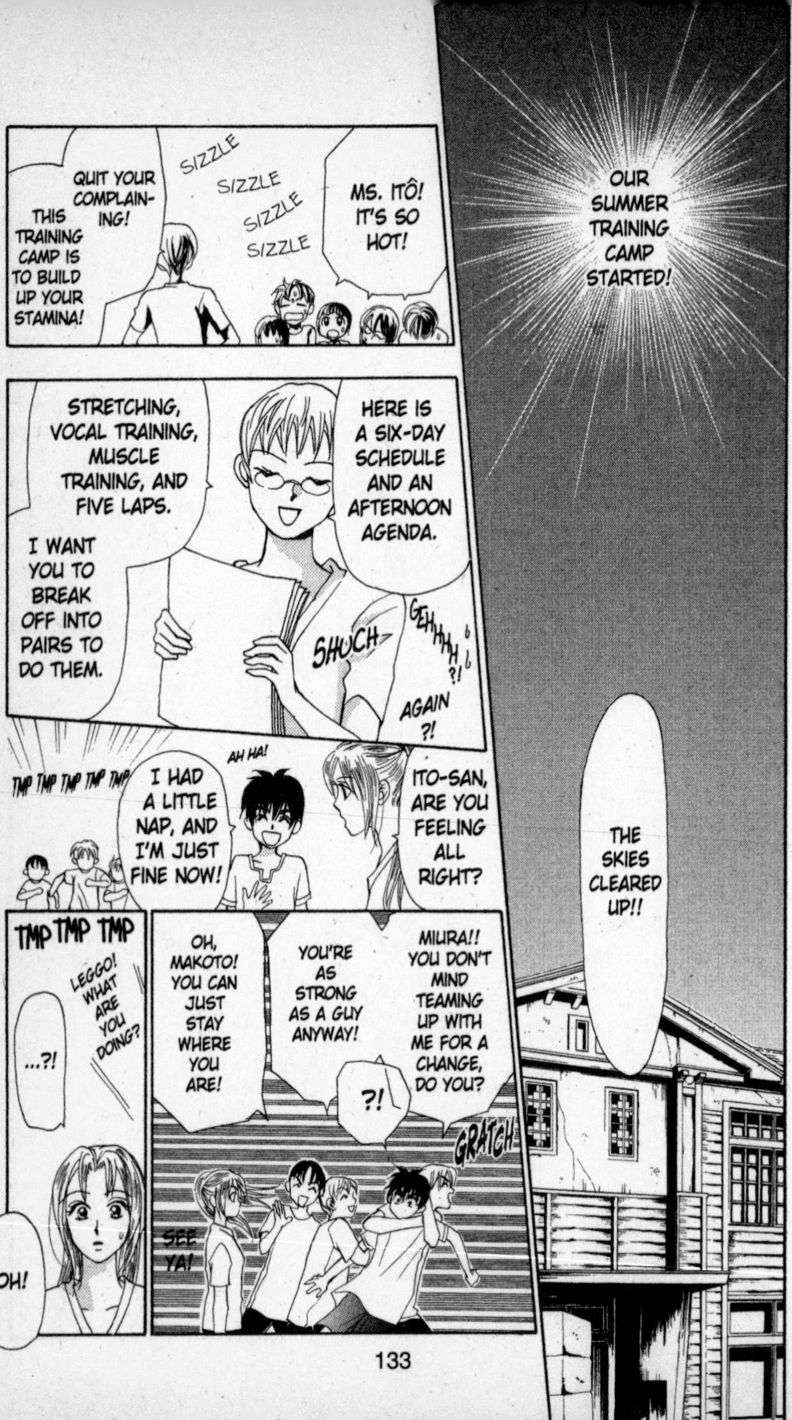

OUR SUMMER TRAINING CAMP STARTED!
THE SKIES CLEARED UP!!
MS. ITÔ! IT'S SO HOT!
SIZZLE SIZZLE SIZZLE SIZZLE
QUIT YOUR COMPLAINING!
THIS TRAINING CAMP IS TO BUILD UP YOUR STAMINA!
HERE IS A SIX-DAY SCHEDULE AND AN AFTERNOON AGENDA.
STRETCHING, VOCAL TRAINING, MUSCLE TRAINING, AND FIVE LAPS.
I WANT YOU TO BREAK OFF INTO PAIRS TO DO THEM.
GEHHHHH?!
AGAIN?!
SHUCH
ITO-SAN, ARE YOU FEELING ALL RIGHT?
AH HA!
I HAD A LITTLE NAP, AND I'M JUST FINE NOW!
TMP TMP TMP TMP TMP
MIURA!! YOU DON'T MIND TEAMING UP WITH ME FOR A CHANGE, DO YOU?
YOU'RE AS STRONG AS A GUY ANYWAY!
OH, MAKOTO! YOU CAN JUST STAY WHERE YOU ARE!
?!
GRATCH
SEE YA!
TMP TMP TMP
LEGGO! WHAT ARE YOU DOING?
...?!
OH!

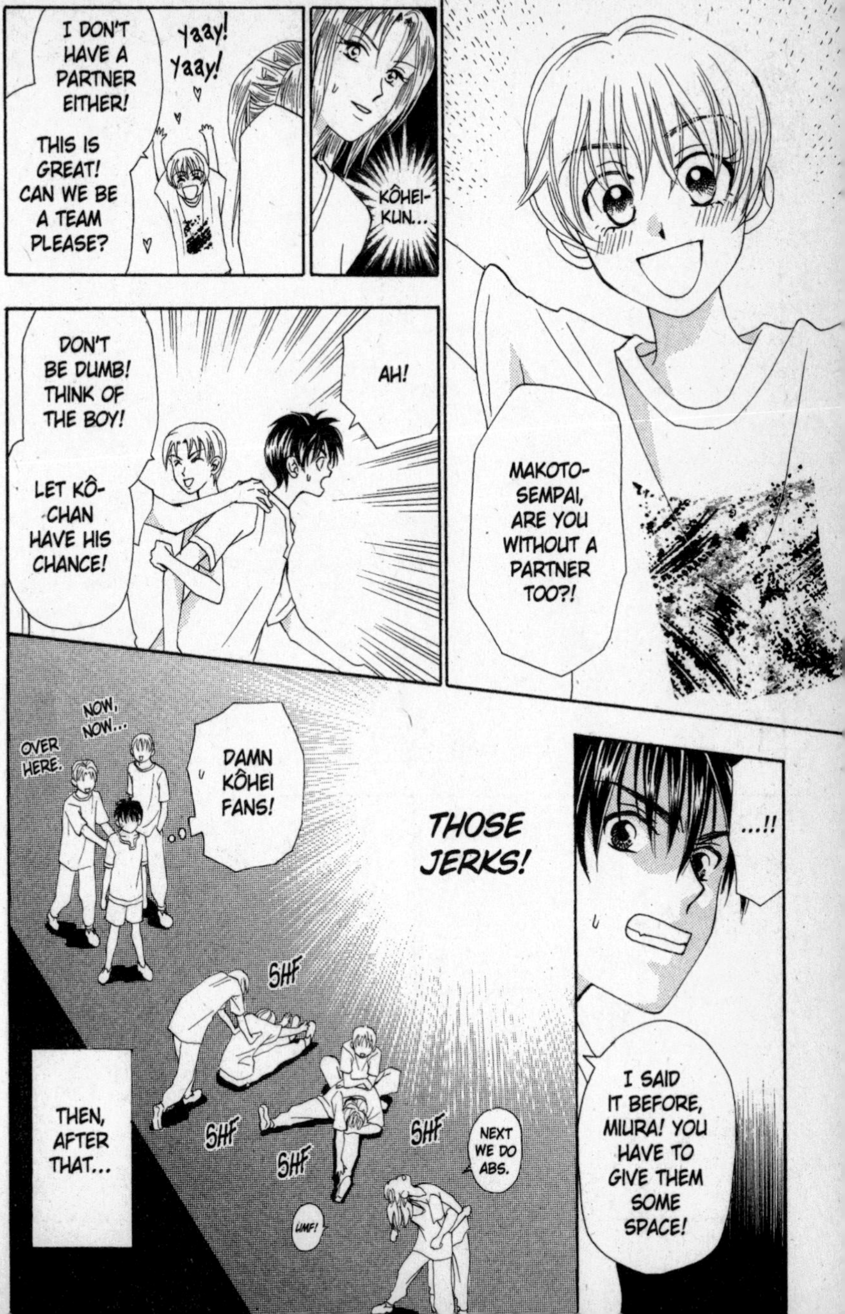

MAKOTO-SEMPAI, ARE YOU WITHOUT A PARTNER TOO?!
KÔHEI-KUN...
Yaay! Yaay!
I DON'T HAVE A PARTNER EITHER!
THIS IS GREAT! CAN WE BE A TEAM PLEASE?
AH!
DON'T BE DUMB! THINK OF THE BOY!
LET KÔ-CHAN HAVE HIS CHANCE!
...!!
I SAID IT BEFORE, MIURA! YOU HAVE TO GIVE THEM SOME SPACE!
THOSE JERKS!
DAMN KÔHEI FANS!
NOW, NOW...
OVER HERE.
SHF
NEXT WE DO ABS.
SHF
SHF
SHF
UMF!
THEN, AFTER THAT...

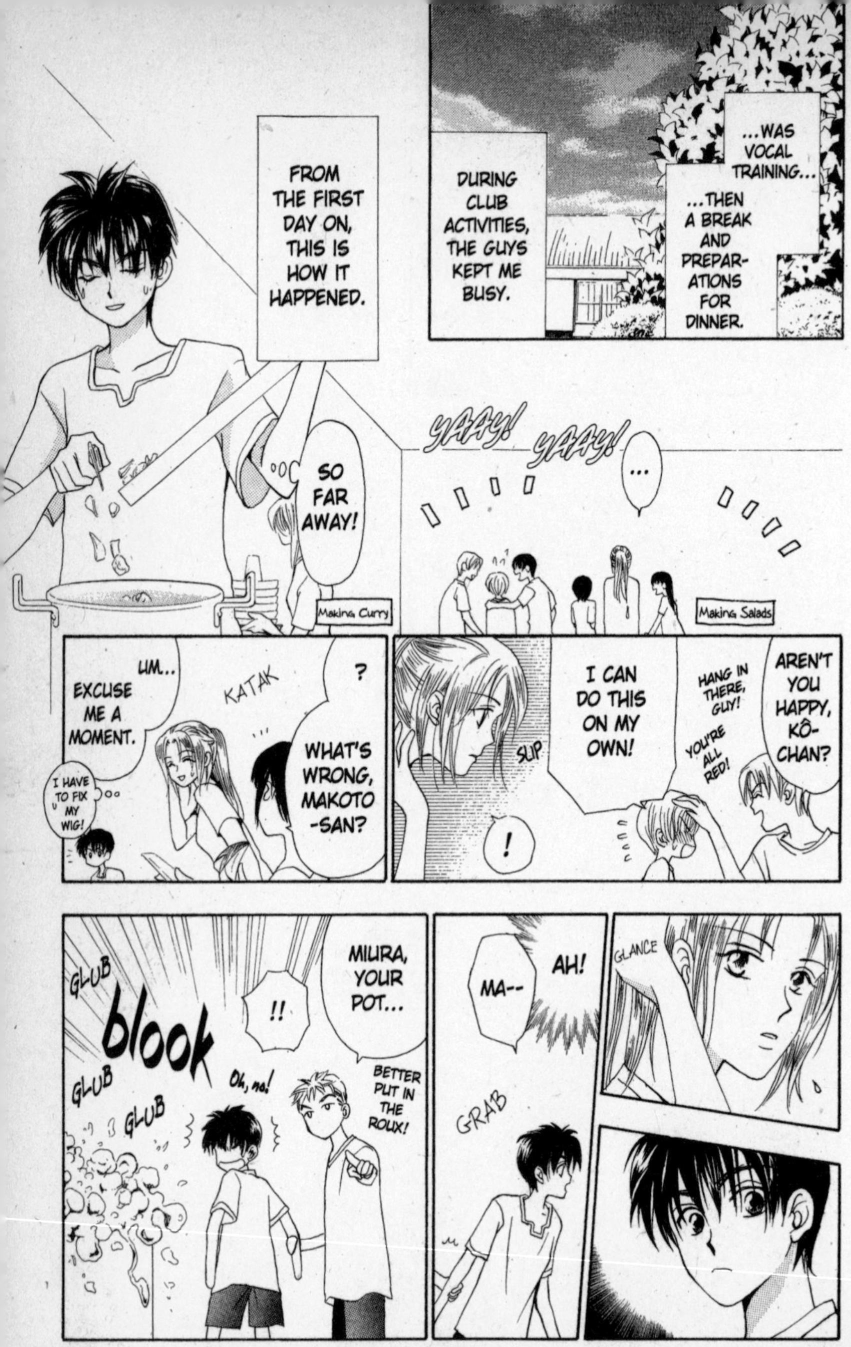
...WAS VOCAL TRAINING...
...THEN A BREAK AND PREPARATIONS FOR DINNER.
DURING CLUB ACTIVITIES, THE GUYS KEPT ME BUSY.
FROM THE FIRST DAY ON, THIS IS HOW IT HAPPENED.
YAAY!
YAAY!
...
Making Salads
SO FAR AWAY!
Making Curry
AREN'T YOU HAPPY, KÔ-CHAN?
HANG IN THERE, GUY!
YOU'RE ALL RED!
I CAN DO THIS ON MY OWN!
SLIP
!
?
WHAT'S WRONG, MAKOTO-SAN?
UM... EXCUSE ME A MOMENT.
KATAK
...
I HAVE TO FIX MY WIG!
GLANCE
AH!
MA--
GRAB
MIURA, YOUR POT...
!!
BETTER PUT IN THE ROUX!
Oh, no!
GLUB
blook
GLUB
GLUB

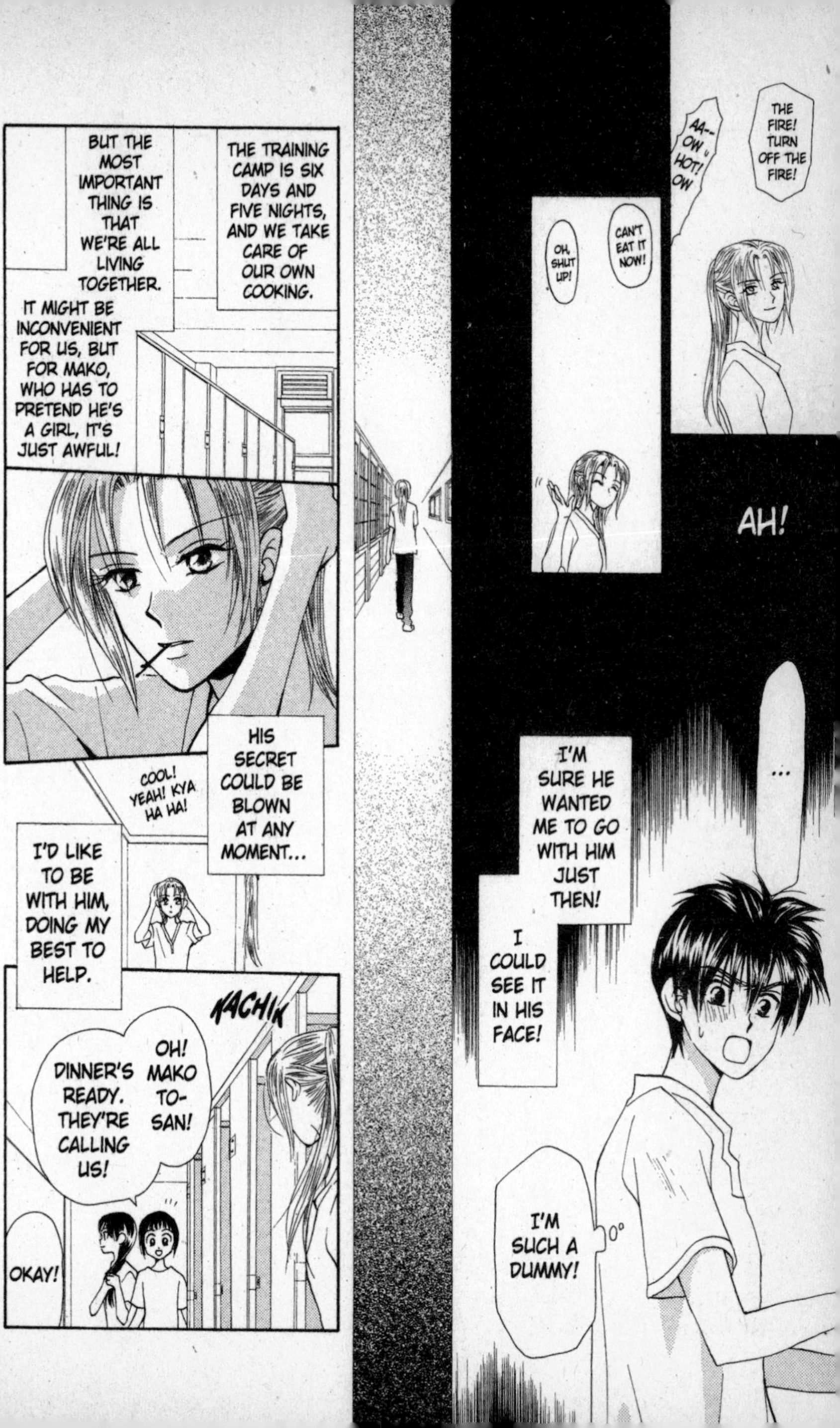

THE FIRE! TURN OFF THE FIRE!
AA-- OW, HOT! OW
CAN'T EAT IT NOW!
OH, SHUT UP!
AH!
...
I'M SURE HE WANTED ME TO GO WITH HIM JUST THEN!
I COULD SEE IT IN HIS FACE!
I'M SUCH A DUMMY!
THE TRAINING CAMP IS SIX DAYS AND FIVE NIGHTS, AND WE TAKE CARE OF OUR OWN COOKING.
BUT THE MOST IMPORTANT THING IS THAT WE'RE ALL LIVING TOGETHER.
IT MIGHT BE INCONVENIENT FOR US, BUT FOR MAKO, WHO HAS TO PRETEND HE'S A GIRL, IT'S JUST AWFUL!
HIS SECRET COULD BE BLOWN AT ANY MOMENT...
COOL! YEAH! KYA HA HA!
I'D LIKE TO BE WITH HIM, DOING MY BEST TO HELP.
KACHIK
OH! MAKO TO-SAN!
DINNER'S READY. THEY'RE CALLING US!
OKAY!

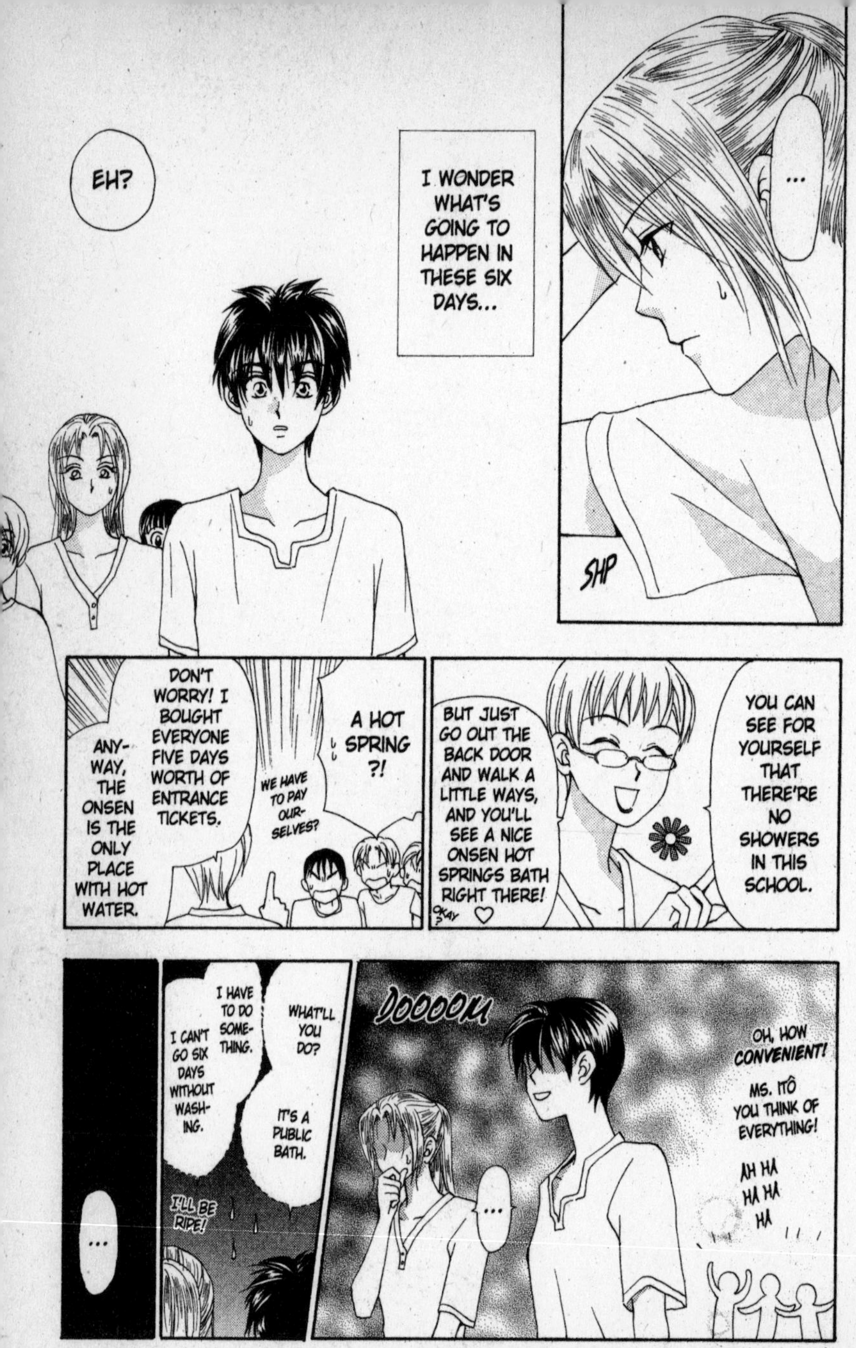
...
SHP
I WONDER WHAT'S GOING TO HAPPEN IN THESE SIX DAYS...
EH?
YOU CAN SEE FOR YOURSELF THAT THERE'RE NO SHOWERS IN THIS SCHOOL.
BUT JUST GO OUT THE BACK DOOR AND WALK A LITTLE WAYS, AND YOU'LL SEE A NICE ONSEN HOT SPRINGS BATH RIGHT THERE!
OKAY?
A HOT SPRING?!
WE HAVE TO PAY OURSELVES?
DON'T WORRY! I BOUGHT EVERYONE FIVE DAYS WORTH OF ENTRANCE TICKETS.
ANYWAY, THE ONSEN IS THE ONLY PLACE WITH HOT WATER.
DOOOOM
OH, HOW CONVENIENT!
MS. ITÔ YOU THINK OF EVERYTHING!
AH HA HA HA HA
...
WHAT'LL YOU DO?
I HAVE TO DO SOMETHING.
I CAN'T GO SIX DAYS WITHOUT WASHING.
IT'S A PUBLIC BATH.
I'LL BE RIPE!
...

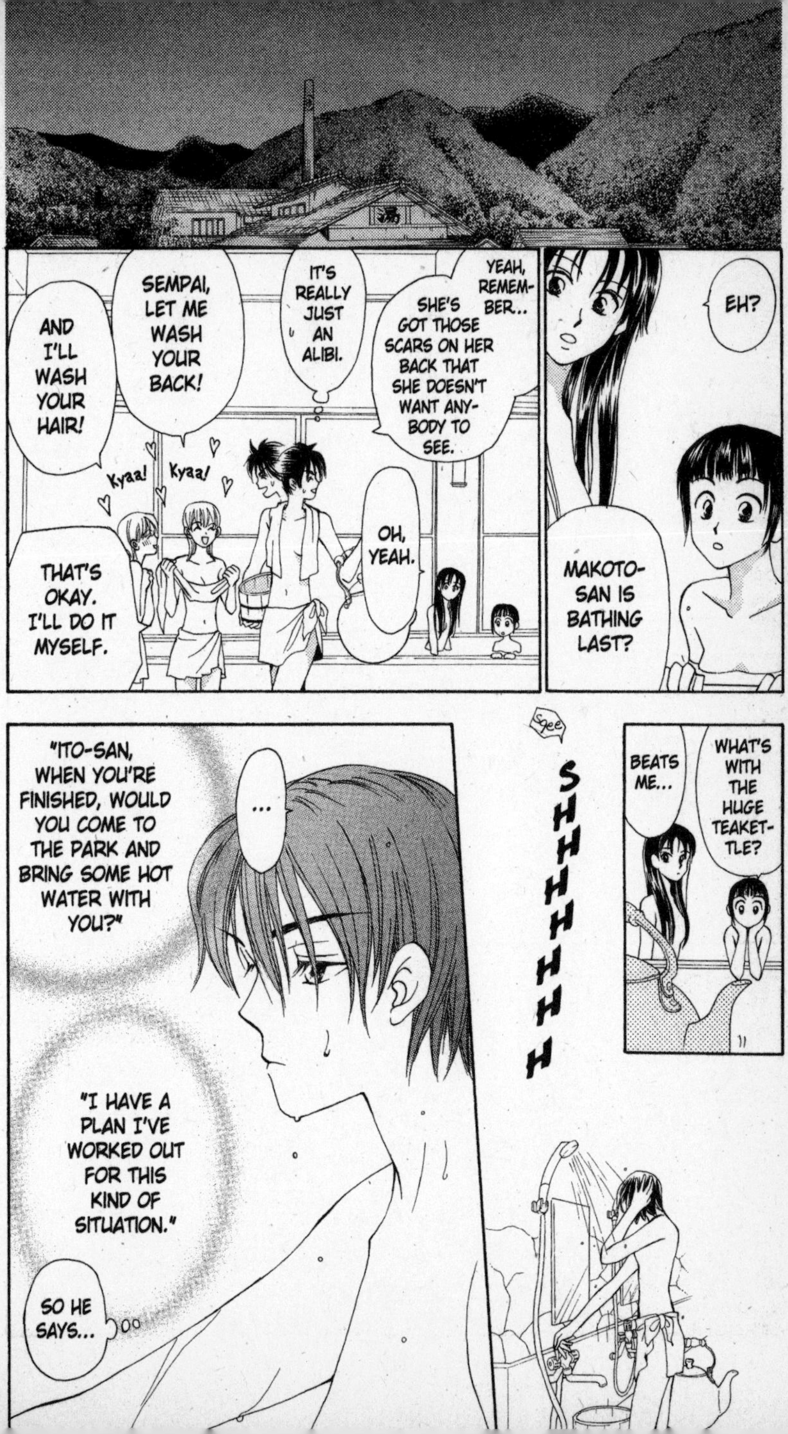
EH?
MAKOTO-SAN IS BATHING LAST?
YEAH, REMEMBER...
SHE'S GOT THOSE SCARS ON HER BACK THAT SHE DOESN'T WANT ANYBODY TO SEE.
IT'S REALLY JUST AN ALIBI.
OH, YEAH.
SEMPAI, LET ME WASH YOUR BACK!
AND I'LL WASH YOUR HAIR!
Kyaa!
Kyaa!
THAT'S OKAY. I'LL DO IT MYSELF.
WHAT'S WITH THE HUGE TEAKETTLE?
BEATS ME...
Sqee
SHHHHHHHH
...
"ITO-SAN, WHEN YOU'RE FINISHED, WOULD YOU COME TO THE PARK AND BRING SOME HOT WATER WITH YOU?"
"I HAVE A PLAN I'VE WORKED OUT FOR THIS KIND OF SITUATION."
SO HE SAYS...

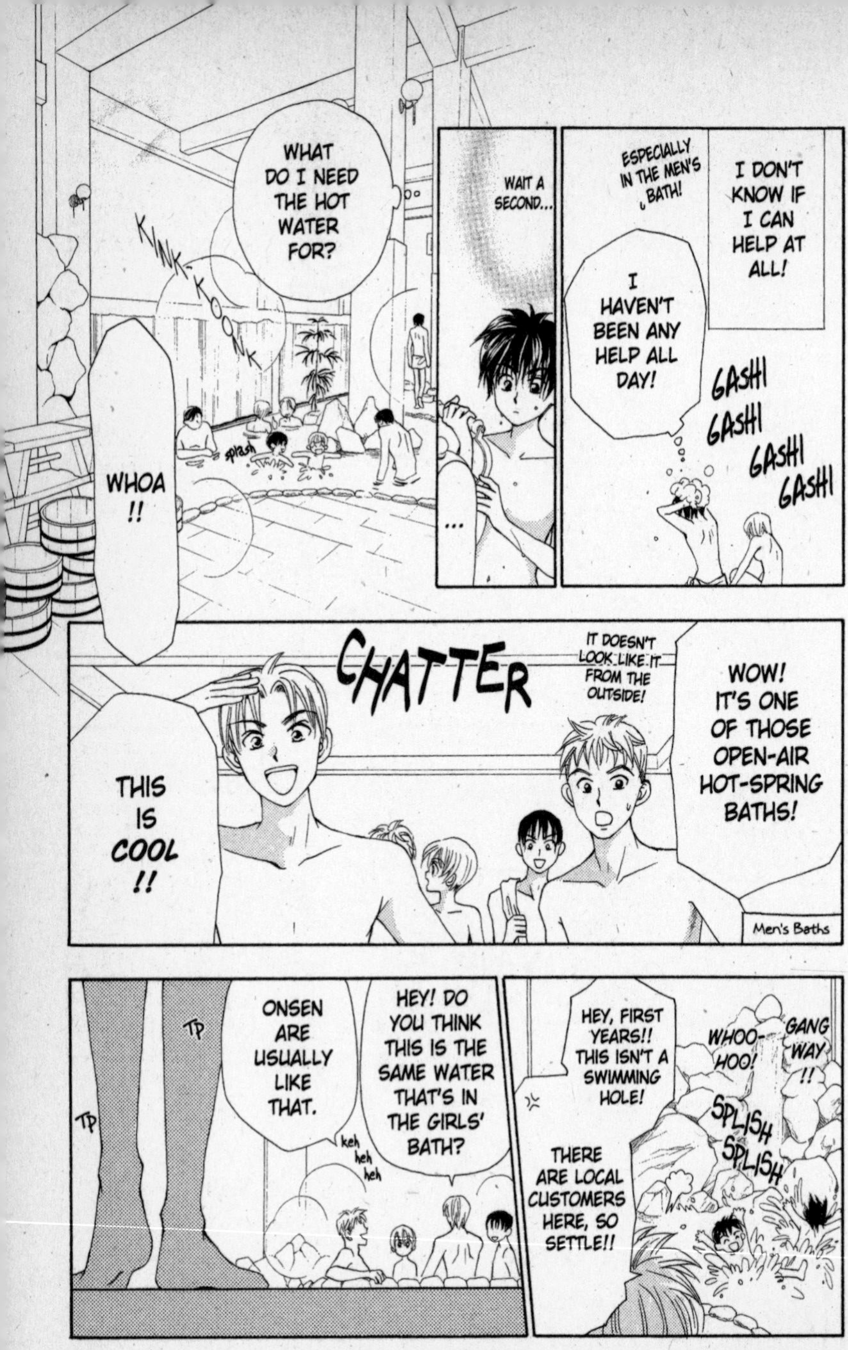
I DON'T KNOW IF I CAN HELP AT ALL!
ESPECIALLY IN THE MEN'S BATH!
I HAVEN'T BEEN ANY HELP ALL DAY!
GASHI GASHI GASHI GASHI
WAIT A SECOND...
...
WHAT DO I NEED THE HOT WATER FOR?
KINK-KOONK
splash
WHOA!!
WOW! IT'S ONE OF THOSE OPEN-AIR HOT-SPRING BATHS!
IT DOESN'T LOOK LIKE IT FROM THE OUTSIDE!
CHATTER
THIS IS COOL!!
Men's Baths
GANG WAY!!
WHOO-HOO!
HEY, FIRST YEARS!! THIS ISN'T A SWIMMING HOLE!
SPLISH SPLISH
THERE ARE LOCAL CUSTOMERS HERE, SO SETTLE!!
HEY! DO YOU THINK THIS IS THE SAME WATER THAT'S IN THE GIRLS' BATH?
keh heh heh
ONSEN ARE USUALLY LIKE THAT.
Tp
Tp

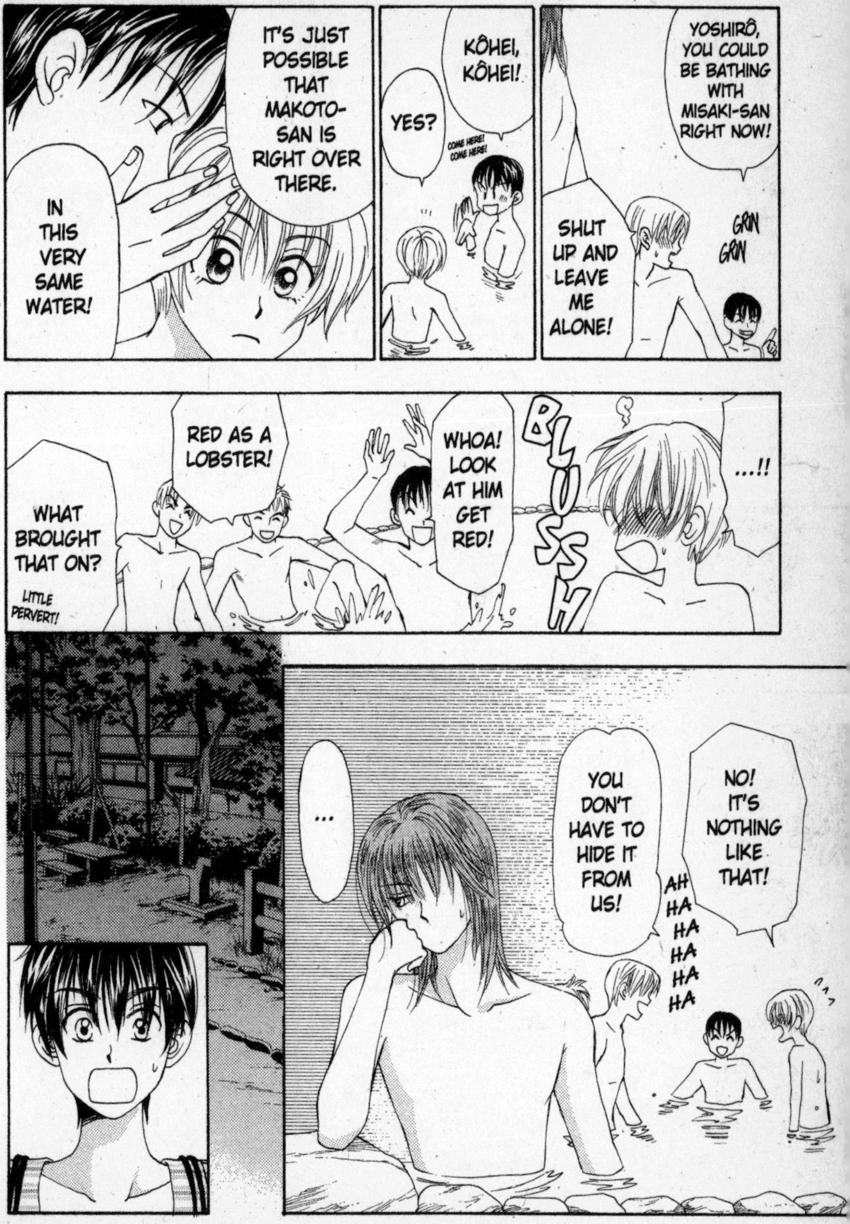
YOSHIRÔ, YOU COULD BE BATHING WITH MISAKI-SAN RIGHT NOW!
GRIN GRIN
SHUT UP AND LEAVE ME ALONE!
KÔHEI, KÔHEI!
YES?
COME HERE! COME HERE!
IT'S JUST POSSIBLE THAT MAKOTO-SAN IS RIGHT OVER THERE.
IN THIS VERY SAME WATER!
...!!
BLUSH
WHOA! LOOK AT HIM GET RED!
RED AS A LOBSTER!
WHAT BROUGHT THAT ON?
LITTLE PERVERT!
NO! IT'S NOTHING LIKE THAT!
AH HA HA HA HA HA HA
YOU DON'T HAVE TO HIDE IT FROM US!
...

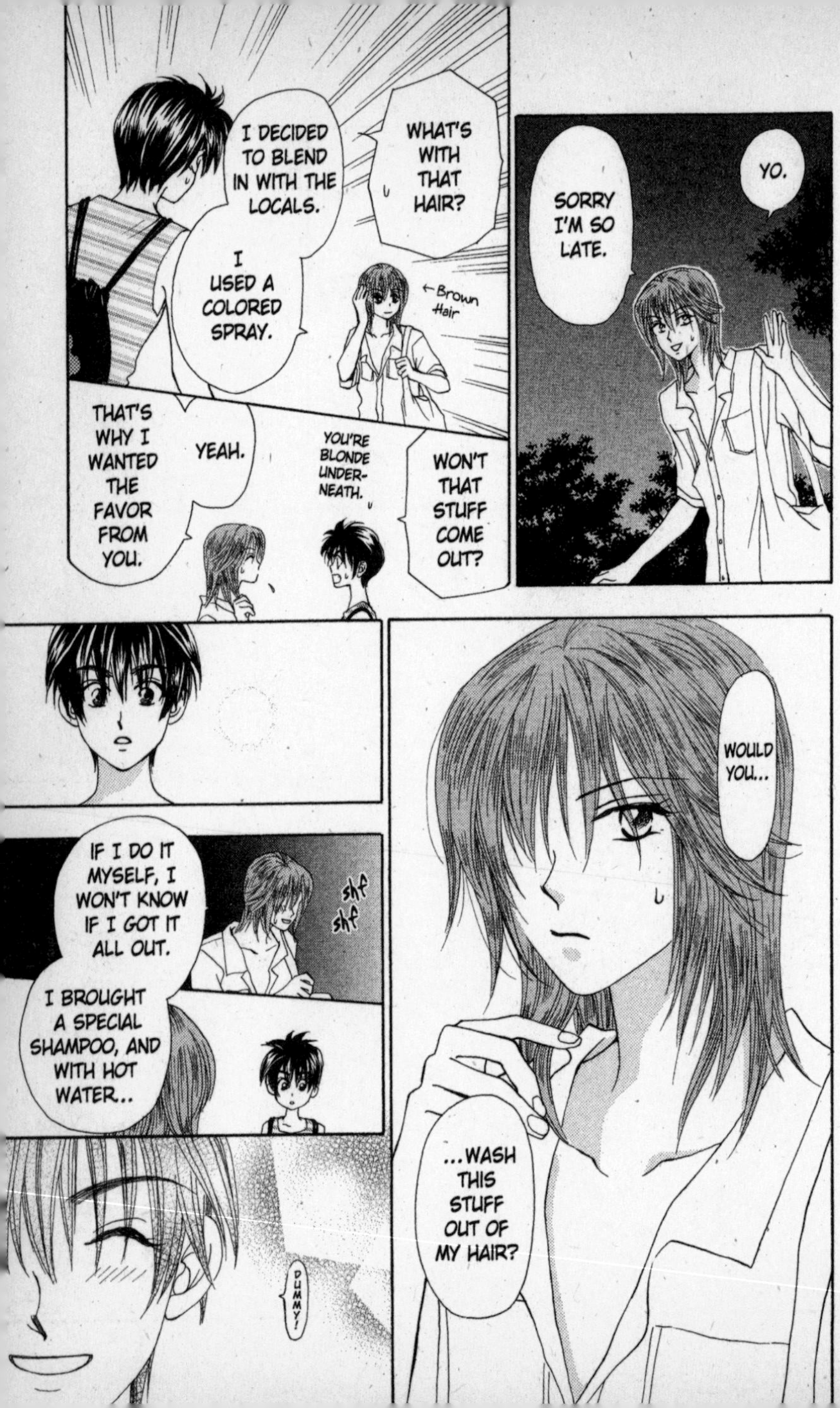
YO.
SORRY I'M SO LATE.
WHAT'S WITH THAT HAIR?
I DECIDED TO BLEND IN WITH THE LOCALS.
I USED A COLORED SPRAY.
← Brown Hair
WON'T THAT STUFF COME OUT?
YOU'RE BLONDE UNDERNEATH.
YEAH.
THAT'S WHY I WANTED THE FAVOR FROM YOU.
WOULD YOU...
...WASH THIS STUFF OUT OF MY HAIR?
IF I DO IT MYSELF, I WON'T KNOW IF I GOT IT ALL OUT.
shf shf
I BROUGHT A SPECIAL SHAMPOO, AND WITH HOT WATER...
DUMMY!

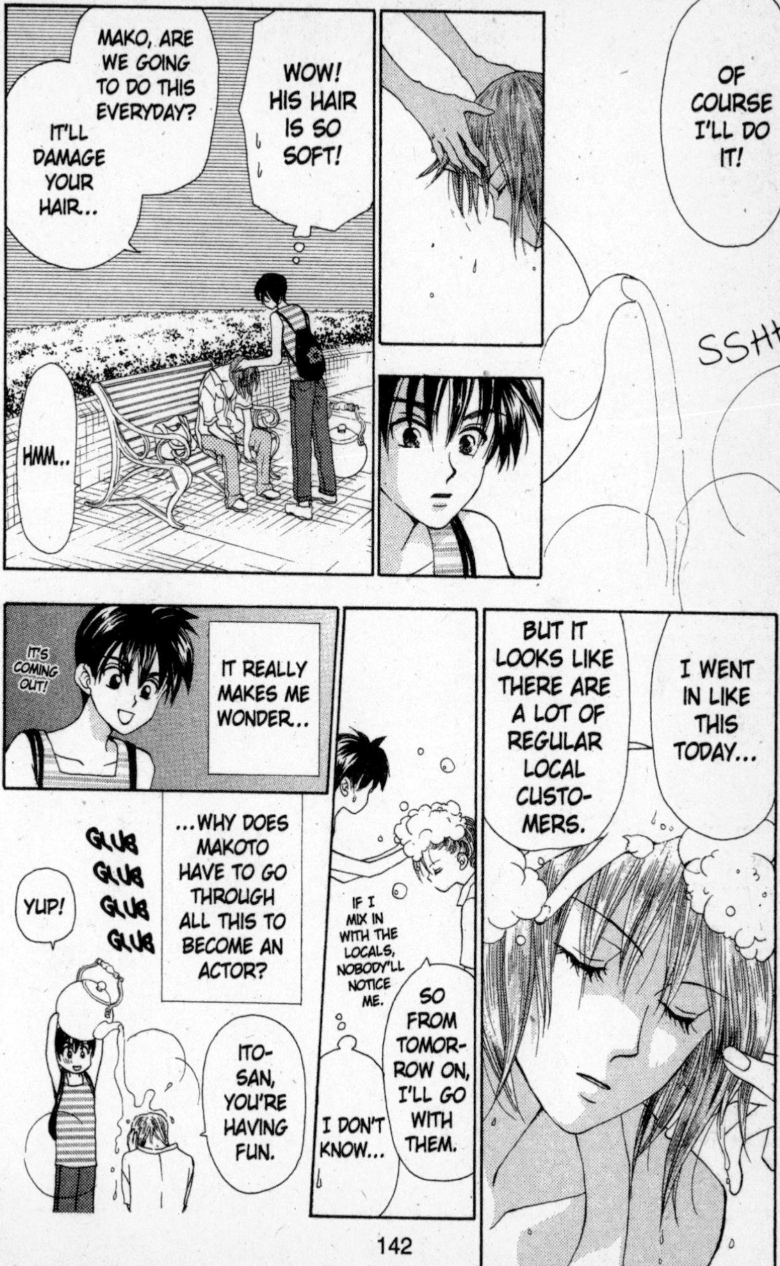
OF COURSE I'LL DO IT!
SSHH
WOW! HIS HAIR IS SO SOFT!
MAKO, ARE WE GOING TO DO THIS EVERYDAY?
IT'LL DAMAGE YOUR HAIR...
HMM...
I WENT IN LIKE THIS TODAY...
BUT IT LOOKS LIKE THERE ARE A LOT OF REGULAR LOCAL CUSTOMERS.
SO FROM TOMORROW ON, I'LL GO WITH THEM.
IF I MIX IN WITH THE LOCALS, NOBODY'LL NOTICE ME.
I DON'T KNOW...
IT REALLY MAKES ME WONDER...
IT'S COMING OUT!
...WHY DOES MAKOTO HAVE TO GO THROUGH ALL THIS TO BECOME AN ACTOR?
GLUB GLUB GLUB GLUB
YUP!
ITO-SAN, YOU'RE HAVING FUN.

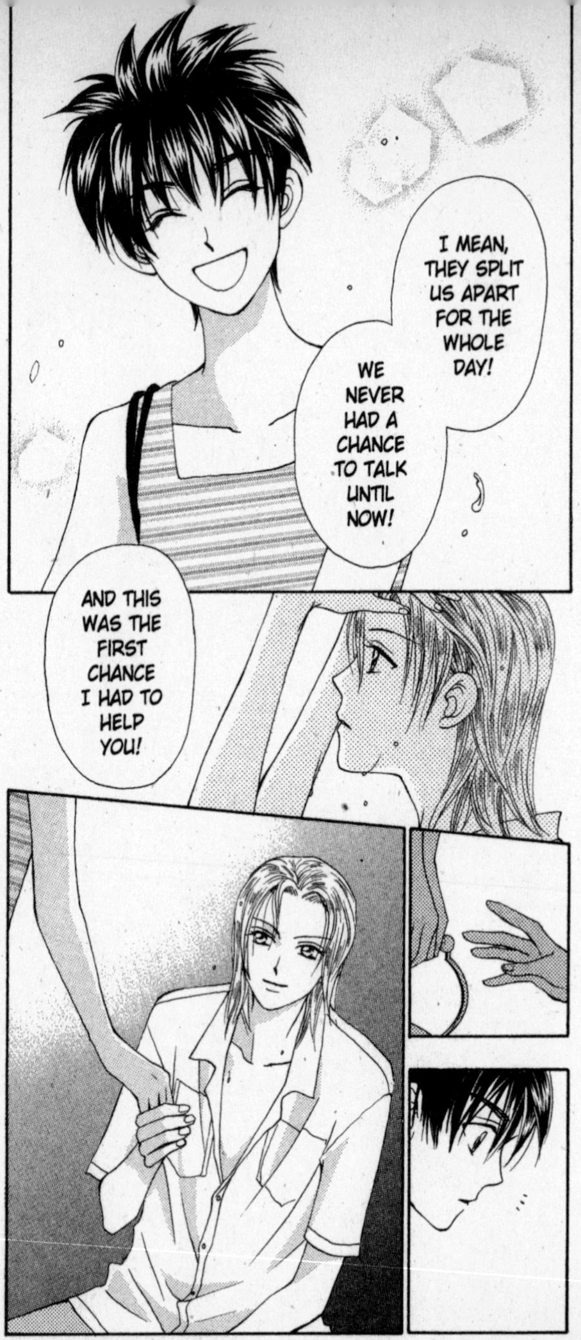
I MEAN, THEY SPLIT US APART FOR THE WHOLE DAY!
WE NEVER HAD A CHANCE TO TALK UNTIL NOW!
AND THIS WAS THE FIRST CHANCE I HAD TO HELP YOU!

Q&A CORNER

Once again, I was thinking that I'd answer some questions from the readers.

● When Mako-chan was tying up his hair in the second volume, was that fake hair?

Ⓔ Yes, it was. I drew a scene like it in this volume too. Mako was given a bunch of items to help him look like a girl from the third eldest sister in his family, Akane. The Pink House frilly clothes that you see Mako wear every now and again were sent him by the second eldest sister, Tsubaki. Makoto's sisters get a small part in the next volume.

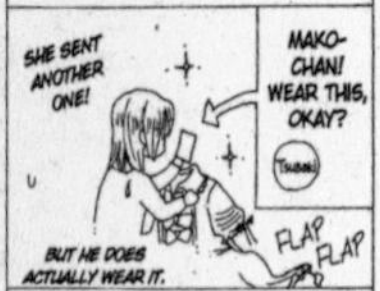
MAKO-CHAN! WEAR THIS, OKAY?
SHE SENT ANOTHER ONE!
FLAP FLAP
BUT HE DOES ACTUALLY WEAR IT.

● So...Mako does wear women's underwear under his clothes, doesn't he?

Ⓔ This question comes up an awful lot! The quick answer is "yes" for above and "no" for below. Below, he wears normal men's underwear and lycra shorts. He stuffs a bra in order to create a bust line.

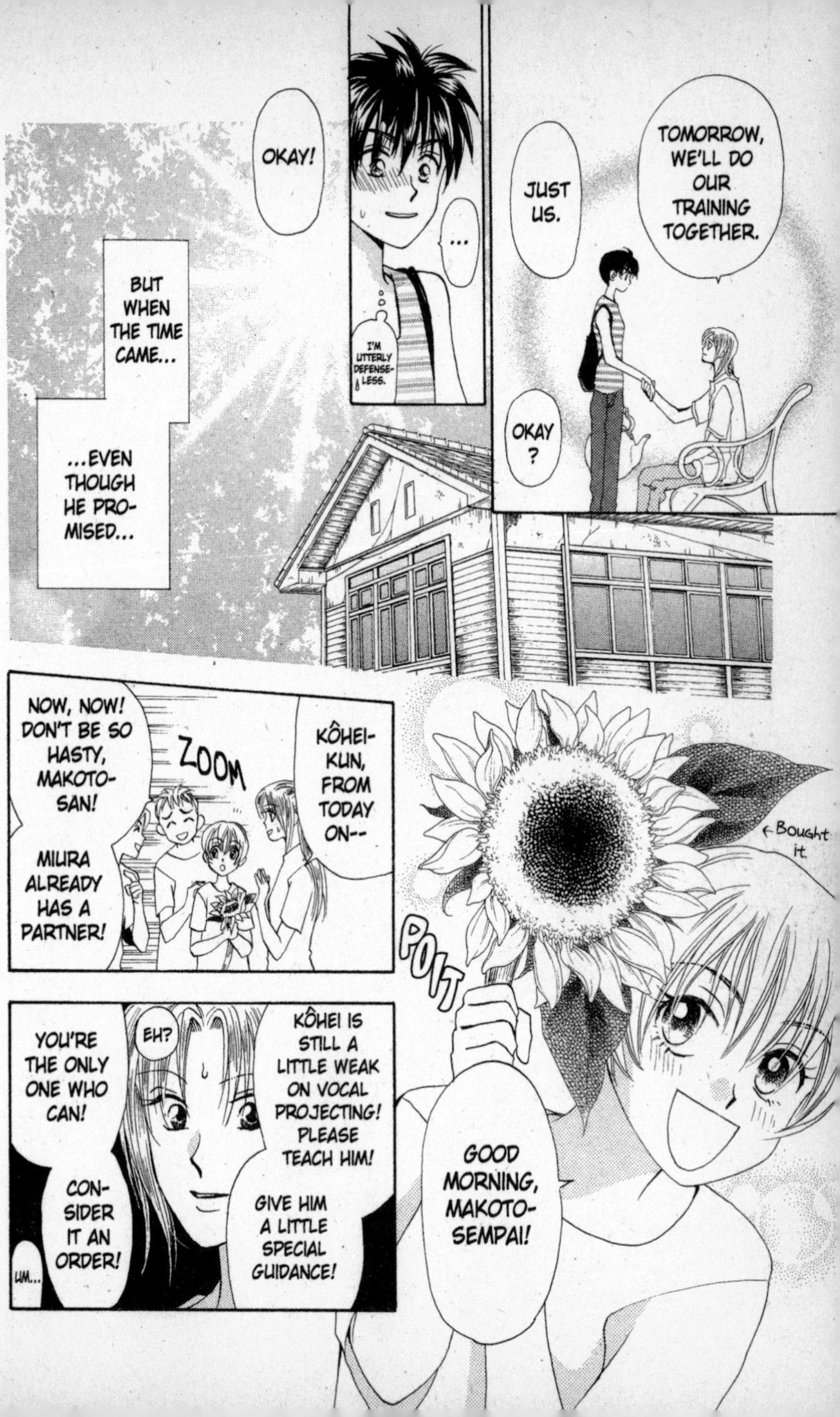
TOMORROW, WE'LL DO OUR TRAINING TOGETHER.
JUST US.
OKAY ?
OKAY!
...
I'M UTTERLY DEFENSE-LESS.
BUT WHEN THE TIME CAME...
...EVEN THOUGH HE PRO-MISED...
← Bought it.
POIT
GOOD MORNING, MAKOTO-SEMPAI!
KÔHEI-KUN, FROM TODAY ON--
ZOOM
NOW, NOW! DON'T BE SO HASTY, MAKOTO-SAN!
MIURA ALREADY HAS A PARTNER!
KÔHEI IS STILL A LITTLE WEAK ON VOCAL PROJECTING! PLEASE TEACH HIM!
GIVE HIM A LITTLE SPECIAL GUIDANCE!
EH?
YOU'RE THE ONLY ONE WHO CAN!
CON-SIDER IT AN ORDER!
UM...

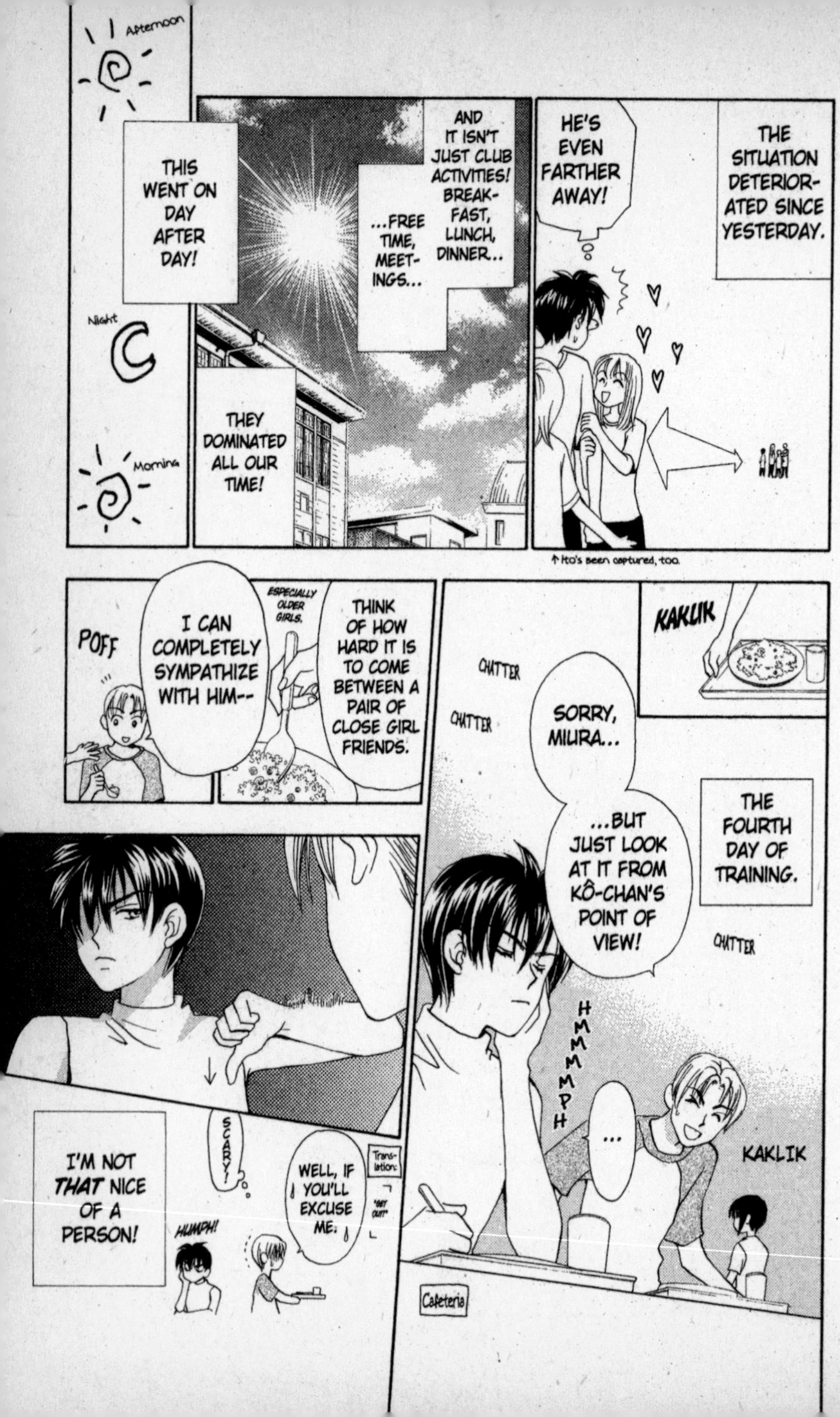
THE SITUATION DETERIORATED SINCE YESTERDAY.
HE'S EVEN FARTHER AWAY!
↑Ito's been captured, too.
AND IT ISN'T JUST CLUB ACTIVITIES! BREAKFAST, LUNCH, DINNER...
...FREE TIME, MEETINGS...
THEY DOMINATED ALL OUR TIME!
Afternoon
THIS WENT ON DAY AFTER DAY!
Night
Morning
KAKLIK
THE FOURTH DAY OF TRAINING.
CHATTER
CHATTER
SORRY, MIURA...
...BUT JUST LOOK AT IT FROM KÔ-CHAN'S POINT OF VIEW!
CHATTER
HMMMMPH
...
KAKLIK
Cafeteria
THINK OF HOW HARD IT IS TO COME BETWEEN A PAIR OF CLOSE GIRL FRIENDS.
ESPECIALLY OLDER GIRLS.
I CAN COMPLETELY SYMPATHIZE WITH HIM--
POFF
Translation: "GET OUT"
WELL, IF YOU'LL EXCUSE ME.
SCARY!
HUMPH!
I'M NOT *THAT* NICE OF A PERSON!

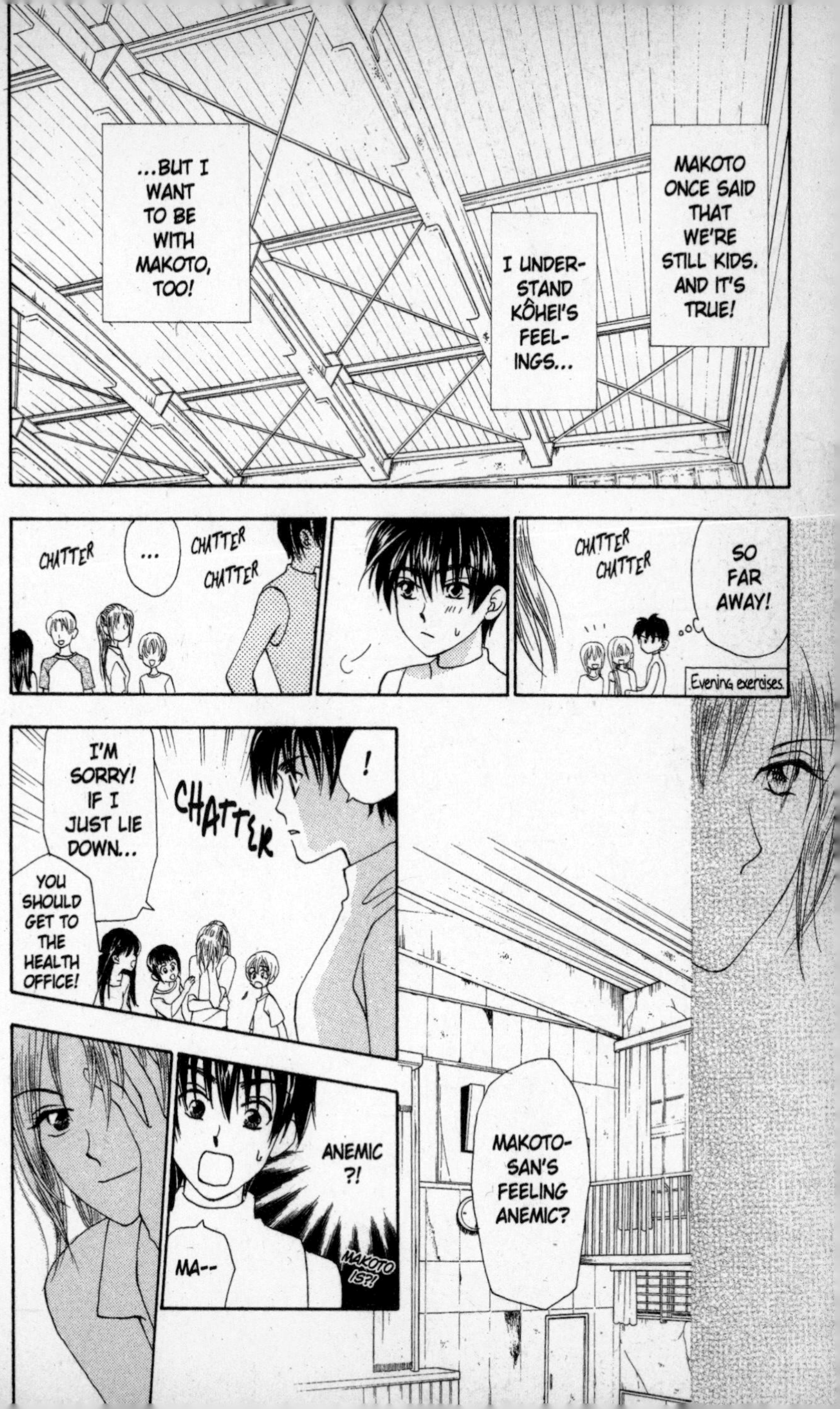
MAKOTO ONCE SAID THAT WE'RE STILL KIDS. AND IT'S TRUE!
I UNDER-STAND KÔHEI'S FEEL-INGS...
...BUT I WANT TO BE WITH MAKOTO, TOO!
SO FAR AWAY!
CHATTER CHATTER
Evening exercises.
CHATTER CHATTER
...
CHATTER
!
CHATTER
I'M SORRY! IF I JUST LIE DOWN...
YOU SHOULD GET TO THE HEALTH OFFICE!
MAKOTO-SAN'S FEELING ANEMIC?
ANEMIC ?!
MAKOTO IS?!
MA--

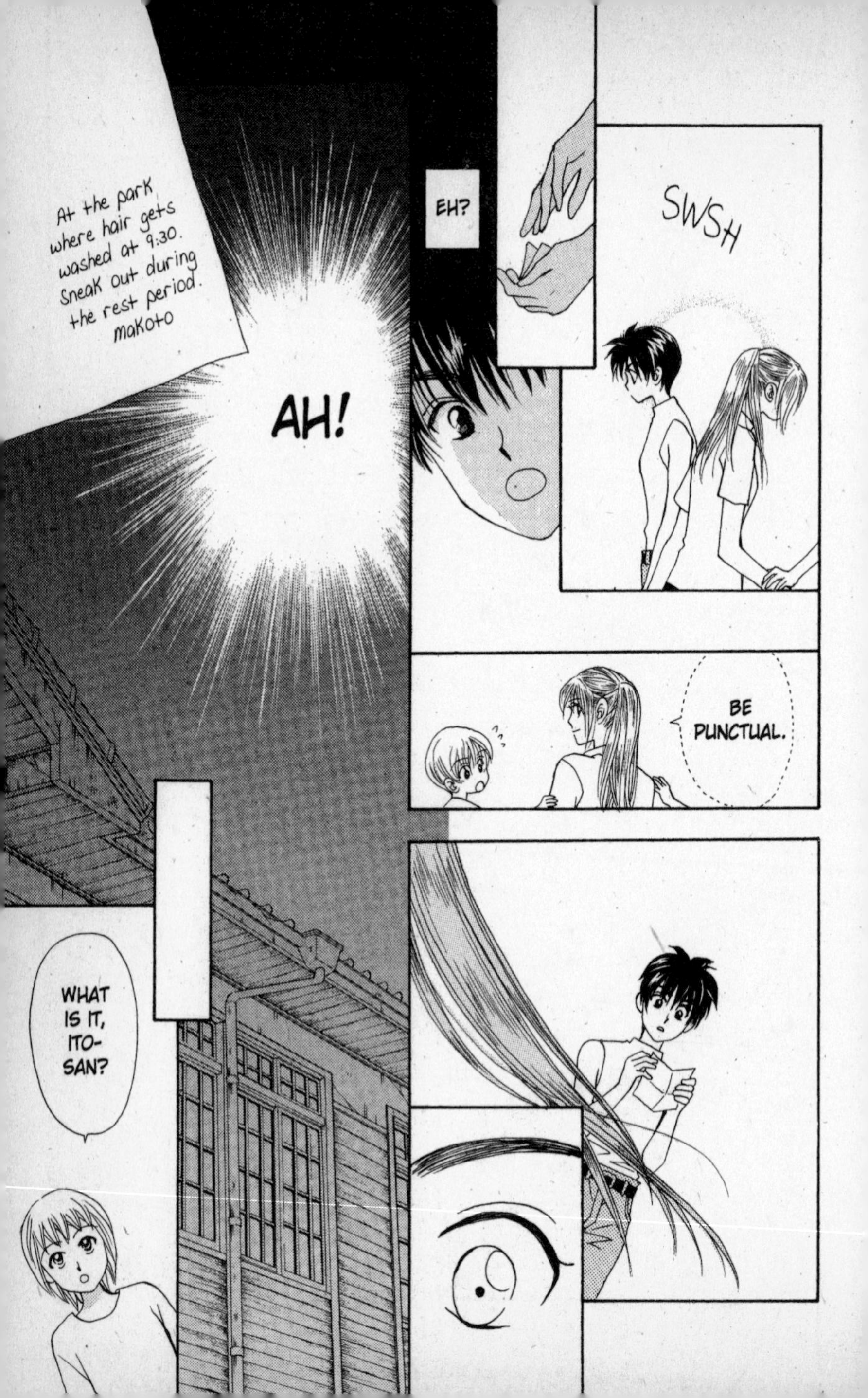
SWSH
EH?
At the park where hair gets washed at 9:30. Sneak out during the rest period. makoto
AH!
BE PUNCTUAL.
WHAT IS IT, ITO-SAN?

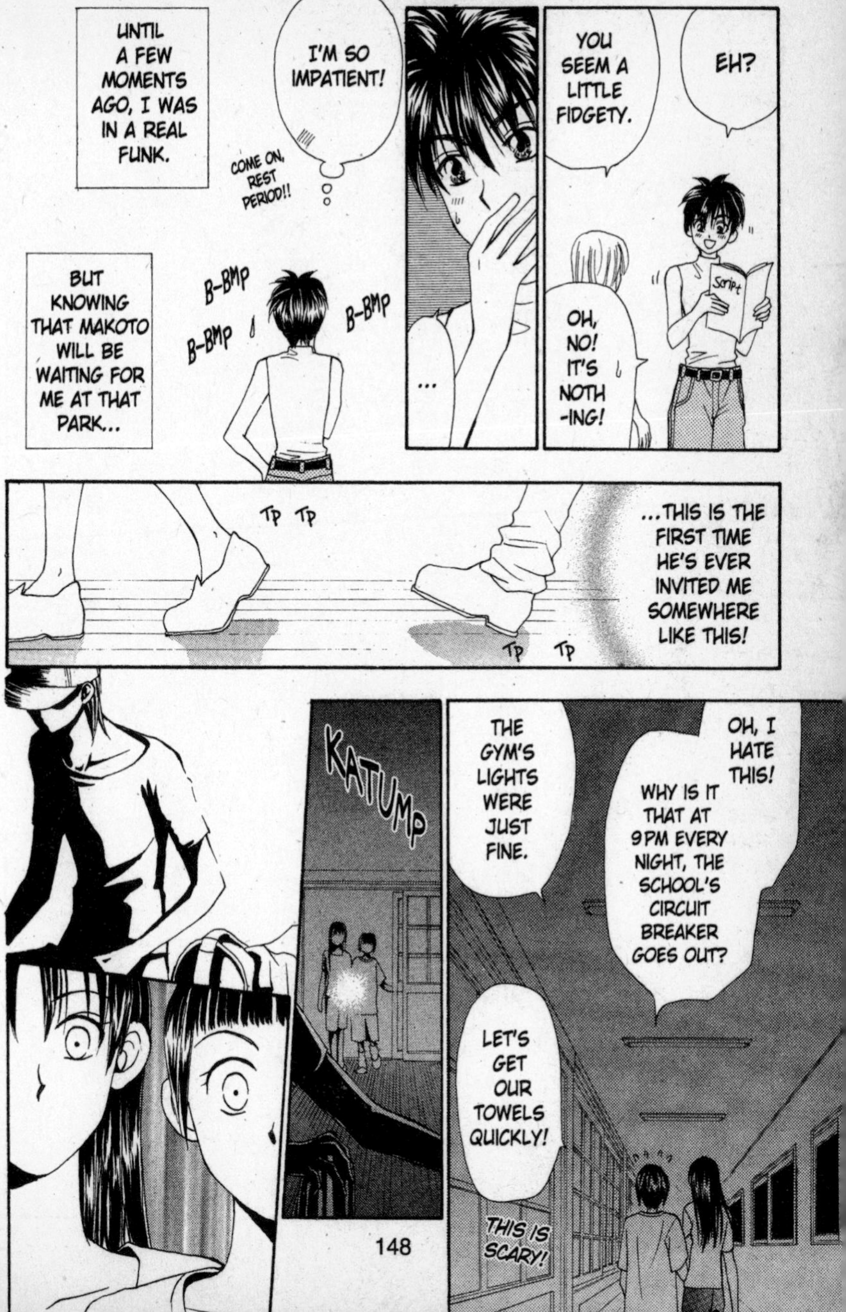
EH?
YOU SEEM A LITTLE FIDGETY.
OH, NO! IT'S NOTH-ING!
...
I'M SO IMPATIENT!
COME ON, REST PERIOD!!
UNTIL A FEW MOMENTS AGO, I WAS IN A REAL FUNK.
B-BMP
B-BMP
B-BMP
BUT KNOWING THAT MAKOTO WILL BE WAITING FOR ME AT THAT PARK...
...THIS IS THE FIRST TIME HE'S EVER INVITED ME SOMEWHERE LIKE THIS!
Tp Tp
Tp Tp
OH, I HATE THIS!
WHY IS IT THAT AT 9PM EVERY NIGHT, THE SCHOOL'S CIRCUIT BREAKER GOES OUT?
THE GYM'S LIGHTS WERE JUST FINE.
LET'S GET OUR TOWELS QUICKLY!
THIS IS SCARY!
KATUMP

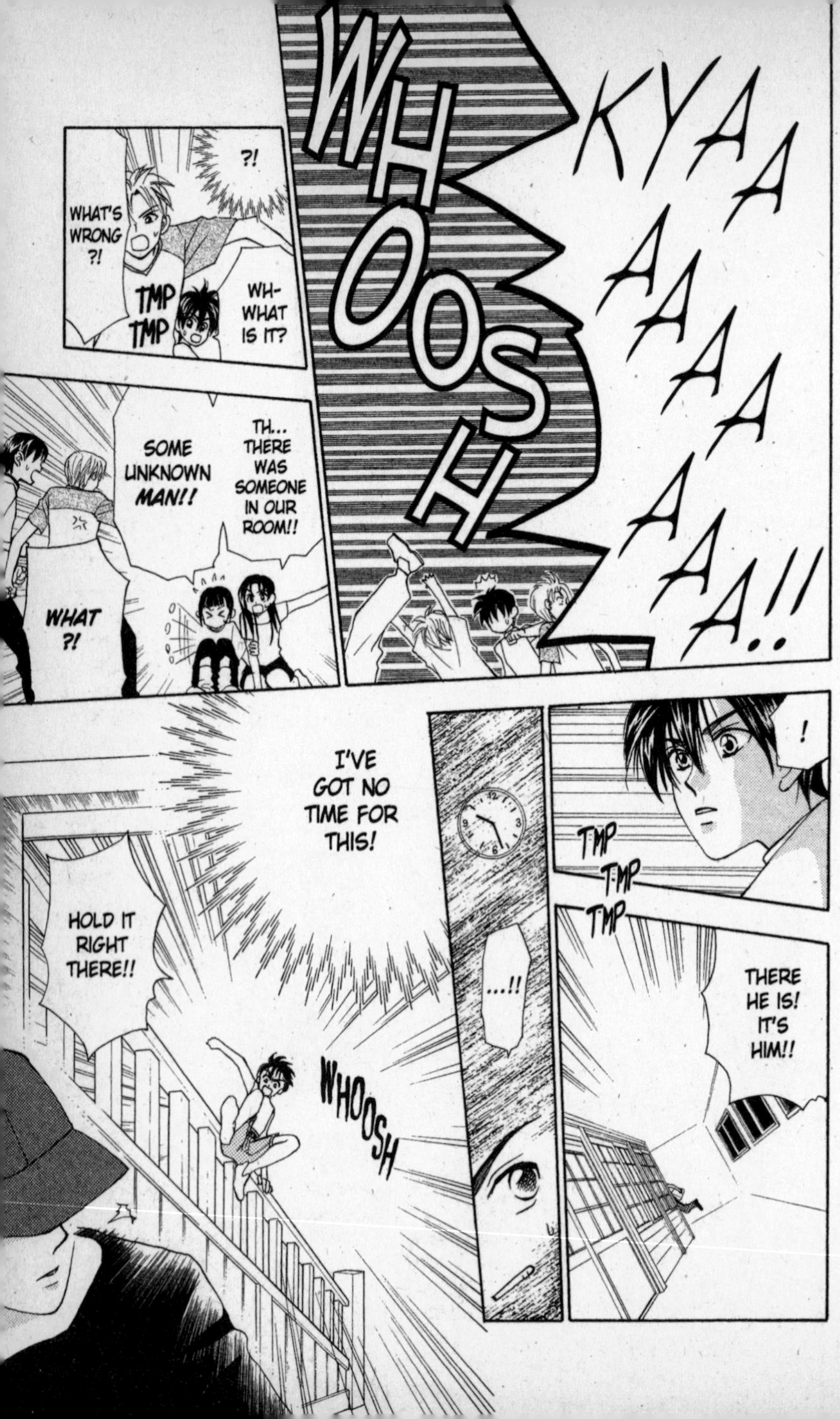
KYAAAAAAAAA!!..
WHOOSH
?!
WHAT'S WRONG ?!
WH-WHAT IS IT?
TMP TMP
TH... THERE WAS SOMEONE IN OUR ROOM!!
SOME UNKNOWN MAN!!
WHAT ?!
!
TMP TMP TMP
THERE HE IS! IT'S HIM!!
...!!
I'VE GOT NO TIME FOR THIS!
HOLD IT RIGHT THERE!!
WHOOSH

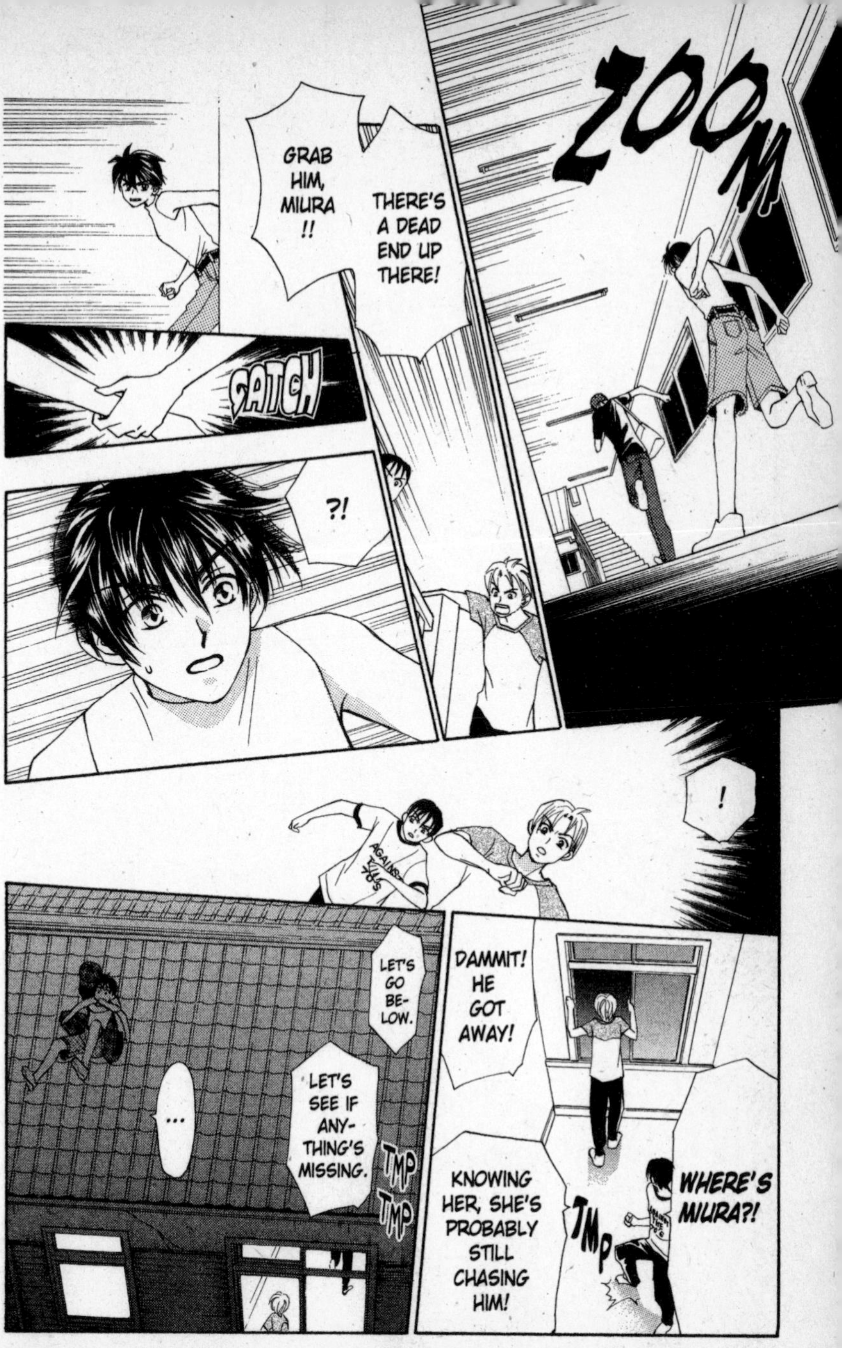
ZOOM
THERE'S A DEAD END UP THERE!
GRAB HIM, MIURA!!
CATCH
?!
!
DAMMIT! HE GOT AWAY!
WHERE'S MIURA?!
TMP
KNOWING HER, SHE'S PROBABLY STILL CHASING HIM!
LET'S GO BE-LOW.
LET'S SEE IF ANY-THING'S MISSING.
TMP TMP
...

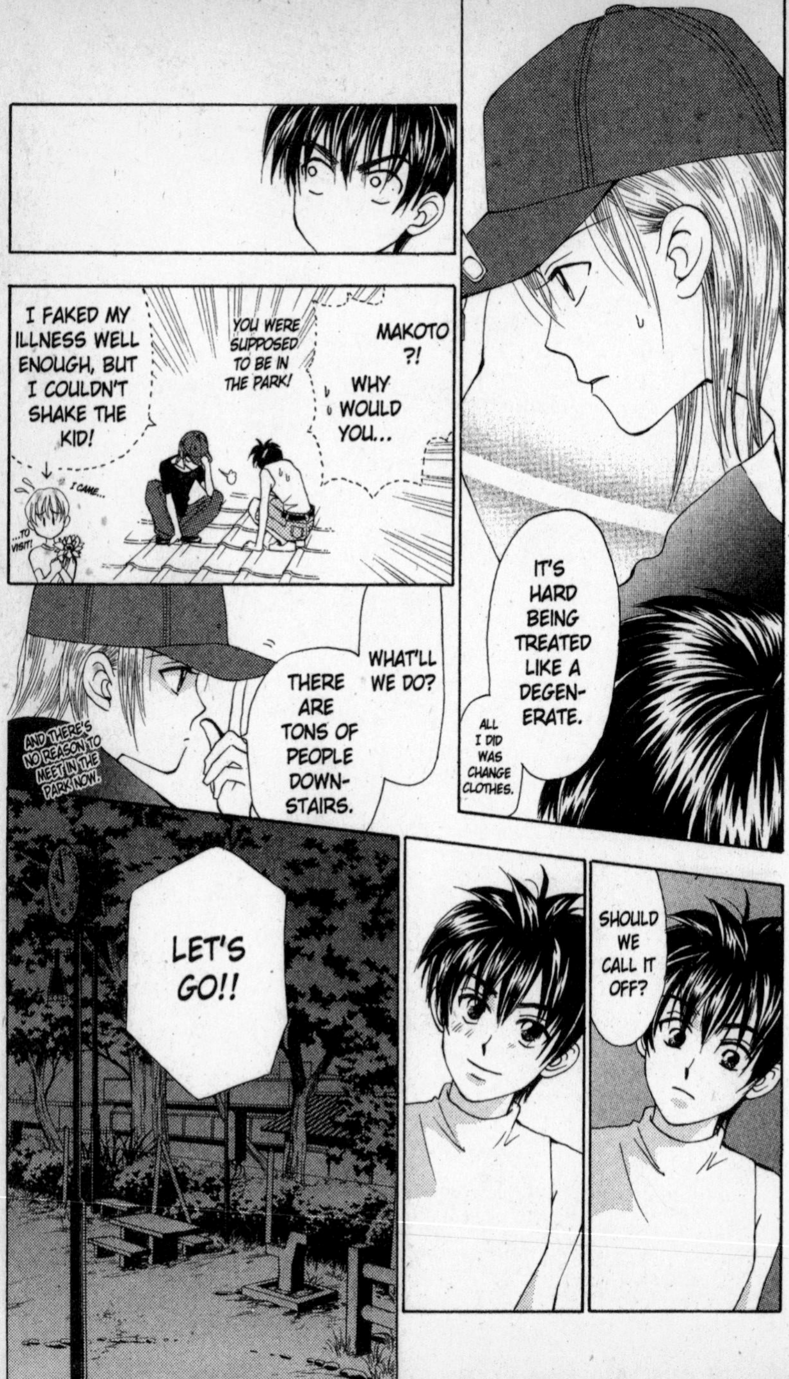
IT'S HARD BEING TREATED LIKE A DEGENERATE.
ALL I DID WAS CHANGE CLOTHES.
MAKOTO ?!
WHY WOULD YOU...
YOU WERE SUPPOSED TO BE IN THE PARK!
I FAKED MY ILLNESS WELL ENOUGH, BUT I COULDN'T SHAKE THE KID!
I CAME...
...TO VISIT!
WHAT'LL WE DO?
THERE ARE TONS OF PEOPLE DOWN-STAIRS.
AND THERE'S NO REASON TO MEET IN THE PARK NOW.
SHOULD WE CALL IT OFF?
LET'S GO!!

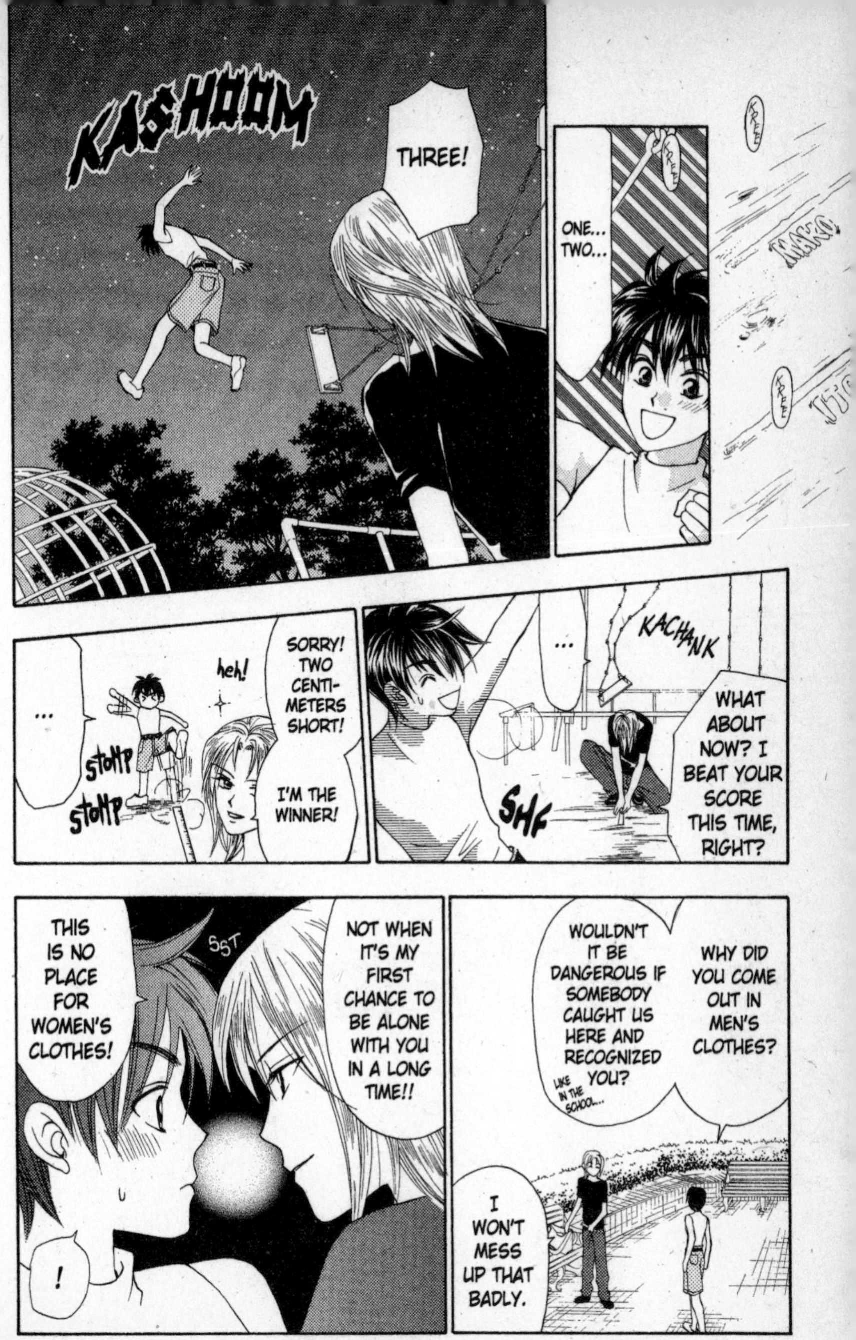
KREE
KREE
ONE... TWO...
KREE
THREE!
KASHOOM
KACHANK
...
WHAT ABOUT NOW? I BEAT YOUR SCORE THIS TIME, RIGHT?
SHF
SORRY! TWO CENTI-METERS SHORT!
I'M THE WINNER!
heh!
...
STOMP
STOMP
WHY DID YOU COME OUT IN MEN'S CLOTHES?
WOULDN'T IT BE DANGEROUS IF SOMEBODY CAUGHT US HERE AND RECOGNIZED YOU?
LIKE IN THE SCHOOL...
I WON'T MESS UP THAT BADLY.
NOT WHEN IT'S MY FIRST CHANCE TO BE ALONE WITH YOU IN A LONG TIME!!
SST
THIS IS NO PLACE FOR WOMEN'S CLOTHES!
!

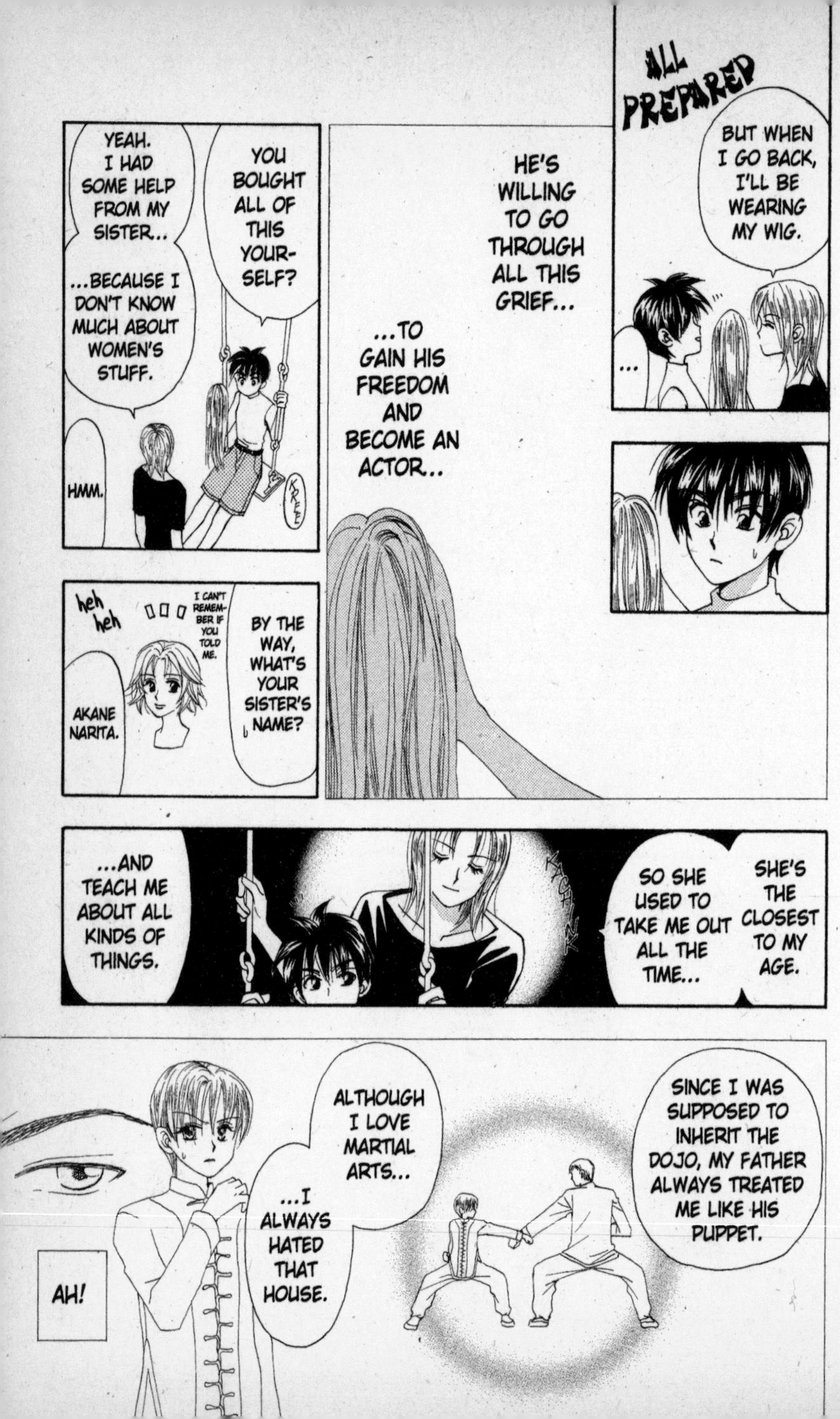
ALL PREPARED
BUT WHEN I GO BACK, I'LL BE WEARING MY WIG.
...
HE'S WILLING TO GO THROUGH ALL THIS GRIEF...
...TO GAIN HIS FREEDOM AND BECOME AN ACTOR...
YOU BOUGHT ALL OF THIS YOURSELF?
YEAH. I HAD SOME HELP FROM MY SISTER...
...BECAUSE I DON'T KNOW MUCH ABOUT WOMEN'S STUFF.
KREE
HMM.
BY THE WAY, WHAT'S YOUR SISTER'S NAME?
I CAN'T REMEMBER IF YOU TOLD ME.
heh heh
AKANE NARITA.
SHE'S THE CLOSEST TO MY AGE.
SO SHE USED TO TAKE ME OUT ALL THE TIME...
...AND TEACH ME ABOUT ALL KINDS OF THINGS.
SINCE I WAS SUPPOSED TO INHERIT THE DOJO, MY FATHER ALWAYS TREATED ME LIKE HIS PUPPET.
ALTHOUGH I LOVE MARTIAL ARTS...
...I ALWAYS HATED THAT HOUSE.
AH!

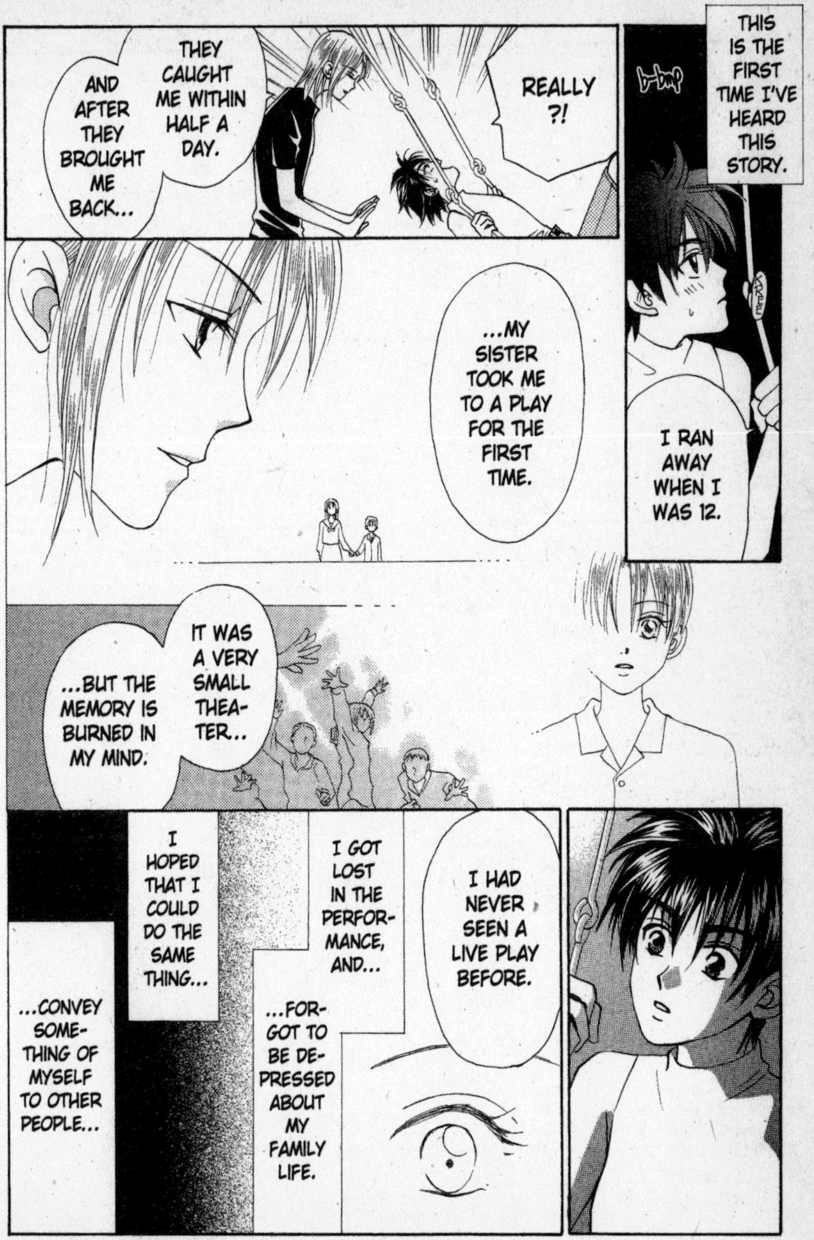
THIS IS THE FIRST TIME I'VE HEARD THIS STORY.
b-bmp
I RAN AWAY WHEN I WAS 12.
REALLY ?!
THEY CAUGHT ME WITHIN HALF A DAY.
AND AFTER THEY BROUGHT ME BACK...
...MY SISTER TOOK ME TO A PLAY FOR THE FIRST TIME.
IT WAS A VERY SMALL THEA-TER...
...BUT THE MEMORY IS BURNED IN MY MIND.
I HAD NEVER SEEN A LIVE PLAY BEFORE.
I GOT LOST IN THE PERFOR-MANCE, AND...
...FOR-GOT TO BE DE-PRESSED ABOUT MY FAMILY LIFE.
I HOPED THAT I COULD DO THE SAME THING...
...CONVEY SOME-THING OF MYSELF TO OTHER PEOPLE...

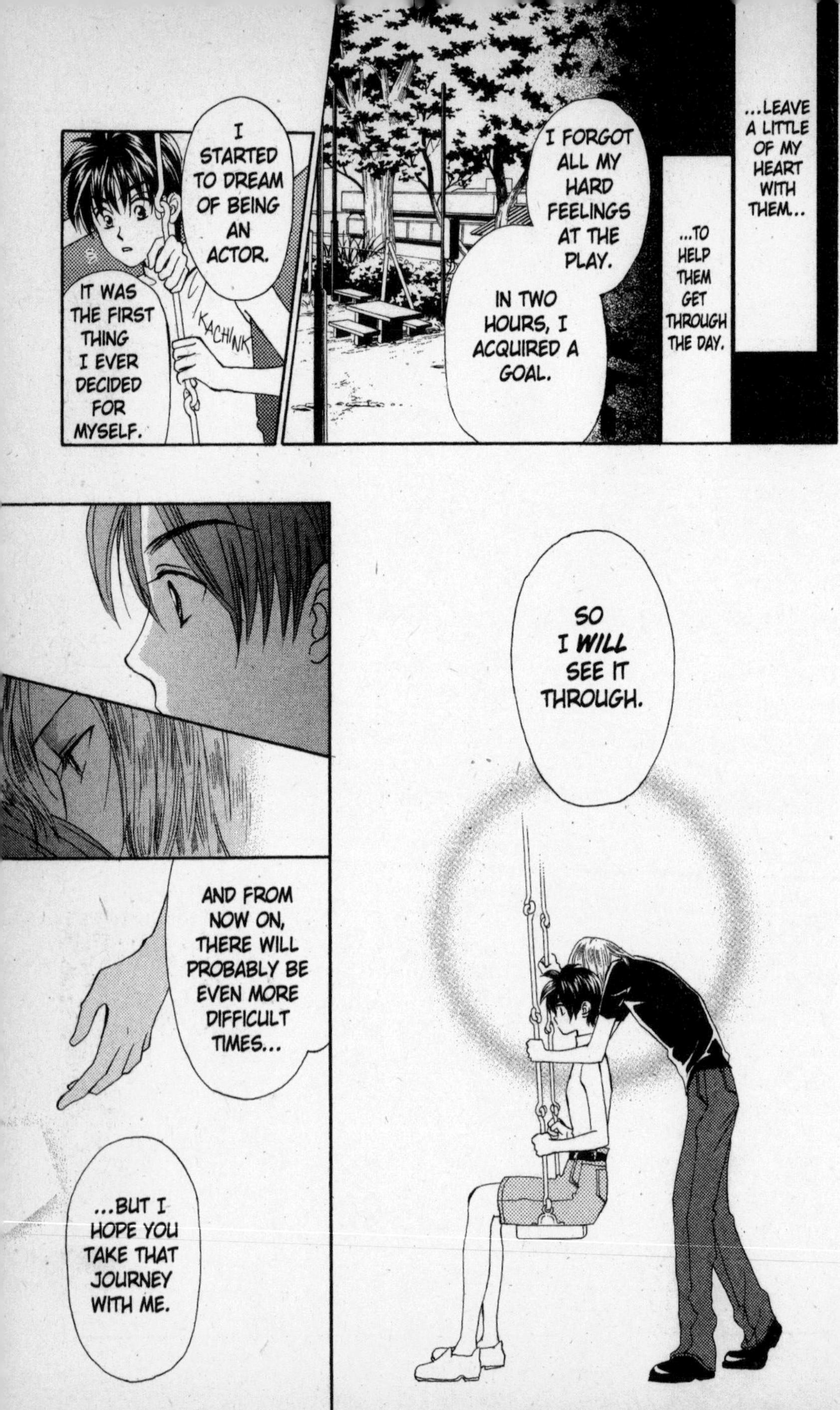
...LEAVE A LITTLE OF MY HEART WITH THEM...
...TO HELP THEM GET THROUGH THE DAY.
I FORGOT ALL MY HARD FEELINGS AT THE PLAY.
IN TWO HOURS, I ACQUIRED A GOAL.
I STARTED TO DREAM OF BEING AN ACTOR.
KACHINK
IT WAS THE FIRST THING I EVER DECIDED FOR MYSELF.
SO I WILL SEE IT THROUGH.
AND FROM NOW ON, THERE WILL PROBABLY BE EVEN MORE DIFFICULT TIMES...
...BUT I HOPE YOU TAKE THAT JOURNEY WITH ME.

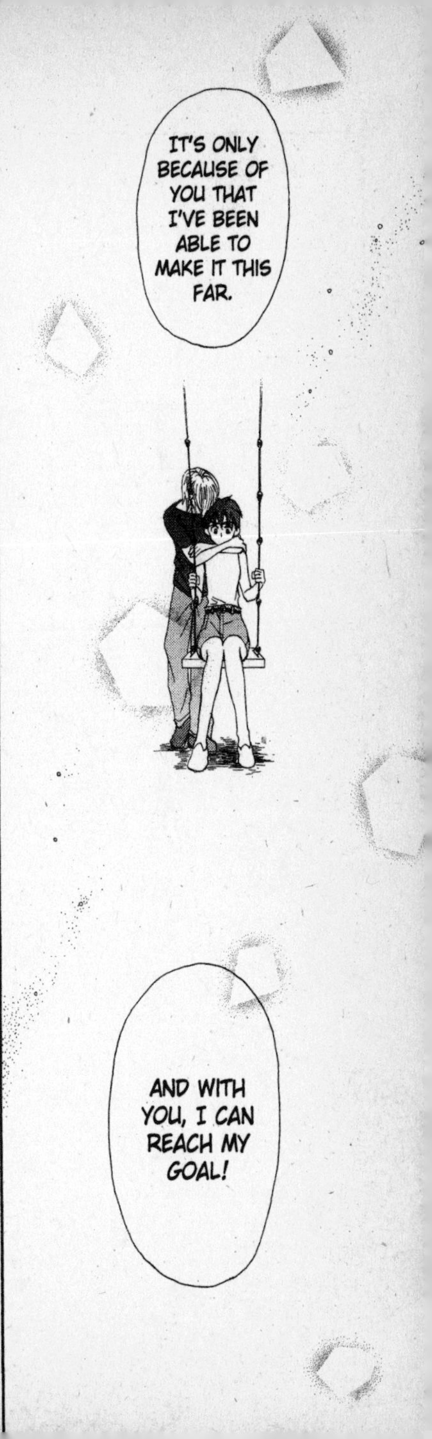
IT'S ONLY BECAUSE OF YOU THAT I'VE BEEN ABLE TO MAKE IT THIS FAR.
AND WITH YOU, I CAN REACH MY GOAL!
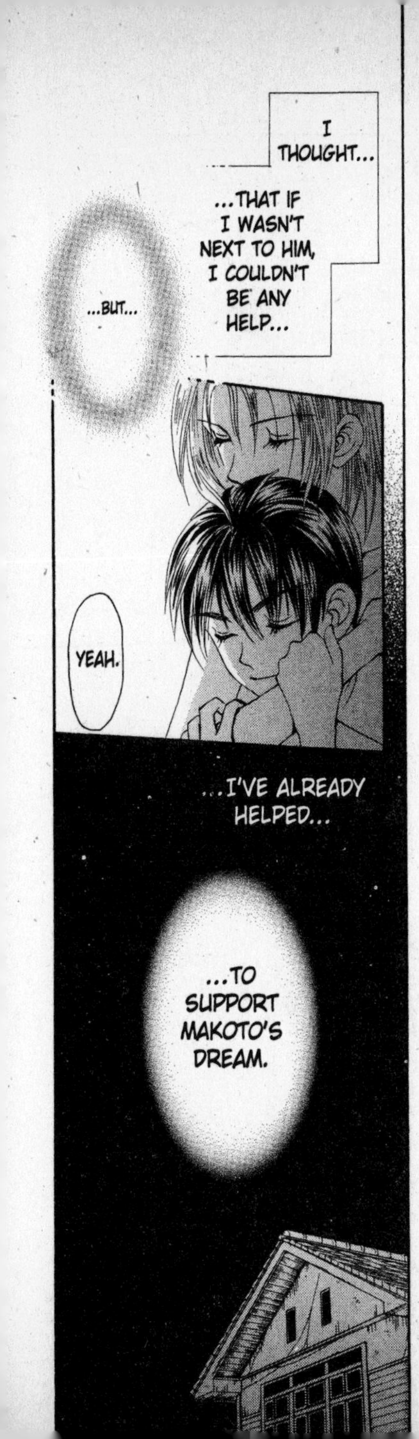
I THOUGHT...
...THAT IF I WASN'T NEXT TO HIM, I COULDN'T BE ANY HELP...
...BUT...
YEAH.
...I'VE ALREADY HELPED...
...TO SUPPORT MAKOTO'S DREAM.

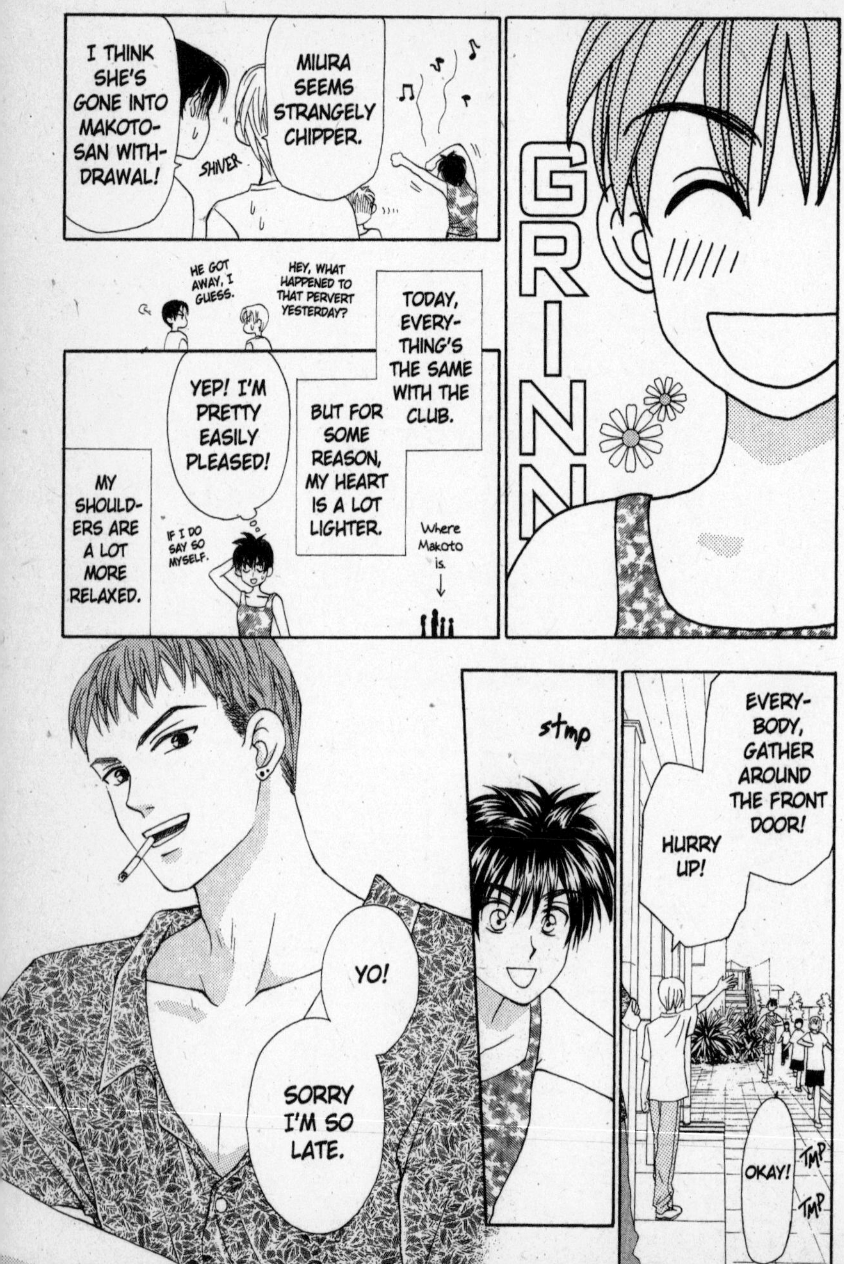
GRINN
MIURA SEEMS STRANGELY CHIPPER.
I THINK SHE'S GONE INTO MAKOTO-SAN WITH-DRAWAL!
SHIVER
TODAY, EVERY-THING'S THE SAME WITH THE CLUB.
HEY, WHAT HAPPENED TO THAT PERVERT YESTERDAY?
HE GOT AWAY, I GUESS.
BUT FOR SOME REASON, MY HEART IS A LOT LIGHTER.
Where Makoto is.
YEP! I'M PRETTY EASILY PLEASED!
IF I DO SAY SO MYSELF.
MY SHOULD-ERS ARE A LOT MORE RELAXED.
EVERY-BODY, GATHER AROUND THE FRONT DOOR!
HURRY UP!
OKAY!
TMP
TMP
stmp
YO!
SORRY I'M SO LATE.

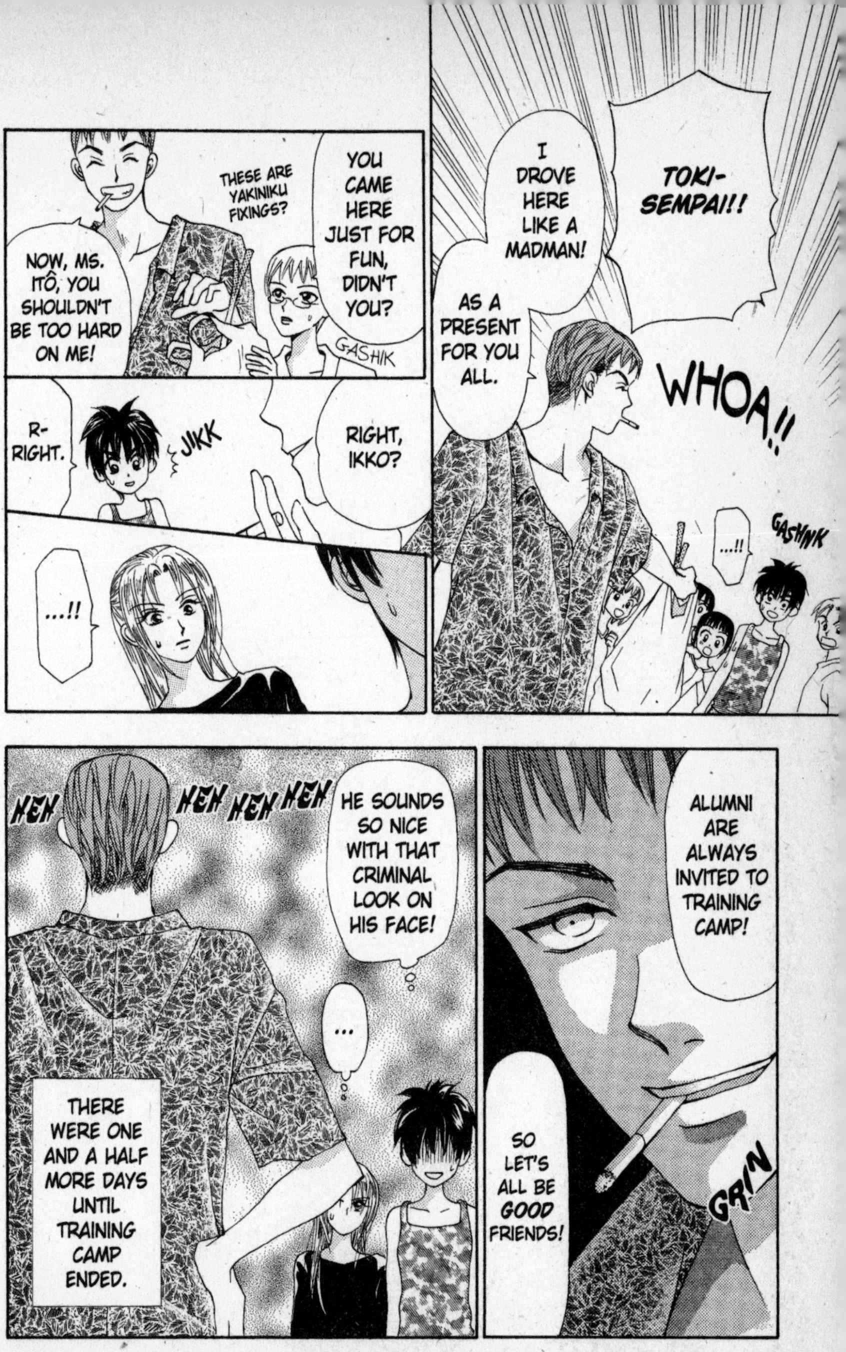
TOKI-SEMPAI!!
I DROVE HERE LIKE A MADMAN!
AS A PRESENT FOR YOU ALL.
WHOA!!
GASHNK
...!!
YOU CAME HERE JUST FOR FUN, DIDN'T YOU?
THESE ARE YAKINIKU FIXINGS?
GASHIK
NOW, MS. ITÔ, YOU SHOULDN'T BE TOO HARD ON ME!
RIGHT, IKKO?
JIKK
R-RIGHT.
...!!
ALUMNI ARE ALWAYS INVITED TO TRAINING CAMP!
SO LET'S ALL BE GOOD FRIENDS!
GRIN
HEH HEH HEH HEH
HE SOUNDS SO NICE WITH THAT CRIMINAL LOOK ON HIS FACE!
...
THERE WERE ONE AND A HALF MORE DAYS UNTIL TRAINING CAMP ENDED.

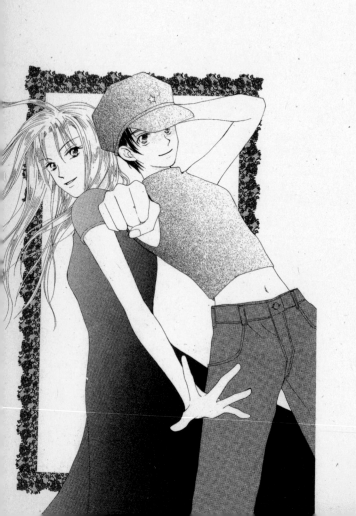

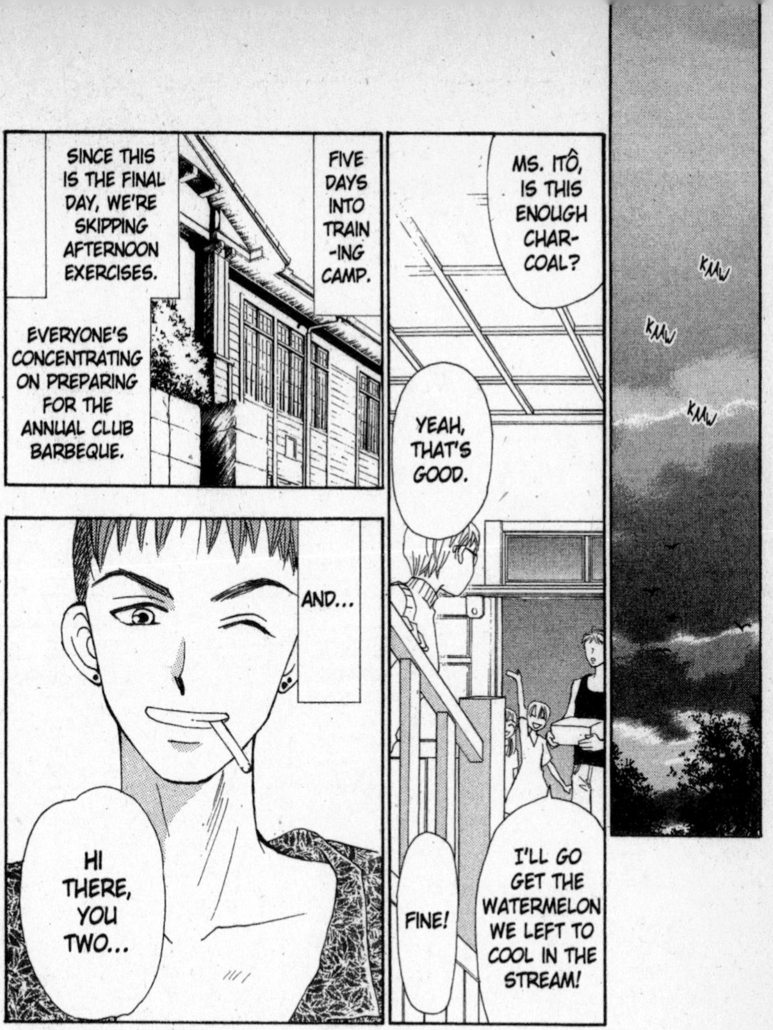
KAW
KAW
KAW
MS. ITÔ, IS THIS ENOUGH CHAR-COAL?
YEAH, THAT'S GOOD.
I'LL GO GET THE WATERMELON WE LEFT TO COOL IN THE STREAM!
FINE!
FIVE DAYS INTO TRAIN-ING CAMP.
SINCE THIS IS THE FINAL DAY, WE'RE SKIPPING AFTERNOON EXERCISES.
EVERYONE'S CONCENTRATING ON PREPARING FOR THE ANNUAL CLUB BARBEQUE.
AND...
HI THERE, YOU TWO...

-Behind the Scenes Story- ⑤

Ito's dream was something I had in mind from the very first, but it took me a long time to finally write it. Sorry if it caught you by surprise! ♡ Both characters are aiming at the same thing. And then there is Nobuko's novel, "Mokugekisha" ("Eyewitness"). There were fans who wrote in to say that they noticed, and I was really happy! "Mokugekisha" was my work that won the B C Award. It was such a sad story that I gave Nobuko, Misaki and Yoshirô a home in W.J., and because I had become attached to them. Their personalities and faces have changed a little though...

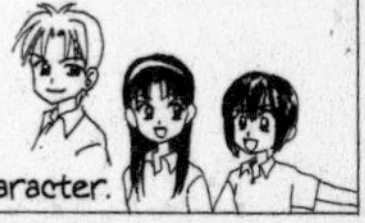

Misaki was the lead character.

The theme is friends forever!

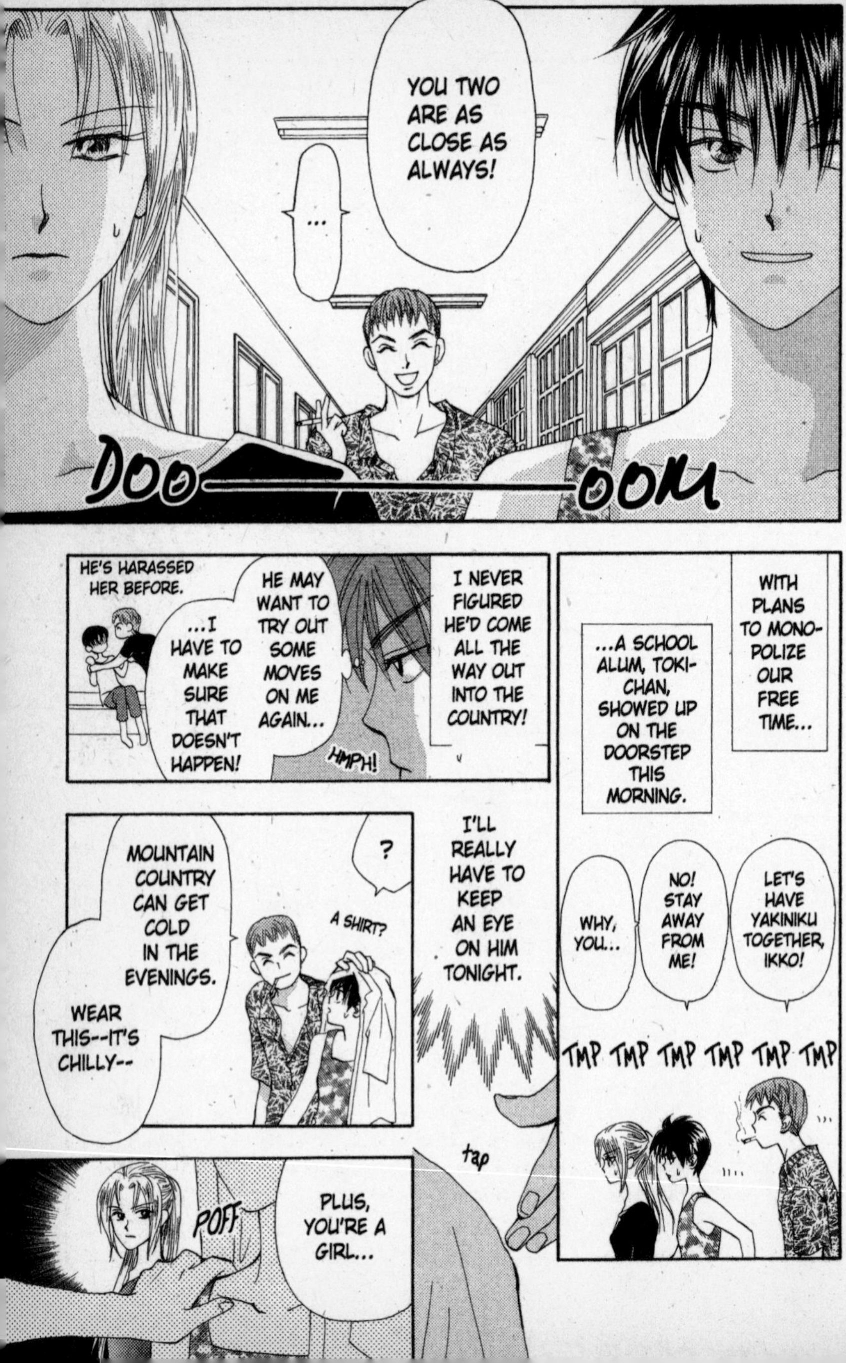
YOU TWO ARE AS CLOSE AS ALWAYS!
...
DOO——OOM
WITH PLANS TO MONO-POLIZE OUR FREE TIME...
...A SCHOOL ALUM, TOKI-CHAN, SHOWED UP ON THE DOORSTEP THIS MORNING.
LET'S HAVE YAKINIKU TOGETHER, IKKO!
NO! STAY AWAY FROM ME!
WHY, YOU...
TMP TMP TMP TMP TMP TMP
I NEVER FIGURED HE'D COME ALL THE WAY OUT INTO THE COUNTRY!
HE MAY WANT TO TRY OUT SOME MOVES ON ME AGAIN...
HMPH!
...I HAVE TO MAKE SURE THAT DOESN'T HAPPEN!
HE'S HARASSED HER BEFORE.
I'LL REALLY HAVE TO KEEP AN EYE ON HIM TONIGHT.
?
A SHIRT?
MOUNTAIN COUNTRY CAN GET COLD IN THE EVENINGS.
WEAR THIS--IT'S CHILLY--
tap
PLUS, YOU'RE A GIRL...
POFF

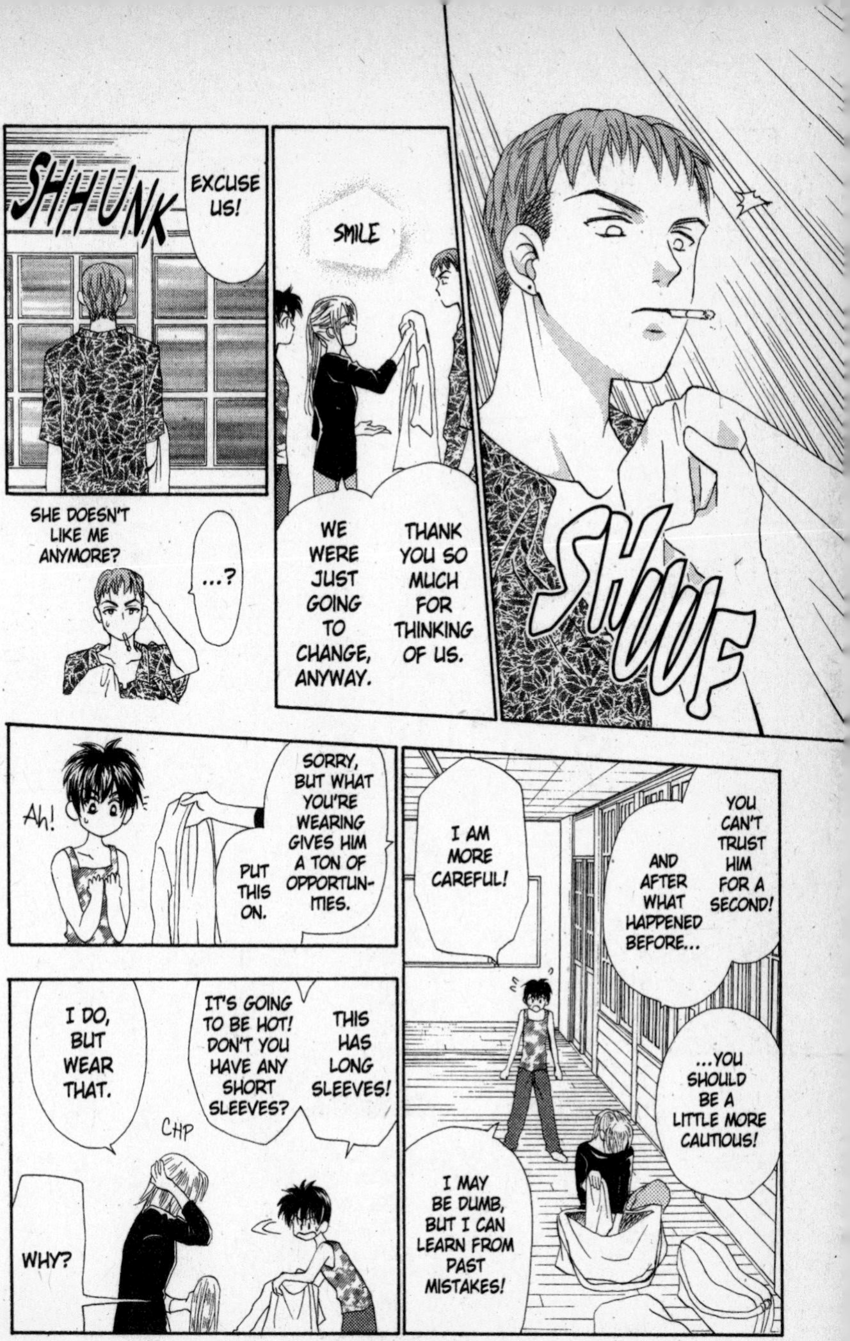
SHUUF
SMILE
THANK YOU SO MUCH FOR THINKING OF US.
WE WERE JUST GOING TO CHANGE, ANYWAY.
SHHUNK
EXCUSE US!
...?
SHE DOESN'T LIKE ME ANYMORE?
YOU CAN'T TRUST HIM FOR A SECOND!
AND AFTER WHAT HAPPENED BEFORE...
I AM MORE CAREFUL!
...YOU SHOULD BE A LITTLE MORE CAUTIOUS!
I MAY BE DUMB, BUT I CAN LEARN FROM PAST MISTAKES!
SORRY, BUT WHAT YOU'RE WEARING GIVES HIM A TON OF OPPORTUNITIES.
PUT THIS ON.
Ah!
THIS HAS LONG SLEEVES!
IT'S GOING TO BE HOT! DON'T YOU HAVE ANY SHORT SLEEVES?
I DO, BUT WEAR THAT.
CHP
WHY?

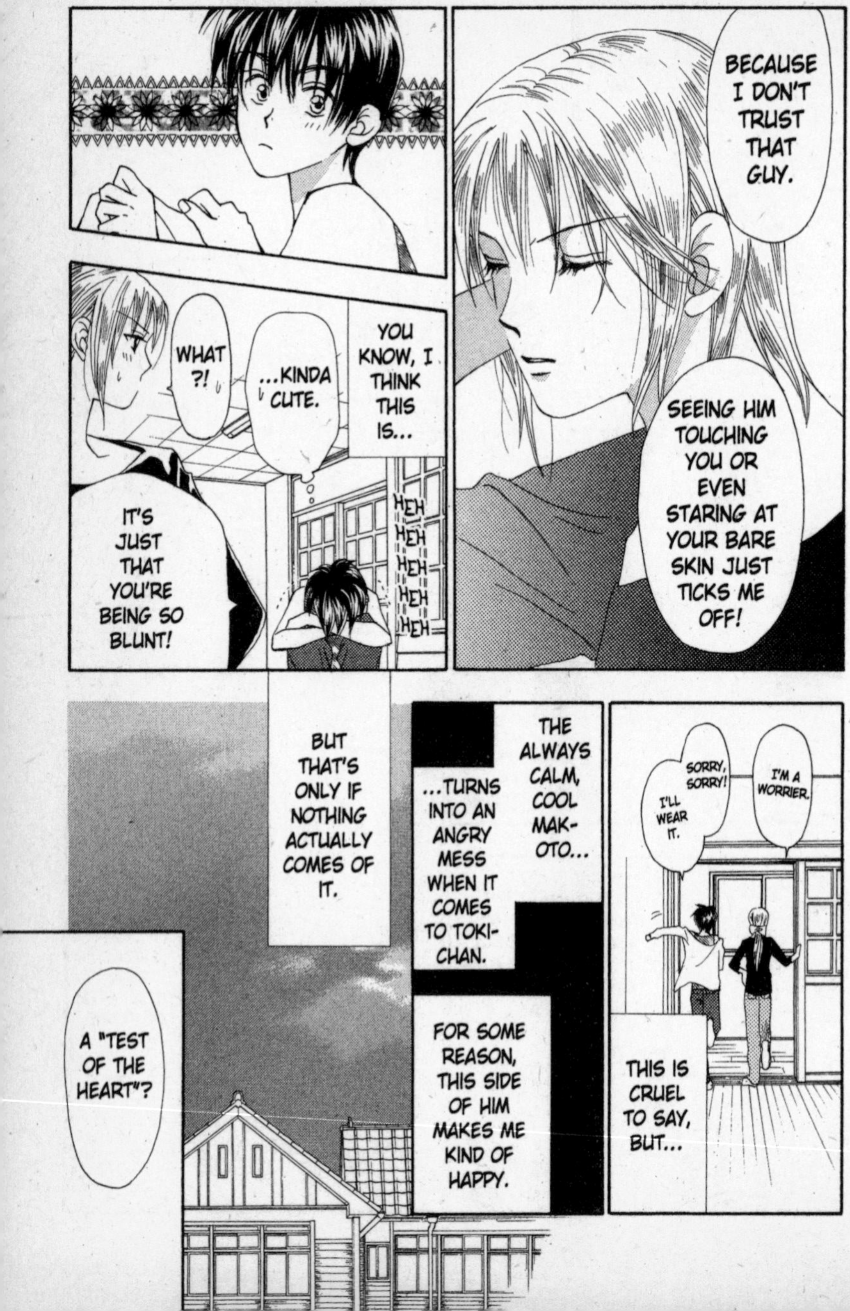
BECAUSE I DON'T TRUST THAT GUY.
SEEING HIM TOUCHING YOU OR EVEN STARING AT YOUR BARE SKIN JUST TICKS ME OFF!
YOU KNOW, I THINK THIS IS...
...KINDA CUTE.
WHAT?!
HEH HEH HEH HEH HEH
IT'S JUST THAT YOU'RE BEING SO BLUNT!
I'M A WORRIER.
SORRY, SORRY!
I'LL WEAR IT.
THIS IS CRUEL TO SAY, BUT...
THE ALWAYS CALM, COOL MAK-OTO...
...TURNS INTO AN ANGRY MESS WHEN IT COMES TO TOKI-CHAN.
FOR SOME REASON, THIS SIDE OF HIM MAKES ME KIND OF HAPPY.
BUT THAT'S ONLY IF NOTHING ACTUALLY COMES OF IT.
A "TEST OF THE HEART"?

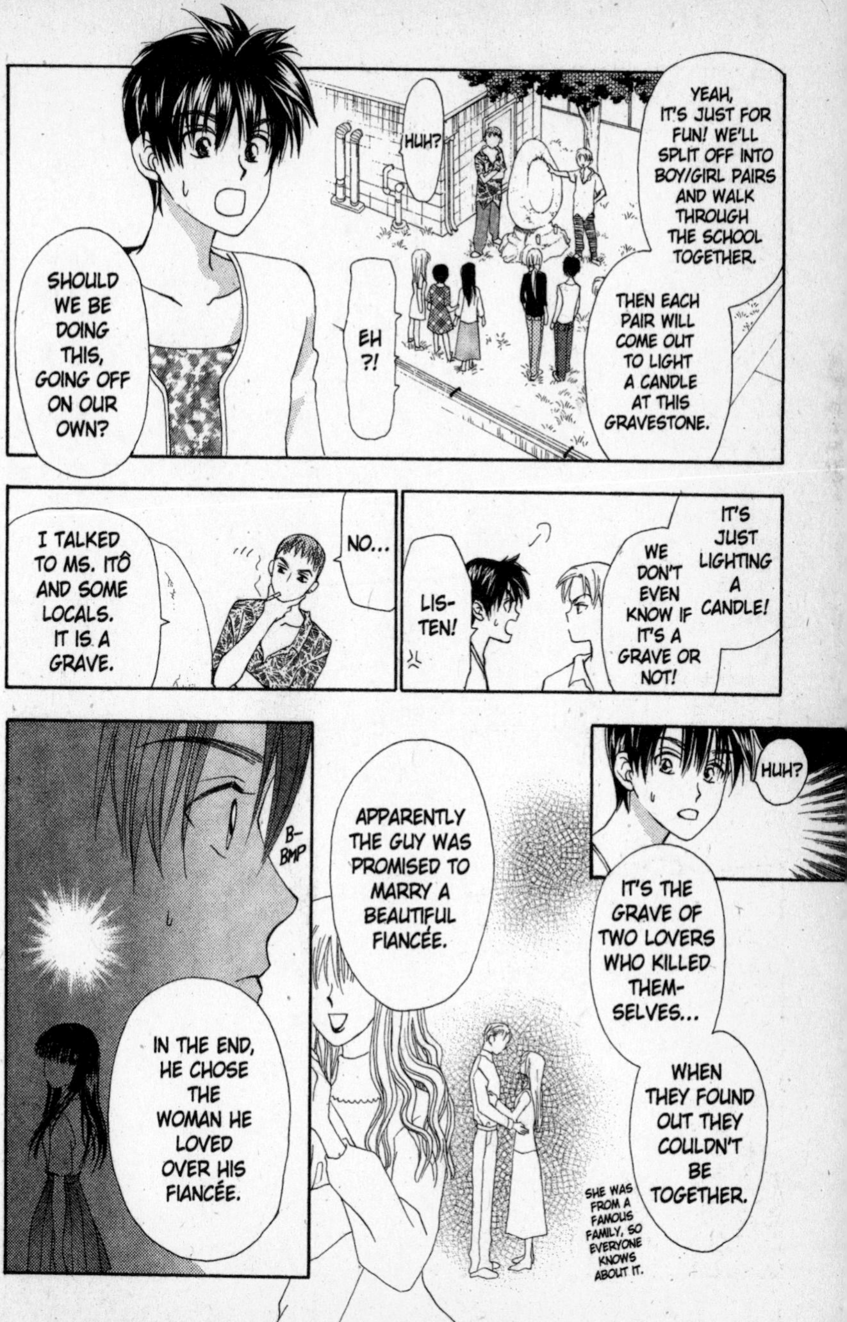
YEAH, IT'S JUST FOR FUN! WE'LL SPLIT OFF INTO BOY/GIRL PAIRS AND WALK THROUGH THE SCHOOL TOGETHER.
THEN EACH PAIR WILL COME OUT TO LIGHT A CANDLE AT THIS GRAVESTONE.
HUH?
EH?!
SHOULD WE BE DOING THIS, GOING OFF ON OUR OWN?
IT'S JUST LIGHTING A CANDLE!
WE DON'T EVEN KNOW IF IT'S A GRAVE OR NOT!
LIS-TEN!
NO...
I TALKED TO MS. ITÔ AND SOME LOCALS. IT IS A GRAVE.
HUH?
IT'S THE GRAVE OF TWO LOVERS WHO KILLED THEM-SELVES...
WHEN THEY FOUND OUT THEY COULDN'T BE TOGETHER.
SHE WAS FROM A FAMOUS FAMILY, SO EVERYONE KNOWS ABOUT IT.
APPARENTLY THE GUY WAS PROMISED TO MARRY A BEAUTIFUL FIANCÉE.
B-BMP
IN THE END, HE CHOSE THE WOMAN HE LOVED OVER HIS FIANCÉE.

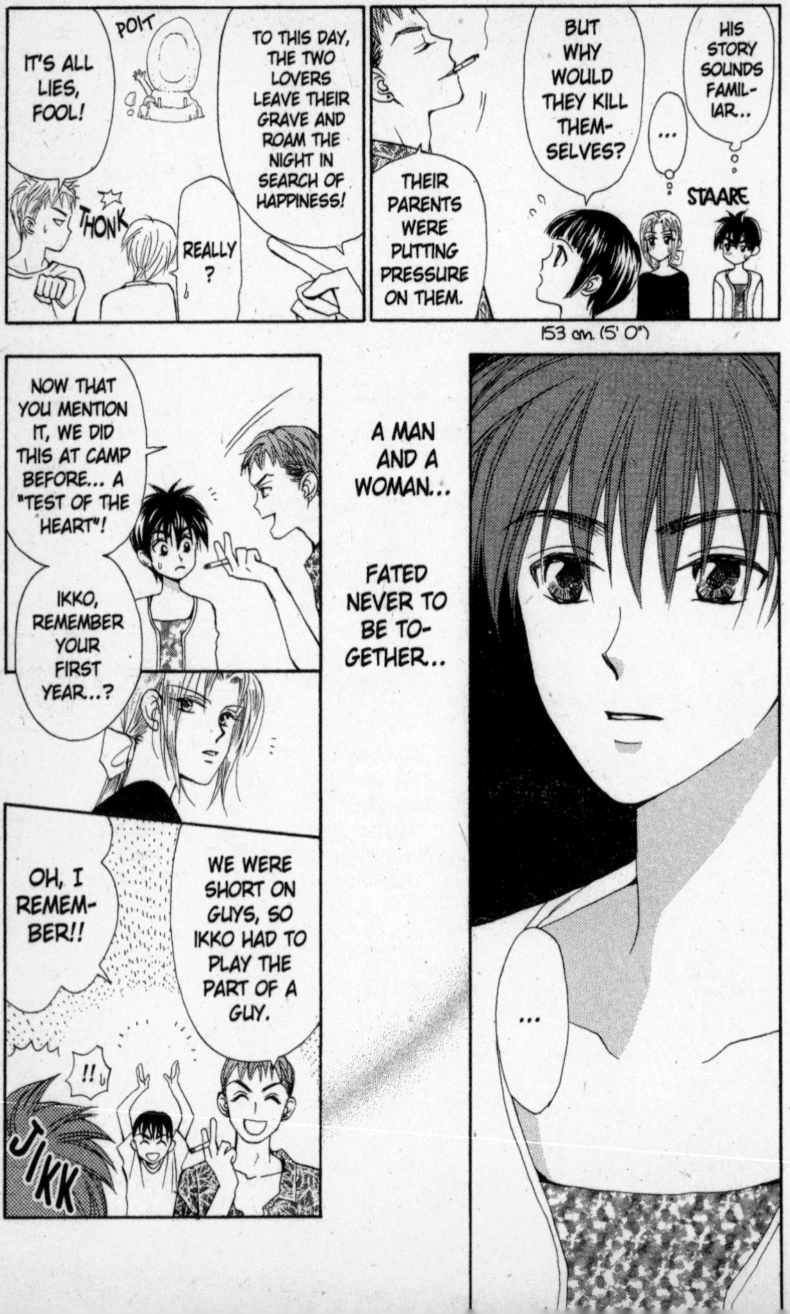
HIS STORY SOUNDS FAMILIAR...
...
STAARE
BUT WHY WOULD THEY KILL THEMSELVES?
THEIR PARENTS WERE PUTTING PRESSURE ON THEM.
153 cm. (5' 0")
TO THIS DAY, THE TWO LOVERS LEAVE THEIR GRAVE AND ROAM THE NIGHT IN SEARCH OF HAPPINESS!
REALLY?
POIT
IT'S ALL LIES, FOOL!
THONK
A MAN AND A WOMAN...
FATED NEVER TO BE TOGETHER...
...
NOW THAT YOU MENTION IT, WE DID THIS AT CAMP BEFORE... A "TEST OF THE HEART"!
IKKO, REMEMBER YOUR FIRST YEAR...?
WE WERE SHORT ON GUYS, SO IKKO HAD TO PLAY THE PART OF A GUY.
OH, I REMEMBER!!
!!
JIKK

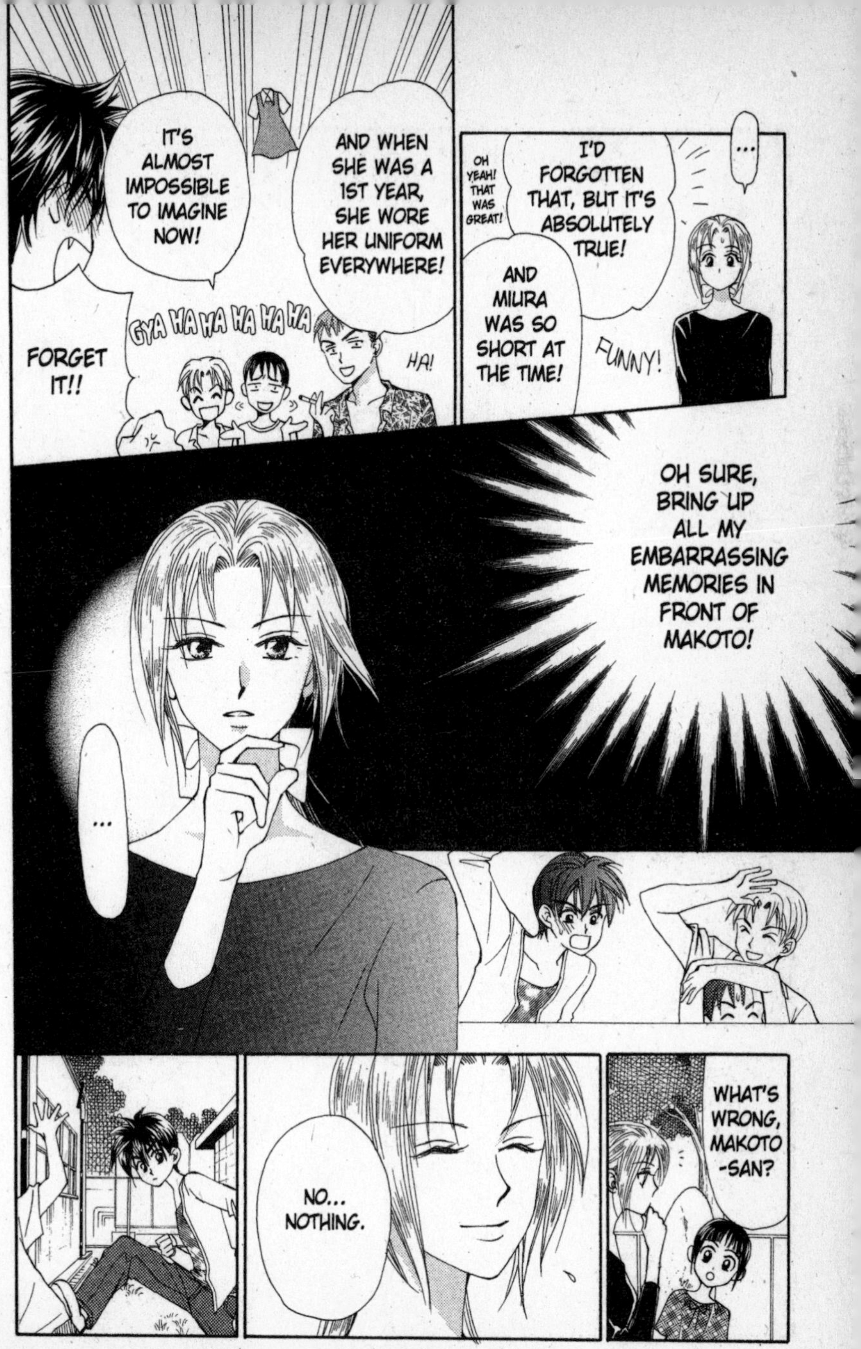
...
I'D FORGOTTEN THAT, BUT IT'S ABSOLUTELY TRUE!
OH YEAH! THAT WAS GREAT!
AND MIURA WAS SO SHORT AT THE TIME!
FUNNY!
AND WHEN SHE WAS A 1ST YEAR, SHE WORE HER UNIFORM EVERYWHERE!
IT'S ALMOST IMPOSSIBLE TO IMAGINE NOW!
HA!
GYA HA HA HA HA HA
FORGET IT!!
OH SURE, BRING UP ALL MY EMBARRASSING MEMORIES IN FRONT OF MAKOTO!
...
WHAT'S WRONG, MAKOTO-SAN?
NO... NOTHING.

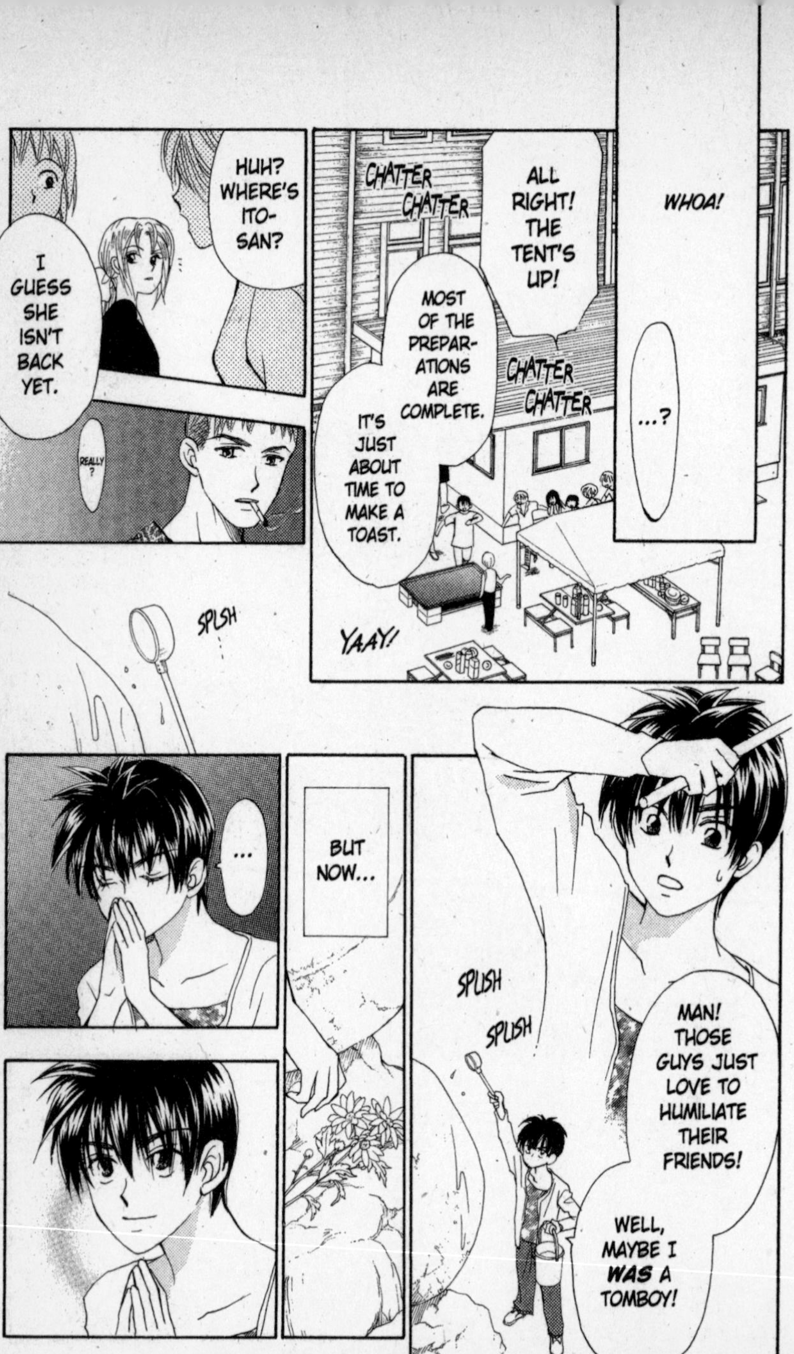
WHOA!
...?
CHATTER CHATTER
ALL RIGHT! THE TENT'S UP!
MOST OF THE PREPARATIONS ARE COMPLETE.
CHATTER CHATTER
IT'S JUST ABOUT TIME TO MAKE A TOAST.
YAAY!
HUH? WHERE'S ITO-SAN?
I GUESS SHE ISN'T BACK YET.
REALLY?
SPLSH
SPLSH
SPLSH
MAN! THOSE GUYS JUST LOVE TO HUMILIATE THEIR FRIENDS!
WELL, MAYBE I WAS A TOMBOY!
BUT NOW...
...

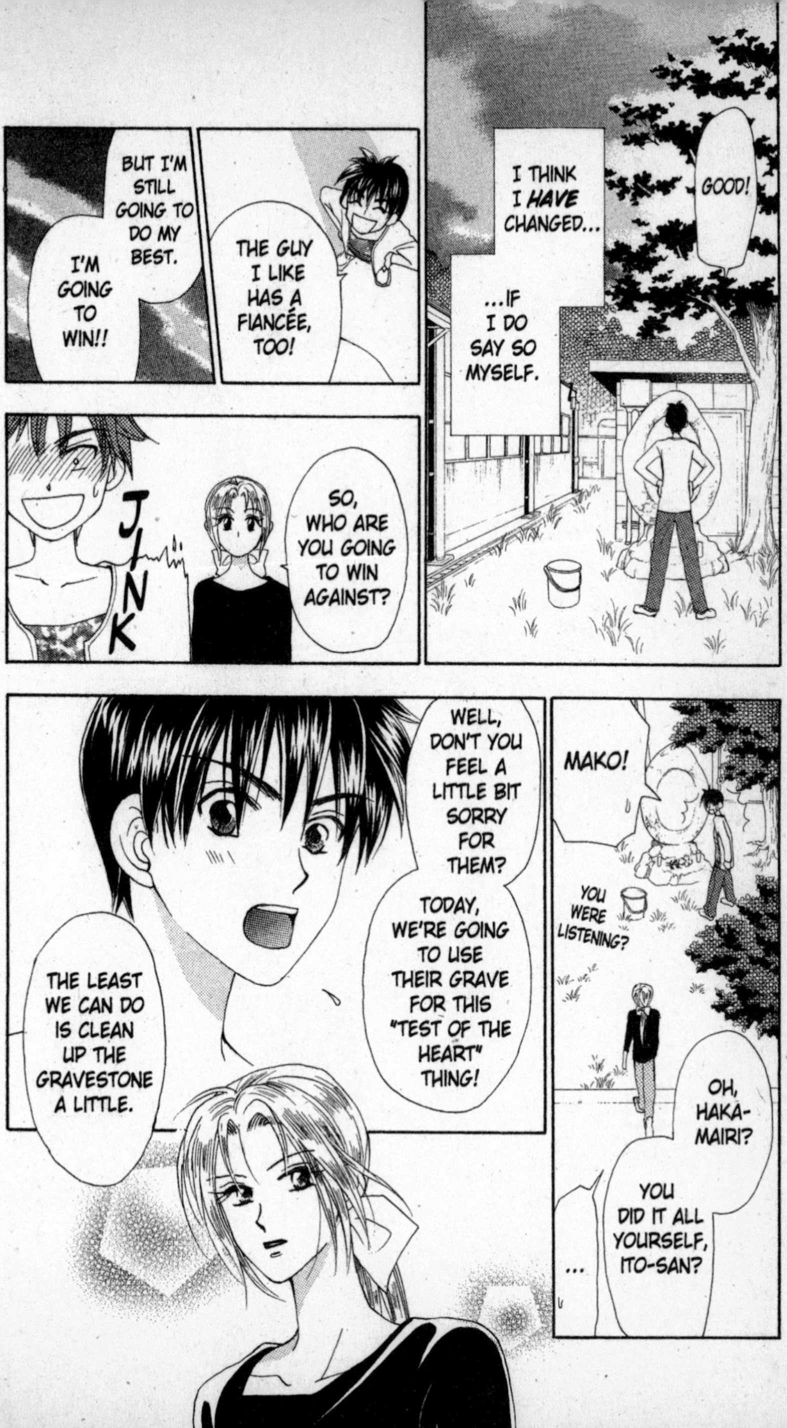
GOOD!
I THINK I *HAVE* CHANGED...
...IF I DO SAY SO MYSELF.
THE GUY I LIKE HAS A FIANCÉE, TOO!
BUT I'M STILL GOING TO DO MY BEST.
I'M GOING TO WIN!!
SO, WHO ARE YOU GOING TO WIN AGAINST?
JINK
MAKO!
YOU WERE LISTENING?
OH, HAKA-MAIRI?
YOU DID IT ALL YOURSELF, ITO-SAN?
...
WELL, DON'T YOU FEEL A LITTLE BIT SORRY FOR THEM?
TODAY, WE'RE GOING TO USE THEIR GRAVE FOR THIS "TEST OF THE HEART" THING!
THE LEAST WE CAN DO IS CLEAN UP THE GRAVESTONE A LITTLE.

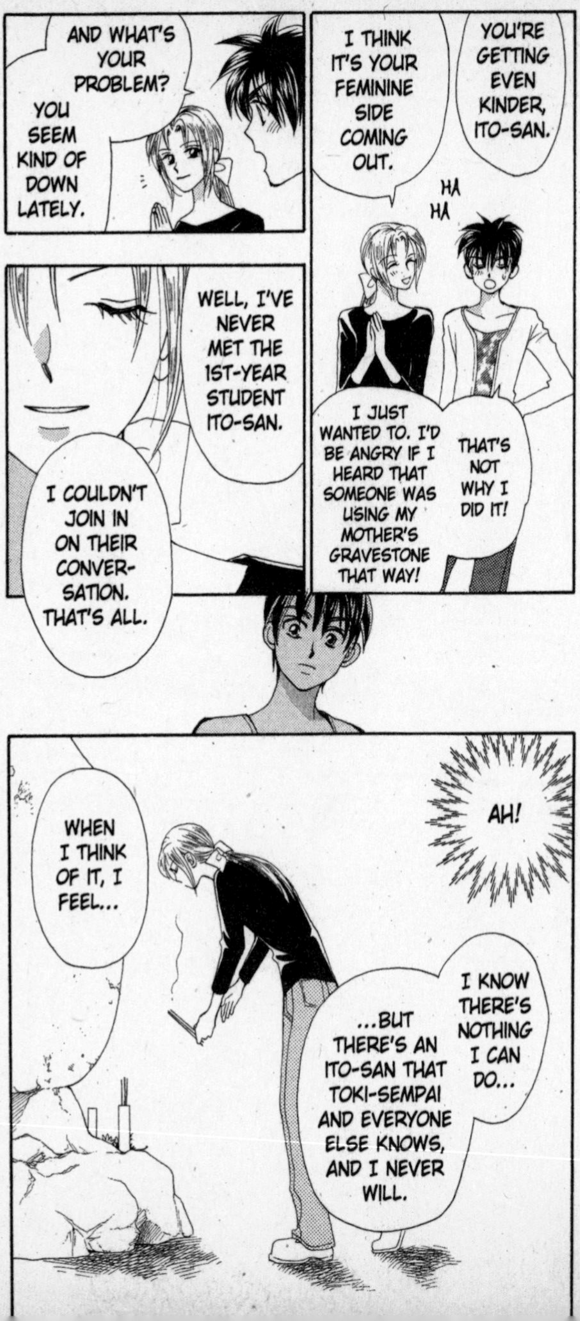
YOU'RE GETTING EVEN KINDER, ITO-SAN.
I THINK IT'S YOUR FEMININE SIDE COMING OUT.
HA HA
THAT'S NOT WHY I DID IT!
I JUST WANTED TO. I'D BE ANGRY IF I HEARD THAT SOMEONE WAS USING MY MOTHER'S GRAVESTONE THAT WAY!
AND WHAT'S YOUR PROBLEM?
YOU SEEM KIND OF DOWN LATELY.
WELL, I'VE NEVER MET THE 1ST-YEAR STUDENT ITO-SAN.
I COULDN'T JOIN IN ON THEIR CONVER-SATION. THAT'S ALL.
AH!
I KNOW THERE'S NOTHING I CAN DO...
...BUT THERE'S AN ITO-SAN THAT TOKI-SEMPAI AND EVERYONE ELSE KNOWS, AND I NEVER WILL.
WHEN I THINK OF IT, I FEEL...

- Is Ito a good cook?

Ⓔ She isn't very good at the complicated stuff. She's especially good with Yakiniku, or fried foods, or other foods that feed a lot of people at one time! She's not completely consistent when it comes to how good it tastes.

- When Toki-chan was a member of the drama club, just what kind of parts did he play?

Ⓔ They must have been pretty evil parts.

- So was **W Juliet** the first of your works that was published?

Ⓔ No!! **W Juliet** was my fifth story after my debut. My debut was... Um... Some day I'm sure you will see it... Have you seen it? If you do, please don't get your hopes up. ♡

The art is a little... heavy handed. Ha ha ha!

To tell you the truth, I'm scared to look at it these days!

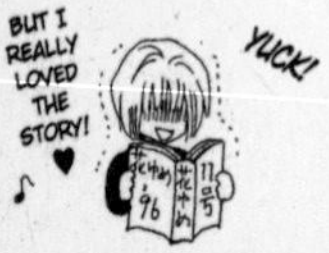
BUT I REALLY LOVED THE STORY!
YUCK!

That's the end of Q&A Corner!

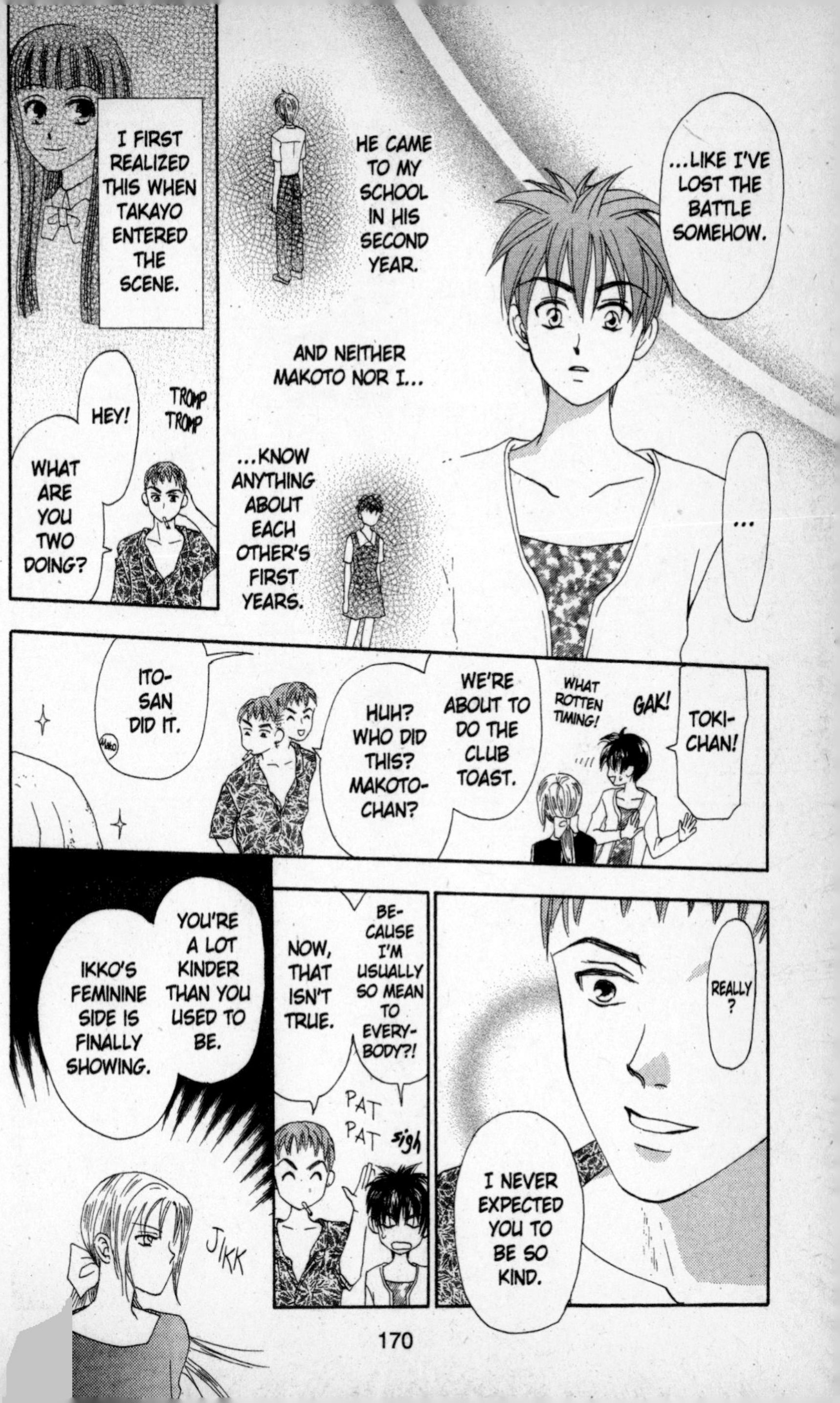
...LIKE I'VE LOST THE BATTLE SOMEHOW.
...
HE CAME TO MY SCHOOL IN HIS SECOND YEAR.
AND NEITHER MAKOTO NOR I...
...KNOW ANYTHING ABOUT EACH OTHER'S FIRST YEARS.
I FIRST REALIZED THIS WHEN TAKAYO ENTERED THE SCENE.
TROMP TROMP
HEY!
WHAT ARE YOU TWO DOING?
TOKI-CHAN!
GAK!
WHAT ROTTEN TIMING!
WE'RE ABOUT TO DO THE CLUB TOAST.
HUH? WHO DID THIS? MAKOTO-CHAN?
ITO-SAN DID IT.
MAKO
REALLY?
I NEVER EXPECTED YOU TO BE SO KIND.
BE-CAUSE I'M USUALLY SO MEAN TO EVERY-BODY?!
NOW, THAT ISN'T TRUE.
PAT PAT
sigh
YOU'RE A LOT KINDER THAN YOU USED TO BE.
IKKO'S FEMININE SIDE IS FINALLY SHOWING.
JIKK

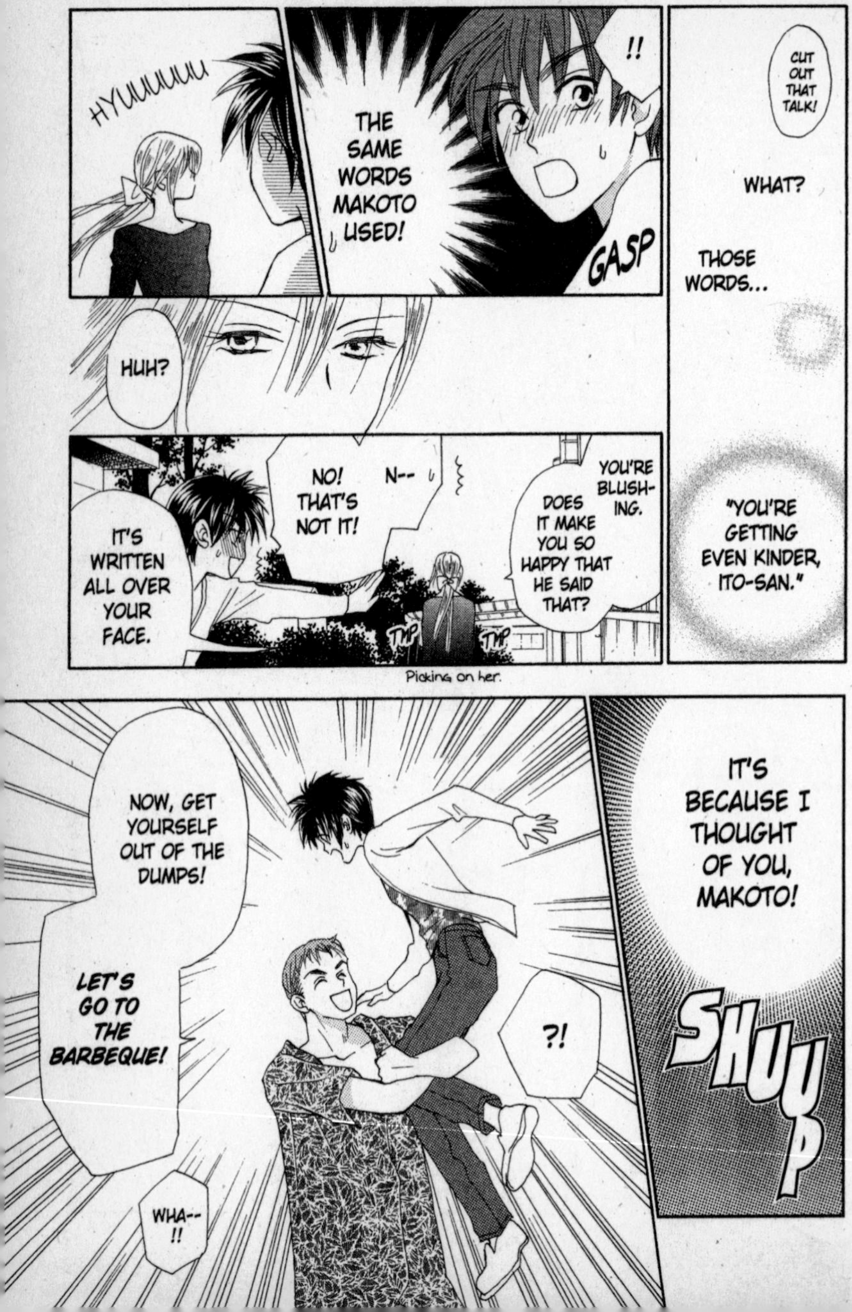
CUT OUT THAT TALK!
WHAT?
THOSE WORDS...
"YOU'RE GETTING EVEN KINDER, ITO-SAN."
!!
GASP
THE SAME WORDS MAKOTO USED!
HYUUUUUU
HUH?
YOU'RE BLUSHING.
DOES IT MAKE YOU SO HAPPY THAT HE SAID THAT?
N--
NO! THAT'S NOT IT!
IT'S WRITTEN ALL OVER YOUR FACE.
TMP
TMP
Picking on her.
IT'S BECAUSE I THOUGHT OF YOU, MAKOTO!
SHUUP
?!
NOW, GET YOURSELF OUT OF THE DUMPS!
LET'S GO TO THE BARBEQUE!
WHA-- !!

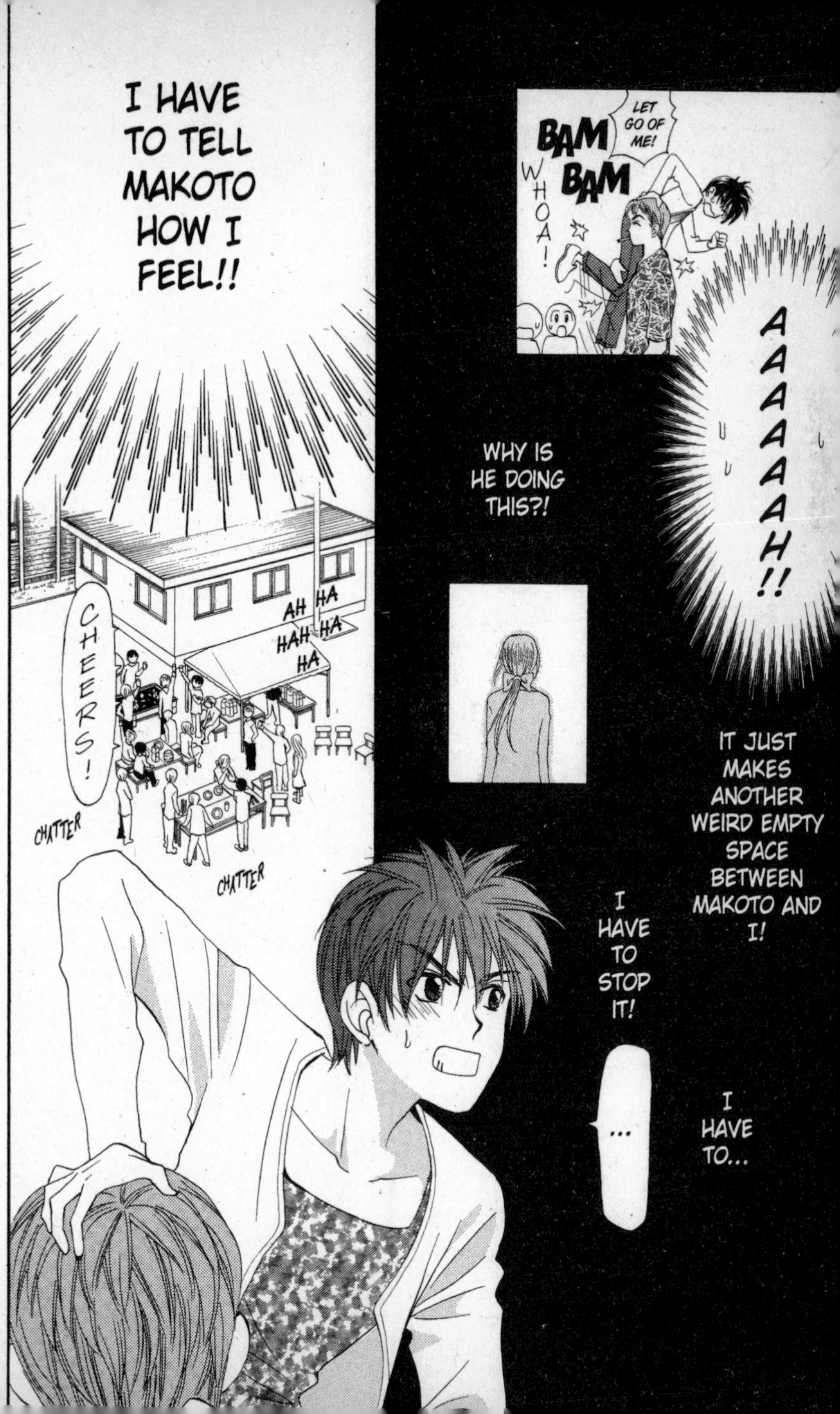
LET GO OF ME!
BAM BAM
WHOA!
AAAAAAAH!!
WHY IS HE DOING THIS?!
IT JUST MAKES ANOTHER WEIRD EMPTY SPACE BETWEEN MAKOTO AND I!
I HAVE TO STOP IT!
...
I HAVE TO...
I HAVE TO TELL MAKOTO HOW I FEEL!!
CHEERS!
AH HA HAH HA HA
CHATTER
CHATTER

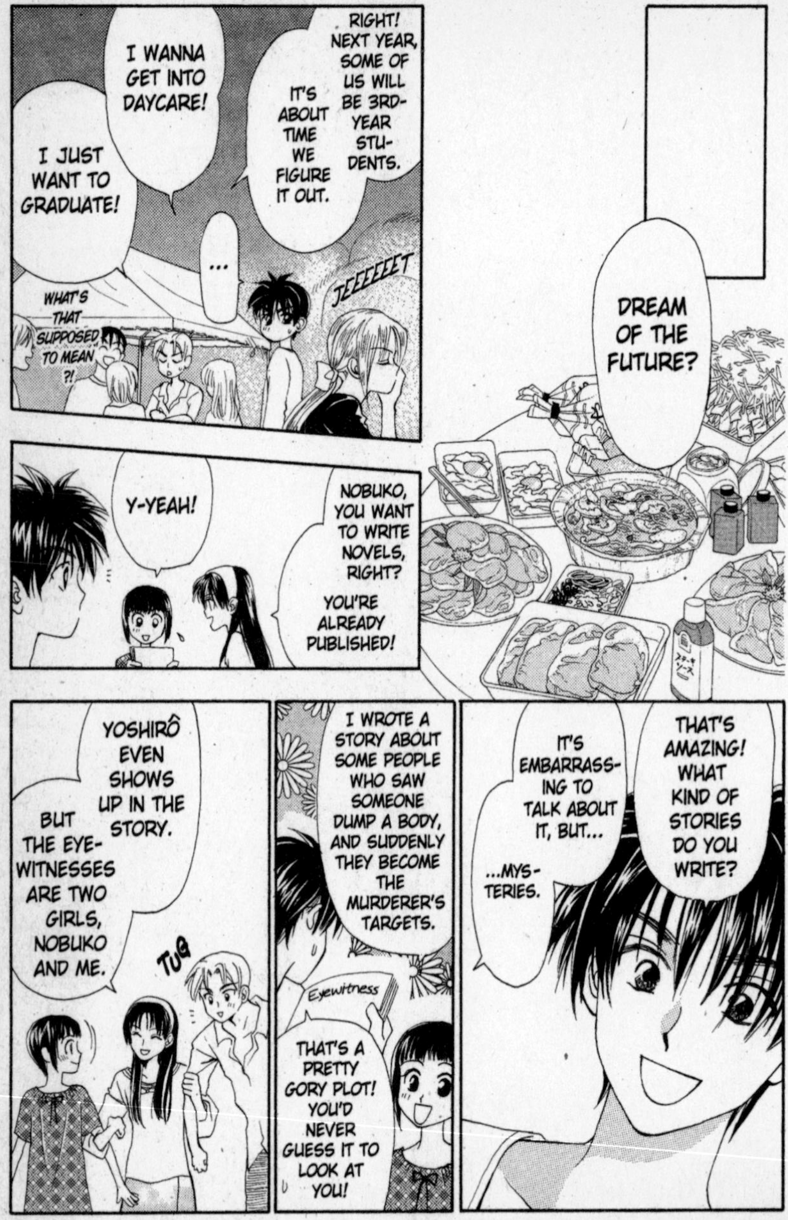
DREAM OF THE FUTURE?
RIGHT! NEXT YEAR, SOME OF US WILL BE 3RD-YEAR STUDENTS.
IT'S ABOUT TIME WE FIGURE IT OUT.
I WANNA GET INTO DAYCARE!
I JUST WANT TO GRADUATE!
JEEEEEEET
...
WHAT'S THAT SUPPOSED TO MEAN?!
NOBUKO, YOU WANT TO WRITE NOVELS, RIGHT?
YOU'RE ALREADY PUBLISHED!
Y-YEAH!
THAT'S AMAZING! WHAT KIND OF STORIES DO YOU WRITE?
IT'S EMBARRASSING TO TALK ABOUT IT, BUT...
...MYSTERIES.
I WROTE A STORY ABOUT SOME PEOPLE WHO SAW SOMEONE DUMP A BODY, AND SUDDENLY THEY BECOME THE MURDERER'S TARGETS.
Eyewitness
THAT'S A PRETTY GORY PLOT! YOU'D NEVER GUESS IT TO LOOK AT YOU!
YOSHIRÔ EVEN SHOWS UP IN THE STORY.
BUT THE EYEWITNESSES ARE TWO GIRLS, NOBUKO AND ME.
TUG

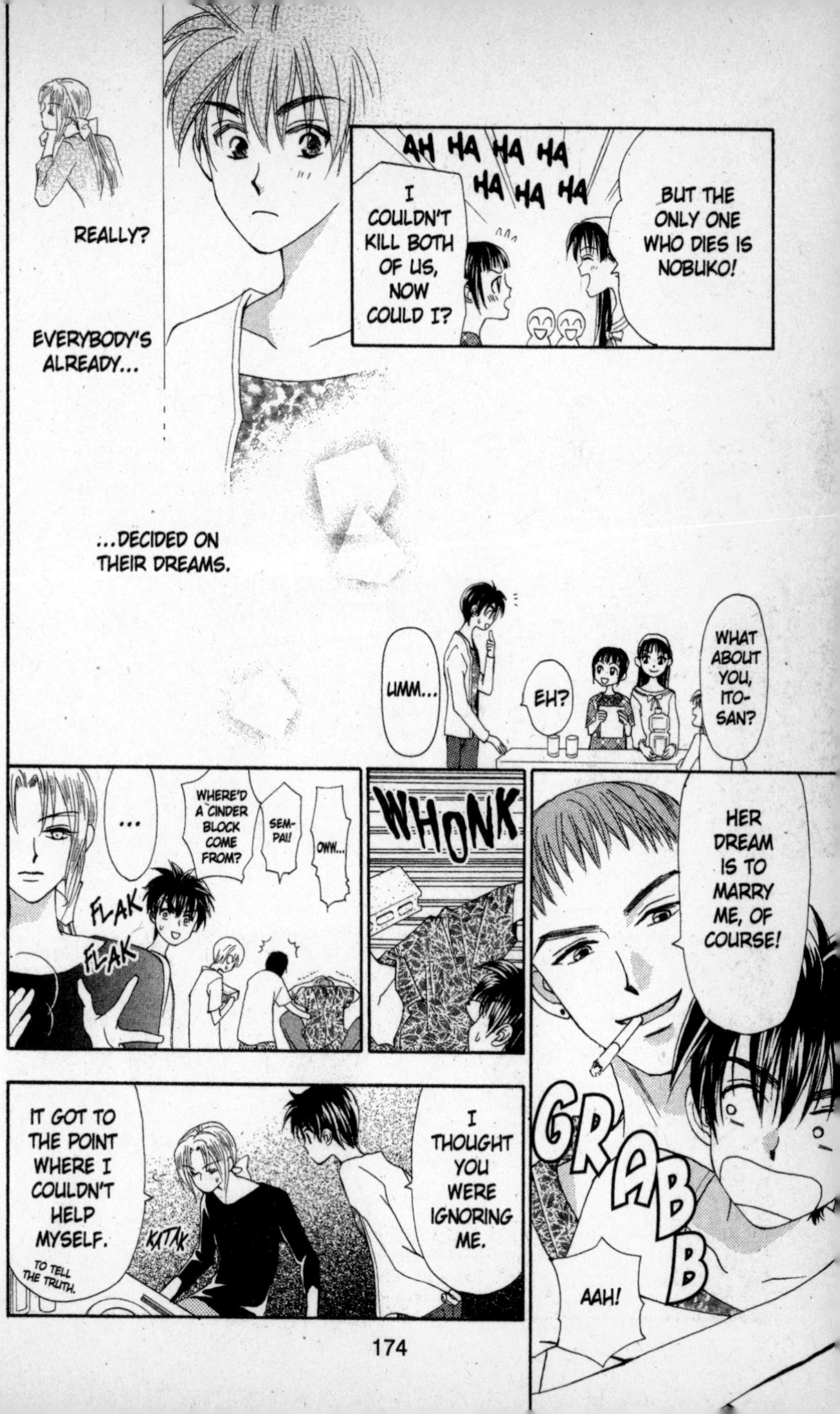
AH HA HA HA
HA HA HA
BUT THE ONLY ONE WHO DIES IS NOBUKO!
I COULDN'T KILL BOTH OF US, NOW COULD I?
REALLY?
EVERYBODY'S ALREADY...
...DECIDED ON THEIR DREAMS.
WHAT ABOUT YOU, ITO-SAN?
EH?
UMM...
HER DREAM IS TO MARRY ME, OF COURSE!
GRABB
AAH!
WHONK
OWW...
SEM-PAI!
WHERE'D A CINDER BLOCK COME FROM?
...
FLAK
FLAK
I THOUGHT YOU WERE IGNORING ME.
IT GOT TO THE POINT WHERE I COULDN'T HELP MYSELF.
KATAK
TO TELL THE TRUTH.

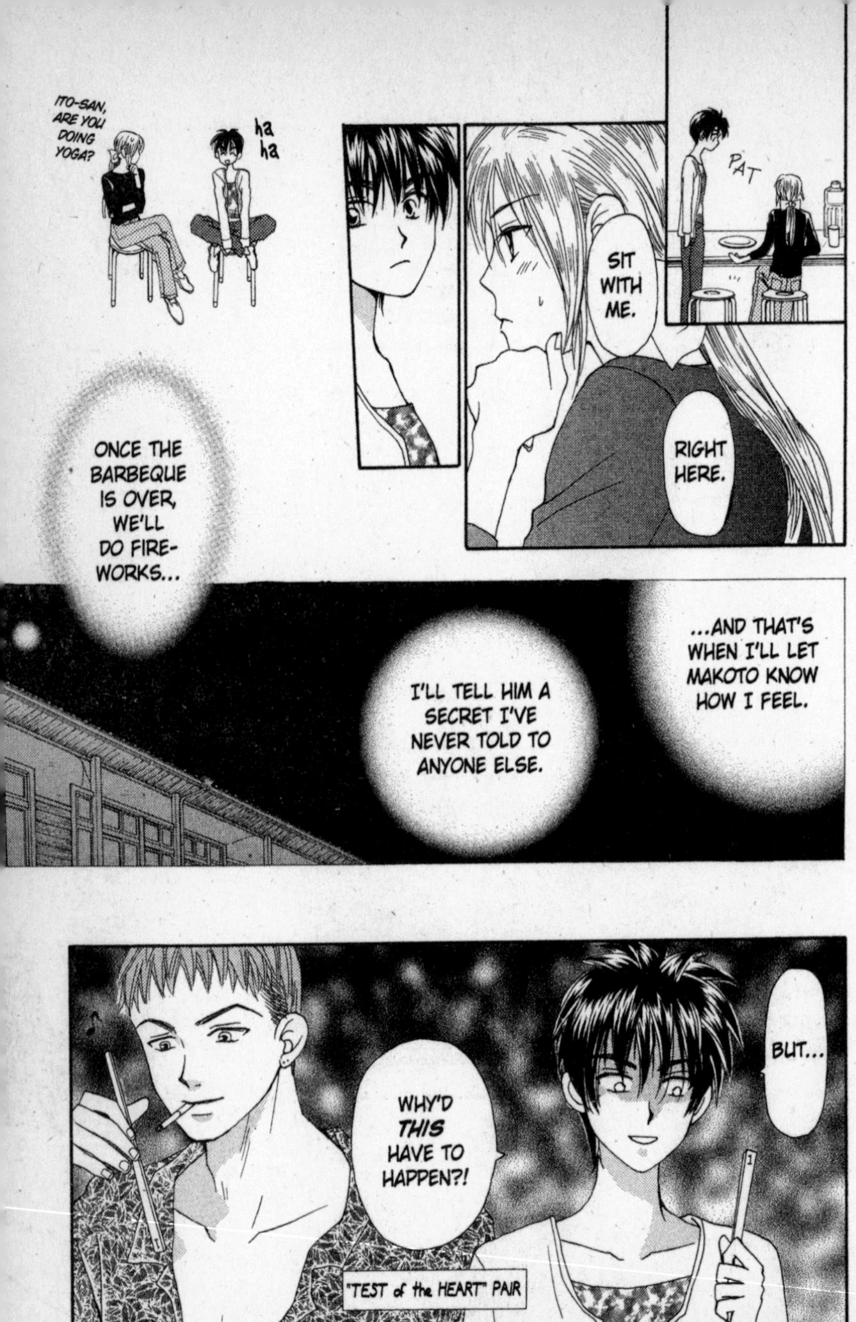
PAT
SIT WITH ME.
RIGHT HERE.
ITO-SAN, ARE YOU DOING YOGA?
ha ha
ONCE THE BARBEQUE IS OVER, WE'LL DO FIRE-WORKS...
...AND THAT'S WHEN I'LL LET MAKOTO KNOW HOW I FEEL.
I'LL TELL HIM A SECRET I'VE NEVER TOLD TO ANYONE ELSE.
BUT...
WHY'D ***THIS*** HAVE TO HAPPEN?!
"TEST of the HEART" PAIR

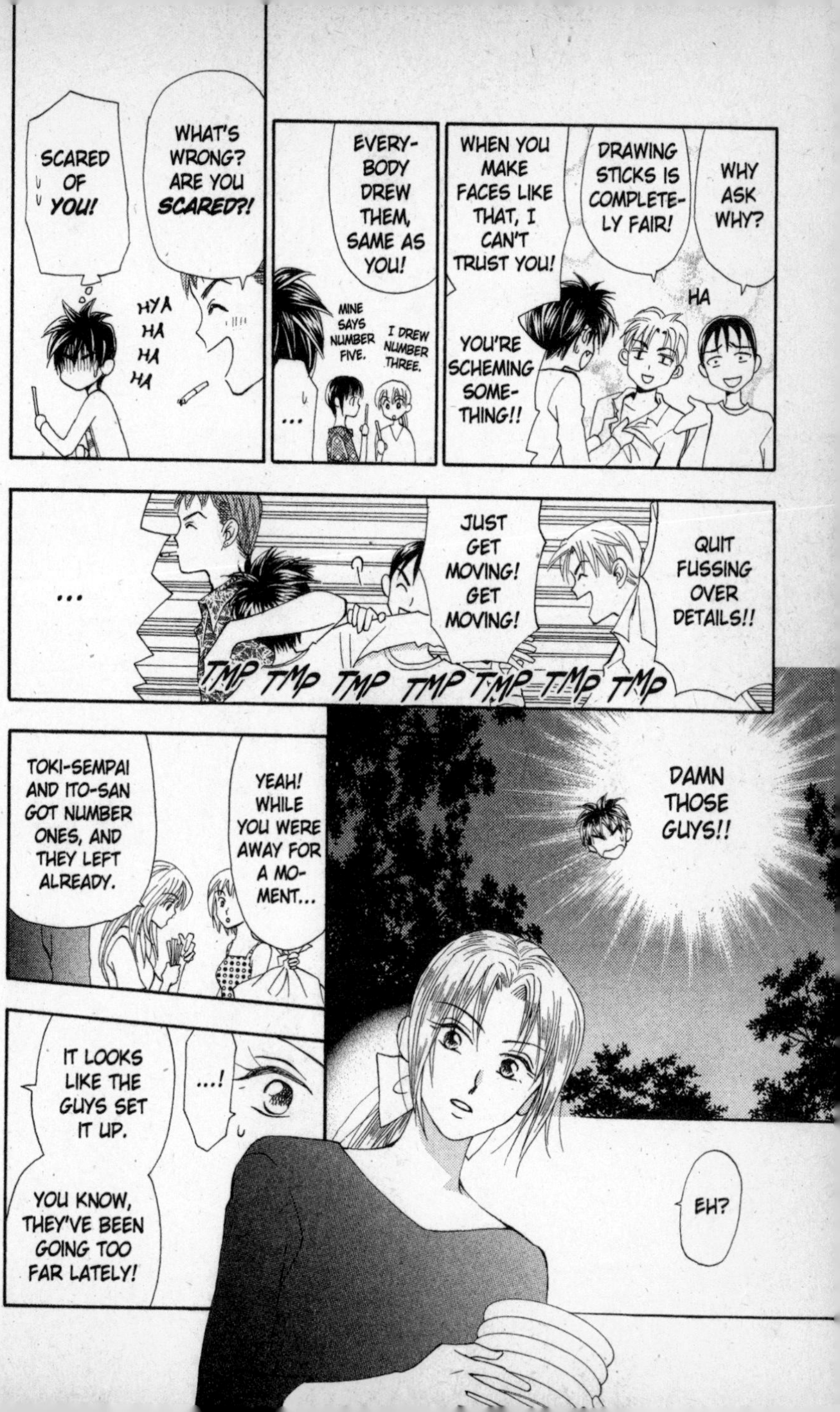
WHY ASK WHY?
HA
DRAWING STICKS IS COMPLETE-LY FAIR!
WHEN YOU MAKE FACES LIKE THAT, I CAN'T TRUST YOU!
YOU'RE SCHEMING SOME-THING!!
EVERY-BODY DREW THEM, SAME AS YOU!
I DREW NUMBER THREE.
MINE SAYS NUMBER FIVE.
...
WHAT'S WRONG? ARE YOU SCARED?!
HYA HA HA HA
SCARED OF YOU!
QUIT FUSSING OVER DETAILS!!
JUST GET MOVING! GET MOVING!
...
TMP TMP TMP TMP TMP TMP TMP
DAMN THOSE GUYS!!
EH?
YEAH! WHILE YOU WERE AWAY FOR A MO-MENT...
TOKI-SEMPAI AND ITO-SAN GOT NUMBER ONES, AND THEY LEFT ALREADY.
...!
IT LOOKS LIKE THE GUYS SET IT UP.
YOU KNOW, THEY'VE BEEN GOING TOO FAR LATELY!

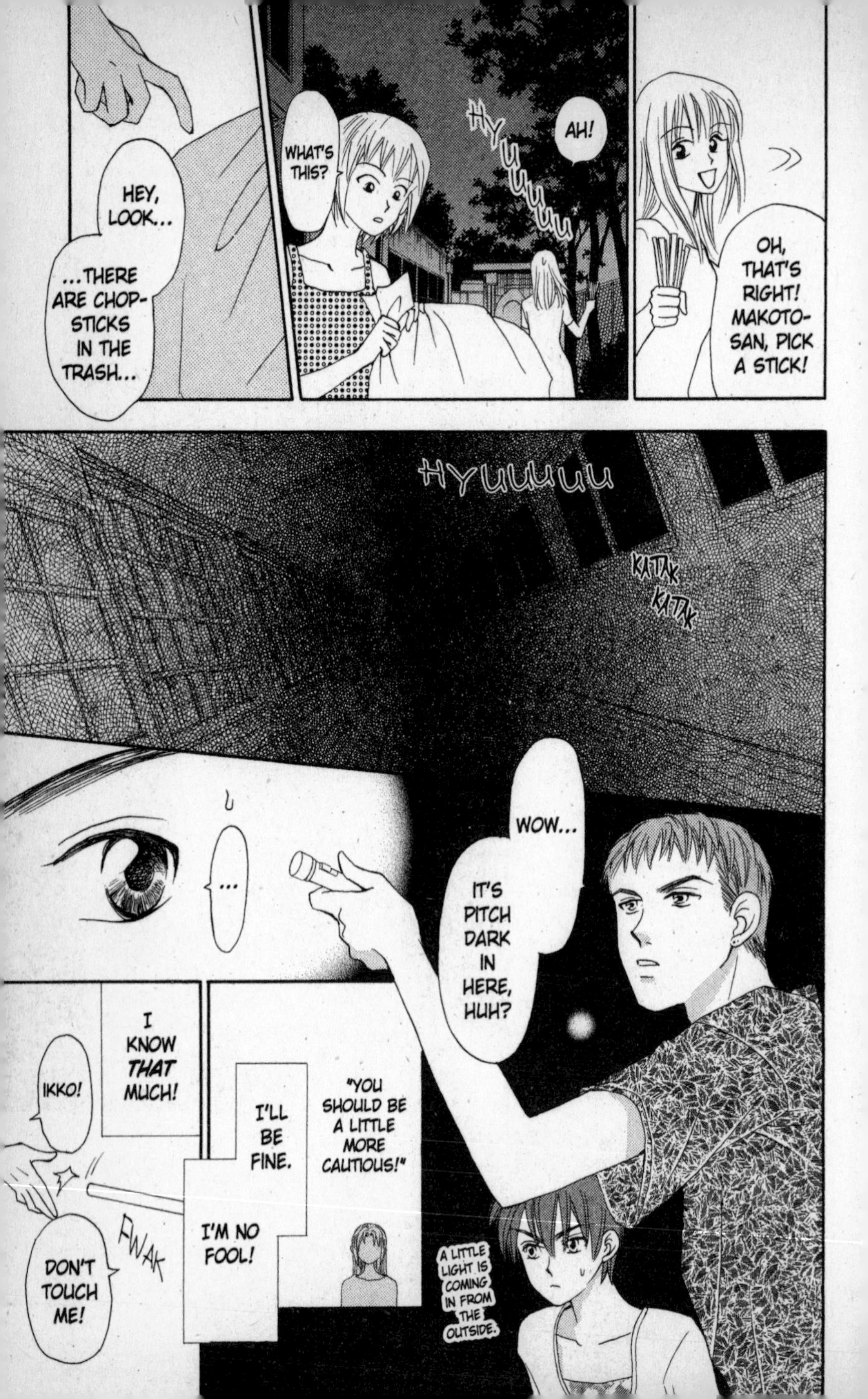
OH, THAT'S RIGHT! MAKOTO-SAN, PICK A STICK!
AH!
HYUUUUUU
WHAT'S THIS?
HEY, LOOK...
...THERE ARE CHOP-STICKS IN THE TRASH...
HYUUUUUU
KATAK KATAK
WOW...
IT'S PITCH DARK IN HERE, HUH?
A LITTLE LIGHT IS COMING IN FROM THE OUTSIDE.
...
"YOU SHOULD BE A LITTLE MORE CAUTIOUS!"
I'LL BE FINE.
I'M NO FOOL!
I KNOW *THAT* MUCH!
IKKO!
FWAK
DON'T TOUCH ME!

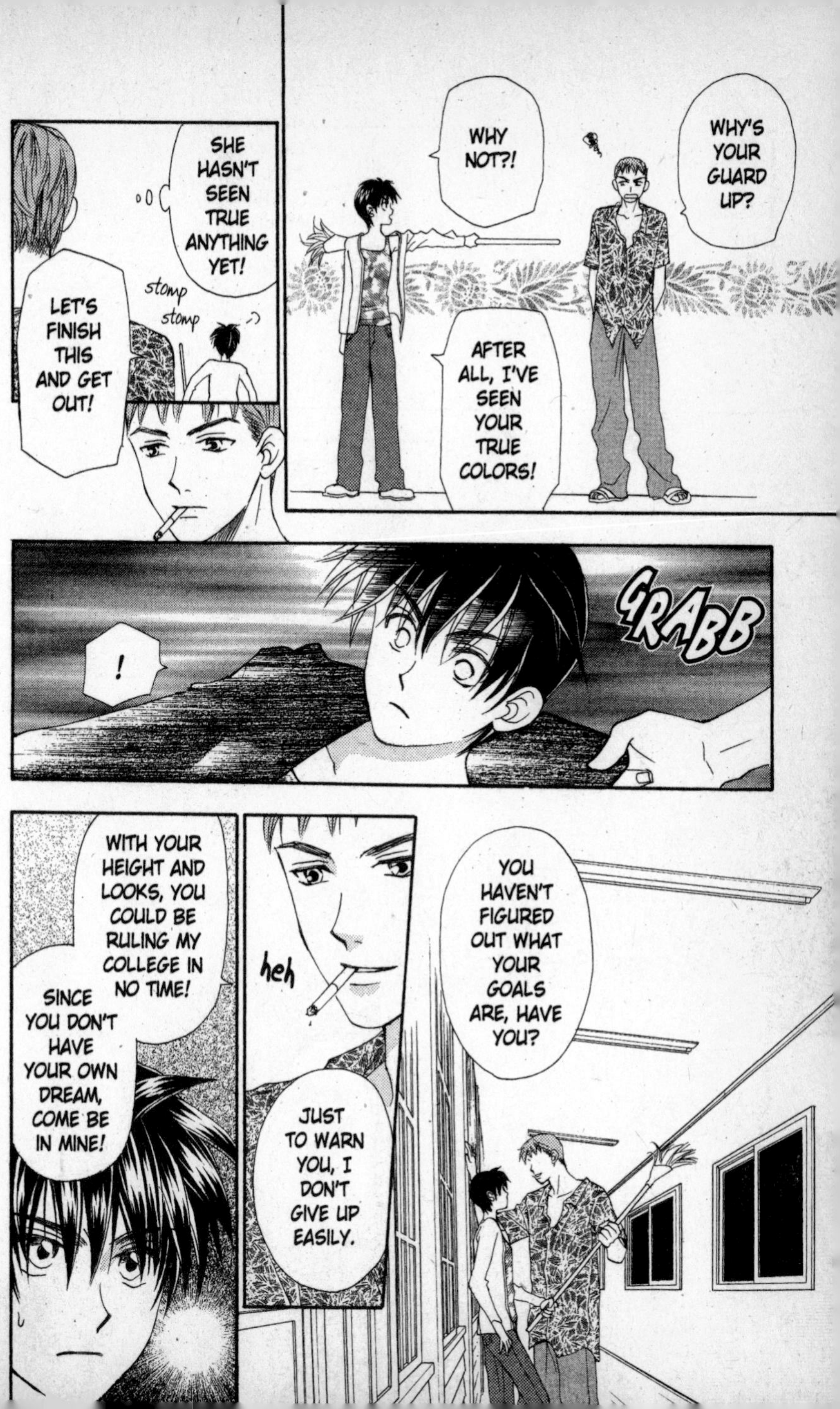
WHY'S YOUR GUARD UP?
WHY NOT?!
AFTER ALL, I'VE SEEN YOUR TRUE COLORS!
SHE HASN'T SEEN TRUE ANYTHING YET!
stomp stomp
LET'S FINISH THIS AND GET OUT!
GRABB
!
YOU HAVEN'T FIGURED OUT WHAT YOUR GOALS ARE, HAVE YOU?
heh
JUST TO WARN YOU, I DON'T GIVE UP EASILY.
WITH YOUR HEIGHT AND LOOKS, YOU COULD BE RULING MY COLLEGE IN NO TIME!
SINCE YOU DON'T HAVE YOUR OWN DREAM, COME BE IN MINE!

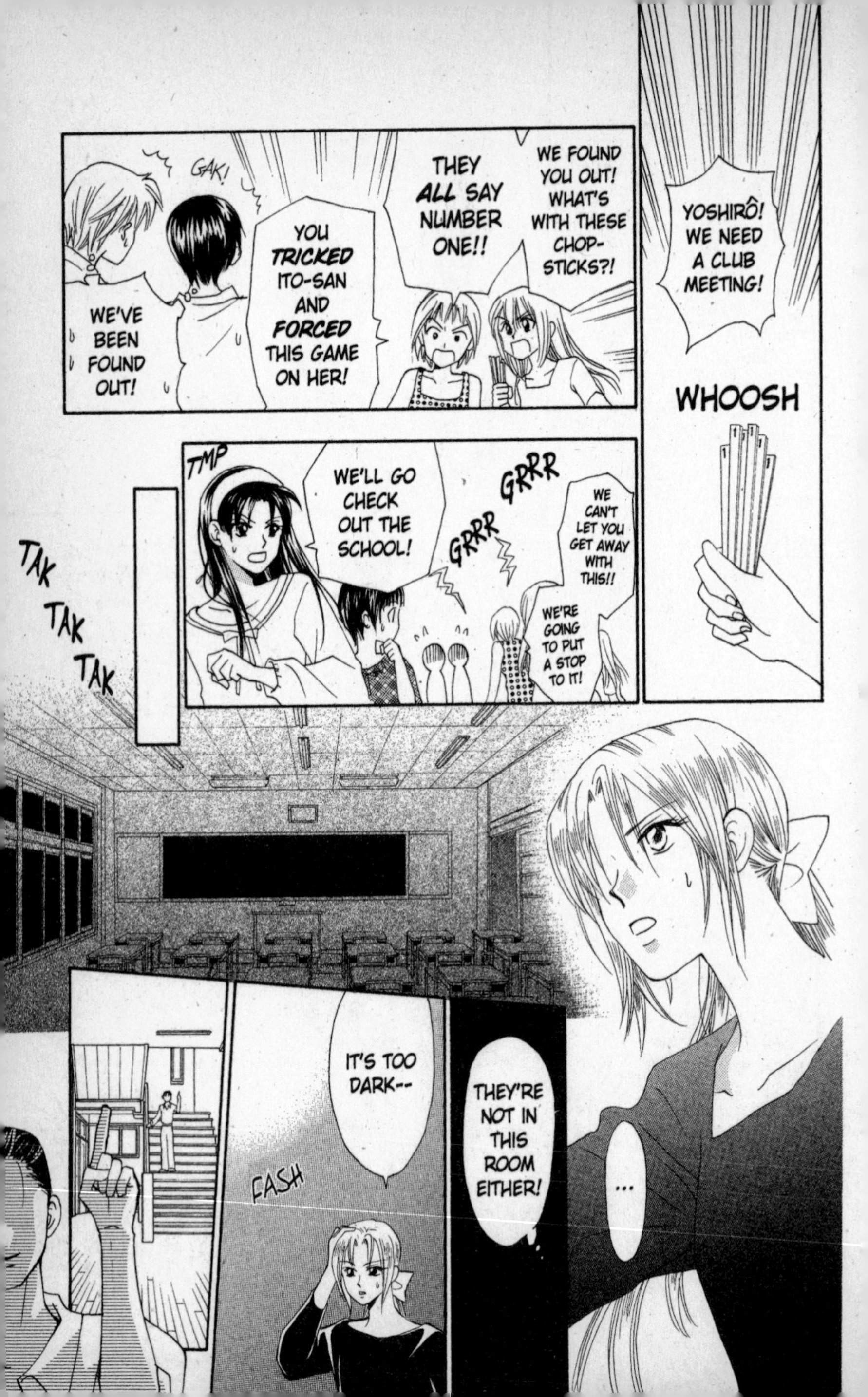
YOSHIRÔ! WE NEED A CLUB MEETING!
WHOOSH
WE FOUND YOU OUT! WHAT'S WITH THESE CHOP-STICKS?!
THEY ALL SAY NUMBER ONE!!
YOU TRICKED ITO-SAN AND FORCED THIS GAME ON HER!
GAK!
WE'VE BEEN FOUND OUT!
WE CAN'T LET YOU GET AWAY WITH THIS!!
GRRR
GRRR
WE'RE GOING TO PUT A STOP TO IT!
WE'LL GO CHECK OUT THE SCHOOL!
TMP
TAK
TAK
TAK
...
THEY'RE NOT IN THIS ROOM EITHER!
IT'S TOO DARK--
CASH

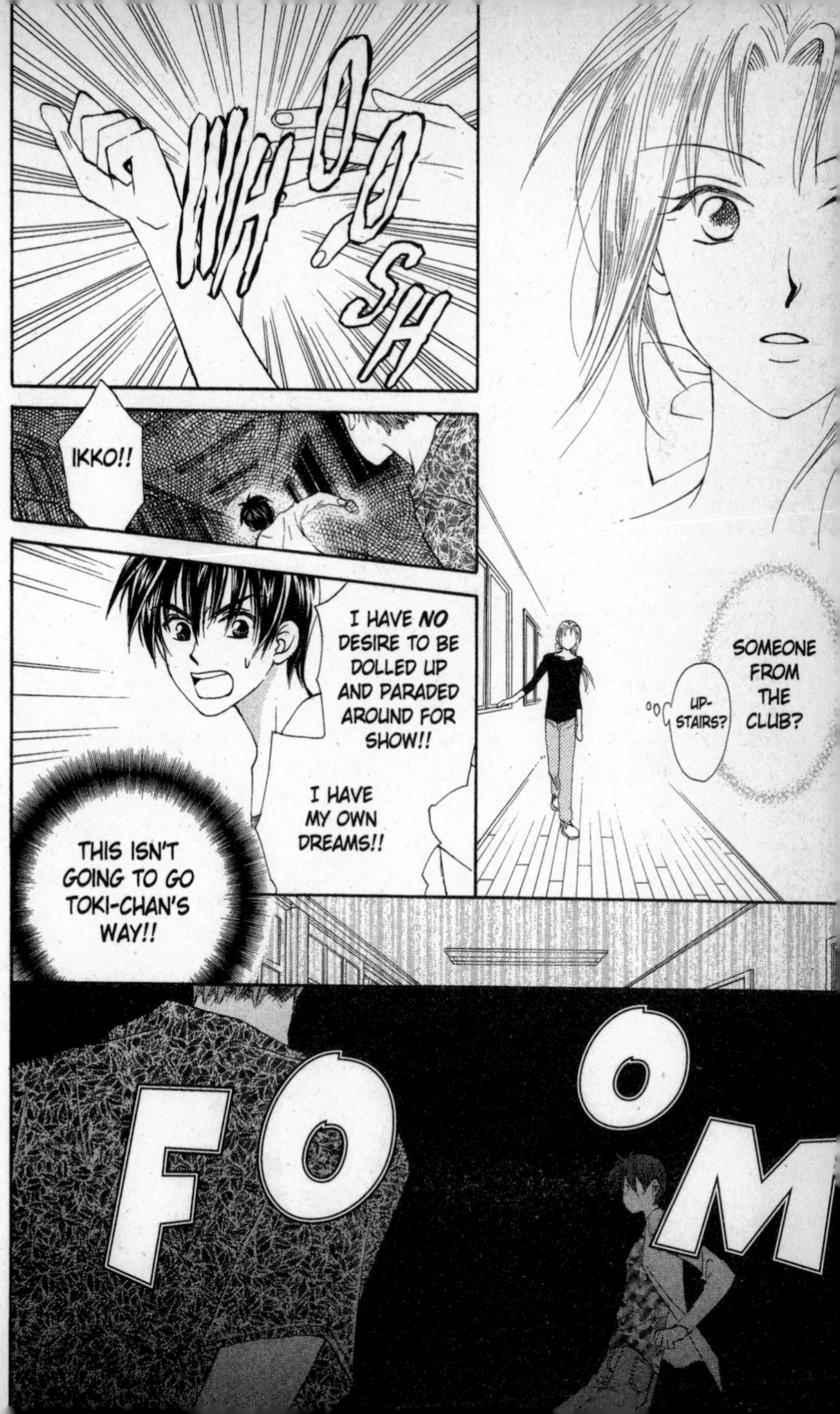
WHOOOSH
IKKO!!
SOMEONE FROM THE CLUB?
UP-STAIRS?
I HAVE NO DESIRE TO BE DOLLED UP AND PARADED AROUND FOR SHOW!!
I HAVE MY OWN DREAMS!!
THIS ISN'T GOING TO GO TOKI-CHAN'S WAY!!
FOOOM

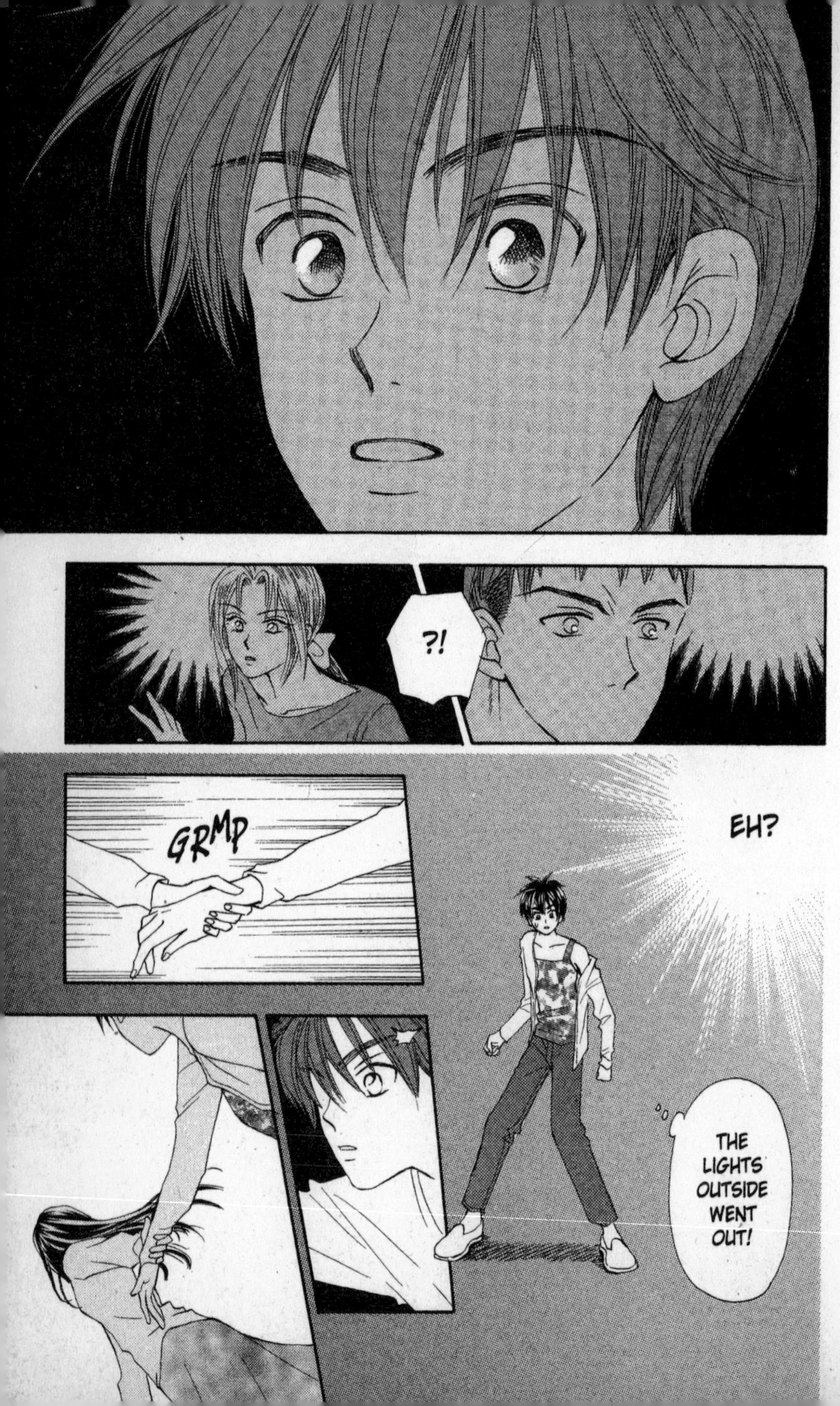
?!
EH?
THE LIGHTS OUTSIDE WENT OUT!
GRMP

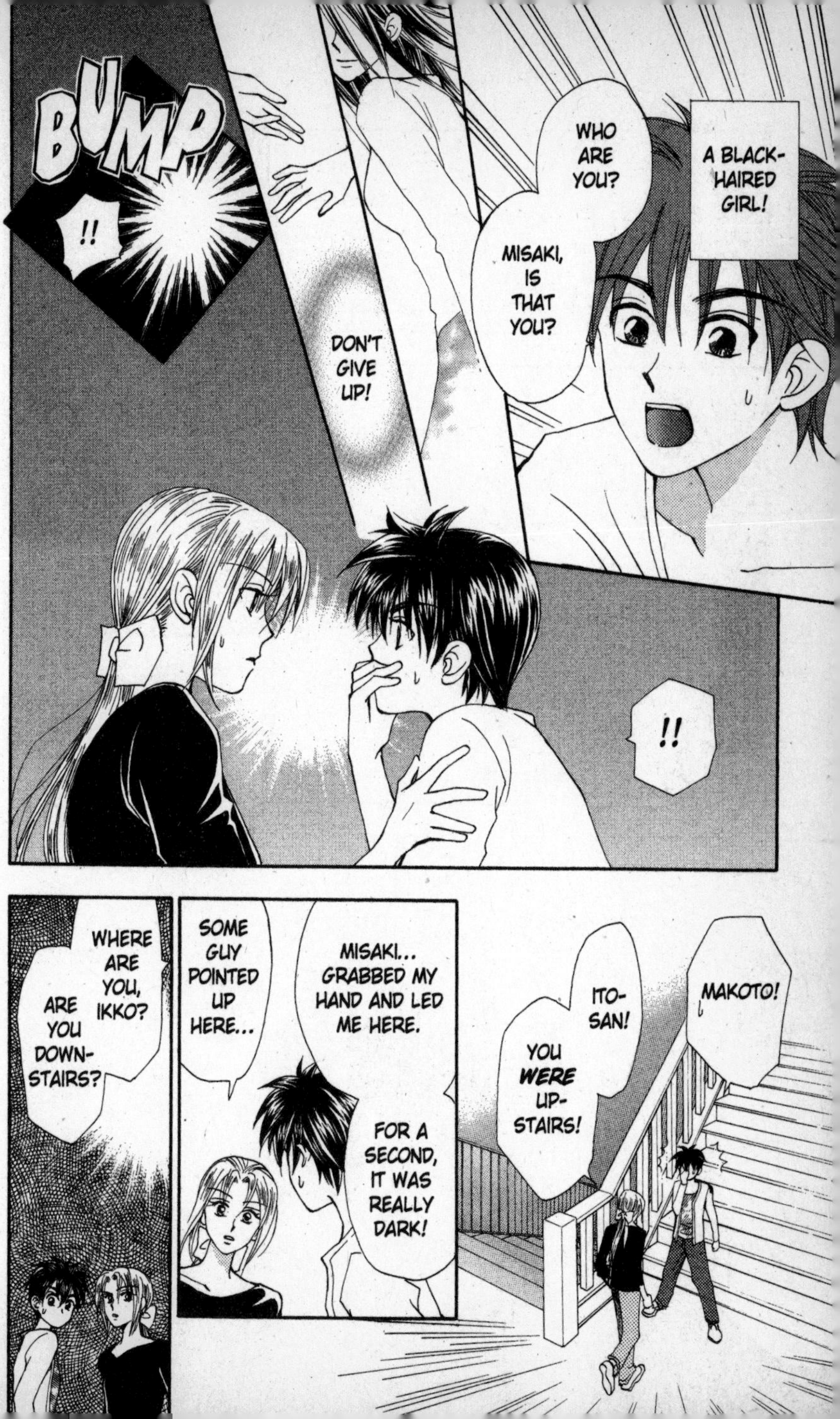
A BLACK-HAIRED GIRL!
WHO ARE YOU?
MISAKI, IS THAT YOU?
DON'T GIVE UP!
BUMP
!!
!!
MAKOTO!
ITO-SAN!
YOU *WERE* UPSTAIRS!
MISAKI... GRABBED MY HAND AND LED ME HERE.
SOME GUY POINTED UP HERE...
FOR A SECOND, IT WAS REALLY DARK!
WHERE ARE YOU, IKKO?
ARE YOU DOWNSTAIRS?

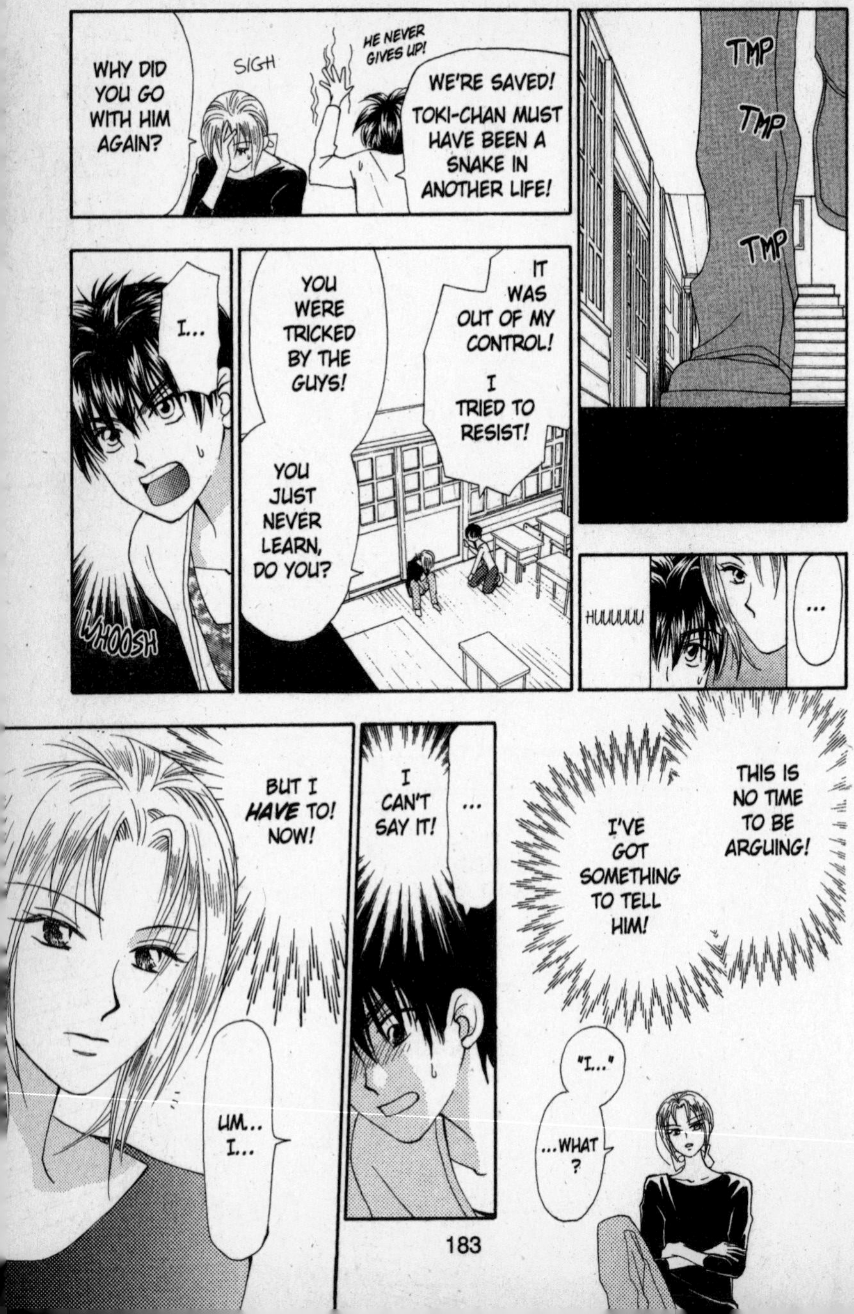
TMP
TMP
TMP
WE'RE SAVED! TOKI-CHAN MUST HAVE BEEN A SNAKE IN ANOTHER LIFE!
HE NEVER GIVES UP!
SIGH
WHY DID YOU GO WITH HIM AGAIN?
IT WAS OUT OF MY CONTROL!
I TRIED TO RESIST!
YOU WERE TRICKED BY THE GUYS!
YOU JUST NEVER LEARN, DO YOU?
I...
WHOOSH
...
HUUUUUU
THIS IS NO TIME TO BE ARGUING!
I'VE GOT SOMETHING TO TELL HIM!
"I..."
...WHAT?
...
I CAN'T SAY IT!
BUT I *HAVE* TO! NOW!
UM... I...

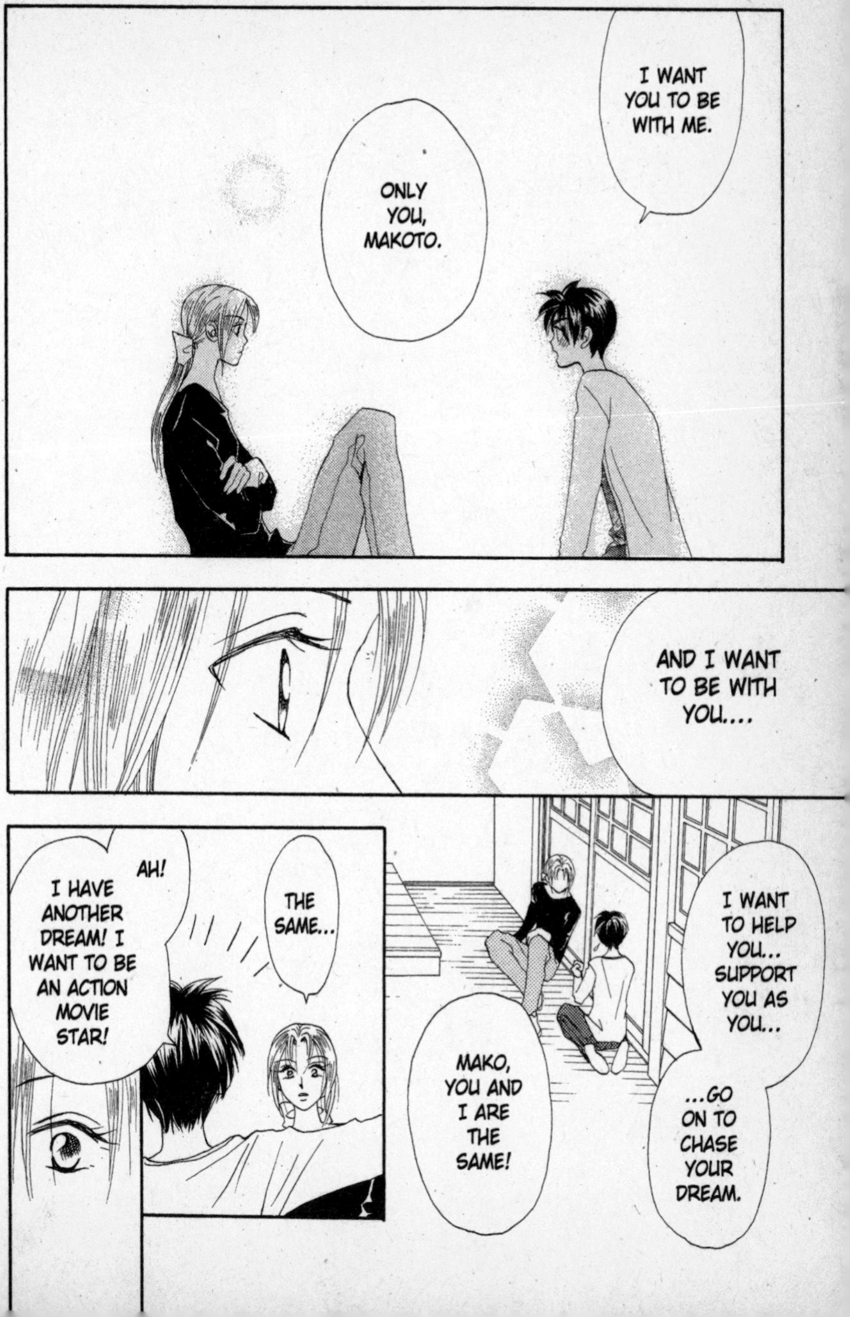
I WANT YOU TO BE WITH ME.
ONLY YOU, MAKOTO.
AND I WANT TO BE WITH YOU....
I WANT TO HELP YOU... SUPPORT YOU AS YOU...
...GO ON TO CHASE YOUR DREAM.
MAKO, YOU AND I ARE THE SAME!
THE SAME...
AH! I HAVE ANOTHER DREAM! I WANT TO BE AN ACTION MOVIE STAR!

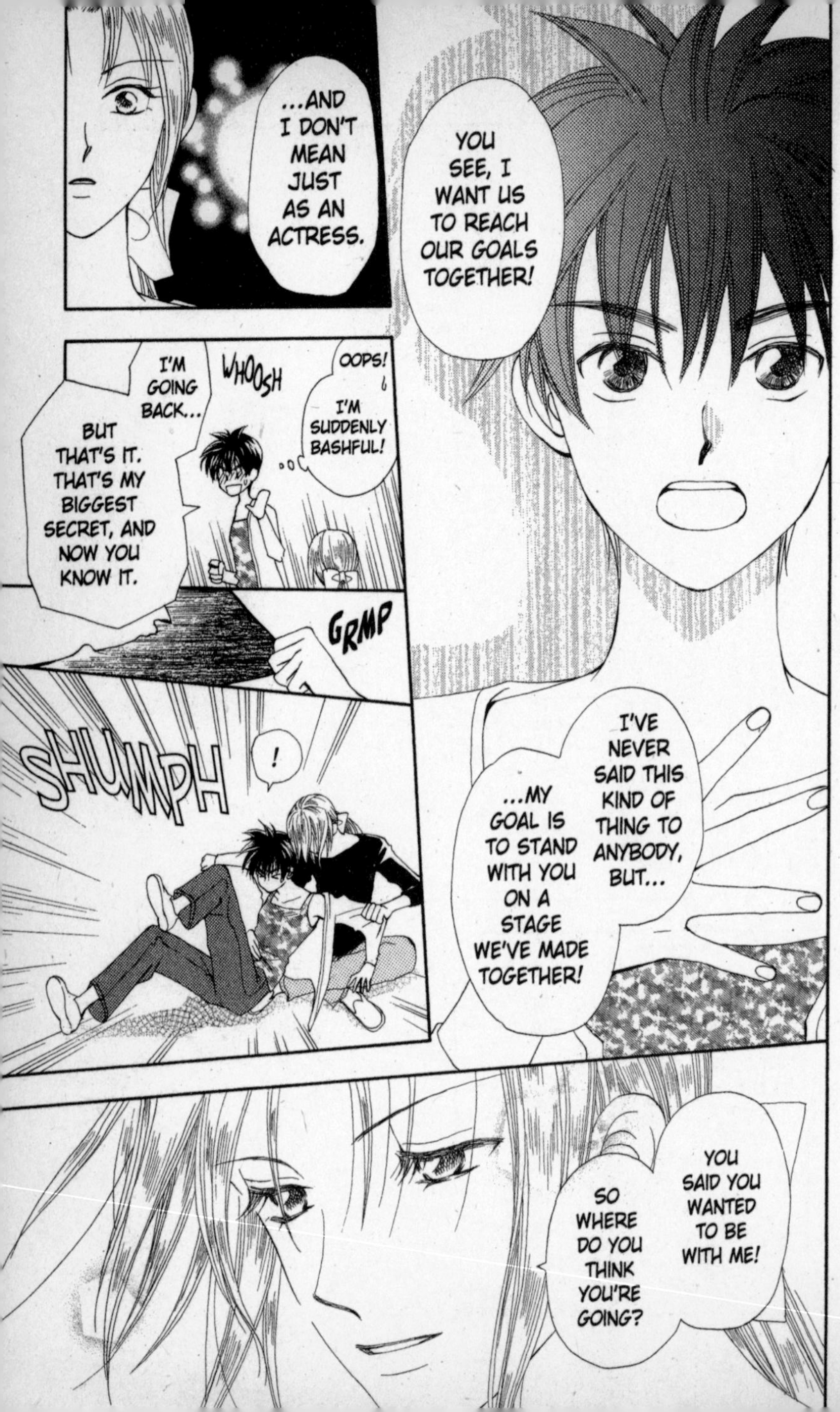
YOU SEE, I WANT US TO REACH OUR GOALS TOGETHER!
I'VE NEVER SAID THIS KIND OF THING TO ANYBODY, BUT...
...MY GOAL IS TO STAND WITH YOU ON A STAGE WE'VE MADE TOGETHER!
...AND I DON'T MEAN JUST AS AN ACTRESS.
OOPS! I'M SUDDENLY BASHFUL!
WHOOSH
I'M GOING BACK...
BUT THAT'S IT. THAT'S MY BIGGEST SECRET, AND NOW YOU KNOW IT.
GRMP
!
SHUMPH
YOU SAID YOU WANTED TO BE WITH ME!
SO WHERE DO YOU THINK YOU'RE GOING?

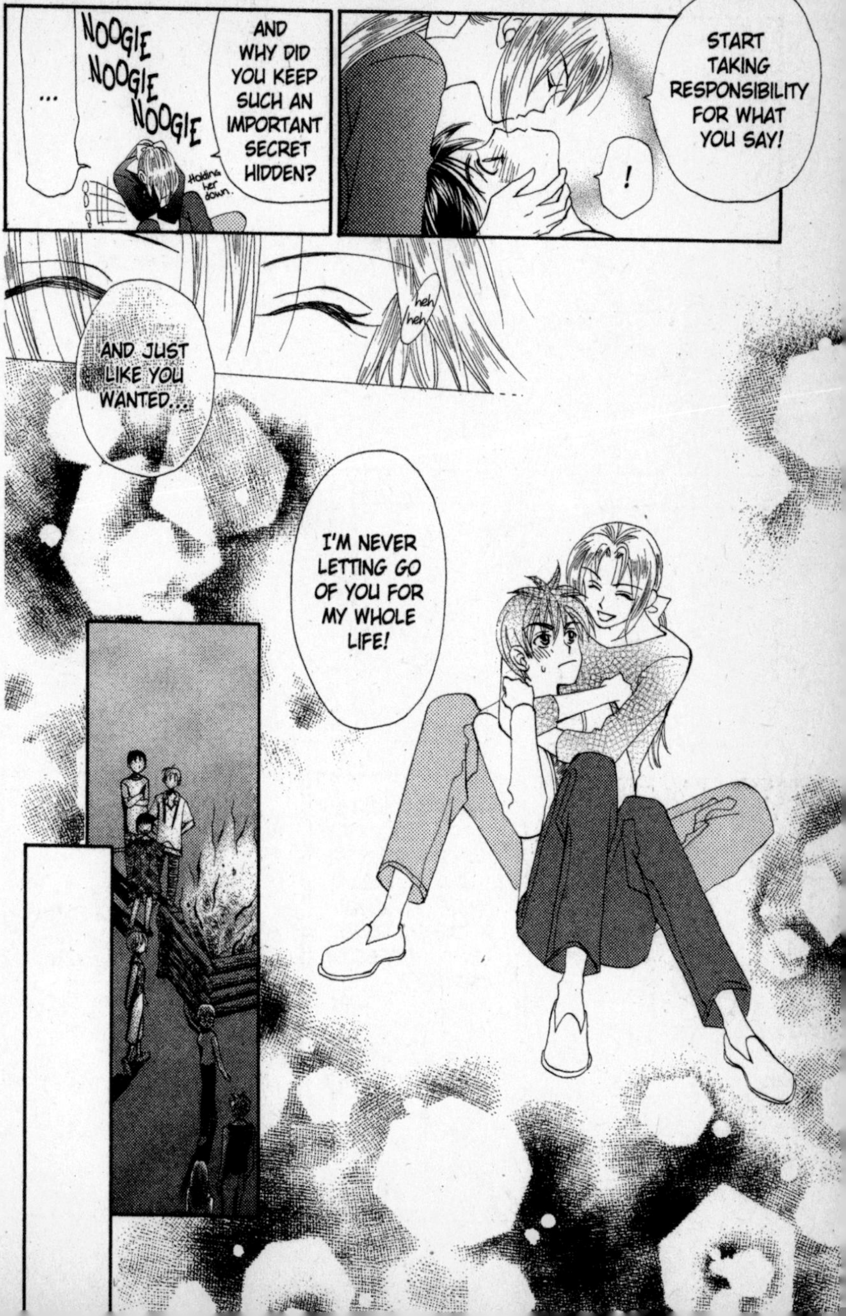
START TAKING RESPONSIBILITY FOR WHAT YOU SAY!
!
AND WHY DID YOU KEEP SUCH AN IMPORTANT SECRET HIDDEN?
NOOGIE NOOGIE NOOGIE
Holding her down.
...
heh heh
AND JUST LIKE YOU WANTED...
I'M NEVER LETTING GO OF YOU FOR MY WHOLE LIFE!

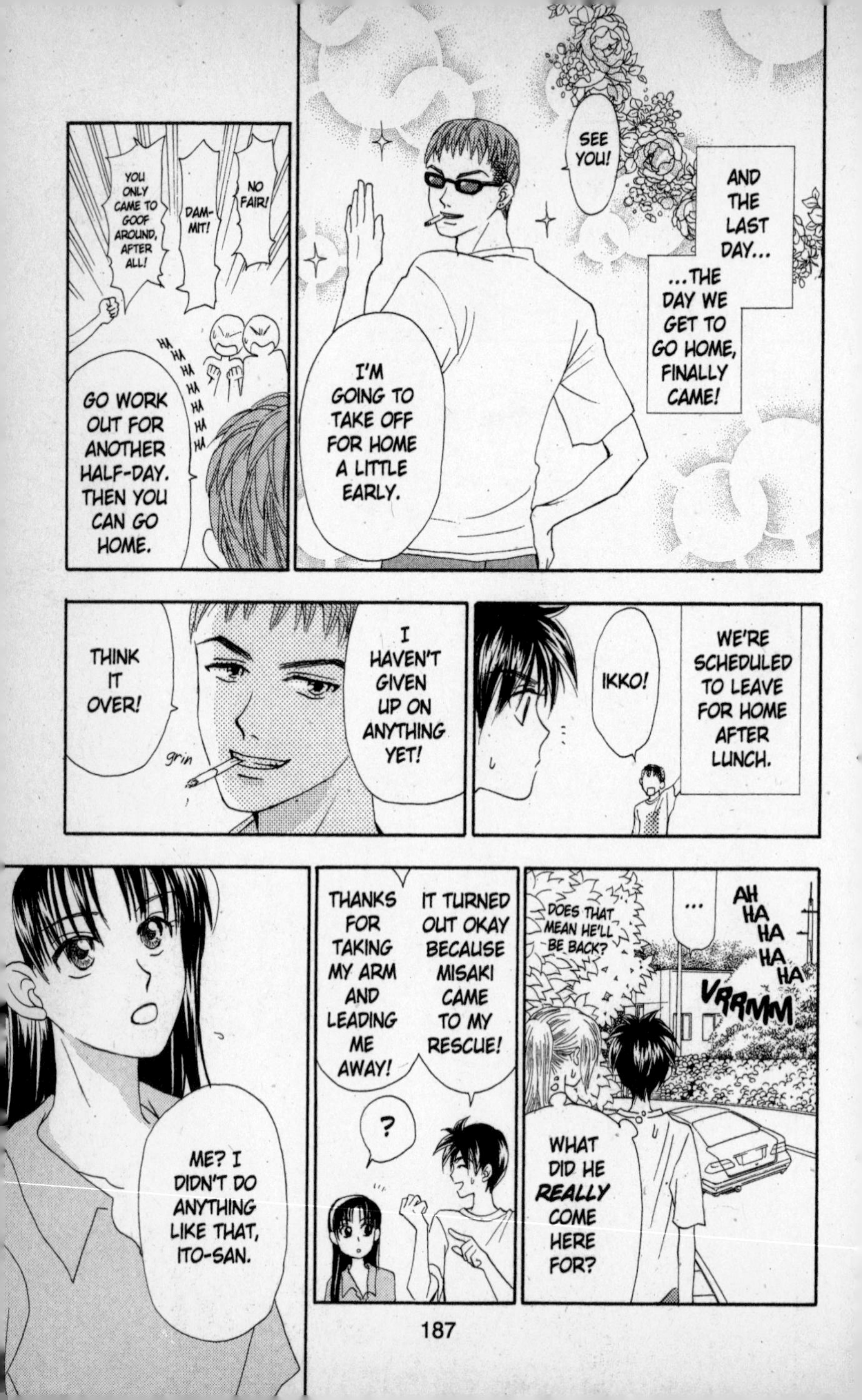
AND THE LAST DAY...
...THE DAY WE GET TO GO HOME, FINALLY CAME!
SEE YOU!
I'M GOING TO TAKE OFF FOR HOME A LITTLE EARLY.
NO FAIR!
DAM-MIT!
YOU ONLY CAME TO GOOF AROUND, AFTER ALL!
HA HA HA HA HA HA HA
GO WORK OUT FOR ANOTHER HALF-DAY. THEN YOU CAN GO HOME.
WE'RE SCHEDULED TO LEAVE FOR HOME AFTER LUNCH.
IKKO!
I HAVEN'T GIVEN UP ON ANYTHING YET!
THINK IT OVER!
grin
AH HA HA HA HA
VRRMMM
...
DOES THAT MEAN HE'LL BE BACK?
WHAT DID HE *REALLY* COME HERE FOR?
IT TURNED OUT OKAY BECAUSE MISAKI CAME TO MY RESCUE!
THANKS FOR TAKING MY ARM AND LEADING ME AWAY!
?
ME? I DIDN'T DO ANYTHING LIKE THAT, ITO-SAN.

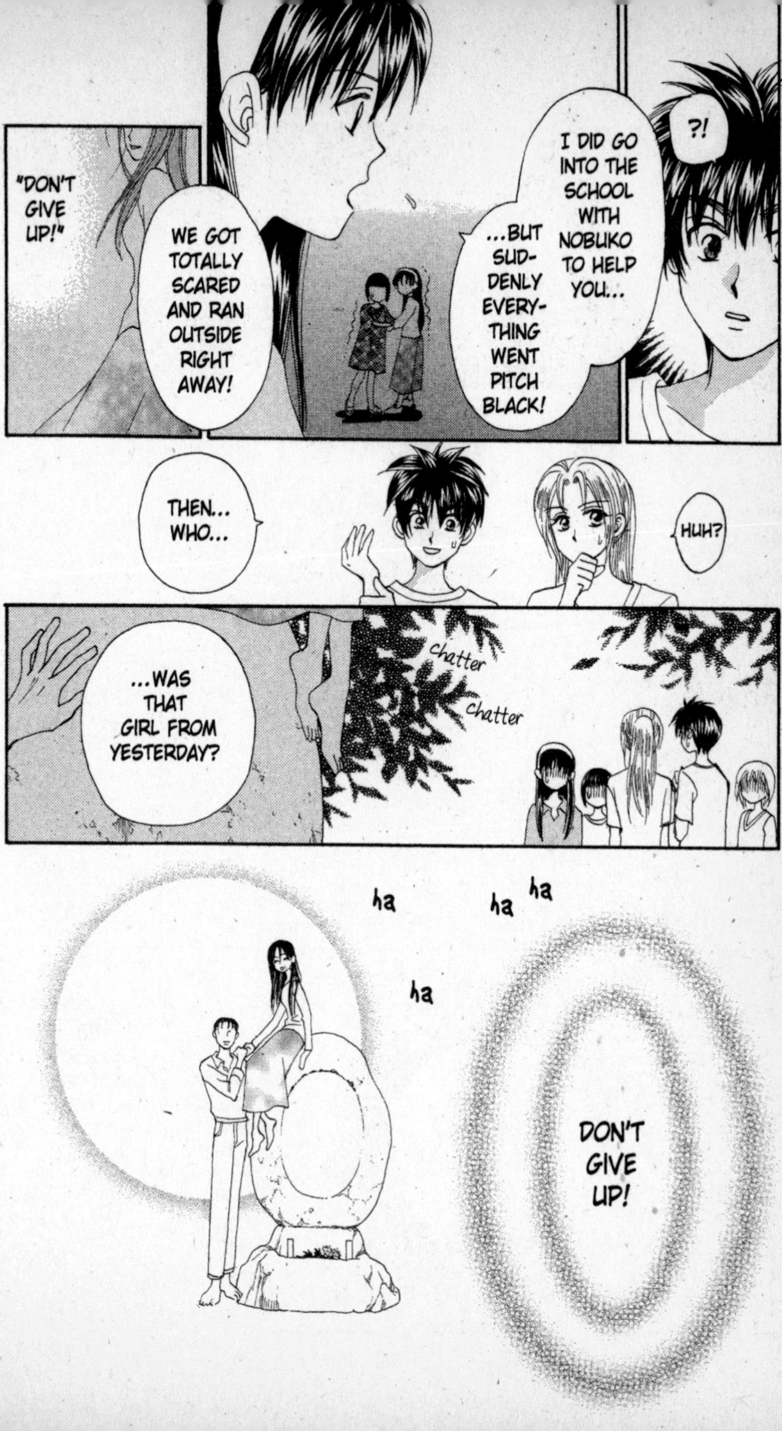
?!
I DID GO INTO THE SCHOOL WITH NOBUKO TO HELP YOU...
...BUT SUD-DENLY EVERY-THING WENT PITCH BLACK!
WE GOT TOTALLY SCARED AND RAN OUTSIDE RIGHT AWAY!
"DON'T GIVE UP!"
HUH?
THEN... WHO...
chatter
chatter
...WAS THAT GIRL FROM YESTERDAY?
ha
ha
ha
ha
DON'T GIVE UP!

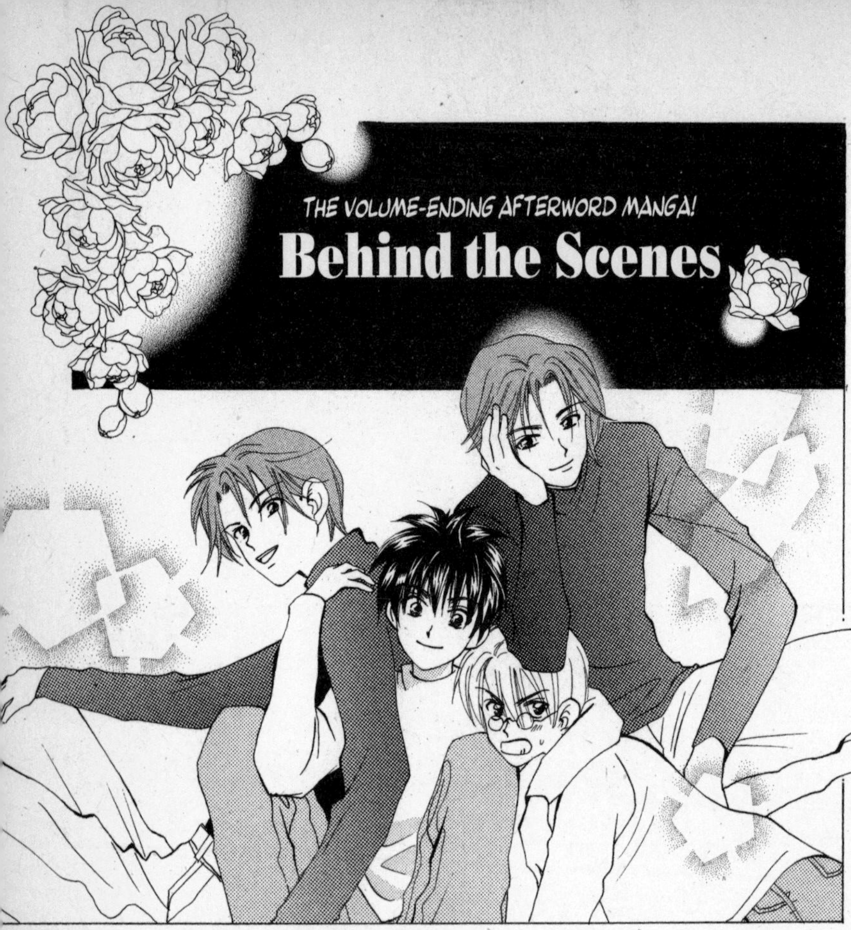
THE VOLUME-ENDING AFTERWORD MANGA!
Behind the Scenes

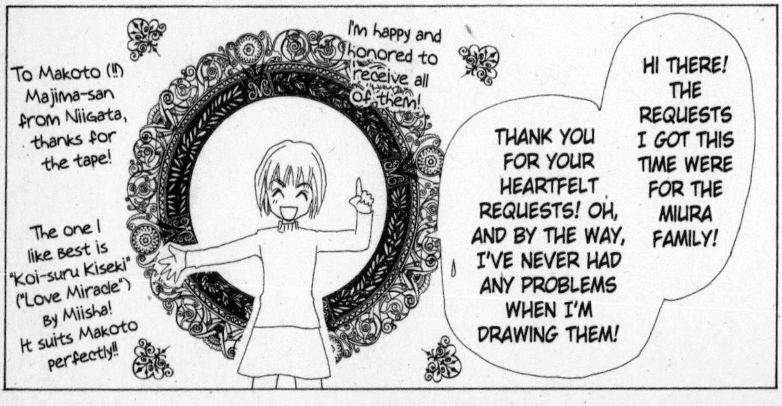
HI THERE! THE REQUESTS I GOT THIS TIME WERE FOR THE MIURA FAMILY!
THANK YOU FOR YOUR HEARTFELT REQUESTS! OH, AND BY THE WAY, I'VE NEVER HAD ANY PROBLEMS WHEN I'M DRAWING THEM!
I'm happy and honored to receive all of them!
To Makoto (!!) Majima-san from Niigata, thanks for the tape!
The one I like best is "Koi-suru Kiseki" ("Love Miracle") by Miisha! It suits Makoto perfectly!!

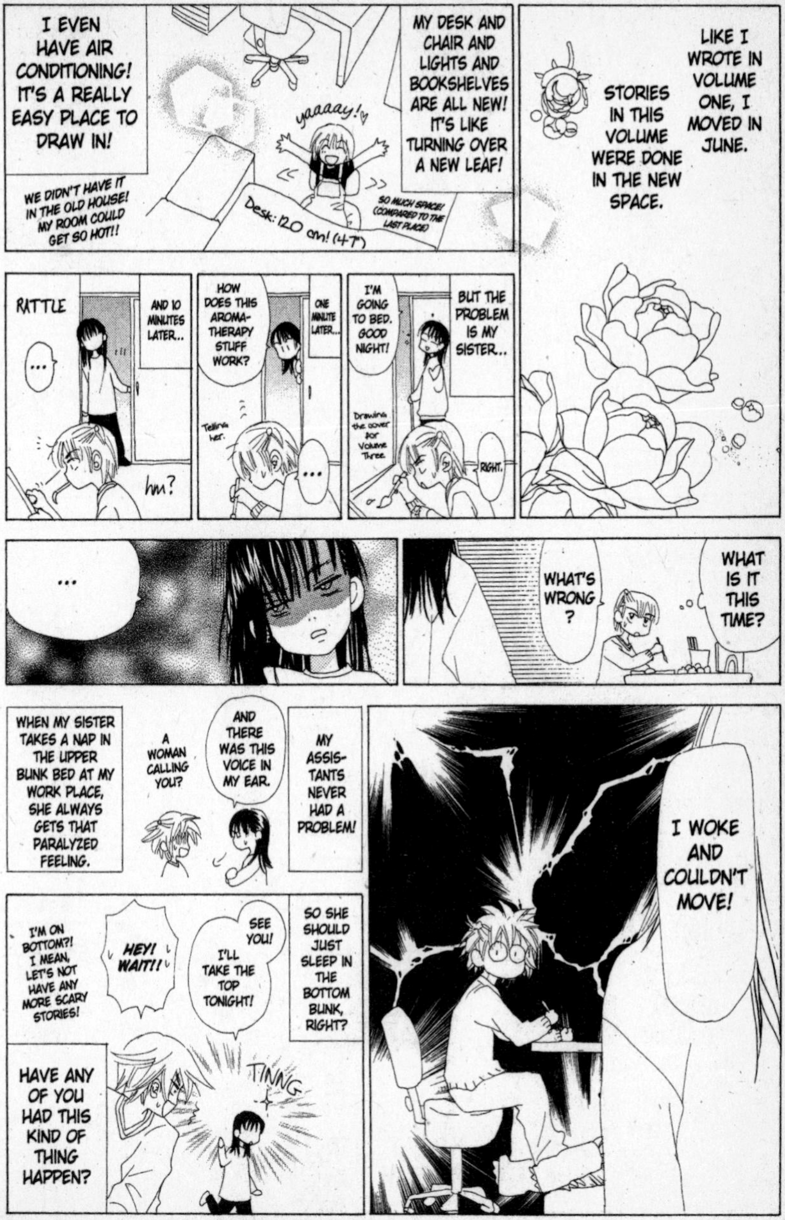
LIKE I WROTE IN VOLUME ONE, I MOVED IN JUNE.
STORIES IN THIS VOLUME WERE DONE IN THE NEW SPACE.
MY DESK AND CHAIR AND LIGHTS AND BOOKSHELVES ARE ALL NEW! IT'S LIKE TURNING OVER A NEW LEAF!
yaaaay!
SO MUCH SPACE! (COMPARED TO THE LAST PLACE)
Desk: 120 cm! (47")
I EVEN HAVE AIR CONDITIONING! IT'S A REALLY EASY PLACE TO DRAW IN!
WE DIDN'T HAVE IT IN THE OLD HOUSE! MY ROOM COULD GET SO HOT!!
BUT THE PROBLEM IS MY SISTER...
I'M GOING TO BED. GOOD NIGHT!
Drawing the cover for Volume Three.
RIGHT.
ONE MINUTE LATER...
HOW DOES THIS AROMA-THERAPY STUFF WORK?
Telling her.
...
AND 10 MINUTES LATER...
RATTLE
...
hm?
WHAT IS IT THIS TIME?
WHAT'S WRONG?
...
I WOKE AND COULDN'T MOVE!
MY ASSIS-TANTS NEVER HAD A PROBLEM!
AND THERE WAS THIS VOICE IN MY EAR.
A WOMAN CALLING YOU?
WHEN MY SISTER TAKES A NAP IN THE UPPER BUNK BED AT MY WORK PLACE, SHE ALWAYS GETS THAT PARALYZED FEELING.
SO SHE SHOULD JUST SLEEP IN THE BOTTOM BUNK, RIGHT?
SEE YOU! I'LL TAKE THE TOP TONIGHT!
HEY! WAIT!!
I'M ON BOTTOM?! I MEAN, LET'S NOT HAVE ANY MORE SCARY STORIES!
TINNG
HAVE ANY OF YOU HAD THIS KIND OF THING HAPPEN?

And still she tries to sleep on the top bunk!

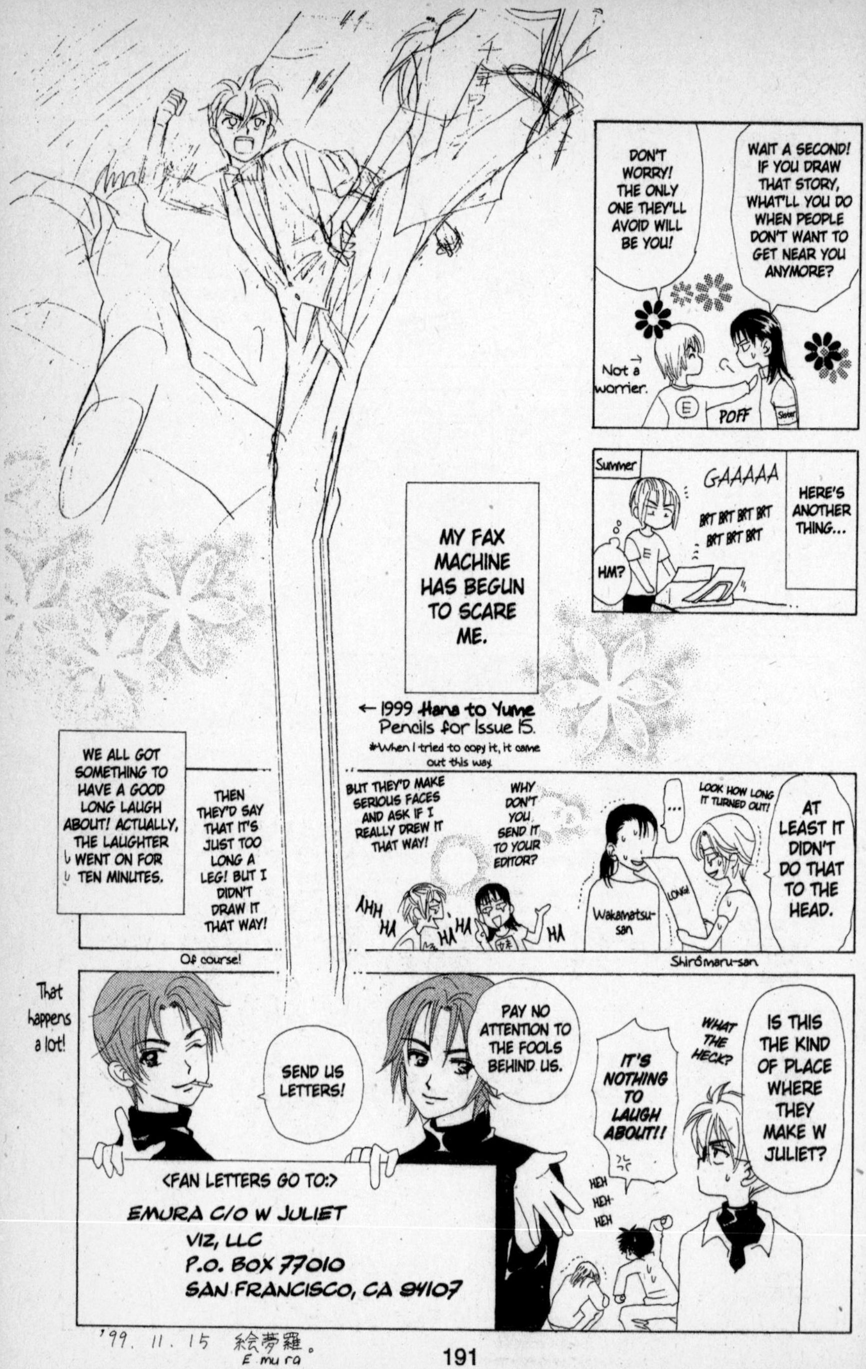
WAIT A SECOND! IF YOU DRAW THAT STORY, WHAT'LL YOU DO WHEN PEOPLE DON'T WANT TO GET NEAR YOU ANYMORE?
DON'T WORRY! THE ONLY ONE THEY'LL AVOID WILL BE YOU!
Not a worrier.
POFF
Sister
HERE'S ANOTHER THING...
GAAAAA
BRT BRT BRT BRT BRT BRT BRT
HM?
Summer
MY FAX MACHINE HAS BEGUN TO SCARE ME.
← 1999 Hana to Yume Pencils for Issue 15.
*When I tried to copy it, it came out this way.
AT LEAST IT DIDN'T DO THAT TO THE HEAD.
LOOK HOW LONG IT TURNED OUT!
...
LONG!
Wakamatsu-san
Shirōmaru-san
WHY DON'T YOU SEND IT TO YOUR EDITOR?
BUT THEY'D MAKE SERIOUS FACES AND ASK IF I REALLY DREW IT THAT WAY!
AHH HA HA HA HA
THEN THEY'D SAY THAT IT'S JUST TOO LONG A LEG! BUT I DIDN'T DRAW IT THAT WAY!
WE ALL GOT SOMETHING TO HAVE A GOOD LONG LAUGH ABOUT! ACTUALLY, THE LAUGHTER WENT ON FOR TEN MINUTES.
Of course!
IS THIS THE KIND OF PLACE WHERE THEY MAKE W JULIET?
WHAT THE HECK?
IT'S NOTHING TO LAUGH ABOUT!!
HEH HEH HEH
PAY NO ATTENTION TO THE FOOLS BEHIND US.
SEND US LETTERS!
That happens a lot!
<FAN LETTERS GO TO:>
EMURA C/O W JULIET
VIZ, LLC
P.O. BOX 77010
SAN FRANCISCO, CA 94107
'99. 11. 15 絵夢羅。
Emura

Cultural Notes

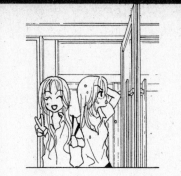

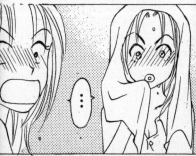

Kogals [reference page 68].
"Ko" comes from the first syllable of *kôtôgakkô*, the Japanese word for high school, and "gal" comes from the English. Kogals all seem to wear the same clothes, wear heavy lipstick and other cosmetics, have hair that is bleached a light brown, talk only of boyfriends and fashion, and are shallow, materialistic, and self-absorbed. They also seem to be the chief interest of perverted middle-aged men.

Haka-mairi
[reference page 168].
Ito is performing a rite called Haka-mairi ("visiting the grave") where one cleanses the gravestone with water, lays flowers, and prays. It is normally done during O-bon (late summer) and at the equinoxes. It is usually performed by family.

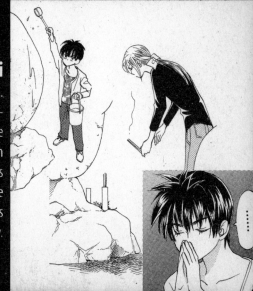

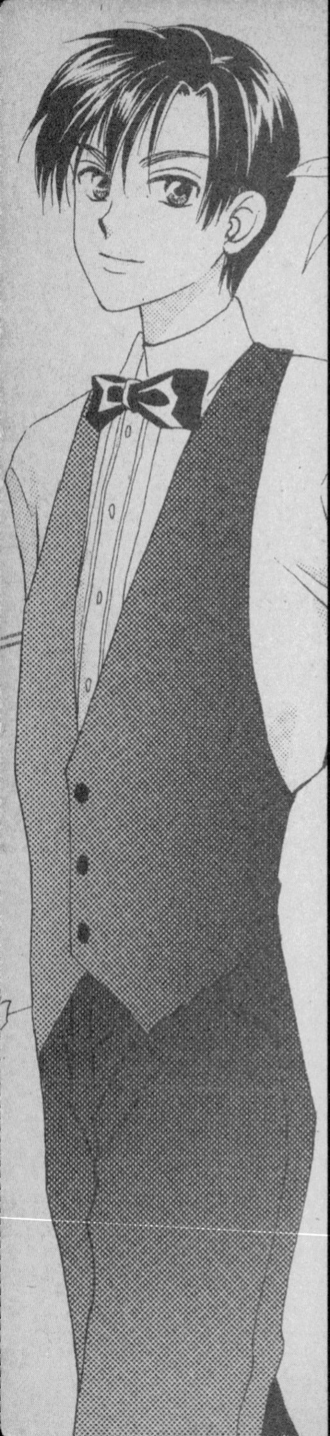

EDITOR'S RECOMMENDATIONS

If you enjoyed this volume of W Juliet then here's some more high-school romance manga you might be interested in.

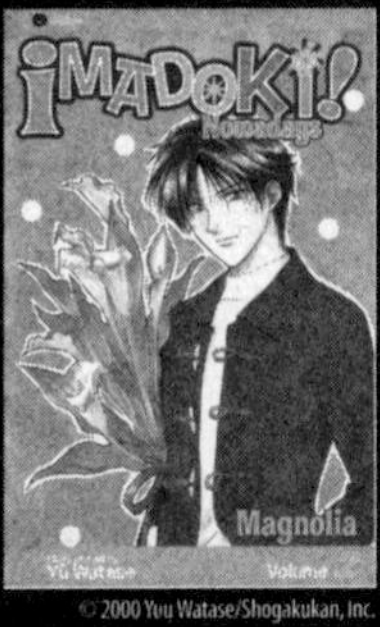
iMADOKI!
Nowadays
Magnolia
Yû Watase
Volume

© 2000 Yuu Watase/Shogakukan, Inc.

Imadoki!

For Tanpopo Yamazaki, life at the elitist Meio Academy starts miserably. The other students torment her, and the cute boy she saw tending a dandelion the day before school started now won't even acknowledge her existence. Hoping to make friends and have some fun, Tanpopo starts up a gardening committee—and the cute dandelion boy is the first to join!

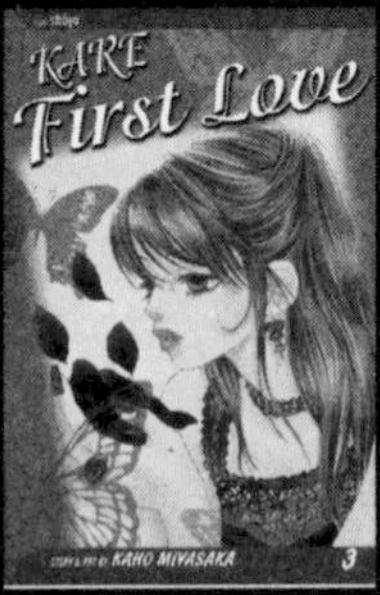
KARE
First Love
KAHO MIYASAKA
3

© 2002 Kaho Miyasaka/ Shogakukan, Inc.

Kare First Love

After a chance meeting, handsome Kiriya happens to notice the exquisite beauty hiding inside of shy and bespectacled sixteen-year-old Karin Karino. The stage is set for true love---but there's one hitch: Yuka, Karin's bossy best friend, has set her sights on Kiriya, too, and will make Karin's high-school life a living hell if she can't have him!

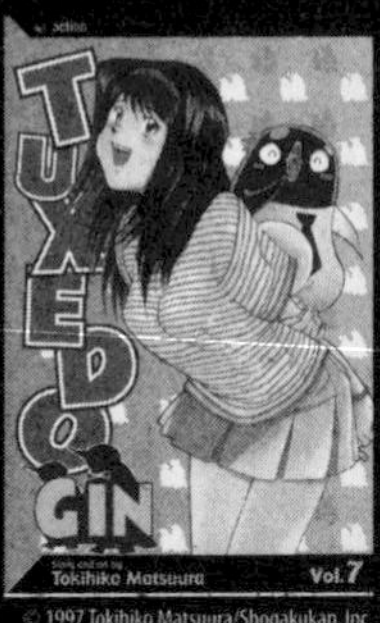
TUXEDO
GIN
Tokihiko Matsuura
Vol.7

© 1997 Tokihiko Matsuura/Shogakukan, Inc.

Tuxedo Gin

High school student Ginji Kusanagi is a tough, motorcycle-riding kid who's about to make his debut as a professional boxer. He's also just met Minako, the girl of his dreams. Tragically, Ginji dies and is reincarnated as a penguin! But that doesn't mean he can't still hang around Minako! Is there a chance for love to bloom between a boxing penguin and a beautiful girl!?

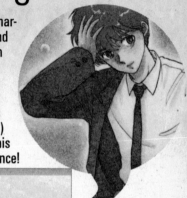

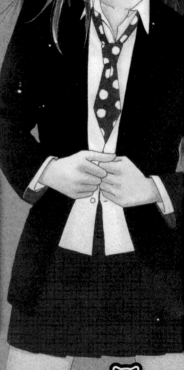
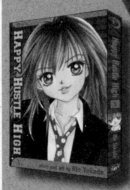

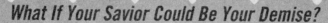
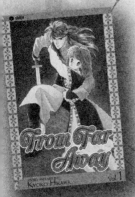

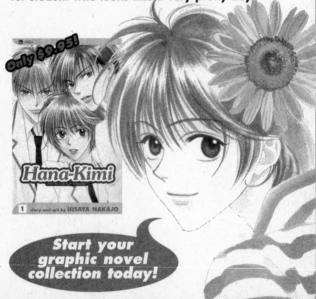

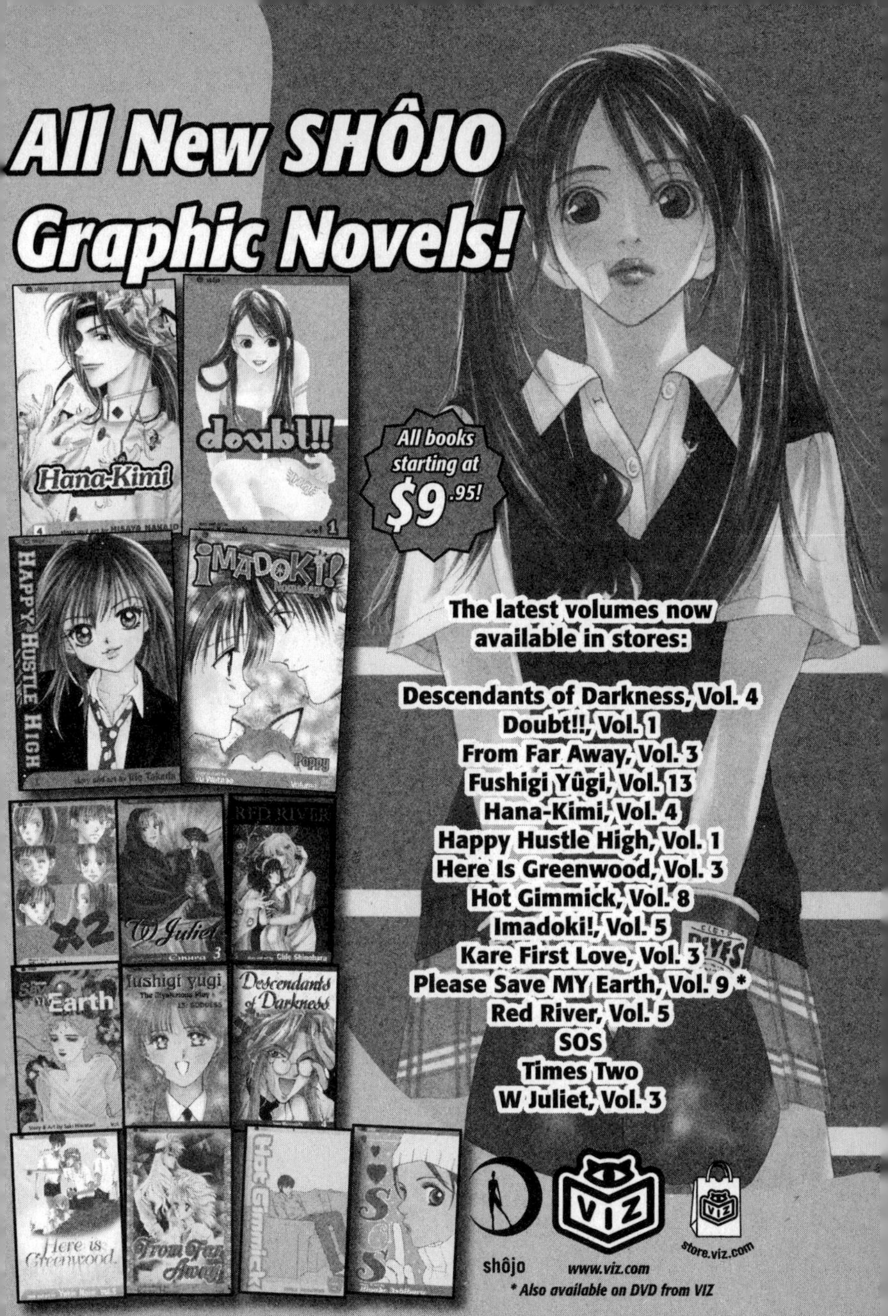
All New SHÔJO Graphic Novels!
All books starting at $9.95!
The latest volumes now available in stores:
Descendants of Darkness, Vol. 4
Doubt!!, Vol. 1
From Far Away, Vol. 3
Fushigi Yûgi, Vol. 13
Hana-Kimi, Vol. 4
Happy Hustle High, Vol. 1
Here Is Greenwood, Vol. 3
Hot Gimmick, Vol. 8
Imadoki!, Vol. 5
Kare First Love, Vol. 3
Please Save MY Earth, Vol. 9 *
Red River, Vol. 5
SOS
Times Two
W Juliet, Vol. 3
shôjo
www.viz.com
store.viz.com
* Also available on DVD from VIZ

COMPLETE OUR SURVEY AND LET US KNOW WHAT YOU THINK!

☐ Please do NOT send me information about VIZ products, news and events, special offers, or other information.

☐ Please do NOT send me information from VIZ's trusted business partners.

Name: _____

Address: _____

City: _____ **State:** _____ **Zip:** _____

E-mail: _____

☐ **Male** ☐ **Female** **Date of Birth** (mm/dd/yyyy): ___ / ___ / _____ (Under 13? Parental consent required)

What race/ethnicity do you consider yourself? (please check one)

☐ Asian/Pacific Islander   ☐ Black/African American   ☐ Hispanic/Latino

☐ Native American/Alaskan Native   ☐ White/Caucasian   ☐ Other: _____

What VIZ product did you purchase? (check all that apply and indicate title purchased)

☐ DVD/VHS _____

☐ Graphic Novel _____

☐ Magazines _____

☐ Merchandise _____

Reason for purchase: (check all that apply)

☐ Special offer   ☐ Favorite title   ☐ Gift

☐ Recommendation   ☐ Other _____

Where did you make your purchase? (please check one)

☐ Comic store   ☐ Bookstore   ☐ Mass/Grocery Store

☐ Newsstand   ☐ Video/Video Game Store   ☐ Other: _____

☐ Online (site: _____)

What other VIZ properties have you purchased/own? _____

_____

How many anime and/or manga titles have you purchased in the last year? How many were VIZ titles? (please check one from each column)

ANIME	MANGA	VIZ
☐ None	☐ None	☐ None
☐ 1-4	☐ 1-4	☐ 1-4
☐ 5-10	☐ 5-10	☐ 5-10
☐ 11+	☐ 11+	☐

I find the pricing of VIZ products to be: (please check one)

☐ Cheap   ☐ Reasonable   ☐ Expensive

What genre of manga and anime would you like to see from VIZ? (please check two)

☐ Adventure   ☐ Comic Strip   ☐ Science Fiction   ☐ Fighting

☐ Horror   ☐ Romance   ☐ Fantasy   ☐ Sports

What do you think of VIZ's new look?

☐ Love It   ☐ It's OK   ☐ Hate It   ☐ Didn't Notice   ☐ No Opinion

Which do you prefer? (please check one)

☐ Reading right-to-left

☐ Reading left-to-right

Which do you prefer? (please check one)

☐ Sound effects in English

☐ Sound effects in Japanese with English captions

☐ Sound effects in Japanese only with a glossary at the back

THANK YOU! Please send the completed form to:

NJW Research
42 Catharine St.
Poughkeepsie, NY 12601

All information provided will be used for internal purposes only. We promise not to sell or otherwise divulge your information.